CW00543796

UTOPIA BRITANN

Volume I

British Utopian Experiments: 1325 to 1945
Written, compiled and edited by Chris Coates

'A map of the world that does not include Utopia
is not worth even glancing at, for it leaves out
the one country at which Humanity is always
landing. And when Humanity lands there, it
looks out, and seeing a better country, sets sail.
Progress is the realisation of Utopias.'

Oscar Wilde
The Soul of Man Under Socialism

Published by Diggers & Dreamers Publications
2001

1

Cover Illustrations:
Front(clockwise from top right: Machynlleth Garden Village, Whiteway Colony, Ruislip Garden City plan, Harmony Hall, Springhead Camp,Abode of Love members,Utopia alphabet by Eric Gill,Charterville, Bournville Pavillion, John Hargrave in front of Kibbo Kift flag, Snigs End Cottage.
Back: Map by Catriona Stamp, Photos - Little Gidding, High Cross House, Silver End & Saltaire Signpost.
Cover Design by Jonathan How - Coherent Visions

c
Diggers & Dreamers
Publications
2001

First Published 2001
D&D Publications
BCM Edge
London
WC1N 3XX

ISBN
0-9514945-8-9
Paperback

Distribution :
Edge of Time Ltd
BCM Edge
London. WC1N 3XX
Printing :
Pagefast
Design & Layout :
General: Catandcoat
Cover design by:
Coherent Visions

CONTENTS:

BY WAY OF AN INTRODUCTION

WHAT IS HISTORY?

History at its best and most basic is storytelling: the story of our collective pasts - part 'fact'; physical & documentary evidence and eyewitness account, part interpretation; the writings of successive generations of historians, with their differing viewpoints, insights and prejudices. Another part is history's own mythology that there is a final true version of what went before and in the end part is what our own world view will allow us to accept about the past.

It is a case of which story you choose to believe.

THE HISTORY OF UTOPIA

Utopia has a chequered history amongst historians. Some would argue that the good place that is no-place has no 'real' history and that its rightful place is in the study of literature. Others have ridiculed utopians and tried to consign them to the footnotes of history. But the utopian tendency has an uncanny resilience - trying to make the world a better place would seem to be a basic human instinct and far from being marginal to our history it has played at times a central and pivotal role.

THE FABRIC OF HISTORY

Historians try to divide history up into manageable chunks - mainly as far as I can see for convenience, otherwise it would be an overwhelming many-headed-monster story with no beginning and no end. The divisions chosen however seem arbitrary; based on specialist fields of knowledge, arbitrary numbers 17th, 18th, 19th centuries or geographic boundaries - English history, Irish history, ... Oh that history were so neat as to arrange itself by subject or in date order, or confine itself to one country at a time. But no, human history, like our own personal histories, is a mixed-up jumble of overlapping stories, layer upon layer of juxtaposed loose ends…that when woven together form the fabric of history. In Utopia Britannica I have divided the history of Utopian experiments into differing historical 'threads' - loosely based on the differing impulses that have caused/inspired people to try and create a better world in the here and now. I have tried as best I can to unravel these threads, to come up with a readable historical story. The threads overlap and interweave through the years - with characters from one appearing in another and the distinction at times between them appearing to be rather thin. In the English Civil War the difference between religion and politics was indistinguishable - religion was political and politics was religious - and the distinction, or lack of it, runs through to Robert Owen - granddaddy of the socialist and co-operative movements - who started off as anti-religious and went on in his later years to become a spiritualist,- right up to the late 19th century Christian Anarchists - surely a contradiction in terms? Such are the vagaries of history. Long may it go on spoiling our attempts to pigeonhole people's acts and deeds!

THE JOURNEY OF HISTORY

This book began life as a history of intentional communities in the British Isles, what were called communes in the 1960s & '70s. As I set off on my journey down the communal memory lane with my baggage of preconceptions I thought I was clearly bound for the footnotes of history, but as I travelled through both geography and time, engaged in the research, I found myself in places that I never knew existed, accompanied by a cast of characters that ranged from the truely strange & eccentric, right through the corridors of power to the dizzy heights of fame & for-

VTOPIAE INSVLAE FIGVRA

UTOPIA

'A Fruiteful and pleasunt worke of the beste State of public weale, and of the new yle, called Utopia.'

The book that gave the world the word Utopia was written in Latin in 1515 by Thomas More, Henry VIII's envoy to Flanders at the time. It was in two parts; the first a conversation between More and his fictional traveller - Raphael Hythloday - about the ills of civilisation and the second a description, by Hythloday, of the Island Commonwealth of Utopia.

'The island of Utopia is in the middle two hundred miles broad, and holds almost at the same breadth over a great part of it; but it grows narrower towards both ends. Its figure is not unlike a crescent: between its horns, the sea comes in eleven miles broad, and spreads itself into a great bay, which is environed with land to the compass of about five hundred miles, and is well secured from winds. ....There are fifty-four cities in the island, all large and well built: the manners, customs and laws of which are the same, and they are all contrived as near in the same manner as the ground on which they stand will allow. The nearest lie at least twenty-four miles distance from one another, and the most remote are not so far distant, but that a man can go on foot in one day from it, to that which lies next it.'

Thomas More, *Utopia*

Utopia had been founded by King Utopus - though he was now long gone and the island a republic, governed by annually chosen officials known as Syphogrants and Tranibors. The fifty-four cities, each surrounded by a greenbelt, had rows of fireproof houses (with no locks on the doors) laid out on a grid pattern. The Utopians exchanged their houses by lot every ten years; ate in communal refectories, all worked a six-hour day and wore identical simple unbleached woollen clothes. All property was owned by the community and everyone's needs were met without the need of money. Gold and silver, being of no use on the island, were used to make chamber pots and prisoners' chains. The cities were supported by community farms where everyone was obliged to go and work.

'Out of every one of these families or farms cometh every year into the city twenty persons which have continued two years before in the country. In their place so many fresh be sent thither out of the city, who, of them that have been there a year already, and be therefore expert and cunning in husbandry, shall be instructed and taught. And they the next year shall teach other. This order is used for fear that either scarceness of victuals, or some other like incommodity should chance, through lack of knowledge, if they should be altogether new, and fresh, and unexpert in husbandry. This manner and fashion of yearly changing and renewing the occupiers of husbandry, though it be solemn and customably used, to the intent that no man shall be constrained against his will to continue long in that hard and sharp kind of life, yet many of them have such a pleasure and delight in husbandry, that they obtain a longer space of years. These husbandmen plough and till the ground, and breed up cattle, and provide and make ready wood, which they carry to the city either by land, or by water, as they may most conveniently. They bring up a great multitude of pulleyn, and that by a marvellous policy. For the hens do not sit upon the eggs, but by keeping them in a certain equal heat they bring life into them, and hatch them. The chickens, as soon as they become out of the shell, follow men and women instead of the hens.'

Thomas More, *Utopia*

Utopia had free hospitals outside every town where the sick got preferential treatment over the healthy. There was universal education with everyone required to learn farming and another craft - masonry, carpentry, weaving or metalwork. There was religious toleration, though the whole population appeared to be slowly converting to Christianity. All in all the Utopians enjoyed an idyllic if somewhat rulebound and conformist lifestyle. It was a place where engineers would be more at home than artists and where there was a death penalty for talking politics in private. More's communism is more primitive Christian and monastic than socialist.

More wrote Utopia as a critique of European society. It was partly influenced by Plato's Republic and partly by travellers' tales of the Americas. It is written in a highly ironic style and it is hard to tell when he is being serious and when he must be joking. It is full of clever allusions, in Greek and Latin, from the title Utopia to the translation of the main character's name, Hythloday - peddler of nonsense. The book, not published in English until 1551, (16 yrs after More's execution), has been far more influential since, than it was during More's own time, becoming a modern classic of literature, inspiring future generations of writers such as the poet Robert Southey and science fiction writer and philosopher, H.G.Wells.

Utopian Alphabet: As it appeared in the first edition of *Utopia.*

VTOPIENSIVM ALPHABETVM. 13

a b c d e f g h i k l m n o p q r s t u x y

tune. What slowly emerged was a Utopian landscape that stretched to the farthest corners of our country and whose influences are embedded so deep into our national culture as to be virtually invisible. I have spent alot of time reading the footnotes of other history books piecing together a jigsaw map of Utopia Britannica, and now when I travel I move through another country; a country of the imagination dreamt into existence by generations of utopian experimenters who refused to accept that there wasn't a better place to be than the one that they found themselves in.

UTOPIAN MAP KEY

What constitutes a utopian experiment? I applied a rough rule of thumb to decide what fitted into the book and what fell outside its remit. To me a community or group was utopian if it was trying to make the world a better place for more than just individuals, which might be for its members or for society as a whole. I have used such a loose definition to be inclusive rather than exclusive, and to avoid interminable arguments about what is or isn't a utopia. I have also tried to let the experimenters tell their own stories and keet my own thoughts and opinions separate from the narrative in 'reflection & commentary' sections at the end of each thread, so as to try and avoid the pitfall of historians' opinion becoming quoted as historic fact by some future utopian researcher. Why stop in 1945? Two reasons; it _is_ a significant utopian date and after it a different sort of historical story can be collected from participants who are still alive.

My own personal journey through Utopia Britannica has been one of travelling in hope of finding signposts to a better world and not being disappointed. I hope your journey is equally rewarding.

Chris Coates. 4.6.2001

Off the south west coast of Ireland from 1325 onwards maps show a perfectly circular island called HyBrasil. Shrouded in mist, it was reputed only to be visible every seven years, when the fog would lift and a land of enchantment could be seen where fairy queens, healers and magicians lived in gleaming cities. Legend had it that if you could touch the island with fire it would remain permanently visible. Celtic mythology from the sixth century onwards tells of magical islands, islands of laughter, whole submarine paradises with psalm-singing birds and magic fountains that spouted wine, islands to which the heroes of legend were spirited away or banished. It is surprising then for an island so obviously located in mythology that anyone ever set sail in search of HyBrasil, but search they did. Christians turned the pagan isle into their own Promised Land of the Saints, one of the islands which St Brendan set out on his epic voyages to find. In the 15th century a number of merchants tried in vain to find the island to use as a stepping-stone to trade with the Orient. And although at least one landing was reported, along with a number of sightings, the Celtic paradise remained lost in the Atlantic mist. It was however to remain on nautical charts until 1865, forming part of a long maritime tradition of mythical island paradises.

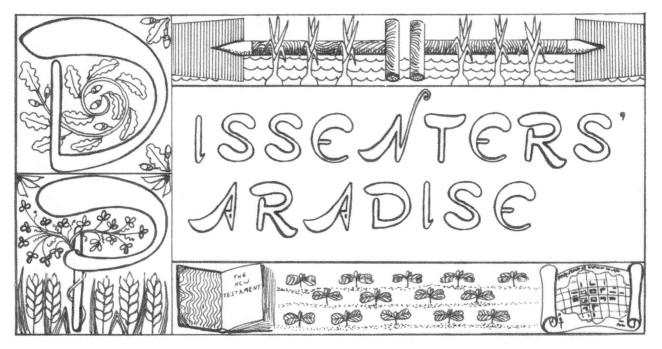

DISSENTERS' PARADISE

EUROPE'S FREE SPIRITS

It is hard now to understand the world view of the 15th & 16th centuries: a view that saw the Classical Greek and Roman civilisations as the pinnacle of achievement and almost everything thereafter a slow decline; a sense that all that there was to be known had been uncovered and that the 6,000 years of the world's span was coming to an end. These views were derived from the Christian belief that man was fallen, the years of plague sweeping the continent, pagan notions of a golden age and biblical prophesies of Armageddon. This all-pervading pessimism was cracked by Columbus's voyage of discovery to the Americas in 1492. Here was a glimmer of optimism on the intellectual horizon, a suggestion that there were new places, new things, new ideas, new worlds to be discovered. Columbus's voyage was the talk of Europe; in the courts, churches, inns and on street corners people discussed the truth, rumour and meaning of the discovery of a 'New World'. From 1492 onwards the western world was a different place and slowly the old order would be changed.

Cracks had already appeared in the old order. Since as far back as the 12th century groups known as the Brethren of the Free Spirit had been preaching a heretical gospel of paradise on earth. Quite who the free spirits were is hard to pin down, the name being applied by church authorities and historians to various groups across Europe. It was the age of the Crusades, and single women far outnumbered men. In the Netherlands there were women, called Beguines, who lived alone, and without taking vows devoted themselves to prayer and good works. About the beginning of the 13th century some of them grouped their cabins together, and formed the first Beguinage. Responding to the spiritual and social needs of the time, these communities spread across the Lowlands. The social status of the members of these communities varied; some of them only admitted ladies of high degree; others were exclusively reserved for persons in humble circumstances; others again opened their doors wide to women of every condition. Several, like the great Beguinage of Ghent, numbered their inhabitants by thousands and were semi-monastic institutions. There was a Beguinage at Mechlin as early as 1207, one at Brussels in 1245, others at Louvain & Bruges, and by the close of the century there was hardly a commune in the Netherlands without its Beguina. The groups were religious and held beliefs varying from the conventional to the heretical. The simple fact that they existed without men, was suspect to the church authorities and they were persecuted as heretics. Most of these institutions were suppressed during the religious troubles of the fifteen-hundreds or during the stormy years which closed the 18th century, but a few convents of Beguines still exist in various parts of Belgium today.

The male counterparts of the Beguines were known as Beghards (giving us the English word beggars). For the most part, though not always, men of humble origin- weavers, dyers, fullers, etc. - they formed communities where they lived together under one roof, ate communally, had a common purse and no private property. Declaring that God is within us all and therefore the church was unnecessary, they acknowledged no authority other than their own experience. They were banned and excommunicated by the church. Hundreds were burned or drowned, refusing to recant or plead lunacy, preferring to die for their beliefs. They also became itinerant preachers passing their message by word of mouth from one small group of like minds to another along the wool and cloth trade routes, down into Spain and Italy, east into Bavaria, and across the North Sea to the east coast of England.

In France a group started by William Aurifex in Paris in 1200 as a rebellion against the power of the church, dressed in a parody of a monk's habit - a patched red cowl - and disrupted church services by entering into debates with priests. Despite their swift execution for heresy the ideas of the free spirit continued to spread.

THE LOLLARD UNDERGROUND

England had its own free spirits known as Lollards. Originally a name applied to the followers of John Wyclif, it was later a general term of abuse for those who held questionable religious views. John Wyclif (1330-84) was a dissi-dent theologian & realist philosopher. Born in Yorkshire, and educated at Oxford, Wyclif started to publish texts in English rather than in Latin, the language of scholars. This was a very novel approach in 1380. His writings placed an emphasis on 'inward religion' and the 'literal' Bible as the Word of God, rather than the mechanics of sacraments and rituals. He put forward anti-clerical views and had a hatred of clerical and monastic endowments.

Early support for the Lollards came from the wealthy classes who advanced similar ideas and wanted to reduce the power and the wealth of the Church for their own reasons. Between 1383-1415 a group of lay preachers or mummers strolled the countryside preaching a reformed doctrine based on Wyclif's writings. They promoted the popular reading of Holy Scripture in common English as the means for knowing the Word of God. The 'Lollard Bible' was an early translation of the Old Testament into English circulated as hand-copied manuscripts.

'The most outstanding representative of the Lollards was John Ball, the mad minister of Kent. Coming from the ranks of the Franciscan monks who sympathised with the Lollard movement, he became one of the leaders of the peasant uprising of 1381 in England. Beginning in 1356, John Ball preached mainly in Essex and in Norfolk, delivering his sermons in city squares and cemeteries. They became very popular. He preached common property, and urged the people to exterminate the nobility. Only then, he said, would people be equal, and the masters would be no higher than the rest. All men originated from Adam and Eve, he said. "When Adam dolf and Eve span, who was then the gentleman?" he queried. He was killed during the suppression of the revolt in 1381.'

Friedrich Engels *The Peasant War*

The Lollard Bible was banned in 1407 and they became subject to the new statute De Heretico Comburendo (1410) which introduced the burning of heretics. A Lollard uprising was planned by Sir John Oldcastle, to remove Henry IV, most of the House of

Lords, and the Catholic Church authorities. Oldcastle was tried and convicted of heresy, and sent to the Tower of London, from where he escaped and became the most wanted man in the realm. He was finally captured and executed in 1417, the last Lollard martyr. After the disastrous results of Oldcastle's uprising and renewed suppression, the Lollards went underground across the nation. Local pockets of Lollard influence continued into the 16th century. Lollard Bibles, hand-written in English, were prized family items to be handed down through generations. Many of these pockets of the free spirit proved to be receptive to many later nonconformist ideas.

Free Spirit ideas resurfaced repeatedly throughout Europe, particularly in Germany. They are discernible in the teaching of Martin Luther, the German founder of Protestantism who was persecuted and excommunicated for his beliefs. They were present in the Anabaptist Free Commonwealth of Munster in 1534 - where, having been overwhelmingly elected to the town council, Anabaptists created a religious commonwealth. John of Leyden, their leader, preached a gospel of common ownership & sexual freedom. Meals were eaten communally in great dining halls, money was abolished and unbelievers were executed for entertainment. Munster was surrounded by the troops of Bishop von Waldeck and the town was besieged for over 12 months. 1700 'soldiers of the prophet' withstood attack after attack upon the town and the city was only taken when, after being forced to the edge of starvation, they were betrayed and soldiers were let into the town. 300 Anabaptists were promised safe conduct if they surrendered. They were then massacred.

GOOD KING HENRY

'Would to God that the Pope and all his Cardinals could set aside their worldly pomp and live according to the simple precepts of primitive Christianity.'

These were dangerous ideas to be expressing in 1529, astonishing ideas to be coming from the monarch of a Catholic nation - but then Henry VIII needed all the arguments that he could muster in his struggle with Rome to get a divorce from Catherine of Aragon for failing to pro-duce a male heir. How far Henry believed any of the ideas he used to bolster his case is hard to know. He was in many ways the good catholic monarch - a religious conservative forced to dabble with heresy to further his personal and political ends. Whatever his personal desires, openly courting heretics, (where their views supported his), and the final break with Rome, was to eventually lead to a climate of relative religious tolerance during the reign of his daughter Elizabeth I.

Henry's attacks on the corruption of the clergy may have been popular in the country, but the dissolution of the monasteries was to prove another matter. The great monastic houses provided a basic form of social welfare, with alms for the poor, hospitals for the sick and employment for many on their vast estates. The closure of the monasteries and the ensuing enclosures of land by the gentry led to poverty and vagrancy on an unprecedented scale. It is estimated that a tenth of the population became homeless, wandering the roads in search of work that did not exist, supporting themselves by begging and stealing. Harsh laws were passed against `sturdy beggars'; penalties were flogging, branding, mutilation and hanging, but this was to no avail; revolt broke out in distant parts of the country where feudalism was still strong. In 1536, in the north, the so-called Pilgrimage of Grace occurred. Many of the gentry joined the common people and great crowds assembled. The rebels opposed the closing of the monasteries and many of Henry's religious innovations. They demanded parliamentary and legal reforms, the restoration of the old Catholic holidays, and an end to enclosures, rack-renting and rising prices.

KETT'S REBELLION

The last great medieval uprising took place in East Anglia in 1549. Country folk had formed 'leagues' to defend themselves against unscrupulous landlords. Rioting had spread across seven counties, with fence-breaking, ditch-filling and hedge-pulling to restore enclosed land to the people. Open rebellion began outside the abbey at Wymondham, Norfolk, in July at the annual fair in honour of St Thomas Becket. A crowd set off from the fair to pull down the fences recently put up round common land by John Flowerdew, an unpopular local landowner. Having torn down Flowerdew's fences they moved on to the land of Robert Kett. Kett however threw in his lot with the rebels, tearing down the fences around his land with his own hands and declaring:

'Many horrible things of late years have ye endured, with many wrongs and miseries have ye been vexed and afflicted. Moreover, I promise that the hurts done to the public weal and the common pasture by the importunate lords thereof shall be righted.'.

Next day a great meeting was held under a prominent oak-tree known ever since as `Kett's Oak', (still standing by the A111 north-east of Wymondham). Here Kett was elected leader of the movement. The meeting went on all day with new supporters constantly arriving. Groups left to clear all enclosed land within a day's walk, and messengers were sent out to rouse the whole country. The rebels moved on Norwich the following day, clearing fences from enclosed land around the town and setting up camp on Mousehold Heath on the east side of the town. They set up headquarters in an old chapel, and occupied the Earl of Surrey's palace that stood on the Heath. Throughout the country men left their farms, shops and families, armed themselves and set out for Mousehold. Within a week the rebels had grown to 20,000 strong.

Over the following weeks a mini-commonwealth was to develop on Mousehold Heath as the rebels negotiated with the gentry inside the city. The camp was fortified with deep ditches and a stockade. Huts were built. The houses and estates of the rich were raided for oxen, sheep, poultry, deer, guns and powder. It is said that 20,000 sheep were consumed with great relish; sheep being one of the chief reasons for the enclosures.

THE OAK OF REFORMATION

On a platform built under the branches of a large ancient oak tree the rebels set up their own 'parliment' where anyone could speak. Even opponents of the rebellion came to speak. The Mayor of Norwich was a frequent speaker, and the Reverend Matthew Parker, later to be Archbishop of Canterbury, preached a long sermon on the sin of rebellion. Daily prayers were held under the oak and the leaders of the revolt made their plans and reports in the full hearing of everybody. A court of justice was set up to try breaches of peace and discipline in the camp.

Under the oak the rebel leaders drew up a manifesto, `The Bill of Twenty-Nine Requests and Demands'. The demands included: the end of enclosures and the restoration of communal land, common rights for fishing and taking game, elections for local law officers and the establishment of a clergyman in every parish to teach children. The manifesto was sent to the king, who promised that when Parliament met in October it would discuss what redress it could offer. Meanwhile the rebels were ordered to break up their illegal camp and disperse. It was at this point that the rebels stormed the city gates and took control of Norwich - the third largest city in the country at the time. The rebellion was now at its peak. Kett dispatched a force to capture Yarmouth, but they suffered heavy casualties and failed to take the port. A number of small uprisings in the south were inspired by Kett's example, but they were put down one by one. The king diverted 12,000 troops from the army raised for the war against Scotland to put down the rebellion. This force easily retook Norwich from the few guards left on the gates by the rebels. After much debate the rebels decided to break camp and face the king's troops in open battle. Out in the open the heavily armoured German mercenary cavalry, supported by the king's cannon, easily smashed through the rebels' massed ranks and by four in the afternoon `Kett's Rebellion' was over. Over 5,000 rebels lay dead on the battlefield with many more wounded and maimed. No mercy was shown; those taken alive were killed on the spot, or hanged from nearby trees. A small band of rebels made a defiant last stand long after the battlefield was cleared. Inside a ring of wagons lashed together they opened a cask of ale from one of the wagons and after a short prayer, solemnly pledged faith to each other and prepared to die. They rejected initial offers of mercy as untrustworthy and it was only when the Earl of Warwick came in person and offered binding oaths that the brave rebels laid down their weapons and were allowed to return home in safety.

Robert Kett was captured, imprisoned in the Tower, tried and sentenced for treason. On 7th December he was dragged through the streets of Norwich to the castle, his body loaded with heavy chains, and hung from the battlements.

Unwittingly Henry the Eighth had set in motion a train of events that would echo through English history for centuries to come. The late 16th and early 17th century saw a proliferation of dissenting sects in England with the Adamites, Brightanists, Thessalonians, Chaldeans, Electrians, Donatists, Panonians, Junonians, Damasians, Saturnians, Bacchanalians, the Pueruis Similes, Liberi, Libertians, Semper-Orantes, Deo-Reclecti, Hetheringtonians, Trakites, Muncerians, Hutites, Bewkeldians, Castilians, Monasterienies, Serventians, Johnsonians, Wilkinsinians, the Scattered Flock, Grindletonians, Etticheans, Monatanists, Pelagians, Notians, Marcians and Nicolatians - to name but a few of the 199 sects estimated to be in existence by contemporary writers in the 1640s, though how many of these were the creation of a worried clergies' imagination, which was apt to find a heresy in every rude utterance and a sect in every commoners' gathering, is hard to say.

Some of these groups were communities of prayer, bands of like minds who gathered together to support each other's beliefs or follow some charismatic leader. Some however went further and attempted to put their ideas into practice, setting up communities where they attempted to live out their ideas.

TYNDALES BIBLE

" I will cause a boy that driveth the plough shall know more of the scripture than thou doest. "

William Tyndale was born about 1495 at Slymbridge near the Welsh border. He gave us the first English version of the New Testament. Educated at Oxford, and a naturally rebellious character, he was influenced by the anticlericalism of the times and saw the Bible as the source of all religious knowledge. In the early 1520s many copies of Martin Luther's German Bible were being smuggled into the country by German traders. Tyndale approached the Bishop of London with the proposal to translate the New Testament. He was turned down, without even an audience, and promptly went to Germany, where sometime in 1525 he finished his own translation from the Greek. Copies printed by Peter Schoeffer in Worms were shipped in bales of cloth down the Rhine, and across into various ports in the south and east of England and sold to avid readers up and down the country. Tyndale hoped to lead his readers to salvation through the Scriptures alone. He hoped they would be moved by what they read, that it would "maketh a man's heart glad and maketh him sing, dance and leap for joy." The Lollards had built up great expectations as to what the Bible could accomplish and many looked to it as a means to a new world.

Ironically, it was Thomas More the author of Utopia who was charged with leading the attack on heretical books. The Bishop of London tried to suppress Tyndale's Bible by buying up every available copy and publicly burning them. He may have been successful in this tactic as only two copies of the first edition survive. However the sight of a bishop burning Bibles made many people assume that it was because the gospel contradicted what the clergy taught and the way they lived, and that they feared being found out. Though saying that he wanted his people to be able to read the Bible in their own language, Henry VIII banned Tyndale's version. Tyndale was caught; betrayed by an Englishman that he had befriended. Tyndale was incarcerated for 500 days before he was strangled and burned at the stake in 1536. His last words were;

"Lord, open the eyes of the King of England."

http://www.williamtyndale.com/index.html

14

THE FAMILY OF LOVE

Followers of Henry Niclaes (H.N. to his friends, which also stood for homo novus - New Man) the Family of Love, or Familists, spread throughout the south of England during the second half of the 16th Century. Niclaes was born in Munster in 1502. The Familists are first found in Kent (in 1552) and later in Cambridgeshire, Essex and London and even as far as Devon & the North. His ideas, spread by wayfaring traders and itinerant preachers, were particularly difficult for the church authorities to root out, as familists were ready to recant when caught, yet not give up their beliefs. They tried, like the Anabaptists, to establish the kingdom of Christ on earth, held their property in common and declared that the essence of religion was love and no other laws were needed.

FREEWILLERS

Free Will Men, Freewillers or New Fryelers were an English movement from the late 1540s to the 1560s. Like the Lollards before them, Freewill Men questioned the "new" reform movement of Protestantism with its clerical manners. Freewill Men became a type of "backseat driver" to many of the religious and political discussions of the period, raising their voices in many different venues to call attention to their concerns regarding the new church reforms and its place in English society. For this reason, some Freewill Men argued for a separation from the 'Reformed Church of England.' Unlike their Lollard ancestors who wanted to reform their Church from within these Free Will Men now became in effect the first separatists in English history. As a movement, the Freewillers probably disappeared during the reign of Mary I, as did a number of other dissident voices.

'JACOBITES'

The Jacobites were an English sect founded by Henry Jacob (1563-1624). An early Puritan, Jacob was an Oxford graduate, and precenter at Corpus Christi College. An ordained clergyman he had been active in the Puritan reform movement within the Church of England for many years. He was instrumental in putting together the Millenary Petition (1603), a list of Puritan reforms submitted to James I when he took the throne. Jacob was called to debate these issues in front of the king at the Hampton Court Conference in 1604. The king rejected the views presented as an affront to his royal authority. Jacob called for reform within the Church of England with his publication, *Reasons taken out of God's Word and the best humane Testimonies proving a necessitie of reforming our Churches in England (1603)*, which promptly landed him in prison. After serving his sentence, he was exiled to Holland where he found other like-minded dissidents. After returning to England in 1616, Jacob started to put into practice his own concepts of a new type of congregational structure, drawing on earlier separatist traditions where authority rested with the local congregation rather than with the national church. Jacob's London congregation in Southwark became a focal point for liberal thought and discussion. Prominent theologians, thinkers and dissenters found a ready audience to discuss the social and political issues of the day. Jacob himself began to consider greener pastures and in 1622, left for the American Colonies, to established his new religious community of Jacobopolis in Virginia. Jacob died there in 1624.

THE SCROOBY SEPARATISTS

In the small north Nottinghamshire village of Scrooby, in about 1606, a group of dissenters known as the Scrooby Separatists, formed their own church. After attempting to set up in Boston, Lincolnshire, where they were discovered and imprisoned, and again near Immingham, on the Humber, and fearing further persecution they fled to the tolerant haven of the Netherlands. Although they were made welcome in Holland they could not find the peace and security they were looking for. Poor living conditions made it difficult for the congregation to recruit more English immigrants and they feared the loss of their English traditions as their children were growing up Dutch.

In 1618, the little congregation made the momentous decision to emigrate yet again. But where to go? England was still closed to them. They discussed settling in

THE RIGHT GOOD OLD WAY

In the last of his Four Quartets, written in 1941, the poet T.S. Elliot used the small church at Little Gidding in Huntingdonshire as a symbol of traditional, Royalist, High Church, English Christianity, harking back to the 20 years from 1626 to 1646 when Nicholas Ferrar was the head of a religious community based in the manor house there. He was born in 1592, the son of a great Elizabethan merchant adventurer - his father was both a friend of Drake & Raleigh and a member of the Virginia Company that oversaw the founding of the colony in America. Nicholas, who as a young man suffered from malaria, which was then rife in the Fens, was sent off on a tour of Europe for his health, during which he made contact with all kinds of religious groups; Anabaptists and Jews in Holland, Lutherans in Germany, and Catholic monastic communities in Italy and Spain. After working for the Virginia Company he entered parliament. He turned down offers of an ambassadorship and a position of clerk to the privy council, to become a deacon and retire along with other members of the Ferrar family to Little Gidding to form a spiritual community based on voluntary poverty, a life of prayer, fasting, and almsgiving. They restored the church which had been used as a barn & pigsty and took responsibility for daily services. Day and night they kept at least one member of the community kneeling in prayer before the altar, so that they might "Pray without ceasing."' Though the community was firmly Anglican in practice they were ecumenical in spirit, reading and studying widely other branches of the Christian faith. From the community they taught local children, and looked after the health and well-being of the people of the district. Nichols Ferrar died in 1637 (aged 45) when his malaria re-occurred, and leadership of the community passed to his brother John.

In the early 1630s King Charles I took an interest in the work of Little Gidding borrowing a number of their prayer books. The king was also to call twice during the Civil War, the second time on the night of 2nd May 1646 seeking refuge from parliamentarian troops. Fearing for the safety of the community John Ferrar hid the King in a nearby house. Shortly after this incident the King was captured. Little Gidding's broad-minded approach to Christian doctrines attracted criticism. A pamphlet describing the community as an 'Arminian Nunnery' and accusing them of all being 'papists' was distributed amongst supporters of the parliamentary cause. And it is thought that some time after the kings last visit, troops from Cromwell's New Model Army forcibly broke the community up and ransacked the church.

The Friends of Little Gidding was formed in 1946 and annual pilgrimages initiated. In 1978 a Trust was formed to buy the farmhouse and since then the small Community of Christ the Sower has grown up at Little Gidding where, with about 20 members, they follow a pattern of simple worship and Christian Fellowship.

'It is the right, good, old way you are in; keep it.' Nicholas Ferrar

South America, but decided that the hot climate would "not well agree with our English bodies". The pilgrims were also dubious about joining the English colony of Virginia for fear of suffering religious persecution once again. In the end they decided to trust their countrymen in Virginia - but at the farthest remove possible. Their goal would be the northernmost boundary of the Virginia Company grant, at the mouth of the Hudson River.

A group of English investors known as the 'merchant adventurers' financed the voyage and settlement. They formed a joint-stock company with the colonists in which the merchants agreed to 'adventure' (risk) their money, and the settlers to invest their personal labour, for a period of seven years. During that time, all land and live-stock were to be owned in partnership; afterwards the company would be dissolved and the assets divided.

They sailed to England in July 1620, where they met other colonists who had hired a large vessel, the Mayflower. Leaving Plymouth, the Mayflower set sail for the New World on September 6th. They arrived at Cape Cod after a 66-day voyage and chose to remain in New England, as it was too late in the season to go on to the northern part of Virginia, where they had permission to settle. They each signed an agreement, known as the 'Mayflower Compact', to guarantee co-operation within their community. An exploring party found the site of the future town of Plymouth. This is celebrated in legend as the landing on Plymouth Rock, a solitary boulder at the foot of the hill on which Plymouth is built. Construction of the new colony began on Christmas Day, 1620.

Winter weather and a poor diet caused half of the colony to sicken and die that winter. In the spring of 1621, the survivors planted their crops and made friendly contact with the neighbouring native Wampanoag tribe. The Wampanoag taught the colonists how to plant corn and a treaty of peace was signed between them, which lasted 50 years. In the early autumn, the colonists' first harvest proved successful. A celebration, attended by the Wampanoag, was held that lasted for three days and at which everyone feasted on turkey, venison and other local foods. It was this celebration, rediscovered in the early 19th century and inaccurately identified as the "first New England Thanksgiving", which brought about the pilgrims' association with the modern American holiday. Before that time they had been chiefly celebrated as the first English colonists in New England, and by implication, in North America. The first English settlement was in fact established at Jamestown in Virginia in 1607, but the Jamestown adventurers were felt to lack the moral fibre and sturdy virtues of the Plymouth families, who better represented the values of the emerging American nation.

Later colonists who arrived on three subsequent ships swelled the colony's population to over 150 people and by 1627 the colony was well established. The English merchant adventurers had broken up in 1624 leaving the colonists in debt. Unable to make their living through cod fishing as they had originally planned, the colonists turned to agriculture and trade instead. Their chief crop, Indian corn, was traded with the Native Americans to the north for highly valued beaver skins. These were sold profitably in England to pay off the colony's debts and buy supplies. The Plymouth colonists were elevated at the time of the American Revolution from simple local forebears to the founding fathers of the entire country. There was a need for symbolic support for the independence of the United States and they became the leading characters in the creation story of the new nation. It was then that they received the name 'The Pilgrims'.

THE STRANGERS

The colony-making traffic was not all one way. In the early 1600s groups of French-speaking Protestants from Spanish-controlled Netherlands and northern France, Walloons & Hugenots, fled persecution and came to England. They were welcomed by Cornelius Vermuyden, an eminent drainage engineer involved in schemes to reclaim land from the fens in Lincolnshire and north Cambridgeshire. The Walloons set up a colony at Sandtoft on Hatfield Chase in the Isle of Axeholme and used their ditching and embankment skills to clear and drain the fens. The local inhabitants had no liking for the 'strangers'. For hundreds of years they had held the right to take wildfowl and fish the pools and rivers, and they were appalled by the idea that Cornelius Vermuyden and his supporters could deprive them of their livelihood by draining the area.

A contemporary account tells the story of what happened to the colonists of Hatfield Chase who;

'did build a town called Sandtoft with a church therein, placing a minister there; wherein two hundred families of French and Walloon protestants ..... who erected and planted two-hundred habitations for husbandry and plowed and tilled much of the said 24,000 and 500 acres of land to the great benefit of the Commonwealth. All which they enjoyed till about the month of June 1642, that some of the inhabitants thereabouts, pretending they had right of common, said they were not bound by the specified degree . . . and began to raise a powerful army . . . They arose in tumults, brake down the fenns and inclosures of 4,000 acres, destroyed all the corn growing and demolished the houses thereon.......And about the beginning of February ensuing, they pulled up the floodgates of Snow Sewer which by letting in the tides from the River Trent, soon drowned a great part of Hatfield Chase, divers persons standing there with muskets and saying they would stay till the whole level was drowned and the inhabitants were forced to swim away like ducks.'

William Dugdale *Imbanking and Draining*

Some of the colonists left immediately and went to join a second colony on the Earl of Bedford's land at Thorney near Peterborough. Others attempted to stay on despite the local opposition, but the colony finally ended around 1650. The colony at Thorney was more successful. Under the protection of the Earl of Bedford and with less local opposition they set about draining the great Bedford level. Along with Dutch and Scottish prisoners of war drafted in by the New Model Army, the colonists carried out the biggest civil engineering project seen in 17th century England. By1653 some 4,000 acres of fenland had been brought under cultivation. The colonists purchased plots around common land at Willow Hall. Some built substantial stone houses and barns using stone from the dissolved abbey at Thorney - some of which still exist today. They shared the local church with the English Congregation and over the years they dispersed into the surrounding countryside setting up satellite settlements at places like Parsons Drove and Guyhirn. By 1727 a separate 'colony' was no longer identifiable.

HOLY NUDISM

Whilst some were busy setting up colonies to usher in the New World others simply acted as if it had already arrived: the Adamites, a small English radical sect active from 1641-1660, believed in an early Christian heresy dating from the fourth century. As Adam and Eve were naked and without sin, so Adamites embraced a type of "holy" nudism. They believed they were in a "divine state of grace", as were Adam and Eve in the Garden of Eden, and so rejected most civil, moral and social restraints on their behaviour. Individuals could regain their innocence by not being fettered by clothing. Some accounts alleged that this sect was dominated by women. Adamites were sometimes mistaken for members of other radical sects.

CALL NOTHING ONE HATH ONE'S OWN

Among those mistaken for Adamites, and vice versa, were the Ranters, who held similar extreme views. Consisting of random groups of individuals rather than forming an organised sect, the Ranters were alleged to have engaged in wife swapping, illicit sex, and other sinful activities. Prominent during the period 1649-54 'Ranterism' was the last major outbreak of the heresy of the Free Spirit. Exactly what they believed is hard to pin down, with huge differences between the groups and individuals accused of being Ranters; Ranter in fact being a term of abuse used by their persecutors. One of the more colourful Ranter characters, Abiezer Coppe, demonstrated against the rich as they passed in their coaches, gnashing his teeth at them and crying;

'Howl, howl, ye nobles, howl honourable, howl ye rich men for the miseries that are coming upon you....We'll eat our bread together in singleness of heart, we'll break bread from house to house.' 'The true communion amongst men is to have all things common and to call nothing one hath one's own.'

Abiezer Coppe. *A Fiery Flying Roll.*

The Blasphemy Act was passed in 1650 aimed at nonconformists in general, and the Ranters in particular. However like the Lollards and Familists before them the Ranters were not by nature martyrs and usually recanted when arrested, whilst continuing to hold the beliefs that so outraged their captors. Ranters were found throughout England, from the northern counties of Yorkshire, Lancashire, Westmorland and Cumberland, through the North Midlands and down into Huntingdonshire, Gloucestershire and Wiltshire as well as in London. As they were never an organised sect we have little idea what happened to the rank and file members after the authorities singled out the more notorious, outspoken ranters and picked them off one by one. They seem to have found their way into other groups such as the Quakers, where they continued to cause scandal by attaching too much importance to

'meat, drink, pleasure and women.'

More is known about the dissenting sects and political radicals existing during the period of the English Civil War than those active previous to this time, due to the collapse of the censorship laws which allowed groups to issue their own pamphlets and broadsheets. In the 20 years between 1640 & 1660 the number of publications that flowed off the uncensored presses exceeded the total published in England in the previous 150 years. This is not to say that groups were not as active before this period, or after censorship was reimposed, just that fewer records of

Ranters - Contemporary woodcut.

their activities are to be found. Out of this ferment of radicalism one group has emerged to hold a special place in the history of utopian experiments. The Diggers were 'rediscovered' by left-wing historians in the 20th century and have become something of a cause célèbre among present day land reformers and political activists, being seen as early English socialists.

THEY HAVE SOME DESIGN IN HAND

On 16 April 1649 the Council of State received a report stating that several individuals had begun to dig and plant vegetables on St. Georges Hill in Surrey and that they had invited "all to come in and help them, and promise them meat, drink, and clothes." claiming their number would be several thousand within ten days. Those involved in digging the common land on St Georges Hill were continuing a long tradition of land squatting by the dispossessed which had been going on with increasing regularity since the dissolution of the monasteries. In the same way that the outbreak of religious radicalism during the Civil

War period was the culmination of years of underground activity, so the Diggers were the latest in a long line of groups demanding land reform that stretches back at least to the Norman invasion. The 'free' presses issued phamplets by Diggers leaders and the movement spread to other parts of the country with evidence of groups 'digging' in Kent, Buckinghamshire, Northants, Leicestershire, Nottinghamshire, Gloucestershire, Hertfordshire and Bedfordshire. Gerrard Winstanley has emerged as the leader of the Diggers as much through the survival of his writings, in which he gave detailed biblical justification for reclaiming the commons, as through historical records of his activities. He was one of a number of men treated as leaders of the group squatting in Surrey by the authorities.

And the other groups around the country were certainly organised independantly there being no evidence for an organised Diggers movement with Winstanley as its leader. The report of squatters digging in Surrey alarmed the Council of State. The threat that they intended to pull down all enclosures and make the earth a common treasury struck at the heart of the new merchant classes who were leading the 'revolution'. The report ended, "It is feared they have some design in hand." This was certainly not a design that fitted the new model order of Cromwell's commonwealth - the report was sent to General Fairfax with orders for the group to be dispersed and any repetition of the event to be prevented.

MARY CARY'S TWELVE PROPOSALS

Mary Cary's Twelve proposals of 1653 mapped out a comprehensive programme of reform including; the abolition of tithes, liberty of conscience, reform of universities, poor relief, establishment of a Post Office with a stamp tax to generate revenue to support the poor, equal justice for poor and rich, a wage limit on government employees, and a violent coup by the 'godly should the ungodly resist this revolution.'

Her Utopia was to be founded on the Puritan work ethic: no lolling or idle cavalier indulgence would be allowed, and no person would be homeless, hungry or unemployed. Women and men would become filled with shining knowledge, unity, and strength. Women so shy in public, would share in the power to prophesy. She wrote of a world in which high infant mortality would be no more, promising that:

'No infant of days shall die; none shall die when they are young; all shall come to a good old age. They shall not be afflicted for the loss of their children; for they shall live till they are an hundred years old.'

Her programme was founded on rational argument, she weighed up issues like vegetarianism, concluding that

`I see no reason to conclude, that man's making use of the creatures in a reasonable and moderate manner, is ... bondage and corruption. Animals cannot suffer violent death in the same way as humans do, for they fear it not.'

Mary's vision of a new golden age was upbeat and optimistic. She thought that if her proposals were implemented by parliament, five years would see a difference,

`but ten years hence much more than now; and twenty years hence far acceding that ... For these are not ordinary times.'

`I do not pretend to be any more exempted from uncertainty, than any other ... I shall not press any to believe these things ... unless they do hear the voice of Christ and his speech setting them home upon them.'

DIGGING FOR FREEDOM

GUEST ARTICLE BY

PETER MARSHALL

This article first appeared in Diggers & Dreamers 2000/01.

Who were the original diggers who tried to live out their dream three hundred and fifty years ago?

After a series of bad harvests and the disruptions of the English civil war, a band of about forty masterless men and women decided to take their lives into their own hands. On April Fool's Day in 1649, they climbed St George's Hill (which they called George's Hill) near Cobham in Surrey to dig up and manure the commons and plant carrots, parsnips, beans, wheat and rye, hoping to eat their bread together by the sweat of their brows. They came with love and peace in their hearts, wanting to turn swords into spades and hoes. Their intentions were simple and clear but profoundly revolutionary:

'That we may work in righteousness, and lay the Foundation of making the Earth a Common Treasury for All, both Rich and Poor, That every one that is born in the Land, may be fed by the Earth his Mother that brought him forth, according to the Reason that rules in the Creation. Not inclosing

any part in any particular hand, but all as one man, working together, and feeding together as Sons of one Father, members of one Family; not one Lording over another, but looking upon each other, as equals in the Creation.'1 They had no intent to fight or to cre-

ate a tumult, but only to get enough bread to eat by working together. They not only tried to love each other as themselves, but made every attempt to love their enemies. Indeed, they insisted; 'we find the streaming out of Love in our hearts towards all... we have peace in our hearts, and quiet rejoycing in our work, and filled with sweet content, though we have but a dish of roots and bread for our food.'2 The Diggers believed that the earth is a common treasury which God intended all to enjoy and saw the commons and wastes of England as a free store-house. In their view, it was 'the cursed thing, called Particular Propriety [private property], which is the cause of all wars, bloud-shed, theft, and enslaving Laws, that hold the people under miserie'.3 They called for the abolition of buying and selling, employment and hire, wages and rent, landlords and tenants. They wanted to see the end of the clergy with their 'tythe-plundering' trade and lawyers with their exorbitant fees who only incite quarrels. With Righteousness in their heart and Reason as their guide (none other than God within) they saw no need for external governments and manmade laws. For them property was theft and the State was tyranny. Their aim was to turn not only England into a common treasury but the whole wide world. They sang:

Then Clubs and Diamonds cast away

For Harts & Spades must win the day. 4

One of their members was Gerrard Winstanley, a former clothing apprentice and hired labourer, who had issued a few months earlier the pamphlet called The New

Law of Righteousness(1649) which defined the law as the pure light of Reason in every individual which comes from God. He argued that before the Fall there had been no private property and that the earth had been created as a "common treasury" for all to enjoy. The time had come to restore the original equality and freedom by cultivating the commons to which the people of England had an ancient claim. True freedom was not just an end to kingly tyranny but the freedom of access to the land for every one.

Winstanley signed with William Everard, John Palmer, Christopher Clifford, Richard Goodgroome, Thomas Starre, Robert Sawyer, Henry Bickerstaffe and other members of the George's Hill colony *The True Levellers Standard Advanced: or; The State of Community opened, and Presented to the Sons of Men* (1649). They claimed that 'Every single man, Male and Female, is a perfect Creature of himself' and being 'subject to Reason, his Maker...[he] needs not run abroad after any Teacher and Ruler without him'.5 In other words, every person is capable of managing him or herself without the entanglement of laws and government. In *A Watch-Word to the City of London and the Armie*(1649), Winstanley further asserted the love of freedom is an inherent part of human nature for 'all men have stood for freedom... Freedom is the man that will turn the world upside downe, therefore no wonder he hath enemies'. But true freedom is not the self-assertion of the rugged individualist but 'lies in the community in spirit, and community in the earthly treasury, and this is Christ the true manchild spread abroad in the Creation, restoring all things into himselfe'.6

The programme of the Diggers was extremely radical, and,even by modern standards, quite anarchist. Since their land, cattle, corn, vegetables and fruits were to be held in common and they would forego the 'cheating intanglements' of buying and selling, 'what need have we', Winstanley asked, 'of imprisoning, whipping, or hanging Laws, to bring one another into bondage?'7. 'The best laws that England hath', he declared, 'are yokes and man-

acles, tying one sort of people to another'. As such, they ought to be cut off with the king's head. Indeed, kingly power, lords of the manor, clergy, lawyers and buying and selling were all linked : 'if one truly fall, all must fall'. When accused that his beliefs 'will destroy all government and all our ministry and religion', Winstanley replied calmly: 'It is very true.'8

THE WORLD TURNED UPSIDE DOWN

The Digger colony on George's Hill was not unique. It was only one sturdy sprout of a complex network of growing roots in the fertile soil of the English Revolution. The poor and dispossessed began to dig up the commons in Iver in Buckinghamshire, Wellingborough in Northamptonshire, Bosworth in Leicestershire, Cox Hall in Kent, Enfield in Middlesex, Dunstable in Bedfordshire, as well as in Gloucestershire and Nottinghamshire. Emissaries were sent out to spread the word. The Diggers of Wellingborough announced in May 1650 that the 'Earth is our Mother, and that God hath given it to the children of men, and that the common and waste Grounds belong to the poor, and that we have right to the common ground both from the Law of the Land, Reason and the Scriptures'. The poor inhabitants in the parish of Iver in Buckinghamshire further declared that there is 'a principle of Reason that teacheth every man to do as he would be done by, that is to live in love, and be at peace with all men'.9

The Diggers expressed themselves in the Biblical language of the day. Winstanley in particular heard a voice in a trance which told him: 'Work together; Eate Bread together; Declare this all abroad.' 10 They interpreted the Bible largely in allegorical terms. They identified the lords of the manor, clergy and lawyers who bent their backs with the 'elder brethren' of the tyrannical Cain and Esau and associated themselves with the 'younger brethren' of Abel and Jacob. Before the Fall, Winstanley claimed that Adam had dressed the earth in 'love, freedom, and righteousnesse'.1 I But covetousness came in the form of the serpent, private property was established and brother began

The Law of Freedom on a Platform.

Gerrard Winstanley

Following the failure of the civil war to bring any real benefits to the common folk Winstanley set out a programme for a state led socialist revolution. Written as an address to Cromwell The Law of Freedom is the first 'communist manifesto' ever to be issued.

His programme included:

- CommonOwnership of land
- The abolition of Money
- Communal storehouses
- Free Universal Education: In the Arts, Science and Languages, everyone was also to learn a manual trade.
- The state to encourage and promote scientific research.
- A national news system: To spread new ideas through out the land.
- Annually elected Parliaments and Civil officials
- A simplified legal system: To control the power of lawyers and judges. Essentially a Bill of Rights. Including: offences for Idleness, waste of resources and slander - punishable by I years community service. And the Death Penalty for : Administering the law for monetary gain, Buying and selling the fruits of the earth (except to a another nation), using religion to get goods or Land, Murder and rape.

The Law of Freedom is available at: **http://www.bilderberg.org/lawofree.htm**

---

to kill brother. Yet all was not lost. The Garden of Eden, where all lived in harmony, could be restored here and now once the serpent of private property and the red dragon of government had been banished.

They found justification in the Scriptures for their conviction that all human beings are born equal and free and that 'particular propriety' was created by murder and theft out of the original 'publick community'. They were no respectors of persons. Robert Coster asserted in *A Mite Cast into the Common Treasury* that 'the great Creator of all things, ordained that the earth, with the fulness thereof should be a common Treasury of Livelihood for all, and that none should Lord over his own kind, but that all should love as Brethren'.12 For Winstanley, God is not only within all beings but Christ is 'the universal Love or Free community' and 'the great Leveller'.13 God is immanent in the world and the whole creation is his clothing. He equated God with Reason, and saw the divine law expressed through human reason.

LIKE PARCHMENT IN THE FIRE

The Diggers were living in a visionary time, a time when 'the present state of the old World' was 'running up like parchment in the fire, and wearing away'.14 For a short spell, it seemed as if the wildest dreams of the poor and oppressed could be realized. The royalists had been defeated and the king had just been beheaded. The levellers in the New Model Army were calling for political democracy in a new constitution and the right to choose their officers. 'True levellers' went even further by calling for economic democracy, for the equality of property and the redistribution of the land. A Leveller pamphlet called *More Light Shining in Buckinghamshire*(1649) called on the soldiers 'to stand everyone in his place, to oppose all tyranny whatsoever', particularly that of the grasping lawyers and the enclosing lords of the manor. The anonymous pamphlet *Tyranipocrit Discovered* (1649) declared that 'God made men and the devil made kings' and went on to upbraid the government of the Republic for not bringing aboot 'an equality of goods and lands' as God and Nature would have it.

Just as the Diggers began to cultivate the commons on George's Hill a group of six soldiers, true levellers to a man, entered the nearby parish church of Walton-on-Thames after the parson's sermon and announced the abolition of the Sabbath, tithes, ministers, magistrates and the Bible. Ranters like Abiezer Coppe, more extreme than the Diggers, believed that they were in a state of purity like Adam before the Fall and could do no sin. Challenging head on the Protestant ethic of work and wedlock for life, some believed in free love and celebrated the joy of leisure as well as sharing the good things of the earth.15

The Diggers and true levellers claimed that by executing Charles I in January 1649 they had at last thrown off the 'Norman yoke' which had been imposed on the free-born English by William the Conqueror in 1066. Abolishing the monarchy meant for them that all the royal charters and grants were rendered null and void, including the tythes to the lords of the manor and the clergy which had been set in the king's name. Moreover, by fighting for the republican cause, they believed that the new parliament had made an agreement with them to make England a free commonwealth:

> A Covenant they did take,
> And promises they did make,
> All burthens to remove,
> And to unite in love;
> Yet we cannot see that good hour,
> The taking down of Kingly power.16

In their pamphlets and appeals to General Fairfax, the Army and Parliament the Diggers reminded those in power of their pledge but their demands fell on deaf ears.

The Digger movement was in many ways the culmination of a century of steady encroachments of the wastes and forests by squatters, commoners, and travellers. By taking up their spades and hoes and digging the commons of England, the Diggers were continuing an ancient tradition. But by making their demands public and taking up the cause of the oppressed they directly challenged the authorities in Church and State. By calling on the poor to organize themselves and to undertake direct action they were a real threat to Cromwell's power and the army grandees. Their demands for the people of England to build an equal and free community at the local level based on the communal cultivation of the land was profoundly revolutionary. The Council of State was right to worry that their communal and egalitarian principles might undermine the security of private property and the rule of the State.

Unfortunately, the grand experiment of the Diggers in communal living and sharing was short-lived. They were harassed by neighbouring free-holders and magistrates. In August 1649 a handful of demoralized soldiers and hired thugs, whipped up by the local parson and lord of the manor, invaded the colony on George's Hill. They trampled on their corn and vegetables, pulled down their simple huts, destroyed their carts and wheels, broke their tools and spades, hit and chased away their cows. Several of the Diggers were cruelly beaten. One poor old man and his wife were turned out of doors to lie in the field on a cold night.

When Winstanley and others were arrested and refused to have a lawyer to represent them in court, they were flung into jail. But whatever the provocation, they refused to fight back, trying, in the most extreme circum-

stances, to love their enemies. In the pamphlet *A New-yeers Gift for Parliament and Armie* (1650), Winstanley reminded the officers that they were 'Servants to the commons of England' but lamented the fact that 'England is a Prison; the variety of subtleties in the Laws preserved by the Sword, are bolts, bars, and doors of the prison; the Lawyers are the Jaylors, and poor men are the prisoners'.17

By the end of 1650 the Diggers had been suppressed. After their rout, they dispersed; it was now simply a question of survival rather than carrying forward the social revolution which had started with the foundation of the Commonwealth. They had cut off the crown of the tree of oppression but the upper branches grew stronger and still kept the sun of freedom from the poor. Like all authoritarian leaders, Cromwell destroyed the movement which brought him to power. Even the anarchistic Gerard Winstanley lost his way, dedicating his blue print for a new society *The Law of Freedom in a Platform* (1652) to Cromwell who had described the Levelers as contemptible 'persons differing little from beasts'. Winstanley even called for a centralized State run by 'Overseers', the death penalty for buying and selling and forced labour for the idle.

STAND UP NOW

Despite the brief shining of their candle three hundred and fifty years ago, the inspiring creed and example of the Diggers lives on, not only in the everlasting gospel of William Blake or the visions of William Morris and Kropotkin, but in the modern co-operative, communal and green movement. The Diggers are the true ancestors of all those who wish to live in harmony with each other and close to the earth and who insist that they can manage their own lives without the burden of external laws and government. They will inspire all those who travel with peace in their hearts & who believe that love conquers all.

Manuring of the common land was a key theme of their writings and almost a sacred act for the Diggers. They wanted to transform the waste land of their own society. Their actions and ideas will undoubtedly fertilize the growing movement which seeks to turn the earth into a common treasury for all to enjoy freely, both humans and non-humans, in the dawn of the new millennium.I for one continue to believe that we are all free-born and have an equal claim to the good things of the earth. We broke the 'Norman Yoke' and ended the monarchy in the 17th century, regardless of the claims of upstart kings and would-be aristocrats in our land, and I look forward to a time when a free commonwealth is established in England and the rest of the world.18

Therefore with the Diggers I sing:

'With spades and hoes and plowes,
stand up now, stand up now
With spades and hoes and plowes stand up now,
Your freedom to uphold...Glory here,
Diggers all!'

Peter Marshall is a writer, philosopher, traveller and founder member of Redfield Community in Buckinghamshire. His many books include : *Demanding the Impossible: A History of Anarchism* (Fontana,1993), *Nature's Web: Rethinking our Place on Earth* (Cassell,1996) and *Riding the Wind: A New Philosophy for a New Era*(Cassell,1998)

NOTES

1 Gerrard Winstanley: Selected Writings,ed., Andrew Hopton(Aporia Press,1 989), p.15. Hereafter referred to as GW. 2 GW, p.20 3 GW, p.32

4 Digger Tracts 1649-50, ed., Andrew Hopton(Aporia Press, 1989), p.24.Hereafter referred to as DT.

5 GW,p.10 6 GW, pp.45-6 7 GW, p.35

8 In Christopher Hill, The World Turned Upside Down (Penguin,1 975),pp.1 33,142

9 DT, pp.29-30,32 10 GW,p.18 11 GW, p.40 12 DT,pp.11,12 13 GW, pp.91,95 14 GW,p.11

15 See my Demanding the Impossible: A History of Anarchism (Fontana,1 993), pp.96-107

16 DT,p.21 17GW, pp.71-2

18 See my Ridhg the Wind: A New Philosophy for a New Era(Cassell,1 998)

RADICAL MYSTICS

John 'Father Abraham' Pordage, and his wife 'Deborah', ran a sort of 'Ranters commune', at Bradfield in Berkshire where he was rector. Here they kept open house or 'family communion' and various notorious radicals are know to have lived there, among them Abiezer Coppe, Thomas Tany and William Everard. Pordage himself was accused of holding Ranter views and called before the Commisioners for ejecting Scandalous, Ignorant, and Insufficient Ministers and Schoolmasters, for making blasphemous statements and having improper intercourse with a woman in London. He was found guilty and ejected from Bradfield.

Pordage was a follower of the ideas of Jakob Boehme(1576-1624) a central European mystic whose visionary works were translated into English between 1644 and 1662, and widely circulated during the period of the Commonwealth. Pordage, who along with his wife had mystical visions of his own, wanted to make Boehme's somewhat obscure Theosophy accessible to ordinary people. Following their ejection from Berkshire he reappears after the restoration of Charles11 in 1660 with his own small nonconformist congregation in London and it is here that he met up with Jane Leade and with her went on to set up the Philadelphian Society.

Jane Leade was the daughter of a well-to-do Norfolk family from whom she had become estranged following a number of mystical visions. She had moved to London where she married a distant relative, William Leade who shared her spiritual devotion. They had four daugthers together, two of whom died in infancy. Mrs Leade was inspired by Dr Pordage's Behmenist teachings and he was impressed by her mystical visions. She soon became to all extents the leader of the group. In 1665 the Great Plague struck London and Dr Pordage and his congregation, now numbering nearly 100, joined the crowds fleeing the city and returned to Bradfield. Following the death of his wife in 1668 Pordage returned to London to resume his work.

Portriat of John 'Abraham' Pordage

Here he found Mrs Leade widowed and poverty stricken. She was also experiencing visions and recording them in a spiritual diary called *A Fountain of Gardens.* She moved into Dr Pordage's house and they started to gather together a small group who, under the guidance of the 'Virgin of Wisdom', would pave the way for the resurection of Christ and the establishment of the glorified church on earth. When John Pordage died in 1681 Mrs Leade struggled to keep the little group going - publishing Pordage's *Theologia Mystica* and her own *The Heavenly Cloud Now Breaking.* Despite her efforts the group dwindled to hardly any more than herself and Dr Pordage's brother Francis.

THE RULES OF PARADISE

Copies of *The Heavenly Cloud Now Breaking* found their way to Germany where they inspired a group of followers to contact her and to offer to publish all her works in German and English. This caused a revival in Mrs Leade's popularity. In 1694 she met Francis Lee, a fomer fellow of St John's College, Oxford who had refused to take the oath of allegiance to William & Mary. Lee married Mrs Leade's daughter and when Leade went blind took on the responsibility of writing all her letters and publications from dictation. By this time her English disciples had formed a community and called themselves the Philadelpians. They published what amounts to the first ever 'new age' monthly magazine entitled, *Theosophical Transactions.* It contained 'Memoirs, Conferences, Letters, Dissertations, Inquiries, etc, For the Advancement of Piety and Divine Philosophy'. Jane Leade died in the spring of 1704, and although her followers attempted to keep the Philadelphians going there is no trace of any activity after 1707. A thread of English Christian mysticism has however continued through the ages and websites dedicated to Jane Leade and Jakob Boehme can be found at :
www.sigler.org/leade/
www.augustana.ab.ca/~janzb/boehme.htm

THE FRIENDS OF THE TRUTH

Out of the many and various groups that emerged in the religious and political ferment that was 17th century England, one has had a long and lasting effect not only on Utopian experiments, but also on wider society. The "Children of the Light" or "The Friends of the Truth", later known as The Society of Friends or simply - the Quakers (originally a derogatory term it is the name by which they have come to be known, though some Friends to this day still dislike the name.) In the late 17th Century loose groups of seekers and dissenters were gathered together by wandering preachers into small fellowships or meetings of 'friends'. George Fox a shoemaker from Nottingham was a particularly charismatic preacher who undertook a religious journey through the north of England during which he had a vision on the top of Pendle Hill, in Lancashire. "As we went I spied a great hill called Pendle Hill, and I went on the top of it with much ado, it was so steep; but I was moved of the Lord to go atop of it; and when I came atop of it I saw Lancashire sea; and there atop of the hill I was moved to sound the day of the Lord; and the Lord let me see a-top of the hill in what places he had a great people to be gathered." George Fox *Journal*

George Fox
from a painting by S.Chinn

The early Friends became a focus for many dissenters providing a refuge for erstwhile Ranters, Levellers, Fifth monarchists and Seekers. This influx of more exterme elements mean't that some Friends' activities were somewhat riotous affairs - disrupting church services, riding into Bristol on an ass, setting off to convert the Sultan of the Ottoman empire - the exploits of the early days seem strangley at odds with the later 'quiet' period of Quakerism with it's plain clothes and its decent honest hard work.

George Fox became the leading preacher in the Society of Friends mainly due to his charismatic personality and indefatigable energy. He was also in no small part helped by Margaret Fell, a judges wife from Ulverston, Cumbria, who was converted by Fox and who later married him upon the death of Judge Fell. Margaret and her daughters were great organisers and it was largely through their efforts that the early 'friends' were organised into communities, or 'meetings', of like-minded individuals, with shared beliefs and goals.

The Friends rejected the formalised structures of the Church of England and its doctrines for a more direct individual experience or personal awakening to God. Fox developed his concept of the Inward Light based on his own personal conversion. A Friends meeting was a time to wait in silence, and to contemplate God. Having no clergy, lay preachers (often women) would officiate. In addition to their religious beliefs, Friends also rejected most of the civil legal authorities and their laws. Public oaths, the payment of tithes to the state, Church or its ministers were considered to be contrary to the will of God. The very fabric of society was being called into question. This brought the Friends into direct conflict with State and the Church. Many Friends were arrested and imprisoned for their beliefs, some repeatedly, some 4000 being imprisoned after the Venner Rising (1661). A number of prisoner support schemes were run where work was found for imprisoned Friends by the local meeting and goods sold on their behalf. Persecution continued until the Toleration Act (1689).

Friends' refusal to swear the oath of allegiance closed off many careers to them. They were unable to enter any university or work in law, medicine or any civic authorities. This meant that they were to concentrate their energies and growing wealth in emerging areas of trade, using the networks of Friends meetings to find both financial support, like minded employees and outlets for their goods. They worked in textiles, mining, iron- smelting & manufacture, banking, clockmaking.... in fact across the whole range of industries building up reputations for being honest, hard-working and fair traders. As some Friends began to prosper marked social differences began to appear between them. Fox, therefore, issued injunctions about Poor Relief. In *The Basis of Truth upon the man of Sin* (1655) he wrote: ' Ye that set your nests on high, join house to house, field to field, till there be no place for the poor, woe is your position . . . The righteous God is coming to give to every one of you according to your works.' And later, in his organization for the Society, he laid down that 'Friends should have and provide a house or houses where an hundred may have rooms to work in, and shops of all sorts of things to sell, and where widows and young women might work and live'.

It was from Quaker schemes for poor relief that many community projects arose. Thomas Lawson, a clerk to a monthly meeting, employed at Swarthmore to teach Mrs. Fell's daughters, addressed parliament on the subject. In an *Appeal to the Parliament concerning the Poor that there may be not a beggar in England* (1650) he set out a 'platform' whereby those who could not support themselves would be maintained by money collected by the parishes. The destitute would be given whatever support was necessary and those in need of work would be helped by a series of labour offices where "(a) handicraftsmen and labourers that want work, and such as want workmen may enquire; (b) masters may find apprentices and servants, and vice versa; (c) maids may find employment, "but none to be put to service until they be first taught to spin, knit, sew, learn some trade, or way of livelihood, who else are neither fit for service nor can in after time do anything for themselves." He suggested that a census be carried out to assess the extent of distress in crowded areas of towns. "I have considered of cities, towns, and villages, but no place have I found where this platform may not be suitable." Lawson's Platform was not taken up by parliament but that did not stop the Friends from pursuing their ideas for social reform.

A PLENTIFUL LIVING FOR THE POOR

John Bellers was specially employed in relief work; he was later made treasurer of a fund for employing the poor, and was soon active in putting forward various proposals. From 1679 till 1696 his fertile imagination evolved numerous projects which he committed to paper. One of them was the *Proposals for Raising a College of Industry of all Useful Trades and Husbandry With Profit to the Rich, A Plentiful Living For the Poor, and a Good Education for Youth, Which Will Be an Advantage to the Government by the Increase of the People and their Riches.* (1696). Bellers' proposed that a community of some three hundred producers should be established, 'a Community something like the example of primitive Christianity, that lived in common, and the Power that did attend it, bespeaks its Excellency'.

In a remarkably thorough and concise 28 pages he presented detailed plans and costing for his scheme. Accommodation was to be in four units, for married couples, for unmarried men, for unmarried women and for boys, with a sickbay or hospital section. Good quality food would be served in a communal canteen. Education and training would be given to both men & women in an apprentices college. He also prescribed that men reaching the age of 60 would leave strenuous work, and become 'overseers'. He calculated that the 'College' could be maintained by - 44 manual labourers and craftsmen; 82 women and girls for housework, tending cattle; 24 agricultural labourers, men and boys; 10 men to look after the fuel supply, maintenance and repair of the property. So impressive was the plan that a century latter Robert Owen would have it reprinted and Karl Marx would praise it as 'a veritable marvel in the history of political economy'.

His proposal was brought before the Friends yearly meeting in 1697 and circulated to different monthly and quarterly meetings up and down the country asking whether they would be willing to support the idea. It was envisaged 'one House or Colledge for a beginning' being 'set on foote by a Joynt Stock by Friends of Estates throughout ye Kingdom (severall having subscribed considerably already)'. It was estimated that it would cost £18,000 to set the community up. Only one district, London, adopted the proposal where in 1701 a Workhouse was established for thirty inmates at Clerkenwell. What might have been the first Quaker community was more like a factory producing yarn and mops and later became a hospital and nursery, and ultimately a school.

William Penn

ATHENS OF AMERICA

As with the puritan separatists before them, the Friends also found new homes in the American Colonies. William Penn(1644-1718), a wealthy merchant and a prominent Quaker establish the colony of Pennsylvania. The son of a British admiral he had been expelled from Oxford, studied law at Lincoln's Inn and at the Huguenot Academy at Saumer. In his mid twenties he converted to Quakerism and quickly involved himself in the Quaker cause being imprisoned several times for his 'radical' preaching on personal, property and religious rights. Whilst travelling in America, in the company of George Fox, Penn wrote a charter for a group of Quaker colonists who were settling in New Jersey. Enshrined in the charter were provisions for religious freedom, the right to trial by jury, freedom from arbitrary imprisonment for debt, and an edict against capital punishment. The Charter is the first clear statement in American history of the case for the supremacy of universal rights over local laws.

King Charles II owed William Penn £16,000, money which Penn's father had lent him, Penn asked the King to grant him a charter for territory between Maryland and New York to pay off the debt so he could realise plans to establish a haven for persecuted Quakers. With the Duke of York's support, the petition was granted. Penn had wanted to call the colony 'New Wales' or 'Sylvania' but Charles II intervened, suggesting instead 'Pennsylvania' after Penn's recently departed father; a name that Penn feared (rightly) would lead people to assume that he had named it after himself.

Although granted all the land in Pennsylvania, William Penn and his heirs chose not to grant or settle any part of it without first buying the claims of the Delaware and Wyandot Indians who lived there and signing a treaty of peace with them. Under the stewardship of the Penn family the colony thrived, with settlers arriving by the score - not only Quakers from England, but Irish and Welsh Quakers, Scots Presbyterians, French Huguenots, German Baptists, Dutch, Swedish and Jewish settlers. Mennonites, Amish and Moravian groups came to set up communities in

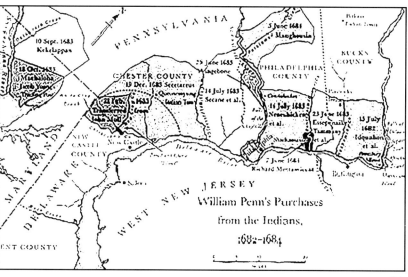

William Penn's Purchases from the Indians, 1682-1684

THE SHAKING QUAKERS

At Manchester, in England,
This blessed fire began, And like a flame in stubble,
From house to house it ran:
A few first receiv'd it,
And their lusts forsake;
And soon their inward power
Brought on a mighty shake.

Millennial Praises 1813

A group of French religious refugees, known as the Camisards, brought a renewed sense of mysticism to the scattered English dissenting sects from 1707 onward. They and their converts toured, gave lectures and brought a new enthusiasm to small groups of seekers up and down the country. One group of Quakers who were enthused by these French prophets was based at Bolton-le-moors 12 miles north of Manchester. Lead by Jane and James Wardley this small group used the techniques of Quaker meetings, but their `silent meditation' was interrupted by 'Mother' Jane's passionate revelations; walking up and down trembling she would declaim the word of God. Because of their dancing and crying out in strange tongues, they were known as the Shaking Quakers.

Attracted to the group was a blacksmith's daughter from Toad Lane (now Todd St) in Manchester. Already known for disrupting church services and disturbing the peace, Ann Standerin a short, stout twenty-two year old would in the ten years from 1758 go from being a lowly member of the Wardleys congregation to Mistress-Messiah and Prophetess of the Sect. The catalyst for this transformation was her marriage to John Lee and subsequent loss of four children. Ann saw the deaths of her children as a series of judgements on her. She reacted with guilt, shame, and an aversion to sex. Avoiding her bed `as if it had been made of embers' night after night she walked the floor in her stocking feet afraid to sleep lest she `awake in hell'. This suffering went on, she denied her self food & drink - that her soul `might hunger for noth-ing but God.' Her health deteriorated until she became so weak that she had to be fed and supported by others. Finally when she had cleansed herself of the `last remains of human depravity' she experienced a spiritual rebirth. From this point she would rise to lead the sect being known to her followers as the `Bride of the Lamb', `Mother Ann' or 'Ann the Word'. Under Ann's leadership the group grew, holding tumultuous meetings that went on throughout the night. Tales of the strange worship, with shakings, tongue-speaking, and dark prophecies disturbed the neighbourhood. They were accused of fanaticism, heresy, even witchcraft. Ann's condemnation of lust and criticism of the established church for condoning marriage brought her into conflict with the authorities and she suffered numerous arrests. Eventually an accommodation was reached whereby the 'shakers' were left alone so long as they didn't disturb the Sabbath.

In 1772 Ann received a vision from God in which she was told that "a place had been prepared" for them in America. A small band of nine believers emigrated to America in1774 and founded the United Society of Believers in Christ's Second Appearing. They lived in New York until they could raise enough money to buy a tract of wilderness for themselves in Western New York State, which they called Niskeyuna. Here they built the first Shaker community in America. In numerous visions Mother Ann formulated a basic philosophy for the group - in one vision it was explained to her that sex was the root of all sin, and that to truly serve God, one must be celibate. She came to believe that God was bisexual because both man and woman were made in his image, and that this was duplicated throughout nature. Every living thing, animal or vegetable, had both a male and female component. She herself was seen to be the female component of Christ's spirit representing the second appearance of Christ on earth. This lead to the belief that all people were equal regardless of sex or race. Although men and women in the communities had separate spheres of activity and responsibilities there was a fundamental spiritual and physical equality, an equality which was extended to non-

Christians and black and native americans who joined the communities. Following Ann Lee's death, the leadership would pass to both men and women. Other tenets of belief were that they must regularly confess their sins, they must separate themselves from the outside world and that they must live communally. These beliefs would eventually become sets of written rules by which they would guide their lives. The Shakers would go on to become the most successful communal sect in America establishing 18 communities. By 1850, they would number almost 4,000 members and over their 200 year history it is estimated that 20,000 Americans spent at least some of their life as Shakers.

Today they have become almost better known for their simple designs for houses and furniture than their spiritual practices which included not only elaborate rituals and dances, but prophetic trances, spirit contact, native American chants and the laughing gift. In the `laughing gift' worshippers held their sides and reeled in their chairs till they became exhausted. Spirit birds brought spirit (ie: Invisible) musical instruments and chosen members would march around playing spirit music.

In the mid-19th century using sales techniques usually thought of as modern, such as the mail-order catalogues and showrooms, the Shakers began to sell their furniture in quantity setting up a factory at the Mount Lebanon community. In 1927 a Shaker rocking chair found its way to Denmark, where it caught the eye of one of the most important figures in the Scandinavian modern movement, architect Kaare Klint (1888-1954). When the Danish Co-operative Wholesale Society began to make well designed, attractive, affordable furniture its designers would draw on Shaker examples for inspiration. Scandinavia began exporting its mass-produced furniture to the rest of Europe and the USA in quantity in the 1950s and the style has gained enormous & continuing popularity, most notably through the IKEA chainstores. The Modern movement mantra 'form follows function' would appear to be an echo of the Shakers from almost a century before - "All beauty that has no foundation in use, soon grows distasteful and needs continuous replacement with something new."

In 1871 FW Evans, the ex-Owenite elder from the Mount Lebanon community, made a speaking tour of England where as well as making a number of converts he set up a recruiting office in London under the name of The Progressive Literary & Spiritual Institution. He was of the opinion that `there are many people in England prepared to enter the Order, and a revival of spiritual life is all that is necessary to inaugurate Shaker Communism on British soil'

Historians have extolled Shaker virtues, their lack of vice, co-operative communities, inventiveness, superb craftsmanship, and self-reliance. But a somewhat different story has started to unfold as archaeologists have begun to excavate Shaker rubbish dumps they have found "widespread evidence for violations of the Shakers' own... laws." 'Contraband' found includes: countless beer, whiskey, wine, and perfume bottles; tobacco pipes; pig bones (pork was taboo); and gaudy material items. These items would appear to come from later periods when it appears from their garbage at least that it is hard to tell the Shakers apart from the mass of middle class America. In 1999 there remained one Shaker community at Sabbathday Lake with only 10 members. Mother Ann, before her death, had a vision that the Shakers would be renewed once they had dropped to five members. The last of the Shakers are awaiting the renewal and continuing to live their utopian lives according to the visions that Ann Lee received over 225 years ago.

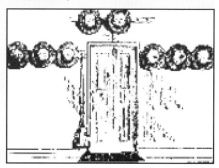

this haven of religious tolerance.

Despite Quaker opposition, by 1730 some 4,000 slaves had been brought to Pennsylvania mostly by English, Welsh and Scottish-Irish colonists. The census of 1790 showed 10,000 African-Americans living in the colony of whom about 6,300 had received their freedom. The Pennsylvania Gradual Abolition Act of 1780 was the first emancipation statute in the United States.

By 1776, the Quaker Province had grown to become the third largest English colony in America with its capitol Philadelphia the largest English-speaking city in the world next to London. The multi-cultural mix of national groups in Pennsylvania helped to create its broad-minded, tolerant and rich cosmopolitan cultural life earning it the nickname of the "Athens of America".

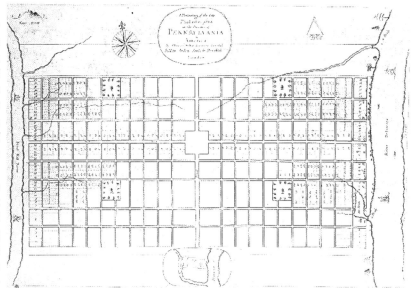

William Penn's plan for Philadelphia

GREENE TOWNE

The Portraiture of the City of Philadelphia, published in 1683 by Thomas Holme carried details of William Penn's proposed layout for a capital city for the colony to be located on a 10,000-acre site at the junction of the Delaware and Schuykill rivers. Penn's designs for Philadelphia were revolutionary for the time and anticipate many future developments in city layout and town planning. On a 1200 acre plot the city was set out on a rectangular gridiron pattern with 100ft wide avenues converging at 'centre square' and dividing it into four quadrants. All houses would have gardens and the core of the "great towne" was to be surrounded by gentlemen's mansions each set in 800-acre estates - in effect a greenbelt. Each quadrant contained additional green-space in the form of a small park. Penn envisioned a 'greene towne' "which will never be burnt, and always be wholesome." He had after all lived through the bubonic plague of 1665 and the great fire of London and so had experienced some of the dangers of

17th century city living first hand. His plans may in fact have been influenced by Richard Newcourt's plans for the rebuilding of London.

Ample space for Philadelphia to expand had been allowed by Penn, which the modern city has done far beyond the original site - building, on the way, America's first hospital, first library, and first insurance company. Though Philadelphia has grown outward beyond Penn's vision, he symbollically controlled its vertical growth until the mid 1980s. Until then his statue atop City Hall was deemed to be the limit for building height in the city.

Penn had planned to stay in the New World, settling at his manor Pennsbury, (up the Delaware from Philadelphia) but whilst back in England in 1712 he suffered an attack of apoplexy that disabled him. His wife managed his affairs until his death in 1718, and after her death in 1727 the proprietorship of Pennsylvania passed to their sons, John, Thomas, and Richard. In 1984, William Penn and his wife Hannah Callowhill Penn were made the third and fourth honorary citizens of the United States, by act of Congress.

The very success of Pennsylvania would by attracting the most persecuted and most radical Quakers contribute to what is known in Quaker history as the Period of Quietism.

WHALING QUAKERS

Not all Quakers fared well in America. During the War of Independence many were persecuted for their neutrality and pacifism. One group of Quaker whalers from Nantucket were offered sanctuary at Milford Haven, in Pembrokeshire, where Sir William Hamilton and Charles Greville were trying to develop the quay and docks. In 1793 they offered the Quaker whalers favourable terms to settle in the town and attempt to set up a whale oil industry to light the lamps of London. Seven families led by a Samuel Starbuck, and the crews to man their Brigantines, some 50 in all, settled in the town building a number of houses and a meetinghouse. In 1843, with the whale oil industry in decline due to the advent of coal gas, some returned to America whilst others stayed becoming traders in the bustling new town. To this day they are remembered in the street names of the town.

The Quaker contribution to the development of the British Isles should not be underestimated. With the advent of the industrial revolution their quiet hard working moral standpoint would make them major players in many walks of life: the Darby family, ironmasters at Coalbrookdale, as the financial bakers of Robert Owen at New Lanark, the Pease family in the North East, coal merchants and sponsors of the Stockton & Tees railway. Not only did they drive the technological change, but along side it pushed for social change - developing model houses for their workforce and sponsoring whole model village developments notably at Caldervale, Bournville & New Earswick. Later Quakers would play key roles in the variety of schemes that would lead to the founding of the welfare state.

LE FRIENDS.

'At the end of the eighteenth century some Quakers set on foot a scheme for a big social experiment in France. The leaders were Jean Marsillac, of Congenies, and Robert Grubb, of Clonmel, and they seem to have been backed by some English Friends. They applied in 1793 to the Council of the Department of Loire et Cher for leave to form in the great Castle of Chambord, schools of moral industry and establishments of agriculture, art, and commerce. They offered to educate free 150 children in morals, reading, writing, calculation, and work relating to agriculture, arts, or commerce; such as were suitable on attaining the age of 15 would, if it were wished, be kept as apprentices until they were 21, or, in the case of girls, married. Then the young man would be given 500 livres and the use of a house, yard, or garden suitable to his trade, rent free for ten years. The school would also be willing to take 300 paying pupils. In return for these advantages to French children Friends asked to be given the Castle at half the estimated value, and that any who became Friends should be freed from the necessity of taking oaths and from military service. They intended to open there eighty or a hundred workshops, "new trades and particular cultures possessed until now only by England:" The Minister of the Interior was most anxious to have the plan carried out, but there was local opposition, and the outbreak of the war between England and France rendered its fulfilment impossible.'

Quakerism and Industry Before 1800 **Isabel Grubb (1950),**

THE QUAKER COMPANY

High up on the moors above the small Pennine town of Alston lies an area of open moorland bleak, windswept and inhospitable at the best of times, where even today the Pennine Way keeps to the valleys. Travelling through this area at the end of the 17th Century two Quaker women were so concerned by the conditions of the lead miners and their families that they sponsored the involvement of the Quakers in lead mining with the formation of the 'Quaker Company' - or so the story goes - though there is nothing in the records of the London Lead company that developed the mines in this area to bear out this legend.

The company was set up by a number of Quakers in 1692 with mining interests in Derbyshire, Lancashire, North Wales, Scotland and Ireland as well as the North Pennines, mining coal and silver as well as lead and at one time (1705-37) supplying so much silver to the Royal Mint that coins were known as the Quaker coinage. From the mid-1750s onwards the company sold off its mines in other parts of the country, concentrating on its operations on Alston Moor in the North Pennines.

Faced with the problems of expanding mining operations in an area where there were no services or accommodation - except for a few remote farms - the company set about designing and building an entire new village called Nent Head, about 5 miles south east of Alston at a height of 1450ft above sea level. As most of the miners lodged at small farms and cottages scattered around the Moor the village was at first small, with a few solidly built houses, for smelters and mine officials, attached to the mine buildings. Nearby a small estate, Cherry Tree Hill, was bought from the Alston Brewery Company and a house was built for the company agent. Considerable effort was put into enlarging and improving many of the local farms, making room for the lodging of miners as well as farm hands, and providing for the care of the miners' children in both day and Sunday schools. However by 1820 it was apparent thst these arrangements were inadequate. With an estimated 4000 people in the area dependent on the company for their livelihood a more extensive and co-ordinated plan was needed if all the Company's workforce were to be housed comfortably. In 1825 a new and larger village was planned, with thirty-five cottages, clock tower, market hall, school and chapel set in a large acreage of fields, gardens and plantations. The old inn of the village, the Miners' Arms, was purchased and on several occasions its rent was reduced as its trade was diminishing, "the miners preferring books to drink".

Some of the Company's mining leases lay between Nent Head and the South Tyne valley, and from an early date the Company took an interest in the hamlet of Garrigill. Experimenting with smallholdings, they built cottages with up to six acres of land attached, and further rights to fifty-acres of pasture. Improvements were made to pasture land by draining and liming, with many experiments on the high level moors up to 2,000 feet above sea level. In an attempt to utilise and improve some of the high level moorland over 650 acres were planted with Scots pine and larch, A nursery was established for young trees, and by 1840 all the timber needed for the mines was being cut in their own woods. In Westmorland, at Dufton and Hilton, a similar pattern was followed - land was purchased, old cottages pulled down and new ones built in their place.

At Middleton-in-Teesdale the second largest estate of the Company was purchased and built in 1815. The situation at Middleton was different from Nent Head. Middleton-in-Teesdale was an old established village and the 'new town' built by the Company was never more than a suburb of the old village. The Company, however, followed its by now customary procedure providing first cottages and gardens, then baths, Company schools, chapels, and all the social amenities that the old village did not possess. After 1880 Middleton became the head office of the Company and the residence of the agent and general manager. A contemporary writer described the part of Middleton built by the Company:

'Masterman Place or as it is sometimes called, New-Middleton, was erected in 1833 by the London Lead Company from the chaste and appropriate design of Mr. Bonomi, and under the direction of Robert Stagg. It consists of several uniform rows of neat and convenient cottages, situated in a spacious garden, a portion of which was appropriated to each dwelling. The increasing population of Middleton had considerably enhanced the rents of dwelling houses there, and it was to diminish this burden that the Company built Masterman Place, in which, as vacancies occur, they place their most deserving workmen, thus combining general utility with the reward of personal merit. The first occupiers took possession of their new abodes in May 1824, accompanied by bands of music, etc'.

Throughout the 19th Century the Company continued to improve the facilities in the villages. In 1833 what was in fact the first free public library in the country was built at Nent Head. Back in 1800 the Company had begun to give regular grants for the purchase of books to loan to the men, and also to subscribe to several small libraries based in the Company's offices. In 1820, libraries were established at first in the schools, then later in purpose built reading rooms at Garrigill, Stanhope, Dufton, Hilton, Lunehead, Egglestone, Harewood, Lune Forest, and Tyne Head. By 1850 the Company were subscribing to sixteen libraries throughout the area.

In 1843 land was donated in Nent Head for a Church of England and a house built for the vicar, a post office was built in 1848, a proper water supply laid on in 1850, baths and a public wash house provided in 1865, and about the same time the old 1750-60 cottages rebuilt. In Garrigill they provided for a Girls' School, two chapels and a Parsonage, provided the curate's salary, and presented a harmonium to the church. The Company was interested in encouraging the miners to supplement their incomes by growing food as an insurance against hard times. Every cottage that they built was provided with a garden adjoining. At an early date Horticultural Societies were formed at Nent Head, and Middleton. Later, similar societies were founded at Garrigill, Dufton and Hilton. Prizes were offered each year by the Company for the two best-cultivated gardens on each estate. At the annual shows everyone from manager down to the horse boys showed some fruit, flowers or vegetables. Demand for land in addition to the cottage gardens increased and under instructions from the Company the agents purchased small plots of ground from half an acre to three acres and let them out to the miners in allotments. Due to the remote location in times of food shortages grain would be purchased by the company and delivered to the villages to keep the price down. This arrangement worked fine until the famine conditions of the 1840s when although wages had been repeatedly advanced to meet the higher cost of food, etc., there was still widespread suffering. The Company urged the miners to form their own Corn Associations. Financed by the advance of a month's wages the miners, through their own committee, purchased corn in bulk at Newcastle market, and with the co-operation of the Company's excellent system of carriers were able to transport it to Nent Head or Garrigill at minimum cost. The mill at Tynebottom was handed over to the corn association and everyone was able to get corn ground there at cost. The Corn Associations were in effect pioneer Co-operative Societies. The company agents reported that the effect of the Associations was to create a closer bond between the men and the Company, and also gave the men a sense of responsibility in running their own concern.

Credit traders preyed on the miners and their families. They would advance goods at ruinous prices on credit to be cleared by the next month's wages. This way many of the families lived constantly in debt. To counteract this and in an attempt to drive the moneylenders out of the villages the company helped finance Ready Money Shops. These were shops built by the Company, and leased to a shopkeeper who was held by a bond not to allow any goods to leave the shop except for cash payment. Provided with ample warehousing and supplied via the Companies transport system the shops were able to carry large stocks, and keep prices stable. With the success of the Ready Money Shops the credit traders practically disappeared. As a result of the Company's polices the people in all their mining localities were well housed, and were fully provided with social and educational amenities. Time after time the agents reported that the miners were content at a time when rioting and striking in other parts of the same mining field were common and they ascribe this in part to the care the Company shows for the wellbeing of their workmen. The Company realised that maximum benefit would be gained, and antagonism avoided, if the whole population of the district had access to Company facilities and from the beginning the Ready Money Shop and the Corn Association, and also the schools, were open to all residents of the area. This policy was fully justified, and was responsible for the tremendous respect in which the "Quaker Company" was held in the district by farmers and miners, alike, even years after the Company left the area.

From 1895 onwards the Company slowly scaled down its whole mining enterprise, partly due to the age of

Coronation procession Nenthead 1902

the main members of the board, or court, but mainly due to the rapidly shrinking lead market at the time. The Company finally wound up in 1905 - selling the mines to the Vieille Montagne Company who worked them for zinc up until the second world war.

'They were far in advance of the age not only in provision of day schools for all the children of the district, but in their recognition of the value and necessity for recreations of divers types-bands, cricket clubs, libraries, lectures, gardens, allotments, etc. etc., and the inevitable provision of work times that would enable miners to enjoy all these recreational facilities. There is a very modern flavour about their " welfare " work. They were seriously concerned for the health of their workpeople and their families, and besides providing medical staff and workman's fund, etc., realized that health must be based on good housing, good and adequate water supply, sanitation, and the provision of baths and wash houses.'   Arthur Raistrick.

The complete story of the Quaker Company is told in :
Two centuries of Industrial Welfare: The London (Quaker) Lead Company. 1692 - 1905 By Arthur Raistrick.
Kelsall & Davis 1988

FROM BOHEMIA TO DROYLSDEN

The 11th century Bohemian historian, Cosmas of Prague, imagined the first settlers of what is now the Czech republic to have lived in a natural state of paradise sharing all things in common:

`Like the radiance of the sun, or the wetness of the water, so the ploughed fields and the pastures, yea even the very marriages, were all in common. . . . For after the fashion of animals they entered on matings for a single night. . . Nor did anyone know how to say "Mine', but, as in the monastic life, they called whatever they had Ours, with tongue and heart and in their deeds. There were no bolts to their shacks, they did not shut their doors against the needy, because there existed neither thief nor robber nor poor man. . . . . . .'

Three centuries later this vision of an original natural order of society was to inspire the Bohemians to try and return to paradise. In the 14th Century the tiny state of Bohemia dominated the political and cultural life of central Europe. King Wenceslas IV was the emperor of the Holy Roman Empire and Prague was home to the empire's most prestigious university. However nowhere in Europe was the church more open to criticism of corruption and abuse of power. John Hus a popular preacher, inspired by the teachings of the English preacher John Wyclif, led a group known as the Hussites in attacks on the church. Hus was arrested and refusing to recant, burnt as a heretic. Hus's execution fanned the flames of social unrest into outright revolution. In 1419 a violent anti-Catholic uprising took place supported by nobles, artisans and peasants alike. From the beginning there were two wings to the Hussites, the Utraquists and the Taborites (named after the Mount of Olives where Christ was supposed to return to earth.). One a moderate reforming group, the other a group of radicals infused with the 'free spirit'.

The Taborites treated many rites of the Catholic Church with contempt and saw nothing to venerate in the relics or images of saints. They believed that every true Christian was qualified to baptise, to consecrate and to hear confession. They refused to take oaths and protested against capital punishment and declared that the Elect must rise up and exterminate their enemies and then go on to conquer neighbouring territories: `For that is what the Romans did, and in that way they came to dominate the whole world.'

Thousands of peasants and artisans throughout Bohemia and Moravia joined the Taborite army or the communities set up in Taborite strongholds. Many burnt their homesteads, sold all their belongings and paid the proceeds into communal chests under the control of Taborite priests. The largest and most celebrated of these communities was on a rocky promontory on the River Luzhnica, near the old radical centre of Usti, a refuge of radical priests fleeing persecution it had become a place of Taborite pilgrimage. Now the radicals fortified the place and built the town of Tabor, which still exists today. Tabor became the spiritual centre of the whole radical movement. Taxes, dues & rents were abolished, as was private property. There was to be no human authority of any kind: `All shall live together as brothers, none shall be subject to another.'. This outpost of Anabaptist anarchy was to last for some 30 years, the Taborite rebellion ending in a combination of internal chaos and military defeat.

When the funds in the communal chests were exhausted the radicals declared that they were entitled to take whatever belonged to the enemies of God - the rich, the clergy, the nobility, and then anyone who was not a Taborite. Moderate Taborites complained `many communities never think of earning their own living by the work of their hands but are only willing to live on other people's property and to undertake unjust campaigns for the sole purpose of robbing' At the battle of Lipan in 1434 the Taborite army was almost annihilated by a Utraquist army and in 1452 the town of Tabor itself was taken by the Utraquists. The radicals may have been defeated and paradise postponed, however a coherent Taborite tradition lived on in a purely religious form in the sect known as the Unitas Fratum, the Bohemian Brethren or as it became known in England the Moravian Church.

NO CHRISTIANITY WITHOUT COMMUNITY

At the begining of the 18th Century attempts by the Habsburg Empire to forcibly re-catholicise Protestant minorities provoked dramatic religious revivals, the suppression of which led to mass Protestant emigrations. In 1722 three men left Moravia with their families seeking a more tolerant place to practise their religion. They made their way to the estate of Count Nikolaus Ludwig von Zinzendorf a pietist who, influenced by the teachings of Wittgenstein and Jane Leade, had formed a German Philadelphian Society. After getting married he bought an estate at Bertholdsdorf, in Upper Lusatia, which he transformed into a model village, with a school, a bookseller's shop, and a dispensary. It was here that the Moravian exiles found sanctuary and set up their own community called Herrnhut (`the Lord's protection'). Moravian exiles flocked to the new community and by 1727 the population of Hermhut had reached 220 and was still growing. The exiles had little knowledge of the traditions of their ancestral church and lack of any organisation began to cause dissension. Taking leave from the Saxon court Count Zinzendorf returned to his estate to attempt to bring some order the community. He instituted fellowship groups, or `bands', as the organisational basis for the community and procceeded to issue both secular and spiritual statutes. He came across accounts of the discipline and practices of the Unitas Fratrum by its most prominent bishop in exile, Comenius, and discovered similarities with the system he had established for Herrnhut.

On 13 August 1727 the community gathered in the parish church at Berthelsdorf for Holy Communion. A quasi pentecostal outpouring of the Spirit occurred giving the whole community a sense of unity. This can be taken as the birthday of the Herrnhut community and of the Moravian Church. Following this profoundly spiritual awakening the Moravians believing that God had acted through them in the founding of their community decided to send `messengers' to communicate news of this to 'children of God' in other lands.

In England Johanna Sophia, Countess of Schaumburg-Lippe, one of the Queen's ladies-in-waiting, was amongst a small number of people who were eager to know more about the events at Herrnhut. In response the Moravians sent three 'messengers' to England. They made contact with the Countess and members of SPCK, an Anglican educational and missionary charity founded in 1698. Other than this they found little interest in their message. It was another six years before the Moravians would return to England, this time to visit the trustees of the new American colony of Georgia with the view of seeking permission to set up a Moravian community there. Despite some anti-Moravian opposition they were granted 500 acres of land on the condition that they would not preach to the 'heathens' without a written licence. 90 Swiss Settlers promptly set off to set up the first Moravians community in the new world. This was followed over the years by other settlements notably at Bethlehem in the Quaker Colony of Pennsylvania where the Moravians undertook missionary work amongst Negro slaves and Native Americans, setting up a school for slave children whose freedom they had paid for. One Native American Moravian, known as Tschoop, would later be characterised as Uncas in *The Last of the Mohicans.*

During the negotiations over the settlement in Georgia the Moravians attracted the interest of a small group of English evangelists. Among them were John & Charles Wesley. John Wesley had first met with Moravians during a voyage to America, and during a two-year stay in

Georgia, he lived in their community and participated in Moravian services. He was moved by the great simplicity and solemnity of the Moravians which he thought "the very embodiment of the spirit and practice of the primitive Church". He requested full membership of the Moravian Church, but was refused. He made a translation of Moravian hymns into English, effectively introducing hymn singing to England - before only psalms were sung in church.

On his return to England Wesley was the Moravians contact in Oxford and their link to a group known as the Holy Club a devotional church network with links far beyond Oxford. It was following a further visit by Moravians from Herrnhut that the Fetter Lane Society was formed. Whilst not officially a Moravian 'band' - the practice and actions of the group were Moravian through and through. The group,s two founding rules were:

1. That they will meet together once in a week to confess their faults one to another, and to pray for one another that they may be healed.

2. That any others, of whose sincerity they are well assured, may, if they desire it, meet with them for that purpose.

These were the rules of a Herrnhut band. Separate bands were formed for youths and men, meeting weekly and combining for a monthly meeting; at these meetings mutual group confession took place followed by prayer for forgiveness and the healing of the soul. Later women's bands were added, a controversial novelty in the all male evangelical world. Members of the group, including Wesley, journeyed to the Herrnhut community to aquaint themselves fully with Moravian beliefs and practices. Throughout 1738-39 the Fetter Lane Society found itself at the hub of religious revival taking place all over the country with Moravian inspired groups and congregations springing up in Basingstoke, Oxford, Bristol, Reading, West Yorkshire & Nottingham. The Fetter Lane Society, by this time some eighty strong, took the step of setting up a house in Islington where they could experiment with community life along Moravian lines.

This revival tapped into radical beliefs that had not seen public expression since the days of the Commonwealth, calls for laymen to be allowed to preach and baptise, calls for separation from the Anglican Church, waiting to receive the direct words of God through 'stillness' and the belief that there was no need to struggle to achieve salvation, but to simply wait for the gift of faith. These were not ideas that came from the Moravians at Hernnhut, and were to eventually lead to the break up of the Society, with the Wesley's separating off to form the Methodists, leaving a much weakened group to continue under Moravian influence. In 1741 a Moravian party from Herrnhut, arrived in London to take over leadership of the Fetter Lane Society. Finding a scattered congregation and no community activity the 'labourers' set about setting up a `Pilgrim House' where they could live together. Other Society members moved to houses in and about Fetter Lane, and four houses were rented immediately around the chapel for congregation leaders in the heart of the city a network of community houses was emerging. This set up however was regarded as far from ideal.

In Yorkshire Benjamin Ingham, an itinerant preacher in the district to the east of Leeds, was carrying out a one-man revival movement preaching in private houses, barns and fields and forming small religious societies wherever he went. Ingham had met the Moravians on an Atlantic crossing and Moravians subsequently travelled to Yorkshire making their headquarters at Smith House, Wyke nr. Halifax. In 1742. at a huge Love Feast held in a meadow near Gomersal Ingham offered the majority of his societies to the Moravians At one stroke the Moravians acquired forty ready-made religious societies with something like a 1000 members.

The story goes that Zinzendorf himself arrived and whilst visiting the sick child of a Moravian missionary found himself looking across a green valley to the southern slope of the township of Pudsey. He 'had such a sweet feeling and deep impression of the place' that he immediately told Ingham that it should be the site of a Moravian settlement, similar to that at Herrnhut, and that it should be named 'Lambshill'. Providentially the 22-acre Fallneck estate was for sale and Ingham bought it for £905. Initially the estate was leased from Ingham by the Moravians. (Later he granted it to the community for five hundred years.) Only after some years was the name Lambshill' dropped and the local 'Fallneck' adapted to Fulneck, the hometown in Moravia of Bishop Comenius.

ENCLOSURE FROM EVIL

A grand quarter-of-a-mile-long terrace cuts across the Yorkshire hillside with gardens tumbling down the hill before it, with adjacent family house, schoolrooms, workshops, inn, & shops. In the centre of the terrace is the chapel flanked by the single sisters and brethren's 'Choir' houses. "Entering the Fulneck (choir) houses by the front door one came straight into the dining-room. From there a grand central staircase led up to the first floor, at one end of which was a large choir hall for morning and evening meetings. The first and second floors also contained rooms for the choir labourers, as well as living-rooms shared by small groups and (in the sisters' case) shared workrooms. The third floor, taking up the whole of the roof space, was one large sleeping hall with room for eighty beds. "

The Moravians at Fulneck **Ruth Strong**

Such an ambitious architectural undertaking almost bankrupted the settlement and it was many years before the various industries set up by the community would do more than pay off debtors. Textiles in one form or another would form the basis of most of the financial ventures attempted at Fulneck. But despite having a 'captive workforce' which was labouring solely for its upkeep the Moravians were no match for small local clothiers whose families worked long hours and who knew the business far better that their Moravian neighbours. Other trades attempted at the settlement were; glove making, marbled paper making (the first in England) and the knitting of stockings, watch-chain making and even considered 'dealing in old Cloaths'. But only the shop and the bakery were to prove to have any lasting success. With bread from the Fulneck bakehouse would continue to be taken by horse and cart for sale over a wide area right up until the late 19th century.

Moravian congregations up and down the country organised 'choir' houses in private homes and set up chapels and schools. At Bedford, Ockbrook (Derby), Haverford West(Wales), Ayr (Scotland), Tytherton(Wilts), Dukninfield (Manchester), and Gloonen (N.Ireland) preparations were made to 'settle' the congregations. Out of these preparations 3 further Moravian settlements would

Fulneck Moravian settlement

be built. In an attempt to settle the London congregation Count Zinzendorf purchased Beaufort house which 234 years before had belonged to Sir Thomas More, the author of Utopia.

A major attraction of the Moravians was their exceptional pastoral care. Organised into 'bands' - small groups that to all extents and purposes would seem to have been self-help therapy groups - characterised by total frankness, (the word `band' often being used by Moravians of conversations where straight talking had taken place) individuals in similar circumstances, single men, single women, married couples, would meet to discuss their problems and offer each other advice.

MARRIAGE MATTERS

The most popular and important feature of the pastoral care was what amounts to the earliest organised programme of marriage guidance and sex education in Britain. The Moravians believed in a sort of Protestant sacred sexuality.

"Because Christ had a sexual organ and was born into the world through the female organ, sexual organs the sexual act could not be regarded as sinful or shameful; such matters should be talked about naturally, rather than treated as taboo."

Earthly marriage was an `interim matter', preparing for and pointing to the heavenly marriage with Christ. In it the husband represented Christ as his `procurator'; he was thus a `vice-man' or `vice-Christ'. Marriage and its consummation could therefore be described as Gottesdienst (the worship or service of God), as a sacramental act; it was the `liturgy of . . . the marriage bed, where two people hold a daily Gottesdienst'   Colin Podmore
The Moravian Church in England. 1728-1760.

This remarkably liberated view of sexuality made possible a programme of sex education carried out through the 'bands' and choir meetings. Each choir was given only as much information as was considered necessary and members were forbidden to talk about what they had heard to those in opposite sex groups. The married choir however discussed sex openly and without shame. In 1743, the London diary recorded that `Br and Sr Prusque were much bless'd together last night in their Fellowship' (the term for intercourse). Sex education was in some ways a necessity as men and women lived in separate communal houses spending little or no time with each other before marriage. Consequently particular care and guidance was attended to the beginning of married life. Before their first intercourse a couple were counselled at a married quarter-hour meeting then `blessed into the marriage state' by laying on of hands by a labourer of their respective sex.

"in 1743: `Hutton spoke with Greening fully about the Marriage Matters, and found him as simple as He could wish, and more Ignorant and unacquainted with those things than could have been possibly thought for in a London Apothecary.' After a further married quarter-

Choir house at Ockbrook

hour, `in which Hutton spoke quite plainly about the Marriage Matters', `Greening and his Wife were carried to their Apartment, and [the Huttons] went and prayed with them.' "   Colin Podmore
The Moravian Church in England. 1728-1760.

Follow up sessions offering further advice & counselling happened after the first 'fellowship' and there is evidence that those who were married and introduced in this way were grateful for the care and guidance they received. The Moravians liberal views on sex would bring them under attack. Some original Moravian Hymns contained passages that reflected their view of sexuality. `May thy, (viz. Saviour's) first holy Wound anoint me for the conjugal Business upon that Member of my Body, which is for the Benefit of my Wife...' When these were translated into English they were viewed with horror by the somewhat more repressed clergy of the Church of England and the Moravians had to rigorously defend themselves from charges of immorality. In turn the Moravians would justifiably attack the Church for its poor pastoral care and lack of discipline.

As well as Fulneck, thriving settlement would grow up at Ockbrook(Derby), Gracehill (N.Ireland) and lastly at Fairfield (Droylsden nr. Manchester). The Moravian settlements would continue as distinct communities until the end of the 19th Century. During the following century the schools at each settlement would come to prominence with other community properties being leased to non-Moravians, a trend that has been reversed at some places in recent years with more Moravians living back at the historic communities. The Moravian Church never became a sizeable part of the Methodist revival in Britain due mostly to the agreement they made not to actively seek converts in this country when the Church of England granted them recognition as a true Protestant church. In America the church with no such restrictions would continue to grow and worldwide would carry out missionary work in such diverse places as Tanzania, South Africa, Australia, in the West Indies and with the Inuit. In the 1950s & 60s the Moravians would seek out and welcome Black Moravian immigrants and offer them support, resulting in the formation of an entirely West India congregation in Leicester.

The Story of the early Years of the Moravian Church is told in: *The Moravian Church in England. 1728-1760.* Colin Podmore. 1998 Clarendon Press.
For further information on the Moravian Church today visit **www.moravian.org.uk**

TREFECA FAMILY

Inspired by the Moravians Howell Harris, a leading light of the Welsh Methodist revival, gathered a community together on his family estate at Trefeca, nr Talgarth. Breconshire. Known as The Family (Y Teulu) from 1750 onwards Methodist families from all over Wales and England flocked to join the little communit, growing to have something like 100 residents. Extra accommodation was built including an infirmary, a bath-house, a dove-cote, a fishpond and a chapel. Trees were planted and grounds laid out. Harris also rented or bought several farms in the neighbourhood. The 'reli-

Old trefeca

gious-industrial' community practiced over 60 trades including spinning and weaving of wool and flax, clog and shoe making, building, tailoring, bookbinding and printing. They lived a disciplined religious life:

'They rose at 4 and went to bed at 10, the day being spent in unstinting work in field or workshop - with no recreation at all - punctuated by three periods of prayer and ' exhorting' by Howell Harris himself or one of the four Exhorters; exposition of the Scriptures and catechising (the asking of " heart questions " as Harris described it) formed a large part of the daily routine.' *There was a man sent.....* **M.Bickerstaff**

Harris was an enthusiastic member of the Breconshire Agricultural Society-the first of its kind in Wales. He is credited with turning it from a 'Country Club for Gentlemen ' into a Society with the improvement of methods of agriculture as its main purpose and through it, and the example of Trefeca, introducing improved methods of agriculture into Wales. After Howell's death in 1773 The Family dwindled down to a few members at the turn of the nineteenth century with the last surviving member dying in 1847. The house passed to the Presbyterian Church of Wales who now run it as a training centre.

THE ENGLISH PROPHETESS

The daughter of a tenant farmer, born in Gittisham, Devon, Joanna Southcott started life as a milkmaid. Her first prophecy came to her at the age of 42 when she proclaimed to a bible class that she was to be 'the Lamb's wife'. She immediately fell into a fit and had to be carried out from the class. Later she discovered a small seal with two stars and the initials "IC" on it. She adopted it as her own, interpreting the initials as those of Jesus Christ.

In 1802 Joanna met William Sharp, a wealthy West London engraver who became one of her disciples. Sharp had been a follower of Richard Brothers another prophet who claimed direct lineal descent from King David and who in his treatise, *A Revealed Knowledge of the Prophesies and Times*, wrote under the direction of the Lord God. He revived the notion, first put forward in 1649 by John Sadler, that the English were one of the Lost Tribes of Israel and that the new Jerusalem was to be built here in England. Brothers went as far as having plans for a new Jerusalem drawn up by Scotsman John Finlayson - it included: 56 squares, 320 streets, 4 temples, 20 colleges, 47 private palaces and 16 markets. Brothers was seen as enough of a threat to warrant his arrest for treason and subsequent incarceration in a lunatic asylum.

A SHARE IN PARADISE

Encouraged by William Sharp Joanna moved to London and soon began to attract other followers of Brothers. From this base her following grew. The first "Southcottian Chapel" was opened in Southwark by William Tozer a dissenting West Country minister. Joanna declared that eternal salvation was to be granted to 144,000 of her followers. To receive salvation all followers would require a certificate bearing the "IC" seal. Salvation certificates bearing the seal were duly prepared and some 14,000 were issued to the faithful. It stated that the recipient was: "...the sealed of the Lord... [and was] to inherit the tree of life - to be made heirs of God and joint-heirs with Jesus Christ;" in short, they owned a share in paradise.

In 1813, after a successful preaching tour of northern England where further chapels were set up, Joanna wrote letters to every bishop and member of Parliament, as well as open letters to the *London Times*, announcing that she was soon to become the "Mother of Shiloh." In March 1814 the prophetess, now 64-years old, was examined by nine eminent doctors. They all agreed that she showed unmistakable signs of pregnancy, and estimated that the child would be born on Christmas Day. This news resulted in a great stir, and gifts of money, jewellery, and clothing poured in from donors eager to foster the goodwill of the second Jesus Christ.

On Christmas Day 1814, growing weaker and beginning to feel that instead of giving birth to Christ she was in fact dying, Joanna gave her last instructions. He body was to be kept warm, then opened up four days after her death. The presents for the Messiah were to be returned. She died two days later. An autopsy revealed no child or any sign of disease.

Following Joanna Southcott's untimely departure various people tried to assume the mantle of the prophetess. George Turner of Leeds initially inherited her followers, but following the failure of the New World to dawn on his prophesied date in 1817 he was eventually deposed by John Wroe.

A MAN OF PECULIAR APPEARANCE

John Wroe, born in the village of Bowling near Bradford, in 1782, was the son of a worsted manufacturer and farmer. After a rather scanty education, he entered his father's business for a time, but later took a farm on his own account. Eventually he married and brought up three

THE MILLENNIAL PANDORA'S BOX

One of Joanna Southcott's legacies to the world is a locked and sealed box tied with cords and kept with great reverence in southern England. In it, or so her followers believe, is the secret of world peace, happiness and the millennium foretold in the Apocalypse of St. John. This box first came to light after the death of the Southcottians' then leader Helen

The secret box being x-rayed in 1927

Exeter, who had formed the Panacea Society to promote Joanna's writings. As the story goes, the box may only be opened in the presence of the full complement of the bishops of the Church of England, 24 of them in all, a stipulation that seems certain to keep it closed forever. The famous psychic researcher, Harry Price, is said to have opened the box in 1927. Among the strange assortment of items he discovered were an old nightcap, a flintlock pistol, some papers and a few odds and ends. The Panacea Society maintains that he could not have opened Joanna's box. There are still groups of Southcottian believers dotted round the world who are awaiting the arrival of the millennium which will coincide with the opening of the mysterious box. Invoking Joanna's formula of "the fourth year after the first decade of the century," the estimated date of the second coming and the new millennium is 2014.

children. In 1819 he was afflicted with a life-threatening fever. Fearing his recovery was unlikely he became seriously concerned about his spiritual welfare. Shortly after a seeming miraculous recovery Wroe started having visions or trances, which were usually preceded by his being struck blind and dumb. During these trances, many remarkable events were revealed to him. He joined the Southcottians at Leeds in 1820 and two years later claimed the succession as their leader. Wroe was 'a man of peculiar appearance who inspired uneducated and wonder-loving people with a strange fascination'

Free Press 28 Feb 1874

At Idle Thorpe in Yorkshire, in 1824, he was publicly baptised before a reported crowd of 30,000 and to demonstrate his divine authority he declared that he would part the waters of the River Aire and walk across. The failure of the waters to part for him seems to have done noth-

ing to undermine his credibility with his followers.

The headquarters of the now Christian Israelite Church were transferred from Gravesend to Ashton-Under-Lyne, where in April 1824 Wroe was publicly circumcised. An elaborate sanctuary, supposedly a miniature version of Solomon's Temple, was opened in Church Street on Christmas Day 1825. Believing that Ashton was to become the New Jerusalem the Christian Israelites built four Holy gateways to the town. In 1830 Wroe reported that he had " had a comand from heaven to take seven virgins to cherish and comfort him." Three local families duly provided the virgins from amongst their daughters and Wroe set off on a preaching tour with them. When he returned one of the girls was pregnant - this scandalized some of his followers and they attempted to hold an enquiry at which fighting broke out; pews, fittings, doors and windows were torn out and broken, and 'pandemonium reigned'. Others were prepared to believe Wroe's word that a Shiloh, or messiah would be born to the girl and great preparations were made for the birth. At Peel Park Museum, Salford, there used to be preserved the magnificent cradle made ready for the Shiloh's reception, described as a "beautiful little ark of blue silk and gold" and said to have cost £200.

IT'S A GIRL!

When the messiah was finally born it was a girl - which somewhat threw the Southcottians' plans into disarray as they were expecting a boy. At this point they finally lost patience with Wroe and he was forced to leave town.

John Wroe now began an energetic life of travel and propaganda. He travelled widely in America, and Australia during the late 1840s and early 50s. It was partly Australian financial support that made it possible for Wroe to build a great house at Wrenthorpe nr. Wakefield. He was also able to attract £2,000 from funds that had been collected with the intention of publishing the *Eternal Gospel*, symbolically, 40years after Joanna Southcott's death.

CHRISTIAN ISRAELITE INSTITUTION

In a dream in 1853 Wroe claimed that the Lord had told him to build a mansion where the Messiah could dwell, along with some of the elect. In the dream he was given detailed instructions on the design of the mansion, but, in the end `Prophet Wroe's Temple' was based more on what he could remember of the design of Melbourne Town Hall. The community was opened on Whit Sunday, 1857, " . . about 250 of the body assembled in Wakefield, from the principal towns in this country America, Germany and Australia, for the purpose of attending the annual conference, and on Sunday morning the ceremony of formally opening the temple was commenced by the entire number; attired in white robes, marching in procession around the grounds in which the edifice is built. They then entered the temple, followed by the prophet; but as no persons were permitted to be present except members of the sect, we are unable to describe the ceremonial observed "

Wakefield Express 6 Jun 1857

The original site was 100 acres in extent;

"Prophet Wroe's Mansion . . . . It stands on a fine commanding eminence which slopes gently to the south from which a view of the whole country for many miles round can be obtained. The grounds, consisting of several acres, are well ordered, and abundantly stocked with beautiful trees, and at each of the four corners there is a porter's lodge, and a carriage drive sweeping round to the south front of the hall. The forcing-houses are extensive and full of vines and various fruits from many lands. The stables furnish abundant accommodation for a numerous stud. The house itself is a fine mansion-like structure with south, east and west fronts; and the principal rooms are said to be panelled with cedar "

Free Press 28 Feb 1874

"The beliefs of the Christian Israelites were compounded from both the law of Moses and the gospel of Christ. They included the specific claim that full and complete salvation (of `body, soul and spirit) would be enjoyed by a chosen few of the world's population, restricted to 144,000. These, the descendants of Abraham, would be immortal, and would be joint rulers with God of the eternal kingdom shortly to be established. Their separation from the rest of society was emphasised by peculiarities of dress and diet; especially noticeable was the fact that they never shaved or cut their hair, a characteristic which earnt them the name of `beardies'. "

Alternative Communities in 19th Century England.
D. Hardy

The hopes of the Christian Israelites were never fulfilled, for Wroe died in 1864 in Fitzroy, Australia. His Australian followers were so angry they demanded their subscriptions back for he had promised them he would never die. Melbourne House which had been built for all the members of the House of Israel, was on Wroe's death transferred to his grandson and the community dispersed. For some years after Wroe's death, a room was set aside with his slippers and a suit of clothes ready should he come back as the Shiloh.

After Wroe's death the leadership of the sect was assumed by an American, Daniel Milton, who continued to claim that the Christian Israelites had the right to occupation of Melbourne House and not Wroe's relatives. His campaign for rightful occupation included pasting bills on the walls of the property. The Melbourne house estate remained in the hands of the Wroe family until the 1930s and today `Prophet Wroe's Temple' is known as the Melbourne House Pentecostal Eventide Home and is used as an old people's home. The Australian wing of the Christian Israelites continued and today has congregations in Sydney, Melbourne, Singleton, Terrigal , Windsor, Brisbane, Kempsey, Australia, as well as missions in Indianapolis, USA, Radom, Poland & Mermansk, Russia.

See: **http//www.cichurch.ans.au**

THE JEZRELITES

Two other adherents to the philosophy of British Israelism set up their own community of followers: Clarissa Rogers the daughter of a sawyer from New Brompton in Kent and James White. White had joined the Gravesend congregation of John Wroe's Christian Israelites in 1875, and sent a `divine message' to the inheritors of the Wroe estate, claiming to be the Sixth Messenger and rightful claimant to John Wroe's position. His letter was promptly burnt and White unsure of his future joined the army and was posted to India. While abroad God revealed to him his `last message to Mankind', which White wrote down as *The Flying Roll.* Clarissa Rogers had made her own preaching tours of America in 1877 and 1878, and on White's return from India in 1879, now under the name of James Jersham Jezreel, the two married, she taking the name Esther Jezreel. A sect formed around the two would-be prophets, and using *The Flying Roll* (A mishmash of Jezreel's own thoughts and the writings of John Wroe) as their scripture they set about preaching their own gospel, holding both secret and open meetings every Sunday where children would recite passages from The Flying Roll and sing hymns accompanied by the sound of harps. They adopted the Christian Isrealite fashion of wearing their hair and beards long, but otherwise they tried to fit in, taking jobs in local industries and opening their own shops.

Whilst waiting for the `ingathering' of the chosen 144,000 the Jezreelites set about building a great temple on Chatham Hill. near Gillingham. Jezreel declared that the location for the temple had come to him through a 'divine message' (though for practical reasons he was forced to take another nearby site.) For the design specifications Jezreel looked to the bible - `the city lieth foursquare, and . . . the length and the breadth and the height of it are equal'. Revelation (21:16).

Jezreel called on his followers from all countries to rally round and support the building of the temple by selling all their property and belongings and converting it into gold to contribute to the building fund. Many of them did and made preparations to move to Gillingham. Unfortunately James Jezreel died on 1 March 1885 with no start made on the temple. This however did not deter his widow. She took the title of Queen Ezreel, the mother of Ezreel, and set about commissioning the building of the temple, laying the foundation stone in the September following her husband's death.

Jezreel's tower prior to demolition

The following description of the plans for the building is based on information given by the architects in a local newspaper report at the time:

'The structure was to be built of steel and concrete with yellow brick walls, and eight castellated towers of the same material. On each side of the outer walls emblems and symbols of the `New and Latter House of

Israel' were to be portrayed in stone, standing out in bold relief. Chief of these were the Trumpet and the Flying Roll, the Crossed Swords of the Spirit, and the Prince of Wales Feathers, signifying the Trinity. A large basement was to be constructed for storage purposes, machinery for working lifts, heating apparatus etc. Above the basement the entire ground floor was to be used for twelve large printing presses, designed to turn out thousands of copies of the Flying Roll and other literature of the sect. Above the ground floor was to be the Assembly Room, which was undoubtedly Jezreel's finest and most original conception. It was to be circular in shape like an amphitheatre, was to reach almost to the top of the building, and was to accommodate 5,000 people. In the roof of this great room or hall there was to be a glass dome, 94 feet in diameter, and invisible from outside the building. The dome, supported by twelve massive steel ribs, was to rise 100 feet above the floor, and in the dome a revolving electric lantern 45 feet in diameter was to be the source of light, since the Assembly Room was not to have any windows..................The tower was to embody a number of remarkable features. Chief of these, perhaps, was the circular platform in the centre of the floor of the Assembly Room. It was to be 24 feet in diameter, and capable of being raised by hydraulic pressure to a height of 30 feet. It was to accommodate the choir and the preachers, and was to be made to rotate slowly so that each part of the congregation in the vast circular hall could be faced in turn.'

Quoted by Dennis Hardy in:
Alternative Communities in 19th Century England.

British Israelism Today

The gospel of British Israelism has carried on. Both Queen Victoria and King Edward VII were patrons of the movement. Today the British Israel World Federation claims some two million followers in Britain and America. British Israelism took off in earnest across the Atlantic when, in 1920, a newspaper owned by car manufacturer Henry Ford published a series of anti-Semitic articles culminating in a book called *The International Jew: The World's Foremost Problem*. The author was William Cameron, a British Israelite. Cameron went on to found the Anglo Saxon Federation of America that has links with the New Christian Rightwing organisations that started to flourish in America in the 1980s. The latest group to use the ideas of the British Israelites is the Identity Christianity movement., which includes such groups as Aryan Nation, the Church of Jesus Christ Christian & America's Promise Ministries. Identity Christianity, like British Israelism, teaches that the lost tribes of Israel left the Middle East and founded the New Israel in Britain. They believe that Jews, blacks, and indeed all non-white people, are sub-human 'mud people'. British Israelite beliefs have received little academic support and Identity Christianity groups are among extreme Nationalist/Racist organisations kept a watch on by anti-racist & anti-fascist alliances.
See: **www.hatewatch.org**

In 1888 'Queen Esther, died with the temple still incomplete and although her followers continued the construction work 'Jezreels tower' was never to reach completion, with the final members of the sect leaving in 1905. The sect had claimed that the temple would withstand all the powers of earth and hell and Jezreel's Tower remained as a local landmark until 1961, when it was demolished to make way for an industrial site.

Scotland's prophetess

'We have been surprized with one of the most extraordinary Phenomena in the moral world, which, I dare say, has happened in the course of this last Century. - We have had a party of the Presbytry Relief as they call themselves, for some time in this country. A pretty thriving society of them has been in the Burgh of Irvine for some years past, till about two years ago, a Mrs Buchan from Glasgow came among them, & began to spread some fanatical notions of religion among them, & in a short time, made many converts among them, & among others their Preacher, one Mr Whyte, who upon that account has been suspended and formally deposed by his brethren; he continued however, to preach in private to his party, & was supported, both he, & their spiritual Mother as they affect to call old Buchan, by the contributions of the rest, several of whom were in good circumstances; till in spring last the Populace rose & mobbed the old leader Buchan & put her out of the town; on which, all her followers voluntarily quitted the place likewise, and with such precipitation, that many of them never shut their doors behind them; one left a washing on the green, another a cow bellowing at the crib without meat or anybody to mind her,...... Their tenets are a strange jumble of enthusiastic jargon, among others, she pretends to give them the Holy Ghost by breathing on them, which she does with postures & practices that are scandalously indecent; they have likewise disposed of all their effects & hold a community of goods, & live nearly an idle life, carrying on a great farce of pretended devotion in barns, & woods, where they lodge & lye all together, & hold likewise a community of women, as it is another of their tenets that they can commit no moral sin. - I am personally acquainted with most of them, & I can assure you the above mentioned are facts.

Robert Burns *The Letters of Robert Burns.*

By the time Robert Burns was "personally acquainted" with the Buchanites they were well established and had gone through a number of trials and tribulations. The followers of Mrs Luckie Buchan (c. 1738-91) had started off in Irvine in Ayrshire where they were part of the Relief congregation of the Reverend Hugh White, a secessionist body which had left the Church of Scotland in 1761. Mrs Buchan, born Elspeth Simpson, daughter of way-side innkeepers at Fatmacken nr. Banff, had separated from her husband and become a seeker in the 1770s. She wandered from fellowship meeting to Kirk in search of salvation - eventually hearing Hugh White preach in Glasgow where her `... soul filled with love for him.' and she followed him back to Irvine. White believed that she was the `Woman clothed with the Sun' (Revelation 12) who had come to disperse the darkness of Antichrist that had long lain over the land and who at the second coming of Christ was to meet Him in the clouds with her followers, and take them directly to heaven without tasting death. These claims split the congregation and in the end White, Mrs Buchan and supporters were not only barred from the church, but eventually forced out of Irvine. Known Buchanite tradesmen were boycotted and labourers thrown out of their jobs. Mrs Buchan herself was attacked by a crowd and run out of town, returning the following morning `bare-headed, bare-footed, with scarcely a rag to cover her nakedness, and all her person covered with blood'. Fearing further disturbances the local magistrate banned her from the town. She left with White and her followers firmly believing that Irvine would shortly be destroyed by a Sodom-like judgement.

Forty-six Buchanites made their way across Scotland in May 1786 to Nithsdale in Dumfriesshire where they lived in an empty barn at New Cample farm whilst they built a rough community house dubbed by locals `Buchan Ha'. Here despite continued harassment from local people they grew in number to 60 members until in March 1787 they were forced to leave when magistrates used the

Poor Laws against them. They moved to Auchengibbert, a wild moorland farm in the parish of Urr, Kirkcudbrightshire where they were able to successfully establish themselves.

'Following the example of the early Apostles they 'had all things common.' Their money was put into a common stock and placed at the disposal of the treasurer; unused clothing was pooled and issued to members as required; and the washing, mending, knitting and cooking were undertaken by the women communally. A rough equality prevailed. All sat at the same table and ate the same food, with the exception of Friend Mother who either served those at table herself or was employed in directing others to do so. No titles were used; members were known by their Christian names; and married women reverted to using their maiden names. At first little thought was given to the economic basis of the community, which lived off the funds provided by the wealthier disciples. Members were happy to work gratuitously for neighbouring farmers, thereby demonstrating their renunciation of worldly considerations. The arrangements were in any case regarded as temporary, since the second coming was imminent. But later, when the funds ere exhausted and when it had become clear that the necessities of life would have to be provided for some years at least, a new regime was introduced. Members hired themselves out to local farmers for work in the fields; and after the removal to Auchengibbert the community set about farming on their own account. Duncan Robertson, a wheelwright and leader of the community, made spinning-wheels, and the women found regular employment in spinning yarn for factories.

The Second Coming. **JFC Harrison.**

The Buchanites were oddities in the locality with their 'uniform' of light green homespun clothes and their unusual habits - such as working on Sunday. But opposition to them eventually died down. The charge most often levelled at them was of sexual immorality; the sects view on marriage encouraging such fears. Declaring that they were no longer subject to `the bondage of what they [i.e. the world outside] call matrimony' members gave up their married status on joining the community. And whilst Hugh White brought his wife and children to live in the community he also shared a bed with Mrs Buchan. Situations that easily lead to Robert Burns' assertion that "they lodge & lye all together, & hold likewise a community of women."

White and Buchan were convinced that the second coming was imminent, and in preparation a forty-day fast was declared, doors bolted, windows nailed down and the community cut itself off from the outside world. For forty days they fasted, singing hymns and reading aloud from the bible to pass the time. After forty days the members of the sect staggered out, weak and emaciated, and climbed to the top of a nearby hill to witness the coming of the Lord and there duly await ascension to heaven. But like other millennial sects before and since their wait was in vain and like other prophets Mrs Buchan explained that it was because their faith was too weak. The messiah's non-appearance sorely dented the faith of some members and when Mrs Buchan failed to resurrect herself following her death in 1791 the sect fell apart. Hugh White and some thirty followers emigrating to America leaving a remnant of 14 members who moved to Larghill taking with them Mrs Buchan's body packed in feathers, keeping her hidden under the kitchen hearth still awaiting her promised resurrection. In 1808 the remaining Buchanites bought 5 acres of land at Crocketford where they built Newhouse. They removed Mrs Buchan's body and after she failed to reappear on the 50th aniversary of her death, Andrew Innes, the last of the Buchanites, buried her in the small burial ground behind the house, where he too was buried in 1846.

THE ABODE OF LOVE

In the quiet Somerset Village of Spaxton four miles from the busy little river port of Bridgewater during the second half of the 19th century lived the 'Holy Ghost' surrounded by his 'soul brides' and accompanied by a 'Devil child'. They lived at the Abode of Love, a collection of houses & cottages with its own chapel surrounded by a 12ft high wall and guarded by ferocious bloodhounds. Set up in 1846 the remarkably successful Agapemone is the prototype of the 20th century cult complete with sex scandals, accusations of brainwashing, dramatic rescues of members by their families, moral outrage from respectable society and virulent attacks in the popular press.

The 'Holy Ghost' and founding father of the community was a defrocked clergyman, the Reverend Henry Prince. Prince had stirred controversy from the start of his career In the church, organising a group of zealous students at St Davids College called the Lampeter Brethren. Hearing voices in his head that he took to be the word of God he led this small devout band attacking the college hierarchy, disrupting services and accusing them of submitting to 'the insinuations of carnal desire...' Keen to see the back of this holier-than-thou troublemaker the church authorities packed Prince off to a quiet rural parish hoping that he would fade away into obscurity. The Reverend Prince had other ideas. From his pulpit in the village of Charlich, a mere stones-throw from Spaxton, he lambasted the local population of sinners sparking a mini-revival in the area with his charismatic preaching and instructions from the Holy Ghost. Prince's identification with the voice in his head grew and he came to believe that he was the embodiment of the Holy Ghost. During his time at Charlich his first wife Martha died. She was a wealthy older friend of his mothers who he had cynically married to finance his way through college. With indecent haste he married his rectors sister, another older woman with her own income. Riding high on the crest of a wave of revival with a full church and a clutch of wealthy patrons, his licence to preach was suddenly revoked by the Bishop of Bath and Wells amid rumours of 'carnal insinuations' with the converted ladies of Charlich.

Prince decided to spread his wings. If Somerset didn't want him he would try elsewhere. Through a friend he set out his stall at Clare in Suffolk where for the next two years he proceeded to rouse the local population to a religious fervour. Eventually the tolerant Bishop of Ely 'requested' that Prince take his services elsewhere - this was the final straw for Prince, if the blind, ignorant bigots in the Church of England didn't want him then he, 'the visible manifestation of God on earth' certainly did not want them. Announcing to the faithful his separation from the Church he moved his preaching operations to the south coast resorts of Brighton & Weymouth. Here amongst the elderly spinsters and young unmarried ladies of Victorian society Prince found his true congregation. In a large house in Belfield Terrace Weymouth he set up an embryonic Agapemone (Greek for Abode of Love). The idea of the Abode of Love was not Prince's. Similar experiments, inspired by the text of the Song of Solomon, had been conceived before and roundly condemned by the church as sinful and degenerate.

"The Abode of Love did not mean, as it seemed to imply, unlimited sexual freedom. Love at Belfield Terrace and later at Spaxton was to be spiritual. In the course of time Prince constructed an elaborate system of Angels and Archangels, a celestial hierarchy promoting and demoting the faithful at will according to their favour and the cash at their disposal. For this was to be a commercial as well as a spiritual venture. Not even the Holy Ghost could build an earthly paradise on faith alone."

C.Mander

The Reverend Prince and his Abode of Love

Sell everything for the lord

In a carefully orchestrated revivalist campaign Prince and his little band of Agapemonites whipped the faithful up into a frenzy with talk of the day of judgement and the imminent arrival of the Lamb of God. Persuading rich and poor alike that 'in the day of wrath all property would be dirt' a sell-everything-for-the-lord programme swelled the group's bank balance - the revelation of the son of God took place at the assembly rooms in the Royal Hotel Weymouth where he turned out to be none other than the Rev Henry Prince himself. Only those who received Prince as the son of God would be saved from Armageddon. It was estimated that 500 souls were saved that day - mainly aging spinsters and children - certainly enough to finance something on a grander scale that a rented house in Weymouth. Two hundred acres of land was purchased in the Spaxton Valley and plans drawn up for a new Abode. Whenever more finances were needed to keep the construction of paradise on schedule Prince exhorted his followers to sell a little more for the Lord, or simply demanded that "The Lord had need of fifty pounds Amen," and finally hit upon marrying his followers to wealthy spinsters to secure the needed funds.

In the summer of 1846 Prince and his entourage moved to Spaxton - the new Abode of Love consisted of a great house with some eighteen bedrooms, sitting rooms, dining rooms and servants quarters. Spacious grounds were dotted with outhouses, stables, conservatories, gazebos and a series of garden cottages. And in one corner its own chapel furnished incongruously with easy chairs, settees and a billiard table alongside the hassocks and hymnboards. All surrounded by a high brick wall designed either to keep prying eyes out, or to keep the faithful in.

Beloved spaxton

The best place to observe the comings and goings at the Abode of Love was the Lamb Inn, conveniently located next door to the main house - separated by 12ft of brickwork of course - whose bar hosted many a journalist covering the numerous scandals that would surround the

Artists impression of the Abode of Love 1850

newly appointed son of God over the ensuing years. Hardly was the house-warming over when the first controversy broke. Prince had married three of his closest 'saints', companions from his Lampeter Brethren days, to the three Nottidge sisters each with an inheritance of £6000. The sisters were steamrollered into the spiritual unions, not allowed to contact their families and bundled with great haste off to Spaxton. Agnes the oldest, and most spirited of the three, was appalled by the whole set up especially when she discovered that on top of it all she was expected to remain celibate. When Prince (now referred to by the faithful as 'Beloved') set his sights on the fourth and youngest Nottidge sister Louisa, and a further £6000, Agnes tried to write a letter of warning to her sister. On the discovery of her betrayal of the Beloved and the further discovery that she was pregnant and not by her 'husband' she was cast out as a fallen woman. Beloved now demanded the presence of

Louisa at Spaxton and lodged her in one of the cottages in the grounds whilst he searched for a suitable spouse. Late one night the locals at the Lamb Inn heard the frantic screaming of young Louisa coming from within the great wall as she resisted the attempts by her two brothers to 'rescue' her. When they got outside they saw the young woman being bundled still screaming into a coach that disappeared into the night. The family liberators promptly turned captors having their sister declared insane and incarcerated in a lunatic asylum. On Prince's orders envoys

Despite the scandals there was no shortage of converts clamouring to pay to get into this Somerset paradise. Prince ruled in despotic style over a membership that varied between 60 and 200 over the first few years. Nobody was paid a penny for administering to his needs and whilst he lived in comfort surrounded by the most attractive women in the main house, the other 'saints' worked on the farm or in the gardens, living in the small cottages, husbands separate from wives.

Members of the Abode of Love - late 1800s
(Prince 3rd from left front row)

"Prince of course, enjoyed himself immensely. He ate well, drank well - he had left his total abstinence period far behind - and stocked his cellars with the best wines, Above all he exercised absolute authority over a large number of men and women who worshipped him as God. Life was pleasant, heavenly perhaps, and some of the women were most desirable."

C.Mander *The Reverend Prince and his Abode of Love.*

were sent out to scour the country for the unfortunate woman. After 18 months of fruitless search word reach Spaxton that Louisa had escaped from the asylum and was hiding in a London Hotel. As she waited on Paddington station with her escort from Spaxton she was picked up by asylum officials and locked up again. Prince made an immediate application to the Commissioners of Lunacy who declared Louisa to be sane - on her release she immediately transferred her inheritance to Prince's bank account and retired behind the walls at Spaxton for the rest of her life. Her inheritance was used to buy two bloodhounds to protect the faithful from further 'kidnappings'.

THE GREAT MANIFESTATION

Tongues wagged not just in the bar at the Lamb, but all the way to the pages of the national newspapers after the most notorious of Prince's exploits and the one that would seal the Abode of Love's reputation. Quite what possessed Prince to carry out the bizarre ritual we can only guess at. Maybe carried away by his notion that he was the son of God he believed in his own infallibility and simply assumed that he could do whatever he pleased. He would later publish convoluted theological justifications for his actions which amounted to the rape of a young virgin in front of his gathered congregation. Described as both the

'Great Manifestation' and a 'divine purification'. Prince had devised an elaborate charade to enable him to carry out one of the obsessions of Victorian men, the deflowering of a virgin. He demanded that a selection of suitable maidens be made available in the chapel for him to choose one to be 'favoured'. Then with due pomp and ceremony he chose 16-year-old Zoe Patterson and in front of the somewhat astonished, if meekly compliant, congregation he proceeded to rape his seemingly hypnotised victim to the accompanying sound of the chapel organ and the singing of hymns.

'Thus the Holy Ghost took flesh in the presence of those whom he had called as flesh. He took this flesh absolutely in his sovereign will, and with the power and authority of God.'
The Testimony of Brother Prince.

The fall-out from this act would shake the community to its core. Whilst some of the 'saints' saw only good in Prince's action others had severe misgivings and started talking of leaving and what was worse taking their money with them. The situation was further compounded when it became apparent that Miss Paterson was pregnant despite Princes claim that his divine union would produce no offspring - he quickly changed his tack to claiming that this was the work of the devil and nothing to do with him; an argument that cut little ice with his disenchanted followers who now left by the score.

And what of Miss Patterson? Well she seemed to have been none the worse for her ordeal. Her 'child of Satan' was born and grew up in the community, a quiet shy

Agapemone (Abode of Love) Spaxton, Som. « Birthplace of Glory »

girl called Eve, whilst Zoe took her place at 'Beloveds' right hand as the first Bride of the Lamb. There were other 'Brides' quite how many is hard to unravel from the so obviously embroidered bacchanalian stories that started life in the Lamb Inn and the cries of moral outrage from society at large that greeted Prince's pamphlets justifying his sacred sex life. A kind of siege mentality came over the community. Locked behind the high brick wall they refused admittance to all comers - a hand would shoot out through a trap to collect goods delivered by local tradesmen. This self-imposed isolation only fuelled the exaggeration of the stories about what went on behind the closed doors.

In 1867 William Hepworth Dixon, a writer and student of religious cults, managed to get permission to enter the Abode of Love and interview Prince. He published a measured account of the community in his book *Spiritual Wives.* Dixon records a picture of a thriving, if somewhat depleted, community with a middle-aged Prince at the centre surrounded by doting billiard-playing beauties. And it seems that things pretty much remained like that for the following 30 years.

HEAVENLY BRIDEGROOM TWO

The Reverend 'Beloved' Prince outlived many of his 'saints' giving credence to his claim that he was immortal and in 1896 aged 85 emerged from behind the walls of Spaxton to initiate the building of an ornate church in Clapton in North London complete with a 155ft tower of Portland stone, intricate oak hammer-beam roof and stained glass windows depicting the submission of womankind to man. The church was dedicated to the Ark of the Covenant and one of the first preachers appointed was the Reverend John Hugh Smyth-Pigott.

Prince's death in 1899 came as a devastating shock to the community. They were thrown into complete confusion and with no funeral plans for one who many seem to have genuinely believed to have been immortal they hurriedly buried him in the front garden in the middle of the

night. Reeling from the shock some members packed their bags and left whilst others tried to contact their Beloved through spiritualist séances. On hearing the news that the bereaved sisters of the Abode of Love were in need of a new heavenly bridegroom a light lit up in the eyes of the Reverend Smyth-Piggot - said by some to be a divine light.

With the help of Douglas Hamilton, Prince's faithful retainer, Smyth-Piggot was enthroned as the new Saviour of Mankind at the Church of the Ark of the Covenant in September 1902 before a not entirely friendly crowd of 6000 who booed and

Smyth-Piggot

jeered during the inauguration and who had to be pressed back by a group of mounted police to allow the new messiah to make his exit - once again the Abode of Love was in the headlines. Smyth-Piggot moved to Spaxton with his wife and slipped into Prince's shoes with consummate ease sparking a mini-revival in the cult's fortunes. Some 50 new young 'soul brides' were chosen, all vetted by Sister Eve Patterson the now grown 'Devil child' who had come to hold a senior position in the community.

Smyth-Piggot set about his new role with great zeal; he bought a motor car and telephone, added a laundry and new cottages, introduced new stock to the run down farm and most of all busied himself in his capacity as heavenly bridegroom. He was "If not a sexual maniac at least a man obsessed with sex in his daily life"

Donald McCormick. *Temple of Love.*

Miss Ruth Anne Preece was chosen to be his Chief Soul Bride with whom he had three children named Glory, Power & Life. A campaign was started against the community resulting in the tarring and feathering of a man thought to be Smyth-Piggot and an undercover masseur being sent to dig the dirt. Catherine Smyth-Piggot the long suffering and scorned wife busied herself with charity in the area and was remembered with great affection by locals for years after.

Following Smyth-Piggott's death in 1927 membership declined rapidly and by 1929 only 33 women, 1 girl and 3 men were left and the community became a sort of liberal finishing school reportedly full of "disillusioned old women and frustrated and disappointed young women." As the old guard died Sister Ruth became the leader and when she died aged 90 in 1956 the community closed and the property was finally sold off in 1958. It is now a series of private houses and flats and still somewhere under the front garden lie the remains of the two heavenly bridegrooms.

The full story of the Abode of Love is told in:
The Reverend Prince and his Abode of Love.
By Charles Mander. EP Publishing 1976
And *Temple of Love*
By Donald McCormick Jarrolds. 1962

A CONTINUOUS THREAD

During the whole of the nineteenth century Christian sects were continually emerging throughout the British Isles: the Lampeter Brethren, the Peculiar People in Essex, the Irvingites in London, the Faith Mission in Scotland, the Church With No-Name in Ireland, the Society of Dependants in Sussex, the Brotherhood Church in Croyden, various Children's of God........the list goes on.........many of these groups believed, like their counterparts back in the 17th Century, in a coming millennium and golden age, or harked back to a primitive Christianity where people lived simply, shared their possessions and preachers 'tramped' the countryside (and other countries.)in search of converts. Some of this ferment of religious evangelism was due to the challenge being made to fundamental Christian beliefs by Science. In other aspects it is a continuous thread of Christian questioning and renewal stretching right from the Lollards to the present day. As in previous centuries some sects were communities of prayer, fairly conventional congregations gathered around a charismatic leader; others chose to separate themselves off from society:

THE COKELERS

In the Sussex villages of Loxwood, Northchapel, Warnham and Shamley Green a series of co-operatively run shops were set up in the second half of the 19th Century. The shops were of considerable size some employing 13 saleswomen in three departments with their own delivery vans. These shops were the economic base for the Society of Dependants, or Cokelers as they were known locally. Set up in 1850 at Loxwood by John Sirgood the group rapidly grew in the locality building a number of cottages, chapels and the chain of shops.

"Their ascetic life included a rejection of alcohol and tobacco, of secular books and music, and of flowers in the home; marriage was tolerated but discouraged as an earthly obstacle to the relationship between the individual and God. They attended three religious services every Sunday and two during the week, the men wearing dark suits, the women in a black costume of straw and velvet bonnets, shawls, coats and long skirts.   D. Hardy
Alternative Communities in 19th Century England

There were 2000 members when their founder John Sirgood died in 1885. Despite their strong economic base the sect went into decline after Sirgood's death though a handful of followers still worship today in the Spy Lane chapel at Loxwood.

ANOTHER FEMALE MESSIAH

Arnewood Tower stands 218 feet high looking down over the Hampshire countryside, an extraordinary concrete construction built by Mr A.T.T Peterson on instruction from the soul of Sir Christopher Wren. Peterson was a follower of the female messiah Mary Ann Girling. Born Miss Cloutery, she married an Ipswich ironfounder and machine fitter. One Christmas she claimed to have received the stigmata on the hands, feet and side. From then on she toured the eastern counties of England preaching in Methodist chapels and gathering a large following. When the Methodists started to refuse her access to their chapels because of her radical interpretation of the Gospel, she started preaching in the street, eventually ending up in London where she and her followers set up a small community at 107 Bridge Rd, Battersea. Calling themselves 'the Children of God' they based their lifestyle on that of Christ's disciples.

Two years later in 1872 following persecution and disruption of their services a wealthy supporter purchased New Forest Lodge, Vaggs Lane, Hordle in Hampshire for the group that now consisted of Mrs Girling and twelve disciples. They were to stay here for three years drawing in members from the local agricultural workers. They earned themselves the nickname 'the Shakers' - to whom they bore some resemblance, not only in their custom of dancing when moved by the spirit, but also in habits which they shared with the American Shakers.

'The group practiced celibacy as necessary to the true worship of God, the children in the community being brought in by newcomers. ………….. the men and women sat at separate tables at meal times and occupied separate apartments, meeting only in connection with the routine of their daily duties and at the religious services. Clothing was made in the community, and the style was strictly regulated. The women wore what is described as a bloomer costume for their work on the land, and white dresses on Sundays. The girls wore their hair in curly ringlets down their back, which apparently gave them an unusual appearance when dancing, and encouraged rumours that Mrs Girling mesmerised them to keep them under her control.'

D. Hardy
Alternative Communities in 19th Century England.

Rumours abounded in the locality of the goings on at the Lodge, sightseers came in carriages every Sunday to gaze at the 'New Forest Shakers' and an attempt was made to have Mrs Girling declare insane. However it was the sect's inability to keep up with mortgage repayments that led to their eviction. The community, now numbering 160, were thrown out into the middle of a snowstorm. The eviction was reported in a local paper;

'…..through all the terrible night they remained in the rain and snow, the sound of their hymns and prayers mingled with that of the storm, and the morning found them half- perished with the bitter cold, but defiant of all consequences and sturdily refusing to leave the spot, saying they were in the Lord's hands and he would do with them as seemed to him best.'

The Hampshire Independent

They eventually took shelter in a local barn and eventually were able to rent a farm at Tiptoe, where they stayed until Mrs Girling died in 1886.

SALVATION FARM

'….take an estate from 500 - 1,000 acres within reasonable distance of London. It should be of such land as will be suitable for market gardening, while having some clay· on it for brickmaking and for crops requiring heavier soil. If possible, it should not only be on a line of railway which is managed by intelligent and progressive directors, but it should have access to the sea and to the river.

W.Booth
In Darkest England and the Way Out .

`General' William Booth, a preacher from Nottinghamshire founded a Christian Mission at Whitechapel in 1878. The ethos behind it was based on the so called `Cab Horse Charter', a belief that, like the working horses of London, every human being should have food to eat and a roof over their head. Out of this Mission the Salvation Army evolved. The Army's early meetings were often controversial with fights and riots breaking out at many of them and Booth and his supporters were often jailed or fined for breach of the peace.

In 1890 Booth published his plan to rescue the poor and destitute from the squalor of London - *In Darkest England and the Way Out.* The foundation of the plan was three types of self-sustaining community, City Colonies, Farm Colonies and Overseas Colonies. The City Colony would take the poor and destitute and give them board and lodgings in exchange for a day's work - they would then progress on to the farm colony where they would be trained to run smallholdings and finally on to the overseas colonies.

SALVAGE BRIGADES

The plan in its entirety amounted to a sort of self-help welfare state, to be financed by a number of imaginative proposals. 'Salvage Brigades' would collect unwanted food from prosperous households, every house in London (over 500,000) would be provided with a tub or sack in which to deposit 'valuable waste' - cast off shoes would be mended and resold, old bottles & tins turned into useful

Frontpage of handwritten newsletter
issued by Hadliegh Colonists 1892

accusing General Booth of acting as if he were the 'Baron of Hadliegh'.

The Army set to work transforming the neglected farms and by the end of 1891 over 200 colonists, were in residence. Existing farm buildings had been renovated, new dormitories erected, a bathhouse, laundry, reading room, a hospital and a Citadel for religious meetings were all built. Along with farming and market gardening 'colonists' were taught brickmaking, pottery and construction skills all in the colony'es own works.

One of the schemes run by the colony included barges taking goods from the colony for sale in London returning with horse manure to fertilise the land; old scraps of tin to be made into toys; and grease and fat from London slaughterhouses to lubricate colony machinery.

Those arriving at the colony had to progress through a series of stages to prove themselves willing and capable. Leigh Park Farm, set up as a mini-colony, was the first port of call for new recruits. Here they were assessed for their willingness to work and the seriousness of their intention to be `saved'. Those successful at this stage could move onto the Colony proper, where the most responsible

utensils and toys, books sold through a chain of second hand stores. The plan also included proposals for a poor man's bank, crèches to keep poor children off the streets, a network of poormen's 'lounges' and even a matrimonial agency.

A trial City Colony had been set up in Whitechapel in 1889 making benches and matting for the 'Army's' meeting houses. Booth found the estate for his Farm Colony at Hadleigh on the Thames estuary in Essex. In 1891 he put down a deposit on 800 acres of land, later expanding it to a total of 3,200 acres, consisting of the Castle, Park and Sayers farms to the south of Hadleigh Village. The people of Hadleigh were not too keen on the prospect of the poor and destitute of the capital descending on them and there was strong opposition to the scheme in the early years. There were disputes over rights of way over the colony land, over traditional 'blackberrying' rights and over the Army trying to get its officers elected to the Local Parish Council, culminating in the local paper

Main gate to Hadleigh colony just before WW1

jobs and the best sleeping arrangements were reserved for the most diligent workers. The colonists were given grants of money for the work they did and the grant was increased as they gradually improved themselves. There was also a system of tokens or Colony `coinage'-which could be used to buy goods at the colony shop.

In the years between 1895 and 1912 the colony flourished. The Army bought other properties in Hadleigh setting up a home for inebriates and a school which local children used. A refreshment room was build for the numerous sightseers who came to view the Army's achievements. The visitors to the colony included Cecil Rhodes, Sir Walter Besant and novelist H. Rider Haggard. Haggard, a Salvation Army commissioner at the time, wrote a very favourable report on the scheme for American Branches of the Army. By the time of the colony's 21st anniversary some 7,000 colonists had been trained by the Army and most had been placed on smallholdings overseas in Canada, New Zealand and the USA.

The years following the First World War saw the colony go through many changes. A shortage of labour after the War reduced the need for the colony and coupled with financial pressure this led the Army to scale down its operations and to sell off much of the outlying farmland, keeping just 900 acres which it used to train boys in 'rudimentary land crafts' before sending them abroad to the British colonies. Some refugees from the Spanish Civil War were housed at the colony in the 1930s and most of the land was requisitioned for anti-aircraft guns and searchlights during the Second World War. After the War ex-borstal boys were trained on the farms alongside a dwindling number of homeless people and alcoholics. By the 1960s any social side of the farms had been wound up and a farm manager now runs the farms on a commercial basis with profits going to general Salvation Army funds.

The rest of the plan had never really got off the ground. The properties bought for the city colonies became the network of hostels still run by the 'Army' today.

LANDLESS PEOPLE ON PEOPLELESS LAND

In 1906 a Mr Herring lent the Salvation Army a sum of money to establish a "labour colony"on Boxted Heath in Essex to put "landless people on the peopleless land." Some 400 acres were divided up into 5 acre plots and semi-detached houses build on them. For the first year implements and seed were supplied free, and a nominal rent charged. After two years the tenants were expected to have made the smallholding profitable. How many of the new smallholders came through the Farm Colony at Hadleigh is not known, but they had little experience of working on the land, after two years their financial situation was worse than when they began. The smallholders became increasingly discontented with the 'Army's' administration of the scheme. A large building (Priory Hall) had been erected near to Priory House, part of it being used as a Citadel and the rest as a packhouse. Produce was brought by the smallholders to be graded and packed, then taken to Colchester to be marketed. The smallholders felt that the Army's superintendents did not try to get the best price for their produce and even suspected them of being German spies. After the eviction of several tenants and a statement in the House of Commons, an inquiry was conducted by the Charity Commision. The inquiry cleared the Salvation Army of maladministration, but the evictions continued with much publicity. The Salvation Army Smallholding Scheme was wound up in 1916. Many of the holdings were bought by Essex County Council to resettle servicemen returning from the war, others were bought by the tenants on 999 year leases.

Information from: *A Short History Of Boxted* By Douglas Carter 1996

Religious anarchy

Guest article by
Dennis Hardy

This article is an extract from Dennis' book:
Alternative Communities in Nineteenth Century England

The influence of religious anarchism can be explained, in part, as a reaction to the association of mainstream anarchism with violence. It is probable that only one death resulted in England from an anarchist bomb (and even that took the form of a home-made device exploding in the possession of a Frenchman who had intended to use it abroad), yet anarchism suffered from what, at times, amounted to hysterical condemnation. There were many who, while sharing their rejection of the State, could not see the way to its destruction by means of bombs or even by mass industrial action. Their strategy, instead, was to `confront capitalist organisation by fraternal organisation' [49], to achieve a social revolution first to ensure that a meaningful political change could follow. It is understandable that this strain of anarchism was a powerful source of inspiration for the communities. The route to salvation was not, in the first place, through mass action, but through gentle co-operation. At the heart of this philosophy are the ideas of Leo Tolstoy.

`A new life-conception'

Although Tolstoy remained in Russia throughout the 1890s and was not involved directly in the practical aspects of any of the schemes, through his writings and through personal contact with a number of the communitarians his influence on the English community movement was profound. In contradiction to his own teachings on humility, the relationship that developed was charismatic - to the point where visits by his followers to his estate of Yasnaya Polyana were described as `pilgrimages', and the communities that were shaped according to his ideas were known as `Tolystoyan'. Such communities were attempts to put into practice the philosophy of Tolstoy as it was then emerging through various translations of books, pamphlets and letters. The Purleigh Colony (1896), the Ashingdon Colony (1897), the Brotherhood Workshop in Leeds (1897), the Wickford Colony (1898), the Whiteway Colony (1898) and the Blackburn Brotherhood (1899) were all attempts to reorganise life on Tolstoyan lines.

A number of Tolstoy's ideas were already well developed and available to English readers before this late nineteenth-century phase of community formation. From as early as 1852 in The Cossacks, Tolstoy was articulating a preference for `Nature's simplicity' in contrast to the artificial sophistication and, as he saw it, futility of city life. It is a theme which was explored in his better-known novels, War and Peace and Anna Karenina - a theme where `. . .Happiness is being with Nature, seeing Nature, and discoursing with her' [50]. It led him to an idealisation, not only of Nature but of the simple life generally, and of the life of the peasant in particular.

There was also, well before the English community phase, a relationship between Tolstoy's developing ideals and practice. In an attempt to reduce the contradictions of his own position as an aristocratic landowner, Tolstoy introduced, first, reformist measures on his estate and, in 1880, a denunciation of property (in effect, more symbolic than real) and a commitment to dress and work in the fields as a peasant.

However, it was from an intensive period of religious writings (between 1879 and 1882), in a series of works where he sought to prove that the State church no longer accorded with the Gospels, that Tolstoy was led into the political realm of questioning (in the words of one of his own works) 'What then must we do?' In examining his religious and political answers, two issues will be explored. The first is to question what there was in Tolstoy's ideas that made them so attractive to the community movement in England, and the second is to consider the relationship between his emerging ideas and the experience of practice. It would seem that two main sets of ideas can be identified, the one relating to a revolution of moral consciousness, and the other relating to a rejection of the State and its associated institutions. It is as a reflection of this duality that Tolstoy is sometimes referred to as a 'religious anarchist'. In practice, the communities offered a way of resolving this division.

Tolstoy's notion of Christianity, a return to the principles of the Sermon on the Mount, is explained in his book The Kingdom of God is Within You: or, Christianity not as a Mystical Doctrine, but as a New Life-Conception (first published in Russia in 1893). In the book, Tolstoy develops three principal ideas, proceeding from an understanding of the essence of Christianity to a call for social action: . . . the first, that Christianity is not only the worship of God and a doctrine of salvation, but is above all things a new conception of life which is changing the whole fabric of human society; the second, that from the first appearance of Christianity there entered into it two opposite currents - the one establishing the true and new conception of life, which it gave to humanity, and the other perverting the true Christian doctrine and converting it into a Pagan religion, and that this contradiction has attained in our days the highest order of tension which now expresses itself in universal arguments, and on the Continent in general conscription; and the third, that this contradiction, which is masked by hypocrisy, can only be solved by an effort on the part of every individual endeavouring to conform the acts of his life - independent of what are regarded as the exigencies of family, society and the State - with those moral principles which he considers to be true [51].

Tolstoy advanced the belief that society had progressed from a state of individualism to one of 'social life-conception' and that a new phase of 'Christian life-conception' was imminent. He argued that society was already experiencing serious contradictions, and that these were manifested along class lines. As such, he provided a spiritual rejection of capitalism:

One needs but to compare the practice of life with its theory to be horrified at the extraordinary contradictions between the conditions of life and our inner consciousness. Man's whole life is a continual contradiction of what he knows to be his duty. This contradiction prevails in every department of life; in the economical, the political, and the international . . . every man in these days knows that in the matter of life and worldly goods all men have equal rights; that no man is either better or worse than his fellow-men, but that all men are born free and equal. Every man has an instinctive assurance of this fact, and yet he sees his fellow-beings divided into two classes, the one in poverty and distress, which labours and is oppressed, the other idle, tyrannical, luxurious; and not only does he see all this, but, whether voluntarily or otherwise, he falls in line with one or the other of these divisions - a course repugnant to his reason. Hence he must suffer both from his sense of the incongruity and is own share in it [52].

It was a revolutionary challenge, where the Christian foundations of life - equality, brotherly love, community of goods, non-resistance of evil by violence - would replace the principles that supported the family and the State as basic institutions of capitalist society. The challenge was sharpened by the messianic prophesy that the time for change was at hand, that 'each man has but to begin to do his duty, each one has but to live according to the light within him, to bring about the immediate advent of the promised Kingdom of God, for which the heart of every man yearns' [53]. The rationale for immediate revolution, of social change in advance of the abandonment of the State, was of obvious attraction to those who were already predisposed towards community formation.

In some of his later works Tolstoy went on to develop his ideas of society without the State, without property and without a need for money, where there would be no exploitation, and where non-resistance would replace violence. Individually, the communities experimented with these ideas which, taken together, provided an overall rationale for their localised efforts. The revolution would occur, not with the sudden overthrow of the State, but through the growth of `rational consciousness'. Tolstoy argued this on the following basis.

He started by noting that exploitation and `slavery', was an inevitable product of capitalism. It had resulted from the dominance of the landowner over those who owned insufficient land, from the imposition of taxes by governments, and from the competition of capitalists who controlled both labour and markets. `So that, in one way or another, the labourer is always in slavery to those who control the taxes, the land, and the articles necessary to satisfy his requirements' [54].

Tolstoy then argued that this slavery was legitimised and perpetuated by legislation which, in turn, rested on the organised violence of the State. It was laws which perpetuated inequalities in property (both land and acquired goods) and which, in legalising taxation, ensured the dominance of State institutions:

It is said that the law defends equally the property of the mill-owner, of the capitalist, of the landowner, and of the factory or country labourer. The equality of the capitalist and of the worker is like the equality of two fighters, of whom one has his arms tied and the other has weapons, but to both of whom certain rules are applied with strict impartiality while they fight [55].

It followed, then, that to remove slavery one had first to remove the State. But the change must not be by means of violence, as this would only sow the seeds for a new form of exploitation. Instead, power must be abolished by the rational consciousness of men, which would expose this power (and its manifestation in the State) as being both useless and harmful. Rational consciousness would itself be shaped, not by materialistic theories, but by a: spiritual weapon . . . a devout understanding of life, according to which man regards his earthly existence as only a fragmentary manifestation of the complete life, and connecting his life with infinite life and recognising his highest welfare in the fulfilment of the laws of this infinite life, regards the fulfilment of these laws as more binding upon himself than the fulfilment of any human laws whatsoever. Only such a religious conception, uniting all men in the same understanding of life, incompatible with subordination to power and participation in it, can truly destroy power [56].

There were immediate, practical steps that could be taken to challenge the State. Individuals should desist from holding any Government post, they should refuse to pay taxes or to receive government pensions, and they should refuse to call on State laws for the protection of their property. He went on to advocate a return to the land for the majority of the population, which he argued would be possible with the cessation of overproduction and without the manufacture of `useless' goods, and with the perfection of cultivation that was possible (acknowledging the arguments developed earlier by Kropotkin). For the communitarians these guidelines for immediate change almost took on the nature of a charter - Nellie Shaw, for instance, describes the solemn burning of the land deeds of the Whiteway Colony, and their collective refusal to pay rates [57].

`FRATERNITY SPELLS REVOLT'

The second question that was posed in the preceding section was to examine the relationship between the ideas as they were still emerging in the 1890s and the experience of practice in the communities at that time. What is interesting to speculate is the extent to which ideas and practice were in a dialectical relationship, with the communities exploring and evaluating the worth of Tolstoy's ideas and, in turn, Tolstoy's later writings benefiting from his knowledge of their experience. It is a difficult proposition to pursue, but possible, at least, to establish the existence of a rich flow of contacts between Yasnaya Polyana and the English communities.

These contacts took one of a number of forms - the circulation of journals to spread the ideas of Tolstoy to an English public, the translation of Tolstoy's works by participants in the community movement, and the `pilgrimages' to the Russian estate by community supporters who would then return with fresh insights and inspiration to disseminate to their comrades. The communities (Purleigh Colony, in particular) also received a number of Russian refugees from Tsarist oppression, including Tolstoy's close friend, Vladimir Tchertkoff.

To explain these various but related contacts it will be helpful to look first at the conjuncture of events that took place in Croydon from about 1890. For it was there, through the Croydon Brotherhood, that an attempt was made to synthesise Tolstoyan philosophy with a growing English sympathy for a notion of brotherhood and peaceful revolution. It was also the base from which the significant Purleigh community venture was launched [58].

The origins of the Croydon movement are twofold. One source is to be found in the movement known as the `New Fellowship' (originating as the `Fellowship of the New Life' in 1883). The Fellowship was convened by Thomas Davidson, a former teacher and educational theorist who had travelled widely in Europe and North America and who had, at one time lectured with Henry Thoreau's mentor, Ralph Emerson. Davidson dreamt of a new form of communistic society composed of people spiritually purer and maintaining a `higher life' than in present society. The Fellowship emphasised the subordination of material things to spiritual, and aimed at the cultivation of a perfect character in everyone. As a reaction to Davidson's commitment to communitarianism a group of the Fellowship hived off to form the `Fabian Society' [59].

From 1889 the New Fellowship spread their ideas to a wider audience through the medium of a new publication Seed Time (originally named The Sower). It was in Seed Time that the links with Tolstoy were demonstrated, and the role of conscience in social revolution was stressed:

We are agreed concerning the diseases and miseries of this present order of society; we are agreed that these are established in the monopolies of property, by which the means of production are put into the control of a limited class, who use them to enslave and exploit the mass of the people. And we see that the remedy can only be found in a reorganisation of society which shall give to all free access to the means of production, which shall secure to each one a brotherly participation in all wealth; which shall destroy the servitude of all menial forms of labour, and establish that honesty and simplicity of life which must distinguish every society of equals. . . . We recognise in the evolutionary processes, more than the mere outward progression of social forms. We know that `conscience' has a part to play in the evolution of the new order [60].

The journal was concerned more with philosophising about a simpler, purer life than with the practicalities of achieving it. It was prepared for an intellectual, middle-class readership and, as well as publishing abstract papers, carried reports of lectures and other activities of the Fellowship. `Rustic gatherings' were popular events, where members were invited to gather at a suitably rural venue to hear a paper, and then to proceed through the countryside to an appropriate tearoom. At one such event the paper was on the subject of `the return to Nature'[61], and amidst `the winds, the woods and water' the author spoke of a new unity between Nature (all that we recognise as not ourselves) and Soul. The rediscovery of this unity would reveal a new understanding of truth, of beauty and of simplicity. The members then returned by railway to the metropolis, but the message of the afternoon was not lost on the later communitarians.

Seed Time was printed at Croydon, and it was there that some of its contributors met. The second arm of the Croydon movement stemmed from the influence of the social mystic, J. Bruce Wallace and, from 1894 the avowed Tolstoyan, John Kenworthy. Wallace had already started a `Brotherhood Church' in North London, with a publication Brotherhood which reported on social issues and on community experiments in various parts of the world. He was described as `a man of intensely devoted and spiritual nature, who was convinced that it was possible to establish some kind of co-operative system in place of the present capitalistic system and commercialism generally' (62).

At the same time, a group known as `The Croydon Socialist Society' decided to emulate Wallace's example, and establish a comparable `Brotherhood Church' in Croydon. The word `church' was used to refer to a number of people inspired by a common aim, but with no established religious or theological imputation. Something of the eclectic origins of the community experiments that followed is captured in Nellie Shaw's memories of their early gatherings:

It may be doubted if ever a more mixed and diverse crowd gathered within four walls than used to assemble weekly at the old Salvation Army tin tabernacle in Tamworth Road. Every kind of `crank' came and aired his views on the open platform, which was provided every Sunday afternoon. Atheists, Spiritualists, Individualists, Communists, Anarchists, ordinary politicians, Vegetarians, Anti-vivisectionists and Anti-vaccinationists - in fact, every kind of `anti' had a welcome and a hearing, and had to stand a lively criticism in the discussion which followed. As many came from a distance, tea was provided at a moderate charge in the adjoining room . . . [63].

John Kenworthy brought with him a familiarity with the American anarchist movement and a firm commitment to Tolstoy's ideas, which he `preached' from the pulpit of the Brotherhood Church. He combined with Wallace in 1894 to establish the Brotherhood Trust, as a means to create a voluntary co-operative system in England. It was a scheme of co-operative trading and industrial ventures, from which the profits were to be used for the purchase of land for communities. Wallace and Kenworthy had hoped to enlist a million participants within four years as the first step towards the dismantlement of capitalism. Kenworthy wrote frequently in Seed Time, urging the establishment of communities as a means of transforming society.

Another important development at Croydon was the new publication The New Order, which from 1895 reported the meetings and ideas of the Brotherhood, and later reported progress in the Tolstoyan communities. The printing activities formed the basis of the `Croydon Brotherhood Publishing Society', which was subsequently relocated in the Purleigh Colony and became the means of printing the Tolstoy translations that were made by Aylmer Maude (who also lived at Purleigh). Tolstoy had granted full printing rights to the press, following a visit by Kenworthy to Tolstoy's estate in 1896.

The New Order was a more evangelical and practical publication than Seed Time, and played a more direct part in the process of community formation. Kenworthy again figured both as editor and regular contributor, constantly reminding readers of the principles of the new life: equality (the socialist idea), fraternity (the communist idea), freedom (the anarchist idea), honest labour (the way of salvation), spreading the truth (the way of Jesus) . . . their fulfilment in practice means revolution to the lives of all who have their places in this unjust and unhappy state of society, the Mammon System. But in time the principles they express will revolutionise society altogether, and overthrow Babylon to bring in the New Jerusalem [64].

The journal also carried regular notices and advertisements, exhorting their members to take immediate and practical steps to revolutionise their lives - coal from the co-operative colliery at Swadlincote, the new vegetable butter at 6s. for a 14 pound tin, and dresses cut and fitted on scientific principles by the Croydon Brotherhood Dressmakers

In addition to the publications, while it does not seem that new points of substance were gleaned from `pilgrimages' to Tolstoy, the process itself certainly contributed an interesting dimension to the relationship. Nellie Shaw claimed that `the connection with Tolstoy became personally intimate' through contact with someone who had visited the master. Aylmer Maude (for long a resident in Russia), John Kenworthy, Tom Ferris (of the northern communities) and Francis Sedlak (who later settled at Whiteway) all made the journey to the Russian interior, the latter two in accord with Tolstoy's `no money' doctrine. Kenworthy wrote a series of letters in 1896, in the first of which he described the purpose of the journey as being to see Leo Tolstoy and friends of his, and to arrange with them ways and means of carrying forward in England the work to which they in Russia gave themselves [65]. Again, it was Nellie Shaw who described something of the excitement occasioned by these visits and by the arrival of others who new Tolstoy:

I well remember the Sunday following Kenworthy's return from Russia . . . how excited we all were to hear first-hand about the great Russian, Count Tolstoy, and to learn that he was a vegetarian, dressed like a peasant and lived so simply and frugally. He had been greatly interested to hear all about our little venture, and particularly about the Sermon on the Mount class. We heard, too, about the poor persecuted Doukhobortsi, interest in whom was shortly afterwards greatly stimulated by the arrival in Croydon of a number of Russians, friends of Tolstoy's - Vladimir Tchertkoff, with his wife and son, Dr Skarvan from Austria, where he had suffered imprisonment for his Tolstoyan principles, Helena Petrovna, a Caucasian princess, with quite a retinue of dependants and two servants ... (and) Mr Aylmer Maude, having left Moscow, arrived in Croydon with his wife and family, settling temporarily at Brotherhood House . [66].

But the focus of activity was already shifting from Croydon. In the winter of 1896 a number of the more active members of the group decided that enough preparations had been made and that the time had come to set up a community. In the first place it was in the Purleigh Colony and the neighbouring Essex communities that this new wave of activity was centred. Later, with the demise of Purleigh, the Tolstoyan trail extended to Whiteway in Gloucestershire. Croydon, Essex and Whiteway were important landmarks of Tolstoyan community activity in the late 1890s, but they were not alone. From April 1898 anarchist groups in the north of England, sharing a similar ideology, circulated a new publication, The Free Commune: `a quarterly magazine of libertarian thought', which carried news of their various activities. In one edition there was news of anarchist groups in Leeds (Brotherhood Workshop at 6, Victoria Road), Manchester (where an anarchist group met every Tuesday in the City Coffee Rooms in Swan Street), Liverpool (at the Wellington Monument every Sunday), Derby (at Comrade McGinnis's in Sitwell Street) and Sheffield (the Norton Colony, advertised as the Sheffield Free Communist Group). The establishment of more communities was urged as a revolutionary deed:

We urge all comrades, that wherever possible, they should group themselves together and acquire land; establishing small colonies adjacent to the towns. They could after the manner of the Clousden Hill Colonists, go in for intensive and glass culture, producing quantities of glasshouse fruits etc. In this manner a large part of their own food could be produced, and the surplus disposed of preferably to the Co-operative Societies - in exchange for labour notes, or drafts upon the stores, which would be a mutual advantage, relieving as it would the necessity of legal tender so often the great difficulty in such enterprises. This would provide for those necessities or luxuries which owing to the exigencies of climate or other circumstances they could not otherwise acquire. If attempts of this character were dotted up and down the country they would prove powerful examples of our principles, and would, no doubt, be largely imitated.

They would help to form the nucleus of a better society, and what is more to the point, find a haven of refuge for those who were victimised in the fight against authority and exploitation.

Agricultural co-operation would produce these results . . . It would remove men from the contaminating influence of commercialism, and by bringing them in contact with Mother Earth, purify and broaden their characters. Everything that purifies life helps the Revolution; the mere change of social forms does not necessarily bring Socialism but Fraternity spells Revolt .

Dennis Hardy is Pro Vice-Chancellor and professor of Utopian History at Middlesex University.UK.

New waves of refugees

Some 350 years after their dissolution by Henry VIII monastic communities reappeared on the British religious landscape. This new wave of monasteries bore more resemblelance to the communities established by the small non-conformist sects than the vast organisations of the 16th century. Even down to being established by those fleeing persecution. Some were set up at the historic sites of previous monasteries.

At Buckfast in Devon a group of French Monks escaping persecution established a self-sufficient community on the site of the old Abbey. Building up a strong economic base based on tonic wine, cider and honey. From 1918 onwards British monks joined the community and in 1937 the set about rebuilding the original monastery church. Other Benedictine communities were set up at Ampleforth, Douai, Downside, Ramsgate, Worth, Prinknash and Quarr. The Cistercian and Carthusian orders established houses at Mount St Bernard Abbey & St Hugh's Charterhouse, and Carmalite & Domonican Priories were established at Aylesford in Kent and Woodchester Gloustershire. Anglican monasteries were also set up during this period; one on Caldey island in the Bristol Channel (who later converted to catholicism.) and another at Mirfield in Yorkshire known as the Quarry, or the Community of the Resurrection, who were proponents of Christian Socialism. At Hillfield, in Dorset, an Anglican community was established based of Franciscan grounds. In a converted farm they ran a refuge for homeless men and in the 1930s became the Society of St Francis running a number of schools for maladjusted children, missions for lepers and friaries dotted over the country.

The culture of religious tolerance that allowed the re-establishment of monastic commiunities would also bring others fleeing persecution to England. Fleeing Russia in the 1890s the Doukhobors found brief refuge amongst the Tolstoyan anarchists both in Croydon and at the Purleigh colony in Essex. Given support by Quakers, who shared their pacifist beliefs, they eventually made their way to British Colombia, via Canada.

A longer period of refuge was enjoyed by the Society of Brothers, or Bruderhof. Founded in the 1920s the followers of German radical Christian Eberhard Arnold were forced to leave the communities they had founded in German and later in neighbouring Liectenstien keeping one step ahead of their Nazi persecutors. They came to England in 1937 buying a 200 acre farm in Wiltshire, where they established a succesfull community based on a combination of agriculture, crafts and publishing.

The appearance of a large number of German speaking pacifists in the midst of rural England with their strange peasant costumes and foreign ways was bound to raise eyebrows and as the countdown to War progressed, so the suspicion of the Bruderhof would grow. Their lifestyle based on simple Chritian principles of charity, humility, poverty, community and unity appealed to many in the English Christians and the community as Ashton Keynes expanded quickly to 250. Following advice from the Hutterites in America, with whom the Bruderhof had close links, they decided to form a second community rather than continue to expand and purchased the nearby 320 acre Oaksey estate. Local landowners alarmed at the sale of 'English' land to German petitioned the Home-Office opposing the sale. The Bruderhof won the support of the Home Secretary, Samuel Hoareand. After arguing that the land belonged to God and they were only its custodians the objections were dissmissed more on the grounds that they had previous permission to settle in the country and were after all pacifist refugees from Nazi Germany, than any case of divine freehold. Following the outbreak of war full-blown xenophobia broke out in Wiltshire with the group being accused of being spys and organising along 'Gestapo lines.' And despite support from parilament at the end of 1940 the two farms were sold and 350 members set sail for Paraguay. English members who were able to stay behind established the Wheathill Bruderhof community nr Bridgnorth in 1942 which acted as a refuge for pacifists during the war and grew to 200 strong by 1950. This community and a further one at Bulstrode in Buckinghamshire lasted until the 1960s and a further community was set up in Sussex in 1971.

Commentary & Reflection.

WHAT A DIFFERENCE A KING MAKES

I never thought that I would be singing the praises of a member of the Royalty in these pages, but without Henry the Eighth's arrogance and greed where would we be? He may have had the creator of the original Utopia executed for treason and he may have been a pretty nasty piece of work up close, but without his challenge to divine authority - well, history would just not have been the same. With no separation of the church from Rome, no dissolution of the monasteries, no enclosures, no disgruntled mobs of displaced peasants wandering the countryside eager for redress, no (relative) religious tolerance, no waves of religious refugees from the continent, no non-conformists, no Ranters, no Levellers, no Diggers, no Quakers! And if you could challenge divine authority and usurp the head of the church, then other heads could be challenged; heads of royal families, heads of state, heads of industry, heads of households......where would it all end? Not that any of this was Henry's intention, far from it. I don't really think that he should get any of the credit for 500 years of Utopian experiment, but then I guess we should be thankful for the unintended consequences of history. What a difference a low sperm count can make! What Henry did was to make it clear that the religious was political and open up an unmendable crack in the whole philosophy underpinning feudalism. From then on, viewed from a distance, the whole history of religious and social reform starts to take on an air of inevitability. You could a put down a rebellion here, suppress an uppity sect there, burn bibles in the streets, come to accommodations & betray promises until the peasants came home. Blow out the candles of hope, but the fire that burned in the hearts of those who thought they had seen a glimpse of the promised land - now that was another matter.

That the dissenting sects that proliferated during and after the English Civil War, practised forms of primitive religious socialism that paved the way for full-blooded social-ism in the 19th century seems undeniable, though with the emphasis on the religion not the socialism. I have a feeling that if we were to meet Gerard Winstanley in the flesh he would come across much more like the leader of a fundamental Christian cult than the proto-socialist so loved by Marxist historians. That the Quakers should hold a special place in the list of sects is also undeniable. Not only have they proved to be the most enduring and successful of the radical 17th century sects retaining much of their radical edge, but in their quiet, industrious, scrupulously-moral way they have underpinned so many of the schemes mentioned in this book and provided the economic and moral starting point for so many technical and social advances in our history that they are almost impossible to catalogue. I would doff my hat and offer three cheers for the Society of Friends if those gestures weren't so disrespectful of their own traditions, so instead I offer my quiet sincere thanks for the efforts of the original ethical producers and consumers.

      Not that we should let the achievements of the Quakers overshadow those of other small groups; the Moravians for instance, who were practising marriage guidance, sex education and what amounts to self-help therapy long before the rest of us had even conceived of the notions and whose communities provided inspiration to a whole generation of Owenite experimenters who followed, or the countless individuals whose spiritual beliefs provided the basis for their belief in democracy, equality and social reform. In our own secular times it is easy to forget that not so long ago the apparent contradiction between radical politics and religious belief wasn't apparent at all. It was quite possible to have a Chartist Church, a Communist Church, Christian Socialists, even Religious Anarchists and far from one set of ideas undermining the other they were seen as mutually supportive. Even the apparent lunatic fringe should not be dismissed too quickly. The likes of the Buchanites and the Southcottians whose belief in the imminent coming of a new millennium and the establishment of heaven on earth was more widespread in the general population than we might like to believe. Arguably kept alive people's aspirations for a better world until such at time as they were considered realisable in this life rather than the next. As for the groups that witnessed such obvious abuses as those of John Wroe & Henry Prince even they could be perceived as having a silver lining for some. Certainly there is little evidence that women were not free to leave the Reverend's Abode if they wanted and perhaps we have to accept that for many of the women life behind the cult's walls was preferable to that on offer outside. Christian community in its various guises, whether in intense communal circumstances or as a looser 'community of prayer' has proved to be a remarkably durable way to follow the path of God. With as many, if not more, Christians drawn to some sort of community life today than at almost anytime since the dissolution of the monasteries despite (or perhaps because of ?) the overall decline in believers.

The World Turned Upside Down Christopher Hill Pelican1975

Essex the rebel: William Covell & the troubles in essex: A sequel to the diggers movement. V.F.Snow. NebraskaUP1970

The Works of Gerard Winstanley. G.H.Sabine Cornell UP 1941

Winstanley: The Law of Freedom & other writings Ed.Christopher Hill Pelican1973

Left wing democracy in the English Civil War. D.W Petegorsky Gollancz 1940 RECOMMENDED

The Digger Movement in the days of the Commonwelth Henry Bewis LSE/B.Museum1906

Anarchia Anglicana Clement Walker London 1649

The Behmenists and the Philadelphians . Nils Thune (Uspala,) 1948

Utopia Thomas More 1517 First english translation 1551

William Tyndale: A Biography by David Daniell 1994 419 pp.

Little Gidding ; An illustrated Guide. Produced by The Friends of Little Gidding1998.

The Pursuit of the Millenuim Norman Cohn 1957 Secker & Warburg also1970Palladin

Unbridled Spirits Women of the English Revolution. Stevie Davies Womens press 1998   RECOMMENDED

Phantom Islands of the Atlantic Donald S.Johnson 1997 Souvenir Press.

The Beginings of Quakerism to 1660. W.C.Braithwaite. 2nd Ed . CUP 1955

The second period of Quakerism. W.C.Braithwaite. CUP 1961

Independent Spirits. Spritualism and English Plebians 1850-1910 Logie Barrow. Routledge Kegan Paul 1986

The Quakers in North-west England. D.A. Rooksby.(3 booklets)

Quakers in Science and Industry. Arthur Rastrick. The bannisdale Press.1930

Quakerism and Industry Before 1800 Isabel Grubb (1950),

The People Called Shakers.   E.D. Andrews New York 1953

The English Rebels. Charles Poulsen. Journeyman Press. 1984

William Penn's "Holy Experiment": The Founding of Pennsylvania 1681-1701. Bronner, Edwin B. Temple UP, 1962.

William Penn and the Founding of Pennsylvania: 1680-1684. Soderlund, Jean R., Ed.U of Pennsylvania , 1983.

The Moravian Church in England. 1728-1760. Colin Podmore. 1998 Clarendon Press.

Ockbrook Moravian Church & Settlement 1750. Pamphlet printed by Ockbrook congregation.

The Moravians at Fulneck. 1744 to the present day. Pamphlet available Fulneck Museum.

I remember,I remember. Reflections of a Fulneck Resident. Hugh L Brook. Pamphlet available Fulneck Museum.

There was a man sent...... An Outline of the Story of Howell Harris of Trevecka. M.Bickerstaff. Phamplet. 1959

The Second Coming. Popular Millenarianism 1780-1850. JFC Harrison. Routlege & Kegan Paul.1979 RECOMMENDED

The Truth will Prevail. The Mormons in the British Isles 1837-1987. Ed.V.B.Bloxham et.al. CUP 1987

Temple of Love. Donald McCormick. Jarrolds 1962.

The Rev.Prince and his Abode of Love. Charles Mander. EP publishing 1976.

ISLANDS OF SOCIALISM

Six hundred kilometres off the coast of Chile lie the Juan Fernandez Islands. Here, in 1704, after quarrelling with the captain and having doubts about the seaworthiness of the ship he was on, Scotsman Alexander Selkirk asked to be put ashore. Selkirk took with him a musket, bullets, gunpowder, a few carpentry tools, extra clothing and bedding, tobacco and a Bible. During the first few months he was so terrified by his isolation and loneliness that he rarely left the beach, sitting for days looking to the horizon hoping to see a ship. Terrified by strange sounds, which he imagined were wild creatures roaming about the interior of the island, (it was actually the wind toppling trees) he remained on the beach until driven inland when his beach was invaded by hundreds of sea lions. The interior of the island turned out not to be inhabited by terrifying wild creature, but instead by feral goats, cats and rats, descendants of those left behind by passing ships. The rats bit his feet and hands at night so Selkirk domesticated some of the cats to protect himself. The goats he shot for food and later,

when he ran out of gunpowder, learned to run them down on foot. Eventually he domesticated a few and fed himself on goat's meat and milk. He built himself several small huts and began to enjoy his island kingdom. The Bible became his most important companion and religion soothed his tortured soul and eased his loneliness. However he dreamed of rescue and daily visited his "lookout" in search of the sight of a sail. Selkirk spent four years and four months on Juan Fernandez Island. On February 1, 1709, he was rescued by Captain Woodes Rogers, the leader of a privateering expedition, who stopped to take on fresh water. Selkirk spotted the two British ships from his lookout and rushed to build a fire on the beach.

For the next two years Selkirk joined a series of "privateering raids" along the coast of Peru and Chile, and did not sight the coast of England until 1711. Booty from the capture of a Spanish galleon made him a well-to-do man and on returning to his hometown, Largo, he was greeted with great joy and surprise by his parents and friends, most of whom had thought him dead. The story of his survival on Juan Fernandez Island became the subject of much talk, due to the story appearing in a book called *Voyage Round the World* . It is these stories that are popularly believed to have inspired Daniel Defoe to write *The Life and Strange Surprising Adventures of Robinson Crusoe*.

Daniel Defoe (1660-1731), was a dissenter, pamphleteer, failed businessman, Jacobite, debtor, secret agent, journalist - inventor of the agony aunt, gossip column & spoof reader's letter - and arguably creator of the English novel with *Moll Flanders, Roxana* and *Robinson Crusoe*. In his story of the shipwrecked slave trader he created the archetype for all island paradises since. Whilst the story has a strong resemblance to Selkirk's, Crusoe's island is quite clearly located somewhere near the Caribbean island of Tobago, an area in which Defoe was involved under the auspices of the South Sea Company in trying to persuade the British Government to set up a colony. Robinson Crusoe has never gone out of print and has been translated into nearly every language. It inspired a whole genre of imitations and sequels known as robinsonades with French, Italian, German and female Robinsons.

COMMUNIST CASTAWAYS

Sometime in the 1920s the Chilean government exiled a group of communists onto Juan Fernandez Island, which had recently been abandoned as a penal colony, and 'invited' them to form a communist colony if the spirit so moved them. Six months later the Chilean Government was petitioned by the group asking leave to return and saying that they were ready to give a solemn pledge to refrain from all agitation against the existing Government and social system. Their request was acceded to. Juan Fernandez Island has recently been renamed Robinson Crusoe Island by the Chilean Government in an attempt to promote tourism.
See:www.brookes.ac.uk/schools/apm/jennings/islomania/

CRUSONIA

Fifty years after Defoe's death Thomas Spence, a radical schoolmaster from Tyneside wrote *A Supplement to the History of Robinson Crusoe, Being the History of Crusonia, or Robinson Crusoe's Island, Down to the Present Time . . .1782.* Spence's utopian travelogue was developed from a lecture that he had given to the Newcastle Philosophical Society on the injustice of existing property relations, a lecture for which he was thrown out of the society.

The main town of Crusonia bore more than a passing resemblance to eighteenth-century Newcastle. "This Town is built on each side of a commodious Harbour, a considerable River falls into it, and at the upper End of the Harbour, there is a most elegant Bridge. The Town extends about a Mile on each Side along the Shore, and about half a Mile outward towards the Country, and contains about fifty thousand Inhabitants. Four Parishes meet and have their Churches in it, two on each Side, whose Steeples are very magnificent, and a great Ornament to the Town. It is full of superb and well furnished Shops, and has every Appearance of Grandeur, Opulence, and Convenience, one can conceive to be in a large Place, flourishing with Trade and Manufactures."

Crusonia was organised under a system of communal land ownership that Spence was to develop and advocate throughout his life. Civic life was financed by the 'rents' or a single land tax, levied on use of the communal land - and industry, schools, the militia and local fairs were all governed by the parish council.

Tyneside in the mid-1700s was a lively radical scene influenced by connections to Scottish dissenting chapels. Spence hawked his pamphlets and balladsheets around the streets of Newcastle. To help working people to be able read, and so better themselves Spence developed a phonetic alphabet and reading system and had his utopian allegory printed in it as *A Suplimint too thi Histire ov Robinsin Kruzo.* Other titles were printed in 'Spencian

English' inc: *Real Reading-Made-Easy* and a cheap anthology of famous authors.

ONE PENNYWORTH OF PIGS MEAT

Spence moved down to London in the late 1780s. One of his first political actions, once he had settled in London, was the countermarking of coins with radical slogans: 'War or Land!', 'Spence's Plan Full Bellies and Fat Bairns!' He threw handfuls of them to the crowds passing on the way to executions at Tyburn. He was one the most enterprising of all issuers of token coinage earning the unintended compliment 'that he alone has done more harm to the coinage than any other person'. He also published broadsides, balladsheets, an allegorical map, and employed placards and chalk graffiti to propagate his ideas. He was not alone in his pursuits, a 'Citizen Lee' issued a number of provocative tracts with such titles as *King Killing, The Reign of the English Robespierre*, and *The Happy Reign of George the Last*. As well as referring to the guillotine in terms of warm approval, 'Citizen Lee' also supported the idea of 'Parochial and village associations'.

Spence started issuing a periodical *One Pennyworth of Pigs' Meat - Lessons for the Swinish Multitude* containing writings from a whole host of radical sources. He was now at the very centre of London's radical culture mounting its defence of the French Revolution and agitating for the overthrow the British Government.

THE PEOPLES FARM

By 1797 Thomas Spence had become one of the most sophisticated theoreticians of revolutionary radicalism in the capital. He published a series of influential radical pamphlets, including *The Rights of Infants* in which he argued for women's rights. In an imaginary dialogue 'woman' declares: 'Our sex were defenders of rights from the beginning. And though men, like other he-brutes, sink calmly into apathy respecting their offspring, you shall find nature, as it never was, so it never shall be extinguished in us. You shall find that we not only know our rights, but have spirit to assert them.' Proclaiming that 'the chains of Hymen would be among the first that would be broken, in case of a Revolution,' Spence saw women organizing for themselves as paralleling and even superseding male-dominated organisations.

In 1801 he published *The Restorer of Society to its Natural State,* an extensive development of his political philosophy that earned him twelve months imprisonment on a charge of seditious libel. Drawing on traditions of the rights of trueborn Englishmen usurped by the 'Norman yoke' he developed the idea that the land of the nation was the people's farm. This was not a harking back to some peasant economy. 'It is childish therefore to expect ever to see small farms again; or even to see anything else than the utmost screwing and grinding of the Poor, till you quite overturn the present system of Landed Property.' How to achieve this Spence was in no doubt: "How lately have we seen unions of the People sufficiently grand, and well conducted, to give sure hopes of success Abroad and at Home; in America, France, and in our own Fleets, we have seen enough of public spirit and extensive unanimity in the present generation, to accomplish schemes of infinitely greater difficulty than a thing that may be done in a day, when once the public mind is duly prepared. . . For who, pray, are to hinder the people of any Nation from doing so when they are inclined? Are the Landlords in the Parishes more numerous and powerful in proportion to the People, than the brave warlike Officers in our mutinous Fleets were to their Crews? Certainly not."

The first Spencean meeting, was held on 18 March 1801, where it was proclaimed, "That the Principles of CITIZEN SPENCE'S THEORY OF SOCIETY are immutable and unchangeable as Truth and Nature on which they are built, and therefore only require universal investigation to be universally acknowledged. Resolved therefore, that it be recommended to all the Well-wishers to that System, to meet frequently, though in ever so small Numbers, in their respective

Neighbourhoods, after a Free and Easy manner, without encumbering themselves with Rules, to converse on the Subject, provoke investigation, and answer such objections as may be started, and to promote the circulation of Citizen Spence's Pamphlets." From this point on a sort of Spencean underground developed which would disseminate his ideas through radical groups for them to re-emerge in later utopian schemes.

Thomas Spence died on 1 September 1814 from a bowel complaint. His funeral cortege was followed 'by a numerous throng of political admirers. Appropriate medallions were distributed, and a pair of scales preceded his corpse, indicative of his views.' The Spencean Philanthropists continued to agitate for an agrarian revolution after their founder's death, being influential in a number of attempted uprisings in London; at Spa Fields, Bartholemew Fair, Cold Bath Fields and in the Cato Street conspiracy. On a cold December day in 1816 at Spa Fields a Dr Watson raised the crowd to fever pitch as they prepared to march on the City and Tower of London with the seemingly unpromising revolutionary cry:

'We have been truly told that Trade and Commerce are at an end - but we still have the Earth - which Nature designed for the support of mankind - The Earth is capable of affording us all the means of allaying our wants and of placing Man in a Comfortable situation - If a Man has but a Spade, a Hoe, and a Rake and turns up his Mother Earth - He will be sure to find the means of averting Starvation.'

Robinson Crusoe was one of the favourite childhood books of the son of an ironmonger and postmaster from Newtown, mid-Wales. In the 1770s this sleepy market town was disturbed from its slumbers only by the intellectual and moral ferment of chapel Methodism. Robert was the precocious sixth child of seven born to the Owen family in 1771. By the age of seven he claimed that he had learnt all the local schoolteacher knew and was appointed as his assistant. During the two years he spent in this position he avidly devoured all the books on the teacher's shelves including; Pilgrim's Progress, Paradise Lost & Robinson Crusoe. And although he was later to view these as 'lost years' it is highly likely that his lifelong interest in education was first awoken whilst trying to teach his fellow pupils the rudiments of reading and writing. Robert Owen left Newtown for good at the age of 10 to become apprenticed to a draper in Stamford, Lincolnshire. In 1784 he went on to join Flint & Palmer, a large firm of London drapers and from there to Manchester to work for a Mr Slatterfield.

GROUND FLOOR OF THE INDUSTRIAL REVOLUTION

All around the young Owen talk was of the cotton trade, the new machinery and the profits that might be made from them. It was a time when anyone with a small amount of capital could hope to make a fortune. Between 1766 and 1785 the inventions associated with Hargreaves, Arkwright and Crompton had been developed and were now being put to use on a mass scale in new spinning mills worked by water power in Lancashire and on the banks of the Clyde at Lanark. Borrowing £100 Owen started making spinning machinery with a rather dubious partner. When the partnership broke up Owen was left with three spinning 'mules'. Employing only three workmen, he was soon making a net profit of £300 a year. These super-profits were due to the use of machine production before it had become general practice.

At the age of twenty Owen gave up his own business to become the manager of Bank Top Mill, a large spinning mill employing 500 workers. 'My name was now up for being the first fine cotton spinner in the world, and this was my standing as long as I remained the manager of Mr. Drinkwater's factory.'

The Life of Robert Owen By Himself. 1857

Peter Drinkwater was a progressive factory owner, and far from the 'sleeping partner' Owen was later to make out. He believed that good ventilation and sanitation were important in factories and is reputed to have asked workers applying for jobs how often a week they were drunk. Drinkwater had much in common with David Dale the owner of the Scottish spinning mills by the Falls of Clyde at New Lanark. Dale had built the mills in partnership with Richard Arkwright the English inventor and businessman. Spinning commenced at New Lanark in 1786 and Dale went on to preside over a highly successful business. By 1800 the mills employed over 1700 workers, easily the largest single factory operation in the United Kingdom at that time. Dale received great attention for his employment of pauper apprentices taken from city orphanages. The conditions and treatment of these 'barrack children' was enlightened for its time with elementary education and religious instruction given and even a slight reduction in working hours introduced.

Whilst on a business trip to Glasgow Robert Owen, then working for a newly formed partnership, met Anne Caroline Dale. Friendship with Miss Dale led to a proposal of marriage, and this, in turn, to Owen moving to Scotland, in 1800, to take over management of the establishment that was to turn him into a national figure.

'NEW' LANARK

'....... I know that society may be formed so as to exist without crime, without poverty, with health greatly improved, with little, if any, misery, and with intelligence and happiness increased an hundredfold; and no obstacle whatsoever intervenes at this moment, except ignorance, to prevent such a state of society from becoming universal.'

Robert Owen. New Lanark Jan 1816

Owen soon made his presence felt, sacking managers who he considered incompetent, and tackling extortionate prices charged by local shopkeepers for goods by opening a company 'truck' store - selling goods in general at 25% less than other stores. He also introduced the 'silent

monitor', a system for assessing a worker's conduct & character. This had been previously used by Quaker educationalist Joseph Lancaster. Owen's innovation to the system was to give the worker a right of appeal to his or her assessment. These changes, along with a 1hour increase in the working day, made Owen unpopular in the mills, a situation that continued up to 1807 when following an American cotton embargo he temporarily suspended production at the mill whilst continuing to pay wages. This act of generosity, very much in the tradition of David Dale, won over much of the workforce to Owen's side.

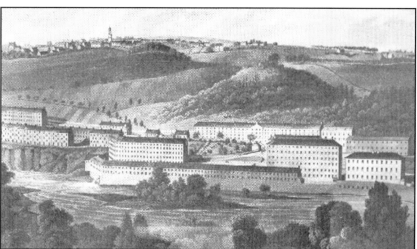

New Lanark Mills 1825

During this period Owen was formulating his ideas on the impact of a person's environment on the formation of their character - a truly radical idea for the time. This led him to propose "the foundation of infant and other schools, to form the new character in the rising population." His business partners were decidedly unenthusiastic about his latest plans and there ensued a dispute that dragged on for years, finally being resolved when Owen was able to form a partnership with a group of mainly Quaker backers and to buy the New Lanark Mills.

INSTITUE FOR THE FORMATION OF CHARACTER

On the back of a successful and profitable cotton business Owen was able to improve the houses and mills and to carry out pioneering educational experiments. On January1, 1816 the Institute for the Formation of Character was officially opened. It was a large two storey building used as a school during the day and as an adult education centre, club, concert room & dancehall in the evenings. Much of Owen's educational philosophy came from the Swiss educator Heinrich Pestalozzi who placed emphasis on the importance of kindness and commonsense in his approach to teaching. Pestalozzi believed that children could learn as much from observation and experience as from formal teaching. The first teacher in the 'new rational infant school' was former handloom weaver James Buchanan, a gentle Swedenborgian, who was described somewhat condescendingly as a 'simple-minded, kind-hearted individual who could hardly read or write himself', but who was to go on to run his own school in Westminster and to be instrumental in the formation of the Infant Schools Society.

STEAM ENGINE OF THE MORAL WORLD

Education was to be the core of the Owenite philosophy. The idea that through the education of future generations a better world would be created - first put forward by the Owenites - is essentially the underpinning idea of all modern education. The example of the 'new rational school' helped to pioneer infant schooling in Britain and a century later many of the subjects first taught there would be found on school curricula throughout the country.

Owen sent his own sons to be educated at Emmanual Fellenberg's progressive school at Hofwyl in Switzerland and the eldest Robert Dale returned to teach at New Lanark and write a book about the school:

'The principal school-room is fitted up with desks and forms on the Lancastrian plan, having a free passage down the centre of the room. It is surrounded, except at one end where a pulpit stands, with galleries, which are convenient when this room is used, as it frequently is, either as a lecture-room or place of worship.

The other and smaller apartment on the second floor has the walls hung round with representations of the most striking zoological and mineralogical specimens, including quadrupeds, birds, fishes, reptiles, insects, shells, minerals etc. At one end there is a gallery, adapted for the purpose of an orchestra, and at the other end are hung very large representations of the two hemispheres; each separate country, as well as the various seas, islands etc. being differently coloured, but without any names attached to them. This room is used as a lecture- and ball-room, and it is here that the dancing and singing lessons are daily given. It is likewise occasionally used as a reading-room for some of the classes. The lower storey is divided into three apartments, of nearly equal dimensions, 12 ft high, and supported by hollow iron pillars, serving the same time as conductors in winter for heated air, which issues through the floor of the upper storey, and by which means the whole building may, with care, be kept at any required temperature. It is in these three apartments that the younger classes are taught reading, natural history, and geography.' Robert Dale Owen.
Outline of the System of Education at New Lanark.

Educational reform would feature in almost all the schemes inspired by Owen leading one contemporary to dub education: "the steam engine of the moral world" George Mudie. *Economist 1826.*

NEW VIEWS OF SOCIETY

At a dinner party in 1812 Owen met the anarchist philosopher William Godwin. In the following months, whilst working on his ideas on how it would be possible to apply the lessons of New Lanark to society at large, Owen not only met regularly with Godwin but was introduced to the radical Francis Place and the political economist James Mill - and although it was never acknowledged by Owen it was Place and Mill who edited his essay and gave it a depth

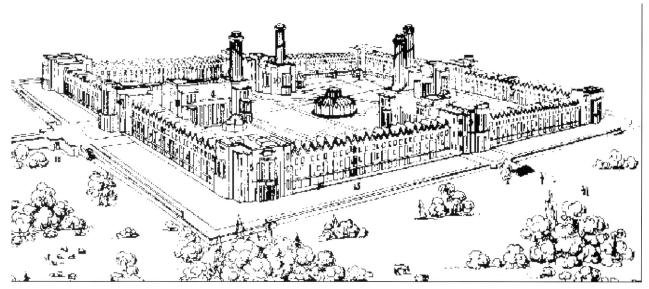

Stedman Whitewell's design for Owenite Parallelogram for 2000 people

and clarity that is missing from his later writing.

New View of Society (1813/16) not only contains a synthesis of enlightenment ideas, but also a detailed plan of 'villages of unity & mutual co-operation'. Owen presented his plan to whoever would listen;

'I now beg leave to solicit the attention of the Committee to the drawings and explanations which accompany this report. The drawing exhibits, in the foreground, an establishment, with its appendages and appropriate quantity of land; and at due distances, other villages of a similar description. Squares of buildings are here represented sufficiently to accommodate about 1200 persons each; and surrounded by a quantity of land, from 1000 to 1500 acres. Within the squares are public buildings, which divide them into parallelograms.

The central building contains a public kitchen, messrooms, and all the accommodation necessary to economical and comfortable cooking and eating. To the right of this is a building, of which the groundfloor will form the infant school, and the other a lectureroom and a place of worship. The building to the left contains a school for the elder children, and a committee-room on the ground-floor; above, a library and a room for adults. In the vacant space are enclosed grounds for exercise and recreation: these enclosures are supposed to have trees planted in them. It is intended that three sides of each square shall be lodging houses, chiefly for the married, consisting of four rooms in each; each room to be sufficiently large to accommodate a man, his wife, and two children. The fourth side is designed for dormitories for all children exceeding two in a family, or above three years of age. In the centre of this side of the square are apartments for those who superintend the dormitories: at one extremity of it is the infirmary; and at the other a building for the accommodation of strangers who may come from a distance to see their friends and relatives.

In the centres of the two sides of the square are apartments for general superintendents, clergymen, school-masters, surgeon, etc.; and in the third are store-rooms for all articles required for the use of the establishment. On the outside, and at the back of the houses around the squares, are gardens, bounded by roads. Immediately behind these, on one side, are buildings for mechanical and manufacturing purposes. The slaughterhouse, stabling, etc., to be separated from the establishment by plantations................'

Robert Owen
New View of Society (1813/16)

Lord Sidmouth, the Duke of Kent and the Archbishop of Canterbury all lent a sympathetic ear. Between 1817 and 1824 Owen was constantly addressing meetings, issuing a stream of pamphlets and travelling incessantly. With all these activities he had less time to devote to New Lanark, and after 1817 the supervision of the factory was increasingly left to subordinates. In 1825 he ceased to be manager of the New Lanark Mills, though he kept his financial interest until 1828.

' Co-operative Shipwrights mill c1760
From a drawing by W.Clifton

CO-OPERATION FEVER

Owen's *New View of Society* was part of an upsurge of 'co-operative' activity that had its beginnings in the late 1700s. As far back as 1760 local bakery owners in Kent had been charged with arson for burning down a mill owned co-operatively by a group of shipwrights & bakers. Early food co-ops had been run by the Weavers Friendly Society at Fenwick, Ayrshire in 1769 & the Govan Victualling Society in 1777. These were followed by others in Middlesex, Leicestershire, Yorkshire & Lancashire(1793-1804). In 1795 on the east coast an 'Anti-mill' opened at Hull, followed by others at Whitby and Beverley. At Plymouth, in 1816, royal dockyard officers and workmen organised the Sheerness Economical Society "for obtaining for themselves and families, a supply of wheaten bread and flour and butchers' meat." A year later they opened the Devonport Union Mill and a bakery and despite intimidatory opposition these both continued in operation until the formation of the Plymouth Co-operative Society.

Much of this co-operative activity was in response to the 'truck' system whereby workers were forced to accept goods - often adulterated & extortionately priced - from company stores in lieu of wages. Given the coastal location of many of the ventures it is also possible that co-operative traditions amongst seamen may have played a part in their formation. It is among these, and other, local self-help schemes that lie the seeds of the co-operative movement. It was also here that the message of the Owenites would find a receptive audience.

The early co-operative movement contained two 'wings'; the wealthy philanthropic theorists who wanted to build a co-operative society on the base of industrial capitalism, and working class radicals who came from a tradition of self-improvement & mutual aid. A third element was a millennialist tendency amongst the poor whom they sought to reform, or organise. Owen's pamphlets and lectures prompted many from all walks of life to try and set up co-operative communities.

COLONIES AT HOME

Quaker William Allen, one of Owen's financial partners at New Lanark, had a considerable knowledge of co-operative experiments. He was a friend of General Contineas, superintendent of the Russian Crimean Colonies. Allen had travelled in Russia visiting the Mennonites at Gorlitz, Greenenthal and Altona; the Dukhobors at Terpania and the Malakins at Simferopol.

In 1821 moved by the signs of poverty in the village of Lindfield near Brighton, Allen came up with his own plan for a co-operative colony. He found willing co-operators in Stephen Wood, the Earl of Chichester and John Smith, M.P. for Buckinghamshire. They first built a school open to pupils of any religion, equipped with a farm, a printing office and workshops. The school was such a success that in 1825 John Smith bought the 100-acre Graveley estate for Allen's `colony'. On the estate Allen built twelve three bedroom cottages with an acre and a quarter of land attached, each with its own wood-house, wash-house, bake-house and piggery. Six larger holdings of 5 to 6 acres were created and Allen took one of these for himself. After the colony had been in operation for nine years it established its own paper, *The Lindfield Reporter*. The colony prospered and conditions were so advanced for the time that the settlement was nicknamed `America'.

In 1827 Allen published a pamphlet *Colonies at Home* outlining a scheme to provide every poor family with a piece of land and a cottage. Allen argued that his `home colonies' were a remedy for poverty far superior to Owenism or emigration. *Colonies at Home* inspired others; Samuel Gurney bought seven acres of land at West Ham and divided it up into allotments and further experiments were begun at Ballinderry near Lisburn in Ireland and Lastadie near Stettin in Germany. A local neighbour of Allen's, Dr. William King became convinced that a co-operative shop could provide the money to finance a community. King established a benevolent fund association and issued a four-page monthly journal known as *The Co-operator*.

'.....a certain number of working-men at Brighton, by clubbing sixpence a week each, which they vested not in a benefit society, or saving-bank, but, as soon as it amounted to a sufficient sum, in a little grocer's shop, carried it on by one of their members, for the benefit of the whole. Of course all the members purchased their goods there. The profits and the continued subscription were next invested in a mackerel boat; then in a garden of 28 acres: thus far the experiment had gone when I obtained my account of it. Their intention is to go on till every member of this society is employed in the service of the whole, and then they consider their society to be complete. They publish a weekly paper explaining their principles and progress, at one penny each; and of this paper 12,000 copies are sold. Already seventy such societies have been formed....'

Robert Southey in letter to W.S.Landor
Selections from the letters of Robert Southey.

Through his magazine Dr King did much to popularise the idea that co-operative communities could be formed from the funds raised by co-operative stores and in the last issue of *The Co-operator* (Aug 1830) it was announced that throughout the country a total of 300 similar societies had been set up.

VILLAGES OF VISION

In 1827 an article entitled *'Interesting Settlement in Wales - an account of the principles and progress of an experiment for improving the condition of the labouring classes of society, in the hills of Monmouthshire,'* appeared in *The Oriental Herald*. The author was John Moggridge a Monmouth magistrate and industrialist. In the article he described the scheme that he had set up on his land in the Sirhowy Valley. Appalled by the living conditions of the colliers in the valley, Moggridge had consulted with Robert Owen and devised a variant of Owen's villages of co-operation. Moggridge's aim was to give working people independence and self-respect. He proposed grants of land for a term of three generations on condition that;

1. The tenant should pay a regular small ground rent.

Cottages in Hall St. Blackwood built as part of John Moggridge's scheme

2. The tenant should personally assist in the erection of a substantial and commodious cottage. This should not interfere with his regular work.

3. Any money advanced by Moggridge should be secured by the premises, and repaid by instalments at regular intervals.

Initially only three tenants accepted the offer of an eighth on an acre plot and in the spring of 1820 three cottages were built and the gardens planted with leeks and onions. Seeing the value of home-grown fruit and vegetables and additional income that could be had from letting an upperstorey 'lodging room' out to single colliers, forty plots were taken up in the next 2 years and by 1828 there were 260 houses and 1550 inhabitants in The Black Wood. As the settlement grew medical services, shops, workshops for craftsmen and small tradesmen, a school and market house - which also doubled as chapel - were all provided. So successful was the scheme that a few miles down the valley the village of Ynysddu was born in the same way with more than thirty houses being built there. Over the hill from Blackwood at Trelyn a further fifty houses were built and in 1829 the total population of the three villages totalled 2000. The scheme obviously brought advantages to the ordinary people of the area, but the greatest beneficiary was Moggridge himself. The total rents from his estate increased significantly, as did its saleable value. A consequence of the social experiment was that a core of the most talented and industrious workmen became tied to the area providing the skills vital to the continued expansion of coal mining in the valley. Folk who had built their own cottages were most unlikely to leave them.

Moggridge's scheme is perhaps closer to the idea of the 'Villages of Co-operation' than any of the other communities set up by Owen and his followers, although it did not have the grand architecture of the other schemes, nor the ardent radicalism of the community members. However it proved to be more resilient than any other Owenite scheme and was to be the foundation of the small town of Blackwood.

CONGREGATIONAL FAMILIES

Inspired by Owen, a Scottish printer George Mundie unveiled his plan for a 'co-operative and economical society' to a meeting of printers at Mitchells Assembly Rooms in London on 23 Jan 1821. He promoted his planned community through the pages of his weekly journal The Economist. A community of 250 families was envisaged with a common kitchen, dining room and a school. As it turned out the venture started on a much smaller scale with a co-operative store and then by renting a number of houses in Islington, Finsbury and Clerkenwell.

Although the community lasted only 3 years it was the only urban community set up during this period. Deliberately situated in London so that it would give 'a greater impetus to the cause of co-operative fellowship than half a dozen villages established at three or four hundred miles from the metropolis. It would be like a pebble thrown into the centre of a pool, village would succeed village, till the circle would at last embrace the whole country.' **George Mundie** in the Economist

Following what would become a common pattern in communities, a printing press was set up and their own paper produced to tell the world of their endeavours. One edition of *The Economist: A Periodic Paper - Explanatory of the New System of Society, Projected by Robert Owen, Esq. ~ and of a Plan of Association for Improving the Condition of the Working Classes, During their Continuance at their Present Employment*, contained a detailed description of the community. Calling themselves the 'The Co-operative and Economical Society of London', they pooled their wages to provide communal facilities.

"The families breakfast, dine, etc., together at the general tables; and in the evenings amuse themselves with conversation, reading lectures, music etc. in the public room. The individuals, however, are at perfect liberty at all times, to take their meals, and to spend their leisure hours, in their private apartments."

Women organised the domestic duties under "a system of combination" with "departments of house-wifery, such as cleaning, washing, getting up linen, etc." Childcare was organised collectively and it was announced that a school would be opened. Some women worked in the community, other had jobs outside.

'The Society already employs its own shoemak-ers and tailors, and will speedily be enabled to perform all its own work within itself. The Society also can now promptly execute, for the Public, in the best and cheap-est manner, orders for carving and gilding, transparent landscape window blinds, paintings on velvet, boot and shoemaking, gentlemen's clothing, and dressmaking and millinery.'

Quite what happened to the Congregationalists is not known, *The Economist* ceased publication in 1822 and by 1824 the community seems to have dispersed with George Mundie going to the Owenite community at Orbiston.

AN ADVENTURE IN SOCIALISM

One visitor to New Lanark in 1820 was so inspired by what he saw and heard that he returned to Edinburgh to embark on a series of community ventures. Abram Combe, a 35-year-old tanner, founded The Edinburgh Practical Society, which quickly grew to claim 500 families as members, some of whom appear to have lived communally. A co-op store was set up and a school planned. After the demise of the Practical Society Combe set up a short-lived, profit-sharing community experiment with the leatherworkers at his tanyard. Dormitories and a kitchen were built but this venture failed too.

Robert Owen had purchased 660 acres of land near Motherwell with the aim of starting a community under the auspices of the British and Foreign Philanthropic Society, but had become frustrated by the lack of support for his grand plans in Britain and departed for America. Combe along with A.J.Hamilton, son of the landowner, bought 291 acres of this land and on the 18 March 1825 building work began on a vast complex of buildings that was to be the Orbiston Community. The first building in the country designed specifically to house the working class was a huge 5 storey block with 2 wings that would house not only 200 families (with their 400 children) but contain kitchen, bakehouse, library, drawing rooms, lecture room, dining room, workshops, a theatre and a school. In the first year a hundred members were attracted to this socialist adventure; weavers, blacksmiths, joiners, cabinetmakers, wheelwrights, printers, painters, tailors, seamstresses and harnessmakers all flocked to the banks of the river Calder.

On the first anniversary of the community a meet-ing was held to discuss self-government. It was decided that all matters would be discussed at a general meeting to be held every Wednesday evening. They then unanimously adopted the principles of the Sermon on the Mount as an ethical code of conduct with additional rules on temper-ance, cleanliness and the sanctity of private rooms. Departments were established for agriculture, manufac-ture, domestic economy and education. And for conven-ience every member was given a number by which they were to be known. The communiarians also decided to complete the building works themselves, dismissing the local tradesmen who so far had done most of the work. The printing, foundry & food growing departments all flourished. The food-producers cultivated 75 acres including vegetable garden and orchard. They also found time to construct roads and walks around the buildings. By June 1827 the *Orbiston Register*, the community's own fortnightly newspaper, could report that 35 acres of oats were rustling in the summer breeze, a wheat crop was in full ear, blossom was on the fruit trees, vegetables were in the garden and the herbaceous beds were a riot of colour.

The experiment seemed to be going from strength to strength; a school was duly established, and managed by Miss Whitwell, who had taught at New Lanark. A drainage system was installed that by use of septic tanks manured the fields with the solids from the sewage and decanted the liquid onto the kitchen gardens. A reservoir for fresh water was built and the foundry water wheel was attached to a sawmill so timber could be planked for community use. Adverts were placed in local papers advertising a whole array of goods and services that could be supplied. The food-growing department and the foundry group were in fact so busy that they started to miss the weekly meetings.

The disparity between the successful departments and others started to be a source of conflict. Jealous of the farmers', foundrymen's and printers' success, one night someone stole their tools. In response to this the successful departments set up what amounted to a group of community vigilantes who patrolled the grounds with guns.

Orbiston, October 1826

Advertisement of articles available of goods in First Style and at Moderate Prices now available to supply.

Printing and Bookbinding

Handbills, cards of address. Magazines. Books of any style or quantity bound. Fancy coloured paper for Stationers.

Boot and Shoemaking

In London and Edinburgh style and much cheaper. N.B. superior blacking.

Carving and Gilding

Looking glass and picture frame.

Turning

Lent wheels and reels made and repaired. Wooden basins,

Painting and Glazing

Paper hangings, sign, house painting, mutations of all woods.

Watch and Clocks

Particularly Repeating watches, musical snuff boxes.

Tailoring

Gents' naval and military uniforms and plain clothes, all kinds of common apparel suitable for working in.

Hairdressing and Perfumer

Wheel Carriage Makers

Barrow, ploughs, cart wheels.

Machinery Makers

Steam engines. Brass and iron castings, apparatus for gas lighting, saws hammered and set. Screw presses.

Upholstery

Mattresses, fringe, etc.

Masons and Joiners

Cabinet and chair making.

Tinsmith

Brazier and tin plate baths.

Weaving

The Community intend, very shortly, to open a Bazaar for Public Inspection. In General Society it too often occurs, that an opposition of interests prevents some part of an undertaking from having the same superior skill employed in the execution of it that the rest may have, but in this Establishment the united intelligence of the whole body will be always employed either in forwarding their respective occupations or concentrated, when necessary, to any given operation. This superiority can only be found amongst persons united for the mutual benefit of each other.

(Printed at Orbiston Press)

Conflict also arose over communal dining arrangements, resulting in the option of private meals being allowed. As a result 21 chose to eat in the mess room; but 77 preferred to draw their rations and cook for themselves. The disparity in consumption was startling, with in some cases the private feeders consuming 3 times as much as those that ate communally. The community was slowly dividing into two camps; those who believe in equal distribution of goods and those who wanted some recognition of their individual contribution. On top of all this Abraham Combes's health was rapidly declining. In the end his brother was forced to take over the management of the community. Unable to cope on his own he convened a committee of the proprietors, who after a close scrutiny of the productive potential of each member adopted a system of piece-work - department superintendents and members were urged to make `economy and industry their watchword'. Three months after this abandonment of the basic purpose of the community Abraham Combe died and following pressure from the mortgagees members were ordered to quit.

The community was bought by the owner of the neighbouring estate, a Mrs Douglas, who had the property razed to the ground, with much of the stone sold to build houses in Bellshill and Motherwell.

A SHORT PERIOD OF IGNORANCE AND MISERY

Whilst Robert Owen was away, the movement he had inspired would continue and flourish under the leadership of the likes of Dr King, Willam Thompson and William Pare. There was an upsurge in working class co-operative activity; with great interest both in small retail societies whose aim was to create enough trading surplus to establish communities on the land, and from the new Trade Unions looking for ways to counteract the worst effects of industrialisation. Thompson in particular developed Owen's paternalistic ideas into a more recognisably socialist set of theories and models. He wrote a number of influential books including a how-to-do-it manual entitled *Practical Directions for the Speedy and Economical Establishment of Communities, on the Principles of Mutual Co-operation, United Possessions and Equality of Exertions and of the Means of Enjoyments.*

Thompson was influenced by Anna Wheeler, a pioneer socialist and early feminist with whom he discussed all aspects of the 'social question'. They collaborated on *Appeal of One Half the Human Race* published in Thompson's name and perhaps the most powerful feminist tract since Mary Wollstonecraft's *Vindication of the Rights of Woman*. Anna Wheeler was a key figure in the early co-operative movement. She had been part of a Saint-Simonian circle in Caen, France after she had fled her family home in Ireland. The Saint-Simonians considered her to be 'the most gifted woman of the age' and hailed her as the 'Goddess of Reason'. She met Charles Fourier the French utopian thinker and writer, and later provided a link between French socialists and the English co-operative movement, translating articles for the co-operative press. So great was her enthusiasm for the French Revolution of 1830 that she was sent a knot of tricolour from the barricades and urged to return to France to argue the rights of women. She urged women 'not to leave the bitter inheritance of ignorance and slavery' to their daughters and along with Thompson saw co-operative communities as a way to combat the inequalities between the sexes.

With all this encouragement from the co-operative press, attempts continued to be made to establish co-operative communities.

"The friends of the system of mutual co-operation and equal distribution will rejoice to hear, that some gentlemen belonging to the Devon and Exeter Co-operative Society have purchased a small estate, and commenced arrangements for the formation of a community, about six miles and a half from that city. The estate consists of thirty-seven acres of excellent land, ……… …..…… thirteen Co-operators, consisting of a Gardener, Carpenter, Quarrier, (there being a stone quarry on the estate), Drainer, Well-sinker, Clay

cont'd P87

COMMUNITY PRINTING

Alongside the innocuously-titled London Chronicle on the counter of Hetherington's bookshop in London in 1817 were other newspapers and periodicals with more intriguing names; The Reformists Register or the Theological Comet. Others had more explicitly political titles like Black Dwarf or the ominous Axe Laid to the Root. In all some 68 radical newspapers were in circulation in the early 1800s. Some lasted for only a few issues others ran for years. They were sold through a network of radical booksellers whose shops, like alternative bookshops today, acted as a focus for political activity in any town. They were subject to frequent government harassment for selling unstamped, blasphemous and seditious publications. They were also frequently printers.

The spread of radical ideas has always relied on effective means of propaganda. As far back as the Lollards, who before they were circulating hand-written copies of the Bible for ordinary people to read in their own language, held meetings where the Bible was recited by individuals who had memorised whole sections of it. And in the 1520s hot off the newly invented printing press came smuggled copies of William Tyndale's English Bible.

BROADSHEET WAR

By the advent of the Civil War in 1640 radicals had set up their own presses and had the technology to take advantage of the collapse of censorship that occurred. A flood of printed matter, newspapers, books, broadsheets, tracts and ballads, flowed off the presses. In the 20 years from 1640 and 1660 the number of known publications printed in England exceeded the total printed during the previous 150 years. Blizzards of ballads printed overnight were scattered in the streets; broadsheets were nailed to posts, church doors, even the House of Commons. And because a printers rights passed to his widow rather than to his son, in the period 1641 to 1660 there were 34 women printers and booksellers. Women

were also writing propaganda, often seeking out women printers to publish their works. Incendiary documents were passed from hand to hand, read and explained by the literate to the illiterate. The prolific propagandist Thomas Spence went as far as to invent his own phonetic alphabet to help ordinary people to learn to read.

COMMUNITY NEWS

By the time of the Owenite agitation of the 1830s access to printing was such that most utopian communities set up at the time were able to print their own paper if not posses their own press. Alongside Robert Owen's own publications, most notably The New Moral World [Ed. `Robert Owen and his Disciples'], The Working Bee was issued from the Manea Fen Community; The Communist Chronicle and Communitarian Apostle was issued by Goodwyn Barmby from the Ham Concordium and George Mundie's printers community in Clerkenwell brought out the Economist. The Owenite propaganda was phenomenal, in addition to the regular newspapers, numerous one off tracts and books were published and over 150 small periodicals were issued.

Wealthy individuals issued their own mass circulation newspapers. James Hill promoted radical ideas in East Anglia through the pages of The Star in the East and Fergus O'Connor promoted the land colony schemes and Chartism in general as editor of the Northern Star. When suppression was particularly harsh corresponding societies were formed who exchanged radical ideas via 'personal' letters.

The Arts & Crafts movement raised printing and propaganda to the status of high art, producing beautifully illustrated books and magazines. William Morris's actual printing press from the Kelmscott Press took on an iconic status being moved to the Guild of Handicraft community at Chipping Camden on Morris's death and from there being bought by Ananda Coomaraswamy.

ANARCHIC PUBLISHING

Seed Time, a small magazine published by the Fellowship of the New Life in Croyden during the 1890s, can perhaps lay claim to being the first paper of a communities 'movement' it carried reports from visitors to communities around the UK and abroad alongside adverts for new members for various colonies, 'associated' homes and co-operative housekeeping schemes.

The works of Tolstoy were translated and printed at the anarchist colony at Purliegh in Essex along with the magazine The New Order. The anarchist press that had produced the influential and long lived paper Freedom was moved to the Whiteway community in 1927 where Tom Keell and Lillian Wolfe kept anarchist propaganda alive by producing the Freedom Bulletin until Freedom reappeared in the late 1930s. The Christian Anarchist Brotherhood Church at Stapleton in Yorkshire still run their own press producing calendars & cookbooks alongside political propaganda. (In the 1960s they branched out into film propaganda touring the country showing peace films from the back of a converted van.)

The Bruderhof along with their own publication The Plough were responsible for the production of The Community Broadsheet in the late 1930s. During WW2 due to the numerous pacifist land communities the Peace Pledge Union paper Peace News became the focus for information about communal living, a link that lasted through to the 1970s & 80s.

The long tradition of radical communal presses continued throughout the last quarter of the 20th century at the Findhorn & Lifespan communities, with the Lifespan press printing both Communes Network and Diggers & Dreamers, Extending support & credit terms without which they would never have appeared. In doing so they joined the countless printers who have given us the 'written' history of a whole movement.

HARMONY IN THE NEW WORLD

In August 1824 a visitor with an unusual offer called at New Lanark. Richard Flower had been sent by the Rappites, a sect of German immigrants, to find a buyer for their lands and buildings comprising the village of Harmony in Beaver County, Pennsylvania. The village, fully equipped for community life, was on offer for a quarter of the sum Owen had estimated for the establishment of minimum size community in the British Isles. It was an offer too good to resist. Owen set off for America almost immediately. On arrival in New York he was feted by American society, from fellow industrialists, educationalists & radicals to national politicians. Active Owenite groups and the long tradition of successful communal sects such as the Shakers had paved the way for him. After a short speaking tour Owen arrived in the village of Harmonie. He was greeted by the son of Father George Rapp and set about a methodical 8-day inspection of the village. Further deliberations and negotiation followed until on New Years Day 1925 Owen told his son William that he had made up his mind. Two days later he became the proprietor of 20,000 acres along with factories, shops, public buildings and housing for some 700 people. Leaving his son in charge Owen promptly set off on a 100-day triumphant whirlwind propaganda tour - taking in New York, Washington, 3 presidents and the Hall of Representatives. He solicited offers of support from numerous leading academics and reformers. Crucially he gained the support of William Maclure, a well-known educational reformer and geologist, who agreed to go into partnership with Owen and invest money in the scheme.

Meanwhile back in Harmonie (now renamed New Harmony) William Owen struggled to set up the community with no guidance from his father. The village was being inundated with applications for membership from all and sundry. No system had been set up for admitting or vetting members. Owen Snr. was sending people he had met and inspired on his tour down to New Harmony and very soon the village was overpopulated and suffering from an accommodation shortage. William Owen managed remarkably well, setting up what was known as the preliminary society as an interim arrangement and getting on with the harvesting the Rappite's crops - which despite the abundant population was hampered by the lack of skilled farmers and gardeners. Goods were not ordered, houses not built; all because no one was sure what Mr Owen intended - it was hoped things would improve upon his return. On his way back Owen was accompanied by a party of 40 that became known as the "boatload of knowledge" a hand-picked group of naturalists, academics, Pestalozzian teachers and their pupils - all persuaded by Owen and Maclure to come and set up a school. The trip had scarcely begun when the boat stuck fast in the ice where it remained a full month. Owen, not one to wait for rivers to thaw, hastened to New Harmony by coach.

The town consisted of; 126 family dwelling houses each with 1/4 of an acre of land, four large communal dwellings, church, steam engine, two large granaries, wool and cotton factories all set out on a grid pattern of manicured gardens and neat tree-lined streets. In addition there was a 5-acre vegetable garden, a 35-acre orchard, a 15-acre vineyard and 2000 acres of highly cultivated land. Owen's arrival heralded a period of hectic activity, a building programme was started, the school inaugurated, and a programme of social events, dances & lectures, was organised. A newspaper *The New Harmony Gazette* was started. A somewhat complicated internal accounting system was set up; with labour credits and passbooks, calculations for working out medical & schooling fees, as well as credits and debits for hours worked, goods taken from the communal store and rents due. The system was supposed to balance at the end of a year, but in the meantime credit had to be advanced to members on a weekly basis. It is estimated that Owen subsidised the running cost of the community to the tune of $30,000 during the first 9 months. A committee drew up a constitution for the New Harmony Community of Equality to supersede the rules of the preliminary society - this proved to be vaguer than the original rules and did nothing to clarify matters. Disillusionment started to set in as people began to realise that this might be the beginning of a New Moral World, but nobody really knew where they were going next, not even Robert Owen.

First to break ranks were a group of Methodists who objected to Owen's religious views - they were granted 1300 acres of scrubland and became Community No 2, or Macluria. They were followed by group of English farmers who were granted 1400 acres of best farm land where they set up community No 3, known as Febia-Peveli. They were both viewed sympathetically by Owen who saw them as branches from the tree of New Harmony. Not all the residents were disappointed by the New Moral World, some like William Pelham would speak highly of his life there; "I have become a Harmonite and mean to spend the remainder of my days in this abode of peace and quietness. I have experienced no disappointment. I did not expect to find everything regular, systematic, convenient - nor have I found them so. I did expect to find myself relieves (sic) from a most disagreeable state of life, and be able to mix with my fellow citizens without fear or imposition - without being subject to ill humor and unjust censures and suspicions - and this expectation has been realised - I am at length free - my body is at my own command, and I enjoy mental liberty, after having long been deprived of it."

William Pelham *Free Enquirer June 10 1829*.

But those who were happy with life at New Harmony were in a minority. The division that was to prove most damaging was the one that brought about the attempt to set up Community No 4 - this was the split between the so called academic 'Literati' and the rest of the members. This involved Owen's two sons, Robert Dale & William, in an attempt to make the community work by taking over most of the buildings in the village with a group made up of those most dedicated to community principles. To those outside this core group, this looked like an elitist coup d'etat and Robert Owen refused to go along with it, making them an offer of a tract of woodland where they could build log cabins - the offer was not taken up. Continued dissension among the Harmonites, coupled with mounting financial troubles would finally bring about the community's demise. Owen never intended New Harmony to be a gift to its inhabitants and hoped to get back the money he had invested. Having by this time already spent $150,000 he was facing financial ruin. From this point on reorganisation followed reorganisation as Owen attempted to find a way for the community to pay for itself. Each change brought further antagonisms, skilled tradesmen vs 'malingerers', libertarians vs. socialists, farmers vs. academics. Everything came to a head when George Rapp came to collect the next purchase instalment. At this point William Maclure chose to buy himself out of the 'partnership' with Owen and make the school a separate body. Either because of the dire financial situation or being faced with the increasing fragmentation of the community Owen decided to call it a day. Whilst New Harmony would carry on as a community set apart, dedicated to high social and academic ideals, as an experiment in Owenite socialism it was dead. Owen left in June 1827. Defeated but not downhearted he set about trying to persuade the Mexican government to grant him a large tract of land stretching from the Gulf of Mexico to the Pacific to carry out his 'Plan'.

The Owenite legacy in America would be a long and enduring one. The glittering 'Literati'of New Harmony would go on to excel in their chosen academic fields. Owen's sons and daughter would make their own contributions to American culture. Robert Dale Owen became an anti-slavery & women's rights campaigner, was editor of the radical newspaper, Free Enquirer. He served in US House of Representatives, where he introduced the bill establishing the Smithsonian Institution. David Dale Owen became a leading American geologist and both Jane Dale & Richard Owen were involved in education.

A further nine Owen inspired communities were set up, the most intriguing and controversial was that set up by a young Scot, Frances Wright. When Owen had arrived in America some had seen his plan as an answer to the problem of Negro colonization. This was an attempt at the peaceful emancipation of slaves. Back in 1822 the American Colonization Society had founded the colony of Monrovia in Liberia with the aim of settling emancipated slaves there. The problem had been how to organise the new colony. However it was not until Frances Wright seized upon the idea of applying Owenite ideas to the slavery question that anything was done about it. During the summer of 1825 Miss Wright formulated her own plan. Citing the Moravians, Shakers, and Rappites as examples, rather than New Harmony, she declared her intention of finding of land where she would gather fifty or a hundred slaves who would earn the money for their emancipation at the same time as they learned the skills and attitudes requisite for freedom. She found a site for the experiment along the Wolf River in Shelby County, Tennessee. Two thousand acres of former Chickasaw land were acquired and the Chickasaw name Nashoba was adopted for the project. A dozen or so slaves, acquired partly by purchase and partly by gift, were installed on the estate and the great emancipation project began.

Through talks with Owen & Maclure, Frances Wright's ideas became more and more radical. Onto the original experiment in Negro education was grafted a communitarian colony open to whites and "founded on the principle of community of property and labor." There was no expectation at Nashoba that racial equality could be realised with the current generation of adults, but the aim would be to achieve it by giving the children of the community, white and coloured together, an identical education. This integrationist approach was a complete break from previous proposals for Negro colonies. In complete defiance of public opinion the community would also embrace Owenite ideas on the irrationality of religion and the tyranny of marriage. Robert Dale Owen joined Miss Wright at Nashoba and accompanied her on a trip to Europe to seek support for her enterprise leaving James Richardson, a fervent Owenite, in charge. The community diary entry for Sunday 17th June, 1827 records: "- Met the slaves - James Richardson informed them that, last night, Mamselle Josephine and he began to live together; and he took this occasion of repeating to them our views on color, and on the sexual relation." White men had had sex with slave women before, but none of them had recorded the fact in the official records of a social institution, and having done so proceeded to publish a transcript to publicise the community's work. Horrified defenders of morality, who had already vented their fury on Owenism, turned upon Fanny Wrightism with a vengeance declaring Nashoba nothing more than "one great brothel." Although Frances Wright put up a vigorous defence of Nashoba's free morality, on her return the writing was on the wall. The community lasted a further year under the watchful eye of Frances's sister then in Jan1830 Miss Wright accompanied the remaining slaves to Haiti where, with their emancipation, Nashoba ended.

The full story of New Harmony is told in: Backwoods Utopias. Arthur Bestor. U.Pennsylvania Press 1950/1970.

Temperer, Moulder, etc. etc., have been set to work, and scores, it is said, are waiting anxious to join them".

Alternative Communities in 19th Century England.

Jasper Veysey, a linen draper and hosier in Exeter was the prime mover behind this West Country Owenite scheme. He had aroused interest in local co-operative circles with his pamphlet, *The proper study of mankind is Man,* in which he put forward a `practical and easy method of immediately banishing poverty from the world, and within a short period ignorance and misery, vice and crime'.

In line with Owen's recommendations there were plans for a community of 2,000. Veysey advertised in the Exeter Flying Post for land of between 100 and 1,000 acres, within 10 miles of Exeter, although he settled for 37 acres, at Rockbeare, near Exeter. In the summer of 1826 after clearing the land and raising temporary buildings for many of the 100 local members who were expected to join them when accommodation was ready, twelve cottages were built.

However 'domestic reasons' caused Jasper Veysey to withdraw his support for the project - and this first manifestation of the community collapsed. Some of the communitarians moved on to form the Dowlands Devon Community. The following summer it was reported that their crops were good, the few trades in operation were paying their way, and there were plans to provide a school for local children. They were however suffering from a shortage of capital and a lack of new members. There is no evidence that they were able to continue beyond the end of 1827.

────────

ALL IS PEACE AND BROTHERHOOD

A co-operative community was formed just outside Chorley, Lancashire, in 1831 by the Calico Block Printers Union. It consisted of Birkacre Mill, a large house formerly occupied by a manufacturer which was converted by the society into apartments, 54 acres of land and 11 acres of reservoirs.

`There is no Mastership, no rivalling one another, all is Peace and Brotherhood. They have their Agent in the market and have more orders than they can supply...'

The society had some 300 members and employed 150 'millwrights, smiths, masons, carpenters, labourers, block and machine makers, printers, cutters, drawers, colour makers, engravers, madder dyers, and crofters, all at work in their different departments . . .' They sent delegates to co-operative congresses and were active in the co-op movement. The scheme was 'managed' for 2 years, from 1831 to 33, by Union Secretary Ellis Piggot after which no record of the co-op exists.

────────

BARNSBURY EXPERIMENTAL GARDENS

The Optimist Chapel, 33 Windmill Street (Finsbury) was for a time a meeting place for Spencean radicals. From here Pierre Baume, a French emigre, ran a bookshop & printing press as well as The Society for Promoting Anti-Christian and General Instruction. In October 1831 Baume sold the 'Chapel' and set about creating a co-operative community on 14-acres of land at Barnsbury Park variously known as 'Frenchman's Island' or the 'experimental gardens'. Baume and a group of radical tailors & shoemakers and their families lived in 'mysterious' cottages and worked the land co-operatively. From his cottage George Petrie a union activist and follower of Thomas Spence wrote articles for the journal *Man* under the pseudonym 'Agrarius'. 'The great evil to be regretted (and is even acknowledged by the legislators themselves) is, that the great bulk of the people have been decoyed from the land and agricultural pursuits into cities and large towns, and there are compelled to submit to their masters' terms, having no alternative. Let them resolve to return to their lawful inheritance; let them take small allotments of land, and act on the principle we are pursuing.'

George Petrie c1830s

The community was financially dependent on Baume a somewhat eccentric character - who carried a live monkey in his pocket to 'deter' pickpockets - and was seen by some as giving co-operation a bad name with his straggling collection of allotments and assorted radicals. The co-operative community seems to have ended on the death of George Petrie in 1836. The cottages and land survived intact until the 1860s. Baume by that time had left London. He died in 1875 on the Isle of Man and left a substantial fortune to Manx charities.

———————

Perhaps the most often cited of the Owenite communities down the years is The Ralahine Agricultural and Manufacturing Association in County Clare Ireland. Maybe this is because its demise was nothing to do with the dynamics of the community - so it could always be seen as a success. It was in many ways the least typical of the Owenite schemes and had very little in common with Owen's own plans. It was very much an imaginative response to the 'Irish Land Question'.

KINGS AND QUEENS OF CLARE

In the early 1830s insurrectionary bands of peasants were roaming the countryside in County Clare.

'..... in particular, all decent persons of all opinions declared that the County was no longer tolerable as a place of residence. The serving of threatening notices, the levelling of walls, the driving off of cattle, the beating of herdsmen, the compulsory removal of tenants, the levying of contributions in money, the robbery of dwelling houses, the reckless commission of murder were driving the better classes of inhabitants to desert their houses and seek refuge in some other quarter '.

Wiliam Pare *Co-operative Agriculture.*

Known variously as Whiteboys, O'Connell's Police, Lady Clare's Boys or Terry Alt's the root of their grievances lay in the land ownership aggravated by famines in the 1820s. On the Ralahine estate peasants working under a particularly harsh and brutal steward were finally driven to murder him whilst he was locking his house after work. In May 1831 the Insurrection Act was applied in County Clare and in all, four men were hanged and ten transported. The owner of the Ralahine estate was the then high sheriff of Clare, John Scott Vandeleur - who had met Robert Owen at a series of meetings held in Dublin in 1822 during an abortive attempt to set up a Hibernian Philanthropic Society to promote Owenite ideas in Ireland.

John Vandeleur decided to try and save his estate by establishing a community on modified Owenite lines. He went to England to seek help in his venture and was introduced to a young Manchester Owenite Edward Thomas Craig who agreed to come and manage the project. Craig's friends feared for his life and his grandfather tried to stop him going, but Craig was undeterred and in Nov 1831 arrived at Ralahine to explain the plans for a community, to be called the Ralahine Agricultural & Manufacturing Association, to the local peasantry. He initially met with an extremely hostile reception, he was assumed to be a spy and was sent a note bearing a skull and cross-bones and informed that an outline grave had already been prepared for him. Even the rest of Vandeleur's family were against the scheme and his servants ridiculed him. Craig faced these difficulties with great patience, diligence and not a little bravery. He went from cabin to cabin, mingling with the people finding out their opinions of the proposed 'New System'. He learnt enough Gaelic to greet passers-by. He finally won over the confidence of the local peasants after treating a coachman after an accident.

When Craig arrived work had already started on preparing the 618 acre estate; a large communal dining room, with a lecture hall above had been erected and a row of six cottages were under way, and Craig pressed on with these works. Craig had no experience of agriculture, but he was a great organiser and anyway the peasants themselves were all experienced at subsistence farming. A constitution was drawn up and the first 40 adults and 12 children were admitted to the association by ballot. Each married couple had their own cottage while youths were accommodated in dormitories with a shared living room. The community was governed by an elected committee and although Vandeluer had the right to expel anyone he saw fit he was never called on to do so. The committee issued printed cardboard labour vouchers worth 8d for each day's work. They could be used in the community shop and were taken by local tradesmen in exchange for work. The community was becoming the centre of much interest both in Ireland and abroad. `It is no longer a theory of Utopia, as in the days of Plato and of More, but a real, tangible verity, waiting only for prudent, practical development and extension by those who comprehend its purpose, and can organise the men and materials necessary for success.'

Edward Thomas Craig, 1882

THE NEW SYSTEMITES

'One day a mail coach traveller found a man up to his middle in water repairing a dam."Are you working by yourself? "inquired the traveller. "Yes" was the answer. "Where is your steward?"

"We have no steward."

"Who is your master?"

"We have no master. We are on a new system."

"Then who sent you to do this work?"

"The committee," replied the man in the dam."Who is the committee?" asked the mail coach visitor.

"Some of the members."

"What members do you mean?"

"The ploughman and labourers who are appointed by us as a committee. I belong to the New Systemites."

G.J.Holyoake. *The History Of Co-operation.1875/9*

'What induced the labourers to work with such profitable zeal and good will was, that the members of all ages above seventeen received an equal share in the division of profits over the above payments. Besides, a co-operative store was established similar to the one at New Lanark, whence they obtained provisions of good quality and nearly cost price. Pure food, honest weight, and reduced prices filled them with astonishment. None had known such a state of things before. None had conceived the possibility of it. The members ate at one table, which saved much expense in cooking food and serving meals. People who had always lived in doubt whether they should have a meal at all, made no scruple of eating with one another when a well-spread table was before them. In addition, care was bestowed on the education of their children. The school was conducted upon purely secular principles, and the results were highly valued by the parents. As was the habit of communities, spirituous liquors were not permitted on the state, and neither was smoking, which was gratuitous and petulant prohibition......'

E.T Craig

The History Of Co-operation. G.J.Holyoake

All went well for two years until disaster struck. Vandeleur was a compulsive gambler; he lost his entire estate on a wager and fled the country. The members of the community received no compensation and Craig sold all he had in order that the members who were leaving with nothing could redeem their community labour credit notes for cash. At the time and for the following fifty years Ralahine was held up as the most successful example of agricultural co-operation. E.T.Craig wrote a very personal account of his experiences in 1882 that was translated into French, German & Italian. The scheme would inspire in turn the Chartists, General Booth of the Salvation Army and the Irish Socialist James Conolley.

––––––––––

On his return from New Harmony, Robert Owen found himself without a vehicle for promoting his ideas and without the bulk of his fortune that was either spent or tied up at New Harmony. What he did find was an emerging grassroots co-operative and trade union movement. Working class organisations were facing up to the challenges of the developing industrial revolution - local trade unions that had grown out of earlier trade guilds were attempting to join together at regional and national levels. Owen addressed the Operative Builders Union, a coalition of building workers at their 'Builders' Parliament' and encouraged them to take over the building industry by forming a Grand National Guild that would replace capitalist contractors with building co-operatives - starting with a contract for a grand 'Guildhall' in Birmingham. Six months later Owen joined together with union leaders to form the Grand National Consolidated Trade Union (GNCTU) to represent all workers whatever their trade - the GNCTU not only drew in existing local unions, but also attracted previously un-unionised workers from chimney sweeps to women gardeners. At Tollpuddle in Dorset 6 farm labourers joined the GNCTU. The local magistrate found them guilty of administering an illegal oath and to make an example sentenced them to 7 years transportation. The later collapse of the GNCTU is seen by some as a low point in union history, but the 30,000 'Trades' who marched to Copenhagen fields in London under their society banners, on 21 April 1834, in support of the Tolpuddle Martyrs, were at a turning point in union history.

"The rules of every single one of those organisations would have barred the men of Dorset, who had served no formal apprenticeship, from joining them. Yet those craft-proud journeymen recognised that brotherhood had a wider meaning than the old exclusive one."

R.A.Leeson *Travelling Brothers*

How much this turning point was reached through the influence of Owenite ideas and how much was an extention of trends already present in union activity is hard to assess. Under Owenite influence the new union movement was now fighting for more than restricted trade issues - it was fighting for a better life for all - in 1833 whilst politicians presented petitions for a 10 hour day, the unions in Lancashire supported by Owen were contemplating enforcing an 8 hour day by a co-ordinated refusal to work any longer. One union activity that Owenites took up and extended was the Labour Exchange. This built on a part of the union tramping system - whereby craft unions supported unemployed members to 'tramp' the country in search of work, and stop at union clubhouses - now remembered in the names of many pubs, the Bricklayers Arms etc. At each clubhouse a register was kept of trade vacancies in the locality which members could consult. The Owenites extended this idea to include the exchange of goods made by tradesmen and co-operatives. They went on to introduce labour notes each representing hours of labour time - goods brought to the exchanges were valued by a committee and accorded a fair price. It was planned to open exchanges in all the main towns in the country starting with those in London and Birmingham. To start with, trade in the exchanges was brisk with labour notes being accepted as currency by some local tradesmen. The exchanges drew together the Owenites, the retail co-operative societies, trade unionists and ordinary working people and for one heady moment Robert Owen found himself leader of the whole working class movement and was moved to announce that the Equitable Labour Exchanges were the bridge over which society would pass to a new and better world.

MARTYRS FARMS

When the Tollpuddle Martyrs returned to England two farms at Greenstead, Essex, were leased for them by the Dorchester Labourers Farm Tribute Fund. Between 1838 & 1845 George Loveless, James Brine and the Standfield family farmed New House Farm and a farm at High Laver. Despite local opposition to the settling of 'convicts' in the parish, the farms became centres for union and chartist activity in the area. When the leases on the farms were due for renewal the families chose to emigrate and start a new life in Canada.

New House Farm, Greenstead.

Unofficial owenism

'You can never be truly happy whilst you are obliged to touch your hat brinks and call those your superiors who live upon your labours, and take all the advantages they can in keeping you in fear and subjection.'
William Hodson *The New Moral World*

A series of National Co-operative Congresses were held in the early 1830s where delegates tried to decide on the best strategy for the formation of communities. Some argued in favour of Owen's increasingly large-scale schemes, others backed the gradualist small-scale approach of the likes of Thompson and Dr King. Some grassroots Owenites became increasingly frustrated with Owen who more and more looked to central control of any community and away from any form of democracy. They were also frustrated by the lack of any action on the community forming front.

A star in the east

The 'orthodox' Owenites formed the National Community Friendly Society in 1837 and started looking for an estate in East Anglia. They were offered the Wretton Estate of James Hill close to Wisbech. However negotiations broke down when Hill insisted that he be allowed to direct the community. Hill was a local banker and editor of a local radical newspaper *The Star of the East*. He had supported the establishment of local allotment associations known as The United Advancement Societies and established a progressive infant school where the daughter of local 'farmer' William Hodson was educated. Hodson had been a Methodist lay preacher and had spent a number of years at sea before settling down to farm at Upwell. He had heard Owen speak and was fired with community enthusiasm and was soon putting forward proposals for a community in the 'official' Owenite paper.

'The present distinctions in society are the cause of more envy and strife than anything that has ever been produced in the world. In order to avoid this calamity, there will be no distinction, no individual property, the motto will be "Each for all."'

William Hodson. *The New Moral World..*

The central committee was cold to Hodson's proposals, but the Owenite branches up and down the country sent their encouragement for 'this important experiment.' After a tour of the country looking for a suitable site Hodson decided to offer his own estate for the community. It consisted of 200 acres on the banks of the Old Bedford River at a place known as Manea Fen (pronounced maynee) and which formed part of the Great Bedford Levels drained some 200 years before by the Walloon & Huguenot colonists who settled at nearby Thorney.

Work began in the summer of 1838. 'Four houses were started, twelve others were rising, and a railway, some 200 - 300 yards long, connected them to the brick kilns. Other buildings finished were the kitchen (with larder, wash-house and oven), the dormitory (for hired labourers) a library, a dormitory, a dining room for fifty people and a dormitory for six married people. There was a compositors room (9 ft. x 9 ft.) for the press, a barn for the joiners and a six-roomed cottage. The clay pit (40 ft. x 12 ft.), now some 22 feet deep, had yielded clay for 100,000 bricks, for which the kiln had been built, and was drained by an "Archimedean screw." But perhaps the most singular feature of all was an observatory on the top of which floated a tricolour with the Union Jack, indicative of conquered tyranny 'cowering below it.' This had two platforms - one housing forty people for tea, and the other sixteen. They announced their intention of building a further set of some seventy-two cottages to form a square, the fourth side of which was to be open to the banks of the River Bedford.'
Pamphlet By W. H. G. Armytage
Manea Fen: An Experiment in Agrarian Communitarianism, 1838-1841

The first 12 months of community life at Manea were somewhat stormy; expectations were high and little attention was given to selection of recruits. One disgruntled ex-resident who left after 3 months condemned the behaviour of his fellow communards.

'They commenced finding fault with one another and with everything about them. At the time of our arrival the first general split had taken place, there had been a fall spent on nothing but useless discussions; previous to this split there were no less than 7 females and 4 males constantly engaged to manage the household department which at that time consisted of about 30 persons. . . . All they (the first colonists) did was look to the provisions, this I assure you was done in the most disgusting manner possible : . . they paid much more attention to the beer shops and the company of the lowest prostitutes that were to be found in the district.'

F Wastney - *New Moral World May1839*

The 'Communionists' (their own description) started a weekly paper, *The Working Bee*, mainly because of the hostility they were getting from the 'official' Owenites who clearly saw the renegade community as stealing their thunder, generally giving communalism a bad name and potentially undermining their own attempts to form a 'proper' Owenite community. As well as reports on the progress of work at the community *The Working Bee* carried articles and letters censored from *The New Moral World*, and the 'Hodsonian Experiment' became something of a rallying point for dissident Owenites critical of the central committees paternalistic pronouncements. This antagonism increased sharply following the commencement of the official Owenite scheme at Harmony Hall in Hampshire.

THE REGISTRAR OF FRIENDLY WINDMILLS

After some of the early 'troublemakers' had left, the community got on with the business of making the new socialist order a reality. Work continued on the buildings, workshops were set up for the production of bricks, floor tiles, drainpipes and pantiles from clay dug on site. A cutter named The Morning Star was purchased to carry goods to market along the fenland dykes. A gymnasium was opened and a cricket pitch laid out. Intensive agriculture was carried out on the fertile fenland fields where 35 acres of wheat, 27 of oats, 24 of grass and 100-acres of fallow were cultivated by the agricultural department. Members were paid in labour credit notes, money having been abolished within the community. At a special meeting on 2 June 1840 it was decided to adopt a community uniform;

'The men wear a green habit . . . presenting an appearance somewhat like the representation of Robin Hood and his foresters, or of the Swiss mountaineers. The dress of the females is much the same as the usual fashion, with trousers, and the hair worn in ringlets. . . . They are quite the lions of the villages round about.'

The Working Bee 28 Nov 1840

Hodson was a believer in the liberation from drudgery through the use of technology, and from the beginning there were plans for the cooking of food by 'scientific apparatus', saving women 'immense labour', centrally heating houses by a system of hot air flues, and thrashing and grinding corn with a steam engine. It was hoped that these innovations would mean the reduction of the working day to a mere four hours. The steam engine doesn't seem to have appeared, but a source of power was obtained by building a windmill that could pump water from the clay-pit, drive a circular saw, lathe & grindstone and operate circular brushes for cleaning boots and shoes, or knives and forks. The windmill was completed on the day that the Communionists received their enrolled rules back from the barrister and so in honour of the Registrar of Friendly Societies, the windmill was ceremonially named 'Tidd Pratt'.

SOMETHING MORE IN THE SYSTEM

There is another version of what happened in the early days at Manea Fen which casts a different light on life in the community - far from being a simple case of drunkenness and debauchery among a few wayward members. In a letter to Robert Owen the then secretary of the colony pointed out that their troubles were due to '....parties not knowing that there is something more in your system than an improved mode of producing and distributing wealth.' Hodson was an opponent of conventional marriage and lived in 'free union' with his dead wife's sister. He claimed that he was only trying to implement Owen's own pronouncements on marriage and that he wished to abolish the ' traffic in human flesh, the buying and selling of each other.' It was this 'something more' that had caused the outburst from E.Wastney and the departure of the first batch of colonists who had felt they had been lured to the community under false pretences. It is likely that the next wave of recruits were aware of the situation when they arrived and were in approval. If anything the pronouncements on the subject in *The Working Bee* became more uncompromising. 'As to being very lax on the subject of marriage, we have the pleasure to ....plead guilty.' The pronouncements coming out of Manea and the unorthodox 'sexual connections' there, scandalised not only members of the local farming community, but many in the socialist movement as well.

'This was as close to genuine "free love" as Owenism ever came, and it is interesting to find that it appeared in a community which, rhetorically at least, was strongly committed to democracy and equality, including female equality. Some of the most militantly feminist statements ever to be voiced within the Owenite ranks came out of Manea Fen, but accompanied by others whose male-centred view of sexual freedom must have lead to tensions.'

Barbara Taylor. *Eve and the New Jerusalem.*

THE COMMUNITY OF UNITED FRIENDS

The apparent success at Manea and subsequent propaganda encouraged others with their own disagreements with Owen to strike out on their own ventures. In Liverpool a breakaway group of Owenites lead by John Moncas leased a 1000-acre estate at Pant Glas in Merionethshire and set about establishing an agricultural and manufacturing community. Registering themselves as a Friendly Society under the name The Community of United Friends they set about community building in a business-like manner, proposing set fees for joining and a weekly subscription, with accounts to be audited on the first week of the month. They set out with an air of optimism for their Welsh hillside paradise. The early reports that described the estate as 'exceedingly fertile' and 'beautifully situated' turned out to be something of estate-agent-speak. The reality turned out to be steeply-sloping, stone-strewn fields that 'the horses can scarcely pull the empty plough up', 2500ft above sea level, that had failed to be productive for the past 16 years. Add to that the inaccessibility, hostile local landowners and a chronic shortage of capital and it is remarkable that the community made it to the end of its first year at all - it dispersed soon after.

THE GRISLY END

Back at Manea, despite outward appearances of a thriving community; promenades along the river bank on summer evenings, trips to local meetings in The Morning Star and a bumper harvest due to an especially good summer, problems were starting to stack up. Hodson who had staked his all in the community was in financial difficulties following the collapse of James Hill's Bank in Wisbech and whilst they may have been effective in the production of goods that now piled up in the yards and workshops they had been less effective in finding outlets for them. Hodson made overtures to Harmony Hall, which was having its own difficulties, suggesting an amalgamation of the two groups. This suggestion was rejected. *The Working Bee* called for support from its readers, pointing out that if every reader bought a pair of stockings from the community, they would keep the stocking makers in work for a whole year.

'The grisly end of the whole experiment was soon painfully documented. The members of the community, convinced of Hodson's unfitness of the post, were powerless to force him out because they depended on him for " pecuniary advances". Three days before Christmas 1840, Hodson gave orders to the meat contractors to stop deliveries to the community. A public meeting of the communitarians decided to take over management, do away with hired labour, dispose of the lighters and to consult a solicitor. Hodson's reply was to seize the books. Another members' meeting was convened on Christmas Day, and the members unanimously condemned his action. There, however, unanimity ended. A pro-Hodson party formed and when, four days later, another members' meeting was convened, to ask for the books, Hodson pointed out that he possessed the money obtained by the sale of the crops, and when they demanded it, he replied that it was in the hands of "a gentleman in March". Tension mounted. The Working Bee ceased publication. The leader of the anti-Hodsonians, the oldest member of the community, William Davidge, was obviously the main target for Hodson's anger and on 30 February, one of the pro-Hodsonians shot at him with a gun. What is worse, the pro-Hodsonians formed a kind of terrorist group. The New Moral World reported "men with bludgeons have constantly been about the premises; the shops and rooms have been broken into and their contents taken out. Nearly all the members have now resigned. ...."'

Manea Fen:1838-1841 **Pamphlet By W. H. G. Armytage**

And so the central committee was vindicated. Owen declared that no community based on his ideas had ever failed, because none had ever been set up that had followed his instructions.

DIS-HARMONY HALL

Owen 'Primo Communist' Flitcroft born in Jan 1842 should hold an honoured place in utopian history, as the firstborn of the new socialist millennium - an occasion commemorated in the letters CM, standing for commencement of the millennium, carved over the entrance to Harmony Hall at East Tytherley, Hampshire. Whilst New Lanark is a World Heritage Site, New Harmony a National Historic Landmark Village and the Co-operative world honours the Pioneers shop at Toad Lane in Rochdale, the only traces of the one 'official' Owenite community are a sawn-off lamp standard and the outlines of some cellars hidden deep in the Hampshire countryside. The story of Harmony Hall has taken on an almost mythical air, often referred to in history books as a lost community, but for six years it did very much exist and carried with it the hopes for the establishment of the New Moral World.

In the 1830's a whole Owenite movement had grown up with branches throughout the country; called variously the National Community Friendly Society, the Association of all Classes and all Nations and finally the Universal Community Society of Rational Religionists, they had established 'Halls of Science' in major towns. The Halls were social centres - with Sunday lectures on the doctrines of socialism, oratorios, festivals, and tea parties. Owenite missionaries went from town to town on propaganda tours. By 1839 they had branches in 350 towns and claimed 50,000 'adherents'. The ultimate aim of the movement was still to establish co-operative communities on the land. Funds were raised through subscriptions from branch members and after what seemed to many members like years of prevaricating the 500-acre Queenwood Farm at East Tytherley was taken on a 99 year lease from Sir Isaac Lyon Goldsmidt at an annual rental of £350.

A MONUMENT OF ILL-TIMED MAGNIFICENCE

'I have named our new Establishment "Economy" and the new Parish "Harmony." .... It will be then "Economy in the Parish of Harmony, Hants."'   R.Owen.*New Moral World Sept 1841*

Economy however was far from Owen's mind when drawing up the plans for the community - and in fact

dence of Sir Robert Peel, and a Fourist Phalanx.

The ground floor included a library and dining rooms, with sleeping apartments for single persons above; the central block contained offices and storerooms; a third section contained schoolrooms and baths. The whole building was equipped with an advanced heating and ventilating system, and a small steam engine to pump mains water to each room. There were various mechanical contraptions including a miniature railway to carry dishes into the

Harmony Hall Illustrated London News 21 June1902

the name was dropped, the place becoming known to all as Harmony Hall. Instead of building 'a village of cottages, each with a garden,' (which one visitor thought would have been more appropriate to an agricultural community), Owen didn't even build a community based on his own 'villages of co-operation' plan, but commissioned Joseph Hansom, architect of Birmingham Town Hall, patenter of the Hansom Cab and founder of the influential architectural magazine *The Builder*, to design a lavish 3 storey red-brick mansion that resembled a cross between Drayton Manor, the resi-

kitchen. Around the building were wide promenades and landscaped gardens. Even in a half-finished state the cost was in the order of a phenomenal £30,000. Yet Owen had his sights on still greater things - a community from whose towers `would be reflected at night, by powerful apparatus, the new koniophostic light, which would brilliantly illuminate its whole square.'

The first colonists arrived in the early winter of 1839, sponsored by their local Owenite branches, mainly from northern industrial towns. By the following February they were busy digging, gardening, manuring and ploughing, excavating clay for bricks, and attending evening classes in dancing, drawing, grammar, geography, elocution, agriculture and music. In contrast to the extravagance of the building works, the colonists themselves survived on little more than subsistence rations.

SOCIALIST TURNIPS

'When we reached the turnip field I remarked to my friend that if these were Socialist turnips they promised well. They were Socialist turnips, and we soon after found seven hundred Socialist sheep, which made my friend exclaim, "Lord bless me! who would have thought it!"'.   Visitor to Harmony Hall

Visitors were impressed by the effectiveness of the organisation and the advanced techniques that were employed in the gardens and fields. The gardener was busy directing operations on a twenty-seven acre market garden, shepherds were with the sheep, nine ploughs were at work, and over a hundred acres were sown with wheat. Compared to local farms the socialists were able to get good yields from the shallow, flinty soil - one of the reasons for this was the systematic manuring they practised - they had constructed a reservoir to store liquid manure and in the woodlands vegetable matter was mixed with lime and piled into compost heaps for use on the fields. It was as much the success of socialist farming that posed a threat to the local establishment as socialist theories and propaganda.

In contrast to all this practical organisation and efficiency the management of the community was fraught with problems from the start - Owen had resigned as Governor before the project was even started. The managers appointed were often at odds with the central committee of the Rational Society, which felt that it should have a say in the day-to-day running of the place. Numbers started to dwindle and by the summer of 1840 they were down to 19 and having to hire local labourers to bring in the harvest. Somehow the remaining members carried on but with little support from the branches and by the end of the following year they were in dire financial straits. At this point Owen reappeared with a group of middle-class investors who were prepared to 'rescue' the community as long as they had the governing control, which in effect meant dictatorship by Owen - Owen then embarked on a spending spree extending the farms and setting up a fee paying school with fees so high that no working class Owenite could possibly afford them. This was done at the expense of other projects; by sacking the Social Missionaries and cancelling grants to the halls of science. When the promised money from his friends failed to materialise he instigated austerity measures sacking all the hired labour, increasing the residents workload and putting them all on a diet of bread and water. Demoralised and disillusioned the rank and file members with the support of socialist in the branches finally revolted and removed Owen as governor at the 1844 annual congress. There followed a series of attempts to turn it into a democratic working-class-controlled community by a succession of managers, but the financial burden was too great. It was left to William Parc to try and sort out the mess. The community officially coming to an end in mid-1845 amid acrimonious scenes. Owen's failure to give a lead when most needed and his seeming inability to carry out sensible financial management after the success of New Lanark had brought the end of Harmony Hall and with it the whole Owenite socialist movement. Harmony Hall was advertised for sale in The Times as suitable for use as a lunatic asylum. It was leased by George Edmunson who ran it as Queenwood College. In 1896 it ceased to function as a college and became a centre for teaching poultry farming and electrical engineering. The entire building was destroyed by fire on 10 June 1902.

'A community was regarded in social mechanics then as a sort of flying machine and it fulfilled the expectation of the day by falling down like one.'
                                        G. J. Holyoake

CO-OPERATIVE PIONEERS

The success of the Rochdale Pioneers in establishing a co-operative retail model would eventually overshadow the very early co-operative experiments, even though the Rochdale men themselves had the ultimate aim of establishing a co-operative community. Once the shops started to pay a dividend to members the writing was on the wall for community building, as no surpluses would be generated to put into them. That is not to say that the Rochdale model was the only one, or that the later co-operative movement did not attempt to set up its own co-operative communities. In the second half of the 19th century a number of local retail co-operative societies made ventures into housing schemes either for rent or sale to members or for housing of their employees. Many of these schemes were concentrated in the Northeast of England.

Retail societies continued to be involved in co-operative communities into the early 20th century.

At Leicester a project initiated by the Anchor Boot And Shoe Co-operative and financed by the local retail society resulted in a small garden suburb being built, in 1906, at Humberstone just outside the city. In 1916 in Northumberland the Co-operative Wholesale Society (CWS) built a number of semi-detached houses with gardens at Shilbottle, a small colliery village it had bought during the wartime coal shortage. The society also gave land for a co-op store, chapel and Aged Miners' Homes. And as late as 1944 retail societies were involved it setting up the South West Co-operative Housing Society, a successful social housing provider established in conjunction with people from Dartington Hall.

WILL THE REAL MR OWEN PLEASE STAND UP ?

Robert Owen has remained a somewhat enigmatic historical character: a highly successful capitalist businessman who is credited as one of the founders of socialism, an autocratic individual who was an inspiration for a whole co-operative movement, a promoter of grandiose schemes as a way to live a simple life and an atheist & anti-church propagandist who not only sparked off the secularist movement, but also became heavily involved in spiritualism. Socialist histories either ignore this later phase of Owen's life or dismiss his ideas as the ranting of a batty old man.

Owen's spiritualist beliefs were not an aberration from his socialist ideas, but had grown out of his search for a 'Rational Religion' - and when in his eighties, having been unable to convince sympathisers either among the ruling class or the emerging working class to follow his Rational System, he turned for support to eminent departed souls. Owen claimed that the spirits of President Jefferson, Benjamin Franklin, Shelley, Dr Channing & the Duke of Kent had expressed their full support for his system. Through the pages of his final publication, The Millennial Gazette, his earthly social millennium slowly transforms into 'Summerland' an egalitarian spiritualist heaven, where you could look forward to your own arrival in socialism, whether socialism had arrived on earth or not. Spiritualist, and secularist, groups kept Owenite ideas circulating amongst their working class & Labour Movement adherents until they would emerge again in the late 1800s to influence a new socialist era.

At the age of 87 after addressing the annual conference of the National Association for the Promotion of Social Science Owen was taken ill and when asked by a minister, sent to give him religious consolation, if he did not regret wasting his life on fruitless efforts? he replied, 'My life was not useless; I gave important truths to the world, and it was only for want of understanding that they were disregarded. I have been ahead of my time.'

Robert Owen died shortly after on November 17th 1858. He is buried in his hometown of Newtown, mid-Wales, where there is a small museum dedicated to him. After he died, or 'passed to Spirit' Owen wrote one last publication influential in spiritualist circles, The Principles of Spiritualism, which he dictated through the mediumship of Emma Hardinge Britten.

MUTINY IN UTOPIA

On 17th Sept 1814 two British Navy vessels called at the remote South Pacific Pitcairn Islands. They found a small community of 10 Polynesian women, 23 children and former able seaman, John Adams, who was the last surviving member of the mutineers of the Bounty who had settled the  island with their Tahitian companions in 1790. Perhaps the best-known mutiny in British Naval history - HMS Bounty under the command of Capt. William Bligh was on a voyage to transport breadfruit trees from Tahiti to the West Indies to provide cheap food for the slave plantations. Following their stay on the idyllic South Pacific Island, ship's officer Fletcher Christian led the mutiny, setting Bligh and 18 crew members adrift in an open boat to make their epic journey, immortalised in Hollywood movies. The mutineers first returned to Tahiti, but following trouble among the islanders and fearing capture nine mutineers, six Tahitian men, twelve women and a baby set sail looking for a safe haven. After two months sailing around the Cooks, Tonga, and the eastern islands of Fiji looking for a home, Fletcher Christian remembered the existence of Pitcairn Island.

On this remote speck of land in the middle of the Pacific Ocean the mutineers thought they had found an ideal home. There was plenty to eat; coconuts and breadfruit on the island, pigs, chickens, yams and sweet potatoes from the ship's stores. To avoid detection the ship was stripped and sunk in what is now known as Bounty Bay. What probably saved them from detection for over 20 years was the fact that the position of the island was incorrectly marked on official maps. The commanders of the British Navy vessels that finally found them were charmed by the 'physique, simplicity and piety' of the islanders. Impressed by Adams and the example he set, they agreed that it would be 'an act of great cruelty and inhumanity' to arrest him for the Bounty Mutiny. John Adams was a gentle man who could barely read and write, he had patterned a simple communistic way of life in the little colony based on basic Christian values. Adams saw to it that every young

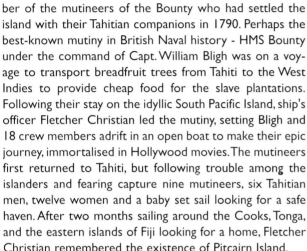

person cultivated the land, cared for the stock and were not allowed to marry until they could support a family. That this egalitarian society should have developed at all is surprising given the early events on the island.

For the first year on the island the mutineers and their companions worked hard. Living in tents made from the Bounty's sails they cleared and planted the land, tended their animals and built a small settlement on the north west side of the island leaving a screen of trees between them and the sea. All the cultivatable land was divided among the nine white men. They also claimed the rock pools, essential sources of salt and good fishing places. The Polynesians seemed not to mind this arrangement and the little colony looked to be a perfect island paradise in the making. However the mutineers treated the Tahitians so badly that in the end they revolted. Five mutineers and all the Polynesian men died in the revolt, leaving only four mutineers leading households of ten women and their children. After this things settled into a period of relative peace and all might have remained harmonious had not William McCoy who had once worked in a distillery, discovered how to brew a potent spirit from the roots of the ti plant. This led to another round of murders & suspicious deaths and by 1800 John Adams was the sole male survivor of the party that had landed just ten years earlier. Adams would preside over the community until 1829 when he died aged 62. The passing of the "Father" of the community was mourned by every member. Under his leadership the community had gone from frontier community hell-bent on self-destruction to an island utopia - governed by customs evolved from a combination of seamen's traditions of sharing, Polynesian customs of communal land ownership & generosity and primitive Christianity.

'Such a society, so free, not only from vice, but even from those petty bickerings and jealousies - those minor infirmities which we are accustomed to suppose are ingrained in human nature - can probably not be paralleled elsewhere. It is the realisation of Arcadia, or what we had been accustomed to suppose had existence only in poetic imagination, - the golden age; all living as one family, a commonwealth of brothers and sisters, which, indeed, by ties of relationship they actually are . . . there is neither wealth nor want, a primitive simplicity of life and manner, perfect equality in rank and station, and perfect content.'   W.Brodie.*Pitcairn's Island. 1851.*

The islanders operated a system of barter amongst themselves. Goods from passing ships and ocean bounty were divided up equally between all. 'Ownership' of land was based on the original division of the island by the mutineers. Plots were sub-divided equally to female and male children through inheritance and on marriage husband and wife were given bits of land by each parent. Simple ownership however never bestowed absolute rights. Islanders were free to plant coconut & fruit trees on anyone's land. It was accepted custom that those who cared for crops had rights to the produce. A family's 'trade mark' was chipped on each tree trunk. Increasing population and fear of crop failure persuaded the islanders, disastrously as it turned out, to return to Tahiti. Suffering from culture shock and decimated by diseases to which they had no immunity, which led to 17 deaths, a fifth of the polulation, they raised the money to return to Pitcairn by selling their possesions. Joshua Hill, a puritanical busybody, arrived on the island in 1832 claiming to have been sent by the British Government. Appointing himself 'President of the Commonwealth of Pitcairn,' he promptly abolished the distilling of liquor, which was welcomed by the islanders, but he also introduced arbitrary imprisonment and severe punishments for the smallest misdeeds. In 1838, his claim to represent the British Government was exposed and he was forcibly removed from the island. Following Hill's dictatorship the islanders felt the need for some sort of con-

stitution. When the small sloop the HMS Fly arrived in 1838 on a routine cruise the islanders pleaded with the Captain, George Elliott, to draw up a constitution for the island and officially establish the island as part of the British Empire. This was an awesome request to a low-ranking naval officer with no official instructions. However the commander rose to the occasion and drew up a brief constitution and legal code. The constitution owed little to British precedent and reflected the custom and culture of the community. A Magistrate (native born) was to be elected annually "....by the free votes of every native born on the island, male or female, who shall have attained the age of eighteen years, ...". He was to be assisted by two councillors, one elected and one appointed by himself. Not only was this the first time female suffrage was written into a British constitution, but it also incorporated compulsory schooling for the first time in any British legislation. These were political rights not enjoyed by other British citizens until well into the 20th century.

In 1856 facing overcrowding again the island was once more abandoned, this time for a deserted penal colony on Norfolk Island. Not all the community were happy on Norfolk Island and late in 1858 16 of the islanders returned to Pitcairn. A box of 7th Day Adventist literature from the USA resulted in the wholesale conversion of the islanders. The 7th Day Adventists in America greeted conversion with great pleasure and in 1890 they raised funds to send a missionary ship to Pitcairn. The islanders were baptised in one of the rocky pools by the shore. With the opening of the Panama Canal in 1914 a liner a week carrying hundreds of passengers to New Zealand started to call and the islanders built up an economy supplying gifts & curios. In 1940 Pitcairn postage stamps were issued and supplying philatelists became a major part of the island economy. Since WW2 the benefits of modernization have been available on the island, starting with wireless communications and electricity. The islands population now fluctuate between 40 & 60.

The story of the early years of Pitcairn Island is told in *Life & Death in Eden.* **By Trevor Lummis. Victor Gollancz 1997.**

Reform vs. revolution

'We drive over to revolution those whom
we shut out from Power.'

Macaulay, House of Lords, 1831

Out of some six million men in England in 1830 only 839,000 were entitled to vote, roughly one in seven. The people of England had watched with great anticipation as both the American and French revolutions had resulted in the establishment of democratic republics with universal male suffrage. Agitation for reform of the British Parliament resulted in the 'Peterloo Massacre' where mounted Hussars cut down peaceful demonstrators at St Peters Fields in Manchester, leaving 11 dead and more than 400 wounded. Further agitation with support from some industrialists culminated in the First Reform Bill being put before Parliament in 1831. It proposed raising the number of voters to nearly 1million by extending the franchise to £10 Freeholders. The Commons passed the bill by one vote, but King William IV dissolved parliament to prevent even this limited reform from becoming law. Rioting broke out all over the country. In Bristol, after burning down the Town Hall and the Bishop's Palace, rioters broke down the prison gates and released the prisoners. Troops opened fire on the rioters killing twelve people. After new elections the bill was finally passed. Employers and middle class property owners who were satisfied having won the right to vote, promptly turned against the mass of common people who had helped them and opposed any further extension of the franchise. This betrayal was to lead to the forming of the first national working class movement - Chartism.

Universal sufferage or univeral revenge

A small group called the London Working Men's Association produced a programme of reform in 1837 it laid out six demands.

· Universal Male Suffrage.
· Equal Electoral Districts
· Annual Parliaments
· Payment for MPs

Secret Ballots

Abolition of the property qualification for MPs These six points made up what became known as The Peoples Charter. (Female suffrage was to have been included as one of the demands, but was dropped as too controversial!) Soon after its issue 150 organisations throughout the country declared their support for its demands. The campaign for the Charter took the form of a petition to parliament. Signatures were collected at mass meetings held across the country. The numbers attending were immense; 150,000 in Glasgow, 200,000 in Birmingham, and 250,000 in Manchester.

The movement had two distinct trends - in the North of England, `Physical Force' Chartism, with demands for armed insurrection should parliament refuse the demands, and in Birmingham, London & the South, `Moral Force' Chartism, emphasising education and legal change. In northern industrial areas, slogans like 'Universal suffrage or universal revenge!', 'Fight to the knife for children and wife!' and 'More pigs and fewer priests!' were heard at great torchlight processions held in support of the Charter. Rumours abounded of stores of pikes, firearms and bullets being collected and meetings at night on the moors for training and drill.

The great petition had 1,280,000 signatures; the pages pasted together, were over two miles long and weighed six hundredweight. It was presented to Parliament on 12 July 1839, by Thomas Attwood, MP. It was thrown out by 235 votes to forty-five. The time had come for `Ulterior Measures'. A `Sacred Month' of agitation had been planned with rents, rates and tax strikes, a boycott of all non-Chartist tradesmen and a 'National Holiday' - in effect a general strike to force the government to accept the charter. In the event the government moved quickly making large-scale arrests of Chartist leaders. The calls for a general strike went largely unheeded, and where it began soon died out. At Newport, Monmouthshire, an abortive uprising was put down by troops and police and although riots and disorder broke out in other areas the great national rising of 'Physical Force' Chartists never occurred.

One Chartist leader not arrested at this time was

Feargus O'Connor, a fiery Irishman whose militant writings in his paper, *The Northern Star*, did much to keep Chartism alive during this period. O'Connor was instrumental in co-ordinating the collection of 3,317,702 signatures for a second petition. It too was rejected by Parliament in May 1842. Chartism was now at a low point. Supporters began to focus on other reforms - the ten-hour day, anti-corn laws and trade unionism.

THE LAND PLAN

In the 7th May 1842 issue of *The Northern Star*, O'Connor proposed two ways to further the Chartist cause; either to ally with the middle classes, or to think of a plan for the settlement of large numbers of working people on the land, each man holding freehold property of the minimum annual value of 40 shillings required to qualify for a county vote. Throughout 1843/44 articles in *The Northern Star* fleshed out the Land Plan. Life on the land was portrayed as a way to escape the ills of industrial society, where you could live a life of freedom without employer or landlord. O'Connor's plans suggested that 20,000 acres would support 5,000 families, divided into some forty estates, each with its own community centre, school, library and hospital. Land ownership would give working people the vote leading to a new government and then universal suffrage.

At the Chartist conference in London in April 1845 O'Connor steered through the founding of a Chartist Co-operative Land Society to carry the plan forward. He then embarked on an intense period of travel, study and public speaking, visiting smallholdings and studying land management. He visited France and Belgium discussing the plan with socialist and communist leaders including Karl Marx & Friedrich Engels, who opposed his scheme. He wrote a book called *A Practical Work on the Management of Small Farms*, which drew on recollections of his estate farms in Ireland. Speaking at meetings up and down the country he continued to develop his ideas for the land plan, everywhere meeting with favourable reactions from ordinary working people. Other Chartist leaders however saw the whole land plan as a distraction from the six points of the Charter and distanced themselves from O'Connor.

In the form that it finally emerged the Land Plan was in essence very simple. People would send in small subscriptions on a weekly basis until enough money had been raised to buy an estate that could be divided up into 2- 4 acre plots. Places would be allocated by a lottery draw of all subscribers. Rents from the smallholders would provide funds towards the purchase of further estates. The only slight problem in the scheme seemed to be in finding a legal structure for it. The failure by O'Connor to resolve this issue was to return to haunt the scheme. Meanwhile money began to pour in. from branches the length and breadth of the country from Newcastle-on-Tyne to Newton Abbot, from Brighton to Bradford. By 1847 there were 600 branches with an astonishing 70,000 subscribers from all walks of working-class life who were sending in their cash, postal orders and cheques for the chance to own their own small plot and to gain the right to vote.

O'CONNORVILLE

The ballot for places on the first Chartist Land Colony took place on Easter Monday 1846 at the old Manor Court Room, Nicholas Croft, Manchester. 1,487 people, with fully-paid-up shares in the Land Company, were eligible for the draw for 35 allotments on the Heronsgate Estate, 6 miles from Watford, that O'Connor had managed to purchase for £2,344. The estate consisted of 103 acres of neglected farm land and cherry woods. Excitement grew as the date for the draw grew nearer. Paying up on shares continued until the close of Saturday, 18 April and many did not sleep that Sunday night. At first light on Easter Monday the small lanes leading to Nicholas Croft were full of quiet crowds of working people making their way towards the hall awed by the prospect of obtaining a passport to paradise. Inside the hall members of the Manchester branch committee guarded the ballot boxes. O'Connor appeared on the platform and spoke to the crowd of the freedom of the birds that they would soon be able to experience, of the cottages, the grass, the trees, plates piled high with bacon, greens and carrots, of children playing in the fields.......... Quietly, painfully members of the crowd wept.

O'Connor raised his hand and the ballot began. The ballot boxes were spun and the crowd waited in silence. When O'Connor indicated, a box was stopped and a name pulled out. The first prize was shouted out! David Watson of Edinburgh. A murmur ran through the crowd. Next out was Thomas Smith of London, then Thomas Bond of Devizes, and at last a Manchester man, Joseph Openshaw. The crowd cheered. Then came a surprise, a female winner, Barbara Vaughan of Sunderland. Winners followed from Worcester, Ashton-under-Lyme, Bradford, Bilston, Northampton, London, Halifax, Wotton-under-Edge, and Leeds. By the end of the draw the crowd were elated - if ordinary working people could have a cottage and some land then anything was possible.

2 A handbill issued by the company early in 1847

Work began on the estate: 'While Feargus planned the lay-out of thirty-five allotments and the school, Cullingham recruited workmen. They tramped over every field, wet to the knees in April rain, plotting the acres. They went to Watford and Uxbridge and chaffered with building contractors.........First, four main estate roads were made, measuring 12 miles, all 9 ft wide. Then labourers were set to make paths giving access to every cottage from the road. Then the building campaign opened - making mortar, digging foundations, cutting timber. Mortar needed vast quantities of water, and this was scarce on the chalky Hertfordshire soil. The one spring and pool were cherished, and a well was dug near the works centre. Oak timber was bought for roofing, and deal for wainscots and walls. Clearing the ground came next, heavy work grubbing out roots of old hedges and felled timber, filling in ditches, demolishing sheds and wheeling away stones and rubble. Anything that would sell or could be used again was saved. Roots were stacked for home fuel. Feargus went to the canal wharf and ordered ten boatloads of London stable dung at 60 tons a load; 103 acres would get 5tons 17cwt each. One of the early pleasures of the estate was finding a patch in the centre of the estate where sand could be dug, `enough to build a town.' On 23 May they read in the hilly streets of Wigan and Hebden Bridge, `On my way I saw a Cow that had just calved, a black cow without horns, and I bought her. She gives 28 quarts A DAY ! ! ! What say you to that?' Milk was not delivered down these hill streets, being 2d a quart. Twenty-eight quarts a day between thirty-five houses meant more than a pint a day each. They looked at their children, and marvelled.'

Alice Mary Hadfield. *The Chartist Land Company.*

The only cloud on the horizon was the continued refusal of the registrar of Friendly Societies to accept registration of the Land Company resulting in O'Connor having to become the 'owner' of the Heronsgate Estate rather than the land company. Work on the estate continued apace. By June 200 men were working on the site, two cottages were nearly up and there was a continual stream of visitors wanting to see for themselves the little piece of paradise taking shape in the Hertfordshire countryside. As well as personally supervising the work at Heronsgate O'Connor was dashing off at short notice to look over further farms and estates. A 130-acre estate near Pinner was bought and sold again at a profit. In October 1846 O'Connor bought the Lowbands and Applehurst Farms at auction in Worcester for £8,100. The 170 acres of good land were in a remote area, 9 miles from Gloucester. Almost immediately work started at Lowbands on what was to become a fairly standard formula for the estates; two, three and four acre smallholdings with model cottages were laid out on a network of lanes around a schoolhouse. The first season's crops were planted, fruit trees provided along with two year's supply of firewood and manure. Each cottage had its own water supply and privy. The new estate had cost 4 times the price of O'Connorville and the size of the transactions obliged O'Connor to seek provisional registration as a Joint Stock Company and to found a Labour & Land Bank to handle the ever increasing subscriptions. These administrative 'difficulties' were overlooked in the rush of enthusiasm as the first estate neared completion.

FROM PARADISE

The last day of April 1847 was, for the allotees of O'Connorville, the last day of wage slavery, the last day of industrial city life, the last day of everything that they understood. What faith they had in O'Connor, in Chartism, in life itself to sign off from their previous lives for a smart newly-built 'model' cottage, with its barley and vegetables sprouting in neat rows and the choicest crop of all, a parliamentary vote ready for the picking. The 1st of May was a glorious day. O'Connor called it 'Englands May Day'.'(The settlers) arrived at Watford . . . and while the sun was still high - the travellers being all seated in vans, in readiness for the occasion, the band struck up "See, the conquering heroes come" - the road for the whole distance, presented the appearance of a Gala Day and never was such a merry May-Day seen in Hertfordshire or in England before. At the entrance to the Holy Land the first settlers were met by many old friends and well wishers and all were conducted to their respective abodes, all anxiously inspecting their castle and their labour field, and tho' tired after a long day's journey, only terminated their research when the sable clouds of night had spread its mantle over their little domains'

Contemporary account.

Charterville Estate, Minster Lovell Illustrated London News. 12 Oct 1850

In June two further estates were purchased; at Snigs End, near Lowbands in Gloucestershire, and an estate in the parish of Minster Lovell, Oxfordshire - named Charterville. An offer was made on an estate at Mathon, near Malvern, but the sale never went through. The indefatigable O'Connor also found time to fight and win a by-election in Nottingham. In the streets of northern towns O'Connor's victory was toasted and Chartist hymns sung; in Barnsley a candle was lit in the window of every working-class home and despite grinding poverty collections were made to cover his election expenses. O'Connor was by now signing off letters he wrote from his cottage at O'Connorville - 'From Paradise.'

O'Connor was now carried away on a wave of popularity. He flirted with communists gathering in London. Marx himself said that if the Chartists could carry the six points of the charter they would 'be hailed as the saviours of the whole human race.' It was said O'Connor envisaged a peasant republic in Britain with himself as president. He set about organising a third Chartist petition. With allegedly 5 million signatures it was to be taken to parliament on a cart specially built for the purpose at Snigs End and pulled by four working horses from the estate. As it turned out the police stopped the cart and accompanying procession at Kennington Common and would only allow 49 people to proceed with the petition to Westminster. From here on a farce ensued. The petition was finally taken to Parliament in three hansom cabs. There O'Connor presented it, only for it to be defeated amid accusations that most of the signatures were forged.

CRACKS BEGIN TO APPEAR

During this time legal wrangles over the company registration were going on in the background. The joint stock company could only be registered if signatures were collected from all subscribers - an almost impossible task. O'Connor petitioned parliament for registration which resulted in a parliamentary enquiry into the scheme being set up. A fifth estate was bought at Great Dodford, near Bromsgrove and plans forged ahead, almost in defiance of the mounting legal troubles. This time plots were allocated by auction - the lottery having been declared illegal under the Lotteries Act. This meant that only better off working people were able to get plots. The scheme also suffered from lack of capital - no school was built, and some land had to be sold off to finance the scheme.

Local landowners, disconcerted by stories of wild northern miners thrashing their hungry pigs for squealing and fearing that the settlers would all end up a burden on the poor rates sent John Revenues, a Poor Law Commissioner, to report on the estates. At O'Connorville he found that conditions were `quite inadequate', crops

Snigs End Estate Illustrated London News 23 Feb 1850

were inferior to those on surrounding farms, livestock had no hay and straw and neighbouring farmers were lending ploughs & implements to help the 'settlers'. On some holdings the work was being done by the local farm labour. Nine of the original settlers had already left, as their 'wives were unused to dairy work and could not bake bread.' He was impressed by the standard of the cottages. Support was forthcoming from some unlikely corners: The Economist was impressed and The Gardener & Florist put its support behind the schemes. However more ominously attacks were starting to come from the estates themselves, where smallholders complained of lack of promised leases and started to withhold rents.

The parliamentary enquiry report condemned the bad management of the Land Company, its almost non-existent accounts and the lack of clarity in its legal dealings. It however cleared O'Connor of any financial misdealings and in fact found in his favour to the sum of £3000. It also declared that the Land Plan did not fall within the scope of the Friendly Societies Act. Amid increasingly acrimonious attacks from all sides O'Connor redoubled his efforts to restore confidence in the plan. However he was forced to instigate eviction proceedings against those smallholders who were withholding rents and in July of 1849, after one final attempt to force through the registration of the company, a bill was petitioned for, to dissolve the Land Company. The final days of the Land Company were chaotic. The settlers at O'Connorville were the only ones to remain loyal to the plan and an attempt was made to save the scheme through them. At Snigs End settlers told bailiffs sent in to collect unpaid rents or evict them that they would 'manure the land with their blood before it should be taken from them.' In the end some managed to claim legal title to their holdings, others ended up at the mercy of the Poor Law Guardians. In June 1852 O'Connor was taken to Dr. Tuke's private asylum in Chiswick rambling about his 'unworthy settlers'. He died on the 30th August 1855 his funeral was attended by over 50,000 people. At O'Connorville he left two sons, born out of wedlock to a local girl. One, Rory, died young, the other, Feargus, lived to be an old man. All the estates exist in some form to this day, the distinctive cottages still recognisable amid conversions and extensions. Smallholding was carried out on the estates to a greater or lesser extent up until the Second World War and at Lowbands, Snigs End and Great Dodford some still continue today. Recent work by historian Dorothy Thompson clearly points to a political conspiracy in the legal wranglings that sank the Land Plan. Had the plan succeeded a whole new pattern of land ownership would have been established and perhaps had working people gained the vote in the 1850s a completely different history of the labour movement and the country as a whole would have followed.

OTHER CHARTIST ESTATES?

Whilst the five estates of the Chartist Land Company are well documented there were others inspired by O'Connor's example. The Worcestershire Chronicle reported in October 1847 a meeting of The Kidderminster Co-operative Independent Land Association. They had purchased the Hoboro, or Hooborough Estate, near Castle Hill in the parish of Wolverley and they intended to locate 25 or 30 families on the 'O'Connor system.' A short time later it was reported that they had purchased an estate in the Wyre Forest.

After being addressed by Feargus O'Connor the Edge Tool Grinders, Britannia Metal Smiths and File Hardeners Unions in Sheffield all set up their own land colonies in the Sheffield area. A similar occurrence happened in Burnley, Lancs., when after hearing a speech by O'Connor a band of unemployed workers set out for Pendle Hill to stake out allotments. Beyond these sketchy details little is known of these communities.
Information from :
Kidderminster Revolutionaries website: http://www.hurcott-rd.freeserve.co.uk/ landclub.htm
And Heavens Below. WHG Armytage.

The full story of the Chartist estates is told in The Chartist Land Company. By Alice Mary Hadfield. David & Charles. Newton Abbot. 1970

DEATH OF AN ISLAND REPUBLIC

The remotest inhabited place in the British Isles lies some110 miles west of the Scottish mainland, a small archipelago of islands known as St Kilda. On the north side of the main island, Hirta, are the remains of the tigh na banaghaisgich, 'female warriors' house' or 'Amazon's house'. Descriptions of the house and St Kildian folklore has lead to speculation that these are the vestigages of an iron age matriarchal culture surviving through oral tradition. - first recorded by Martin Martin in 1698 in his detailed description of

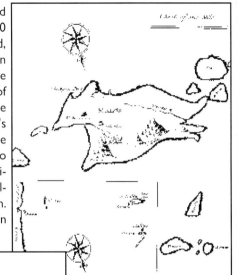

the island and it's community - the story of the survival and eventual demise of this idyllic community is in danger of itself passing away into folklore.

"If St Kilda is not the Eutopia so long sought, where will it be found? Where is the land which has neither arms, money, care, physic, politics, nor taxes? That land is St Kilda. No taxgatherer's bill threatens on a church door-the game-laws reach not the gannets. Safe in its own whirlwinds, and cradled in its own tempests, it heeds not the storms which shake the foundations of Europe - and acknowledging the dominion of M'Leod, cares not who sways the British sceptre. Well may the pampered native of happy Hirt refuse to change his situation - his slumbers are late - his labours are light - his occupation his amusement. Government he has not - law he feels not - physic he wants not - politics he heeds not - money he sees not - of war he hears not. His state is his city, his city is his social circle-he has the liberty of his thoughts, his actions, and his kingdom and all the world are his equals. His climate is mild, and his island green, and the stranger who might corrupt him shuns its shores. If happiness is not a dweller in St Kilda, where shall it be sought ? " Lachlan Maclean 1838.

Who knows how long it had taken the St Kildans to develop their communal republic, observed by Martin in 1698, or where these traditions had come from? Certainly without them their very survival would have been at risk. On the islands, consisting of 1575 acres of Hirta, a further 244 acres on Soay & 79 acres on Dun, the 180 islanders had developed a self-sufficient communal economy based on seabird (meat, oil & eggs), Soay sheep, fishing, and small scale crofting. A form of primitive socialism prevailed on the island. All grazing land was held in common. All property on which they depended for their livelihood was held in common; including boats, climbing ropes and fowling gear. All the island's produce of seabirds and fish was divided equally according to the number of households on the island, with provision made for the sick and elderly. And later gifts brought in by tourists, philanthropists and visitors were divided as equally as possible between the families.

The main settlement on the island, at village bay, was rebuilt in 1836-8. It consisted of 25 stone built cottages with barns & outbuildings in typical Hebridean style. The islands are also dotted with distinctive stone built/turf roofed cleits, or storehouses. Decisions concerning all matters were made by an informal meeting that took place each weekday morning - known as the `St Kilda Parliament' it consisted of all the adult males on the island. It had no rules, no chairman and 'members' arrived in there own time. Once assembled the 'parliament' would consider the work to be done that day. The islands' schoolmaster in 1889 wrote that the parliament 'very much resembles our Honourable British Parliament in being able to waste any amount of precious time over a very small matter while on the other hand they can pass a Bill before it is well introduced'. The islanders had a thriving cultural life with their own music, dance, poetry and sports. Martin reported that they were `very fond of music, dancing to an old wretched fiddle with great delight. They were also good singers, and accompanied all their duties with suitable songs, generally of their own composition.' Shinty was a favourite game & rock climbing was as much a sport as a skill needed birding.

Whilst some of their customs showed a possible early Christian influence - the beliefs of the islanders were seen as a mixture of 'popery and druidism,' prompting the Church of Scotland to send out a series of missionaries from 1705 onwards. Some of the missionaries had a beneficial effect on the island improving housing and living conditions. However in 1844 the islanders were won over to the doctrines of the Free Church and from 1863-1889 came under the severe rule of a Rev John Mackay whose adherence to a strict Christian doctrine played a large part in the eventual downfall of the island republic. Mackay's autocratic rule undermined the traditions that had grown up on the island to such an extend that religious worship often left little time to carry out the essential tasks necessary for survival on the island. In the late 1800s the island economy was given a boost by becoming part of the Victorian cruise itinery. This introduction to the cash economy (the tourists bought tweeds, knitwear & sheepskins) further undermined the subsistence economy of the island and also led to emigration from the island to the mainland. As the cruise ships declined in the early 1900's the islands dwindling population was supported by trawlermen fishing the seas around the island and from public funds. On 10 May 1930, a petition was signed by 20 islanders `We the undersigned . . . hereby respectfully pray and petition Her [sic] Majesty's Government to assist us all to leave the island this year and to find homes and occupation for us on the mainland.'

The evacuation took place on 29 August 1930. The Surgeon of HMS Harebell recorded the death of the community: ".....all the houses were locked and the people taken on board. Shortly afterward they were looking their last at St Kilda as the Harebell, quickly increasing speed, left the island a blur on the horizon. Contrary to expectations they had been very cheerful throughout, though obviously very tired, but with the first actual separation came the first signs of emotion, and men, women and children wept unrestrainedly as the last farewells were said."   A. Pomfret

So ended the longest surviving 'Communal Republic' on British soil. Somewhat ironically many of islanders found work with the Forestry Commission at Ardtornish in Morvern, where these refugees from a treeless island, found that their climbing skills were in demand to tend trees.

The story of St Kilda is told in: St Kilda. and other Hebridean Outliers. Francis Thompson. David & Charles.

After the riots - the aftermath of Chartism

All but one of the six points of the Charter would become law by 1911. The immediate effects of the first mass movement of working people were felt in many areas. Many Chartists went on to take leading roles in trade-unionism, local government, education, the co-operative movement and friendly societies. Some emigrated and joined Garibaldi's fight for an independent Italy and the struggle for reform in Australia. Other influences are harder to trace, but were in many ways equally far reaching.

In the Staffordshire potteries Chartism never recovered from the events of 16th August 1842 when a rally in Burslem to commemorate the Peterloo massacre turned into a riot that lasted for 2 days. Police stations at Hanley, Stoke, Fenton & Longton were demolished and houses of magistrates, lawyers and members of the clergy burnt down - brutal sentences were passed on rioters with 54 people being transported and 146 imprisoned with hard labour. The effect was to turn the potters against Chartism to such an extent that when Feargus O'Connor came to speak about his Land Plan they rejected it out of hand - they however had their own plan.

"To make labour scarce."

The Potters Joint Stock Emigration Society was the brainchild of William Evans who ran a newsagents in Shelton from where he published the *Potters' Examiner and Workman's Advocate* and sold copies of works by Mary Wollstonecraft, Rousseau and Emerson. Evans persuaded the Trades Union of Operative Potters that the answer to the problems of unemployment and competition from new machinery was to create a shortage of labour through emigration.

'Upon the foundation of this Society, the details of the scheme were disclosed to the potters· generally. It was proposed to purchase, in one of the Western States of the North American Union, twelve thousand acres of land, payment for which should be made by instalments extending over a period of ten years. As soon as the funds of the Society were sufficient to pay the first instalment on the land, the land would be divided into allotments of twenty acres each, and five acres of each allotment would be cultivated, and buildings erected thereon. Then lotteries were to take place amongst the shareholders of the Society, and the successful ones would be sent out to their allotment, and all the expenses of their migration paid. The lotteries, thereafter, would be continued until the colonisation of the twelve thousand acres was completed, and then more land would be bought, and the operations of the Society continued indefinitely.'

Harold Owen *The Staffordshire Potter.*

Funds were to be raised from £1 shares paid in instalments by union members. The plan was to target any pottery owner who installed new machinery with the threat of the emigration of his workforce. The plan receive a boost when this appeared to work on a Mr Mason who had introduced a machine known as the "rolling monster.". The machine was mothballed before the scheme was up and running. The scheme was also boosted by letters from individual potteries families who had already emigrated who sent back glowing letters from America telling of a land of liberty and plenty which were published in Evan's Paper.

Pottersville

Twelve months was spent cajoling subscriptions from union members and canvassing support from branches until almost the only activity of the unions was the promotion of the emigration society. Early in 1846 a small advanced party of 'Land Officers' set out for Wisconsin to purchase land. Having identified available land they wrote asking for money to be sent out - this was slow in coming and when it arrived finding the owners of the land entailed a long journey during which they got lost in forests, had to sleep out under the stars and encountered 'Red Indians'. They eventually bought 1600-acres that they named

Pottersville - back in the Potteries an Estate Committee was formed of eight 'persecuted' potters, who along with their families made ready to depart for Pottersville. Farewell entertainments were laid on and as the families, numbering forty in all, departed in canal boats to Liverpool. Thousands of people lined the banks to wish them well and for some miles up the canal they were accompanied by boats containing bands of musicians. As the Estates Committee was on route to the promised land the first ballots for plots were held and others made ready to set sail.

In the following two years only 134 people were to settle in Pottersville the scheme was beset with problems ; the Estates Committee came into conflict with the land officers over allocation of plots, with one officer describing the committee as less wise-men-of-the-east and more foolish-men-of-the-west and accusing the early settlers of only being interested in hunting and fishing and not prepared to do any work. Funding the scheme was slowly bankrupting the union back home and the unity of the potters was being undermined as some came to terms with the new technology and broke away to form a rival organisation. William Evans doubled his efforts to save the scheme opening it up to workers from other trades, canvassing support from cotton workers in Lancashire and proposing an extension of the scheme on a new plot of land on the Fox River. However a trickle of returning emigrants turned into a veritable swarm and the end finally came at a meeting held at Fort Winnebago on 8 June 1850, where included in a grand indictment of the project were charges of misrepresentation, corruption, and incompetence. By January 1851 the Emigration Society was dead and along with it any effective union organisation for the Potteries - a state of affairs from which it is said the union has never really recovered to this day. The Wisconson census for 1860 however showed 76 Staffordshire families settled in Columbia and Marquette Counties, most of them `prosperous farmers'.

"VOTINGHAM"

Other people saw the logic of acquiring the vote through the property route. The Liberals in particular promoted tactical vote acquisition. In marginal constituencies they supported the formation of Freehold Land Societies or Land Clubs.

"If we seek to get the franchise without property they tell us we are revolutionary: if we get it with property, then we are revolutionary too!"   James Taylor 1851

The first Freehold Land Society was started in Birmingham in 1847 by James Taylor, a temperance campaigner, who was the most vociferous advocate of the Freehold societies. From small beginnings in Birmingham it grew quickly into a national movement. At the end of its first year there were six independent societies at Dudley, Stourbridge, Coventry, Worcester, Wolverhampton and Stafford in which with the Birmingham Society 2,108 members had subscribed 2,837 shares. By December 1852 the movement was claiming that there were 130 societies with 85,000 members with 120,000 shares that had purchased 310 estates and had allotted 19,500 freeholds.

In 1850, John Merridrew, a conservative in Birmingham published an alarmist tract about the impact of the movement, which actually overstated the impact that the so called 'Votingham' estates were to have on local elections. Conservatives in Birmingham responded by forming the Victoria Freehold Land, Building and Investment Society. The societies bought land wholesale and sold it retail at wholesale prices, dividing the property up into plots just large enough to enable the buyer to qualify to vote. Some societies developed housing estates with street names such as Ballot St or Franchise Street to show their purpose. Elsewhere plots on some estates remained unbuilt on until the 1920s. In Kidderminster direct links can be traced from those involved in the Chartist agitation in the town through the Freehold Land Society, which eventually turned into the Local Kidderminster Building Society.

In 1848 The Northampton Town & County Benefit Building and Freehold Land Society was formed with the aim of enabling "every mechanic or working man, by small weekly contributions, to purchase a piece of land, on which he may erect a cottage, cultivate a garden, &c, &c., either occupy it himself or let it to others, so that he may possess a stake in the country, and a voice in the election of members of parliament.'

Land Society Circular.

The first land developed by the Society now comprises Freehold St, Primrose Hill, Elysium Terrace, St George's Place & Terrace in Northampton. Over the years through numerous mergers the Society became the Anglia Building Society then the Nationwide Anglia and currently the Nationwide - the worlds largest building society.

PHILANTHROPY RULES OK

Watching the Chartist agitation from the sidelines was a Bradford millowner with a social conscience. A radical dissenter, sympathetic to electoral reform, but horrified by the violence of the chartist campaign, Titus Salt was one of Bradford's largest employers and a pioneer in the use of new fibres in the woollen industry. Active in the political life of the town through the Anti-Corn Law League and the National Reform League he was a magistrate, a Deputy Lieutenant of the West Riding, a Liberal MP and President of the Bradford Freehold Land Society.

Towards the end of 1850 Salt conceived the idea of building a model industrial village, possibly inspired by a fictional model village described in Benjamin Disraeli's novel Coningsby but more likely as a result of conversations with his friend and Owenite Samual Bower. Salt was about to join an established tradition of paternalistic model villages. The tradition was instigated by Quaker industrialists in the 1700s, at Nenthead by the London Lead Company, and the Darby's in Coalbrookdale. And as the industrial revolution was kick-started in the early 1800s so too from a combination of philanthropy and pragmatism the concept of the model village was developed by David Dale & Robert Owen at New Lanark, Richard Arkwright at Cromford, Jerimiah Strutt at Belper, Thomas Ashton in Hyde, the Quaker Jackson brothers at Caldervale in Lancashire, Robert Gardiner at Barrowbridge, the Ashworths in Bolton, John Grubb Richardson, also a Quaker, at Bessbrook N.Ireland. And shortly before Salt started his venture one of his business associates Edward Akroyd built the small village of Copely next to his works in Halifax and later went on to built the larger Akroyden on the other side of Halifax.

These early industrialists were on the one hand having to provide the infrastructure necessary for the smooth running of their new industries and providing decent conditions for their workforce either out of firmly held religious beliefs or from the relatively new idea that peoples morals were formed by their surroundings. On the other hand by providing facilities under their control the mill owners obtained a docile workforce less likely to disrupt the smooth operation of the factories by strikes and 'unreasonable' wage demands.

By 1850 in Bradford the industrial revolution was getting into its stride and some of the worst impacts were starting to be felt. Death rates were rising, canals turning into open sewers, there was chronic overcrowding, people sleeping 15-20 to a room. All this was accompanied by intense class conflict. The chartists had found a well of support for their cause in Bradford. Salt, then Mayor, had watched as in 1848 the chartists had taken over parts of the town, patrolling the streets with armed guards and talking of a democratic republic of the North. Following the defeat of the chartists and a cholera epidemic in the town. Salt became a leading figure in the promotion of a policy of reconciliation. He realised that social harmony was only possible if working people could be persuaded that the new world of industry had something to offer them. In an example of what the *Bradford Observer* called 'Practical Christianity' Salt took his entire workforce of 3,000 on a day out to Malham Cove where he treated them to a grand picnic accompanied by brass bands.

WONDER OF THE INDUSTRIAL WORLD

Titus Salt's vision of a model village was grander than any that had been built before. A site on the edge of Shipley at the point where the River Aire, the Leeds & Liverpool Canal and the London to Glasgow Railway all cross was chosen and work on Saltaire started in the autumn of 1851. The crowds that gathered for the grand opening on 20th September 1853 were confronted with one of the wonders of the industrial world. Six storeys high and spread out over ten acres stood a huge T shaped textile works with a stunning 250ft high Italianate chimney modelled on the campanile of the Venetian Church of Santa Maria Gloriosa. Around the works, covering another 26 acres, Salt had built 800 houses, each with a kitchen, living room and scullery, a pantry, cellar and at least three bedrooms. In addition a row of 14 shops, a public baths and washhouse, a communal dining room, a church, a three-ward hospital, 45 almshouses, a high school for girls and boys, and a multi-purpose club and institute were all provided. On the top floor of the mill in what was claimed to be the largest room in the world the 3000 guests that attended the opening were treated to lavish hospitality.

In 1870 on the other side of the River Aire 11 acres of land were turned into a park where his workers could stroll, play cricket, tennis, bowls, and even practise archery. Salt was buried in the family mausoleum in the church at Saltaire. Thousands lined the streets of Bradford to watch his funeral cortege pass. Since then Saltaire has had a somewhat chequered history. By 1892 only sixteen years after Salt's death the great enterprise he had founded was filing for bankruptcy - in part due to changes in world textile markets, but also due to lack of interest in the business by his sons. It was taken over by a syndicate of Bradford businessmen - one of whom, James Roberts became the sole owner from 1899 to 1918 when he sold the mills and village on to another syndicate for £2 million. The inter-war years saw a revival in the company's fortunes with mohair in demand for car upholstery and alpaca for imitation skin jackets and coats. During WW2 the looms at Saltaire churned out khaki, navy & airforce blue fabric by the mile. and the village welfare dept was extended to deal with wartime refuges. Post-war Pakistanis, Sikhs and Hindis came to work in the mill as the firm tried to keep wages down to remain competitive. The last owners of Salts(Saltaire) Ltd were Illingworth Morris and Co who ran the company from 1958 until it finally closed as a textile mill in 1986. The fortunes of the firm mirroring the decline in the textile industry as a whole, the most colourful moments of the era being provided by boardroom battles involving Pamela Mason - ex-wife of Huddersfield born movie star James Mason - who had inherited a controlling stake in the firm in 1975 and despite the fact that the last strike had been in 1926 saw the whole place as a hotbed of industrial unrest. By this time the village had become a desirable part of Bradford's commuterville. On closure in 1986 the mill was striped of all the equipment and the magnificent temple of industry stood empty as schemes for turning it into a transport museum and then a leisure complex came and went.

PATRON SAINT OF SALT

Salt's vision however refused to lie down and die - it would shortly arise from dereliction. revived by the combined efforts of a twentieth century philanthropic entrepreneur, a pioneering new technology firm and Bradford's most famous living artist. Jonathan Silver, who had made his name in the 1970s with a chain of northern clothes shops and then in partnership with Ernest Hall in the groundbreaking redevelopment of Dean Clough Mills in Halifax, bought the Salt mills complex in 1987 in a calculated gamble that paid off when he later persuaded Pace Micro Technology to move to Saltaire and the Artist David Hockney to back the opening in the mills of a gallery dedicated to his work. Today Salts mills once again hum with sound of industry and thousands of visitors flock to see not only the largest collection of Hockney's work in the world, but also to wander the streets and marvel at Titus Salt's wonder of the industrial world.

The full story of Saltaire is told in *Salt and Silver.*
By Jim Greenhalf. Bradford Libraries 1997.

Utopia Erupts

After 2 months of minor earth tremors the tiny volcanic island of Tristan Da Cunha erupted on October 8 1961. 260 British citizens were evacuated, via Cape Town, to Southampton where they were accommodated in empty RAF married quarters at Calshott at the mouth of Southampton Water. The British Colonial Office had made earlier attempts to persuade the inhabitants to leave this remote South Atlantic island and they used the eruption as justification for their plans for a final evacuation. The islanders saw things somewhat differently. Instead of welcoming the sudden advent of 20th century creature comforts, they were appalled by modern society and became virtual prisoners in their homes (now renamed Tristan Close) longing to return to the life they had been forced to leave behind.

The community on Tristan owed its existence to the occupation of the island at the end of the Napoleonic Wars. Fearing that the French would attempt to rescue Napoleon off St Helena from a base that they might establish some 1300 miles away, a small British garrison was set up on the island. The unlikeliness of this scenario was soon realised by the Admiralty and the orders given to evacuate. At this point a Corporal William Glass requested that he and his wife be allowed to stay on the island. This request was granted and along with two civilians an embryonic new colony was left as the military departed. The settlers signed an 'agreement' which on the surface was a simple business partnership, but its commitments to equality and freedom laid the foundations for the community on Tristan to the present day.

William Glass was a gentle Scotsman under whose guidance the little community flourished. He earned himself the nickname of the 'Governor' and island tradition views him as the venerable patriarch and founding 'father' of the community. 'The house where he lived with his young wife and children - there were now six of them - was a social and religious center of the little settlement, commonly called "Government House." Here, each Sunday, Glass would conduct a short service, reading a passage from the Bible. And every night, the little group of settlers would gather in Glass's sitting room "round a large and cheerful blaze," each telling his story of adventure or singing an old sailor's song.'

THE TRISTAN DA CUHNA 'AGREEMENT'.

We, the Undersigned, having entered into Co-Partnership on the Island of Tristan da Cunha, have voluntarily entered into the following agreement-Viz

1st. That the stock and stores of every description in possession of the Firm shall be considered as belonging equally to each.

2nd. That whatever profit may arise from the concern shall be equally divided

3rd. All Purchases to be paid for equally by each.

4th. That in order to ensure the harmony of the Firm, no member shall assume any superiority whatever, but all to be consiclered as equal in every respect, each performing his proportion of labour, if not prevented by sickness.

5th. In case any of the members wish to leave the Island, a valuation of' the property to be made by persons fixed upon, whose valuation is to be considered as final.

6th. William Glass is not to incur any additional expence on account of his wife and children.

Somerset Camp Tristan da Cunha 7th November 1817.

From the start the island was multi-cultural. Mrs Glass was a black from the Cape and through shipwrecked sailors, those jumping ship, settlers & adventurers the community would grow to also include; Americans, Italians & Englishmen. The preponderance of bachelors amongst the new settlers resulted in the captain of a passing ship being persuaded to go in search of 5 marriageable women who would be prepared to return to the island - the captain had no trouble finding candidates on St Helena despite reservations from the authorities about the propriety of the venture. And so the islanders welcomed a boatload of wives most of whom were of mixed race. This racial mix has led over the years to what is know as the Tristan type - or more aptly put in a song popular on the island -' *Some wus white and some wus black and some wus the color of chewed tobac.'*

On the death of Glass, Peter Green was seen by the outside world as the new 'guvernor' of the colony - Green however saw himself as no such thing. The anarchistic traditions on the island were so strong by this time that 'leadership' was frowned upon and Green was at pains to point this out to visiting ships' captains. Outside authorities repeatedly tried to foist some sort of official structure on to the islanders, unable to comprehend how a community could function otherwise. Green did in the end accept a role as 'referee' in island disputes and spokesperson to outsiders, but this was a role he earned through the respect of the other islanders and not by appointment.

Life on the island revolved around a combination of subsistence farming and fishing, supplemented by trade with passing ships and salvage of wrecks. Tristan's isolation was lessened during the Second World War when after rumours of German U-boat activity a naval garrison was established officially, titled HMS Atlantic Isle, but known to the islanders simply as the Station. After the war the military establishment was abandoned, but the South African government decided to maintain a meteorological station on the island insuring continued radio contact and regular visits by supply ships. Rev. C.P. Lawrence, who had served on Tristan during the war *"... had been entranced by the unbelievable riches of the fishing grounds around the island, was impressed by the fact that the Tristan community was living on such a narrow subsistence margin, ...with these incredible riches remaining practically unexploited right at its doorstep.'* Lawrence initiated the Tristan Da Cunha Development Company and launched an ambitious plan to make the island 'self-reliant'. This included building two canning factories, with a road or railway between them, a hydroelectric power plant, estab-

Islanders wait for a bus Fawley 1962

lishing a fish waste fertiliser business and reorganising the islanders subsidence farming into a centralised 'Scientific' farm. The Plan however hadn't taken into account the islanders, who were not all that keen to exchange their co-operative economy for a 'contract'. A few improvements were carried out and by being flexible the company managed to run a small fishing industry from the island.

Until the fateful day in 1961 when their world erupted Tristan continued with its anarchic 'sub-marginal' economy - despite repeated attempts by the Colonial office to get them evacuated. Back in Tristan Close after a long and sometimes bitter campaign permission was granted for a small group to return to see if the island was still inhabitable. And finally after winning the support of the British Press the majority of the islanders set sail in April 1963 to return to their South Sea Island, gladly leaving behind most of the trappings of 'modern life'.

"the most eloquent and contemptuous rebuff that our smug and deviously contrived society could have received." **William Connor** *Daily Mirror*

The story of the Tristan Islanders is told in :
Crisis in Utopia. The Story of Tristan Da Cunha.
By Peter Munch. Longman 1971.
Quotations in text are from Crisis in Utopia.

Commentary & Reflection.

THE SEA OF CAPITALISM

The early socialist utopian communities are all a response in one way or another to the rising tide of industrial capitalism; whether it be on the one hand the benevolent mill owners looking for a more humane way to manage capitalism or simply being pragmatic in providing a contented workforce, or on the other hand self-help workers' groups organising to claim some of the benefits of the new order for themselves or to alleviate its worst excesses. Occasionally schemes develop into coherent alternatives to the current society as in the plans of Thomas Spence or the later phase of Owenism.

The early model industrial villages present a very mixed bag of experiments. Some were certainly little more than efficient ways of organising an industrial work-force whilst making more money for the factory owners through rental income. Others appear as grandiose acts of personal vanity carried out by men whose chequebooks matched the size of their egos. And then some seem to be genuine attempts to improve the living conditions of the newly industrialised worker, in par-ticular those with Quaker involvement. Most in fact look like a mish-mash of all the above it being hard to tell where one motivating factor ends and another starts. The picture is further complicated by the fact that in some places, notably Egerton and Bank Top on the outskirts of Bolton, the reality of what was built does not match the model village propaganda with some back-to-back housing even being built to look like better model housing. And whilst it is tempting to point a finger at the nasty capitalist mill owners pulling the wool over gullible investors' eyes - there is evi-dence that workers didn't want to live in the new improved model housing which not only came with higher rents, but also with a whole load of middle-class Christian ideological baggage attached.

114

A more clearly utopian picture is presented by the early co-operative movement that grew out of and around Owenism, giving rise to a pattern of small scale self-help groups of workers combining co-operatively to improve their conditions, through collective ownership of small plots of land, the odd workshop and chains 'fair trade' shops with the ultimate aim of raising enough surplus to establish a co-operative commonwealth on the land. Somewhere along the way the idea of the co-operative commonwealth got lost as the myriad of small societies learnt to swim in the capitalist sea, but it could still be argued that even today the ultimate aim of the movement is still to establish a co-operative commonwealth and that the 100 year adventure in retail shopping is merely a lengthy side-track.

Chartism may have been the first and singularly most successful working class campaign that this country has ever seen, with all but one of the six points of the charter being eventually achieved. Votes for women - dropped from the original charter as too extreme - has followed. The use of the link between property ownership and the right to vote used by the Chartists and by later campaigners through the freehold land clubs as leverage in their demands, may well go some way to explaining the peculiarly English cult of the owner occupier, not really seen anywhere else in Europe - if in the minds of the population, home ownership was clearly linked with having the vote in one generation, when their grandchildren were encouraged by Prime Minister Stanley Baldwin to become part owners of middle England in the 1920s perhaps at the back of their minds lingered the connection between property rights and voting rights. An English'man's' home may never have been a castle, but it may have been one of the keys to the ballot box.

Whoever said that you couldn't build islands of socialism in a sea of capitalism obviously hadn't come across some of the characters in the previous pages who, despite their achievements appearing to be a list of heroic failures, set in motion chains of events that have moulded society as we know it today, and provided inspiration for future generations.

"We take some inspiration from the ill-fated early co-operative movement which resolved .... - " Let it be universally understood that the grand ultimate aim of all co-operative societies...is community on the land." (our underlining).....We see ourselves as a fifth column within capitalism and just as the 'workers friendly societies' could be said to be forerunners of the welfare state, so the 'workers co-operative living group' could be the forerunner of a new social creation."

From: A brief summary of our history and aims. People in Common. Feb 1975.

Islands of socialism : bibliography

The Life and Strange Suprising Adventures of Daniel Defoe. Richard West. Harper/Collins 1997

A Supplement to the History of Robinson Crusoe. Thomas Spence(English and phonetic edns., Newcastle, 1782).

The Peoples Farm English Radical Agrarianism 1775-1840.Malcom Chase. Clarendon Press 1988. RECOMMENDED

The Life and Ideas of Robert Owen. A.L.Morton. Lawrence & Wishart. 1962

Historic New Lanark. I.Donnachie & G.Hewitt.Edingburgh Univercity Press. 1993

Co-operation & the Owenite socialist communities in Britian1825-45. RG Garnett. MUP 1972. RECOMMENDED

Robert Owen & the Owenites in Britian & America. JFC Harrison. Routledge&Kegan Paul.1969. RECOMMENDED

Independent Spirits. Spiritualism and English Plebians.1850-1910. Logie Barrow. Routledge & Kegan Paul1986.

Robert Owen & his Relevance to our Times. Co-op. College Papers. Co-op Union ltd. 1971RECOMMENDED

The History of Co-operation. GJ Holyoake. 1906

Travelling Brothers. R.A.Leeson. Granada. !980

William Pare Co-operator & Social Reformer. R.G.Garnett.Co-operative College Papers. Co-op Union ltd. 1973

Dr William King: A Co-operative Pioneer. S. Polland, Loughborough, 1959.

William Thompson (1775-1833) Pioneer Socialist. R.Pankhurst. Pluto Press. 1991.

Adventures in Socialism: New Lanark Establishment & Orbiston community. A.Cullen. Glasgow 1910

The New History of the CWS. P.Redfern. Dent & Sons ltd. 1938

Eve & the New Jerusalem Barbara Taylor. Virago 1983 RECOMMENDED

Manea Fen :An Experiment in Agrarian Communitarianism, 1838-1841. W. H. G. Armytage. John Rylands Library.

The English Rebels. Charles Poulsen. The Journeyman Press. 1984.

Backwoods Utopias Arthur Bestor, University of Pennsylvania Press 1950/1970.

Frances Wright and the 'Great Experiment' Margaret Lane. MUP

A Century of Co-operation. G.D.H Cole. Manchester 1944

The Making of the English Working Class. E.P.Thompson. Penguin

Taming the Tiger :The struggle to control technology. W. Rybczynski Penguin 1983

The Chartist Land Company. Alice Mary Hadfield. David & Charles: Newton Abbot. 1970. RECOMMENDED

The Chartist Land Colonies. 1846-48 W.H.G Armytage. Agricultural History.Vol32.No4 1958

A Practical Work on the Management of Small Farms. Feargus O'Connor. A Haywood.Manchester 1843.

The Staffordshire Potter Harold Owen 1901(reprint 1970) Kingsmead Reprints

William Evans and the Potters Emigration Society. University of Keele Thesis 1974

Saltaire An Introduction to the village of Sir Titus Salt. Jack Reynolds. Bradford Art Galleries & Museums 1976.

The Great Paternalist Jack Reynolds. Bradford University. 1983

Salt and Silver. A story of hope. Jim Greenhalf.Bradford Libraries. 1997.   RECOMMENDED

Life & Death in Eden. Pitcairn Island & the Bounty Mutineers. Trevor Lummis. Victor Gollancz 1999

Bounty : Beyond the Voyage Julie Pearson. Trusson Publications. 1989

St Kilda. and other Hebridean Outliers. Francis Thompson. David & Charles. 1970.

Crisis in Utopia. The Story of Tristan Da Cunha. Peter Munch. Longman 1971.

WHAT GOOD IS AN ARTS DEGREE?

"Twelve gentlemen of good education and liberal principles are to embark with twelve ladies in April next, first having become as well acquainted as possible and having settled every regulation of their future conduct. Their opinion was that they should fix themselves at - I do not recollect the place, but somewhere in a delightful part of the new back settlement; that each man should labour two or three hours a day, the produce of which labour would, they imagine, be more than sufficient to support the colony. The produce would be stored and shared out communally. They would assemble a good library and spend their leisure in study, liberal discussions, and the education of their children. The women would care for the children and engage in other occupations suited to their strength; at the same time the greatest attention is to be paid to the cultivation of their minds. All members would be free to hold whatever political or religious opinions that they pleased. Anyone could withdraw from the society whenever he chose."

Thomas Poole on Pantisocracy.

Artists have always counted visionaries amongst their number. Painters, writers and poets have imagined other worlds, better worlds in their work - some have tried to create those imagined worlds in reality. Oxford undergraduate & poet Robert Southey contemplating his future in 1794 - having ruled out careers in medicine (he was unqualified), in government (his Jacobin views.), considered emigrating to America - lamenting, "What is a liberal arts degree good for ?" At the peak of his despair Southey met a Cambridge undergraduate - recently discharged from the army where he had enlisted under the false name of Silas Tomkyn Comberback - better known as Samuel Taylor

Coleridge. Southey had started to imagine a way he could emigrate and set up a community in the new world based on his reading of Plato's Republic. Swept along by Coleridge's enthusiasm the two poets dreamed of an enlightenment utopia, and 'Pantisocracy' (equal government by all) was born.

Coleridge waxed eloquent on the practicality of such a scheme, and within a few weeks had convinced Southey and several friends to establish a settlement on the banks of the Susquehanna River in Pennsylvania, where there were no hostile Indians and where the mosquitoes were not as bad as English gnats. Southey promptly set himself to finish a poem, Joan of Arc, to raise money for travel and implements. 'This new pantisocratic scheme has given me new life, new hope, new energy; all the faculties of my mind are dilated'. Coleridge, not to be outdone, wrote a poem on 'The prospect of establishing a pantisocracy in America'.

Where dawns, with hope serene, a brighter day
Than e'er saw Albion in her happiest times,
With mental eye exulting now explore,
And soon with kindred minds shall haste to enjoy
(Free from the ills which here our peace destroy)
Content and bliss on Transatlantic Shore!

The two poets fleshed out their pantisocratic utopia in a series of letters and lectures. On land that they hoped to purchase for some £2000 on the banks of the Susquehanna River they would work only 2 or 3 hours a day to provide their simple needs - spending the rest of their time in intellectual pursuits amongst equals. Southey hoped to be able to "Criticise poetry when hunting buffalo and write sonnets whilst following the plough."

Coleridge believed that the experiment would only be completed in the second generation, when their children had grown up in an environment purged of the corruptions of vice, wealth, and inequality. Because of this conviction great emphasis was to be placed on education not only of the children but also the adult members. In later plans for a school he hinted at the Pantisocrats' curriculum.

" ...they would study the evolution of society, beginning with Savage Tribes and ending with revolutionary states and Colonies."

The scheme quickly attracted others. One, a young Quaker poet named Robert Lovell, was married to Mary Fricker one of five daughters living with their widowed mother and supporting themselves with their needles. In August 1794, Southey became engaged to Edith Fricker and in a mad moment of enthusiasm Coleridge proposed to, and was accepted by, Sara Fricker; a decision he was to have second & third thoughts about in the coming months. Southey forged ahead with plans to take his family out to America. Coleridge was none too happy with either his rash engagement, or the prospect of trying to found Pantisocracy with Southey's relatives and the Fricker women. Whilst theoretically he believed in equality of the sexes, in practice he saw the women as potential spoilers of his utopian system - in one of his letters to Southey he outlined the role he imagined for the women. The two older women "can at least prepare the Food of Simplicity for us" and "Let the married Women do only what is absolutely convenient and customary for pregnant Women or nurses - Let the Husbands do all the Rest," including "Washing with a Machine and cleaning the House." He was still having grave doubts over his rash proposal of marriage. That Christmas, he confessed to Southey that he did not love Sara Fricker and asked how could he marry a woman he did not love. On the other hand he declared;

"Mark you, Southey! I will do my Duty."

MOUSE OF THE MOUNTAIN

Southey was starting to have his own doubts about the scheme. Things came to a head when Southey started to hint that maybe the American venture was a little too drastic and perhaps they could try things out on a smaller scale on a farm in Wales. Oh, and he also wanted to take his aunt's servant, Shadrach Weekes, with him. Coleridge was outraged. 'SHAD IS MY BROTHER', he wrote in large capitals in a letter to Southey protesting at this attempt to introduce 'slavery' to pantisocracy. As to the idea of a small-scale trial in Wales - this amounted to no more that a petty farming venture. "This was the Mouse of which the Mountain Pantisocracy was at last safely delivered!" The quarrel caused a breach between the two men that, while not permanent, was to take many months to heal. "You have left a large Void in my Heart", said Coleridge; "I know no man big enough to fill it". Southey replied that he would go to Wales or whatever place Coleridge chose. In reality he had decided to honour an uncle's wishes and take up a church career. Almost exactly a year after the scheme was first fully worked out it was over. Southey accompanied his uncle to Portugal, vaguely promising to join Pantisocracy in fourteen years time. Coleridge honoured his commitment and married Sara Fricker, moving with his wife and infant son, not to America, but to Nether Stowey in Somerset, where he hoped his friend Thomas Poole would instruct him in agriculture. Meanwhile he would spend the rest of his time in literary pursuits and the education of his child.

Years later he would reflect on the dream of pantisocracy:

" What I dared not expect from constitutions of Government and whole Nations, I hoped from Religion and a small Company of chosen Individuals, and formed a plan, as harmless as it was extravagant, of trying the experiment of human Perfectibility on the banks of the Susquehanna; where our little Society, in its second generation, was to have combined the innocence of the patriarchal Age with the knowledge and genuine refinements of European culture: and where I had dreamt of beholding, in the sober evening of my life, the Cottages of Independence in the undivided Dale of Industry. . . . Strange fancies! and as vain as strange! yet to the intense interest and impassioned zeal, which called forth and strained every faculty of my intellect for the organization and defence of this Scheme, I owe much of whatever I at present possess, my clearest insight into the nature of individual Man, and my most comprehensive views of his social relations. . . ."

Coleridge, *The Friend*, II.

Robert Southey became poet Laureate in 1813 and upon meeting Robert Owen in 1816 he remarked that Owen was 'neither more nor less than such a Pantisocrat as I was in the days of my youth'. `Had we met twenty years ago the meeting might have influenced both his life and mine in no slight degree'.

LETTER FROM AN ANCIENT MARINER

Fuelled by the publication of such titles as "Letters From Mr Fletcher Christian Containing A Narrative Of The Transactions On Board His Majesty's Ship Bounty Before And After The Mutiny, With His Subsequent Voyages And Travels In South America" rumours of the whereabouts of the crew of HMS Bounty circulated in England at the turn of the 19th century. One persistent rumour was that Fletcher Christian was being hidden by his first love, Isabella Christian Curwen on Belle Island in the middle of Lake Windermere.

In 1798 Coleridge and Wordsworth collaborated on a book of poems entitled "Lyrical Ballads". One of Coleridge's contributions was an early version of the 'The Rime Of The Ancient Mariner'. Wordsworth had attended the same school as Fletcher Christian at Cockermouth and it is likely that their families were acquainted. This has led to speculation that the Ancient Mariner is none other than Fletcher Christian himself, or at least a version of Wordworth's reminiscences seen through Coleridge's opium-induced haze, and, if the mutineer really was holed up on Belle Island, that the two poets could have made an undercover visit to the island and talked directly with the renegade seaman!

Egality, liberty, poetry

All the romantic poets were radicals in their own ways before their reputations were sanitised by the Victorian literati. From Southey & Coleridge through to Keats & Byron and none more so than Percy Bysshe Shelley. The son of minor Sussex landed gentry he was something of a troublemaker from the start - being expelled from Oxford for amongst other things sending copies of The Necessity of Atheism to all the bishops & heads of college. At Oxford he was given a copy of the Histoire du Jacobinsme, a witch-hunting attack on a continental secret society known as the illuminists. This was a group dedicated to spreading a worldwide revolutionary conspiracy. The illumiinists' doctrine was one of militant egalitarianism dedicated to the destruction of private property, religion and 'superstitious' social forms such as marriage. Shelley wrote a letter to Leigh Hunt the editor of The Examiner suggesting that a society should be set up along the lines of the illuminists to co-ordinate all the different reform groups active in England at the time. Shelley received no reply to his letter, but a vision of a 'completely-equalized community' was firmly planted in his mind.

Shelley further scandalised his family by eloping to Scotland with Harriet Westbrook, the daughter of a coffee house owner - in his family's eyes tantamount to marrying a servant. Shelley was now beginning to move in Radical circles. He had struck up a friendship with the anarchist philosopher William Godwin. And in 1812 he went to Dublin and immersed himself in the cause for Irish liberation. This was a Dublin still reeling from the defeat of Wolfe Tone and the United Irishmen in the 1790s and the English repression that followed. Shelley published two pamphlets during his Irish stay; An Address to the Irish People and Proposals for an Association of Philanthropists. Both showed a naive comprehension of the complexities of Irish politics, something that Shelley was to eventually realise. He was invited to speak to a meeting at the Fishamble Theatre. Here the pale young Englishman, still barely 19, spoke to several hundred 'respectable' Irishmen & women. They listened for over an hour, cheering loudly whenever he expressed anti-English sentiment or attacked the Prince Regent, but booing & hissing with equal enthusiasm when he brought up political and religious reform. In the audience were two informers working for the English who sent a report of the meeting to Lord Sidmouth's Home Office. William Pitt had set up the Home Office in order to deal with the possibility of revolution spreading from France. A nation-wide network of spies and informers was built up using Customs & Excise officers, postmasters and local mayors to keep a watch for seditious activity. The Shelleys left Dublin feeling demoralised, realising the enormity of the task facing the Irish radicals and appalled by the conditions of the ordinary Irish people under English Rule.

Rendezvous for the friends of liberty

In need of respite and a place to relax and recover from their Irish agitation they found themselves looking around the substantial country house and estate of Nantgwillt a few miles west of the town of Rhayader in central Wales. Within a mere 48 hours they had fallen in love with the romantic charm of the place and instigated negotiations to take a lease on the property.

Shelley set about writing to his father for an advance on his inheritance so he could enter into the lease. He also wrote to his 'friends of liberty & truth' painting a vision of the possibility for a commune of romantic radicals `...embosomed in the solitude of mountains, woods and rivers, silent, solitary and old... '

He wrote to William Godwin and tried to persuade him to join them. Leigh Hunt and his wood-sculptor wife were also canvassed to consider the benefits of mountain air and radical companionship. An old Sussex companion of Shelley, Elizabeth Hitchener, who had shared his radical views and wanted to set up a free-school was written to with encouragement to found her school at Nantgwillt. For eight weeks while Shelley tried to convince the estate staff of the merit of his egalitarian scheme, introducing communal meals and talking of self-fulfilment & the betterment of man, Dan Healy - an Irish orphan taken in by the Shelleys - would ride to and from the mail-coach with correspondence. Neither money nor companions seemed to be forthcoming. His father sent a curt refusal of help. Other friends were promptly written to, to try and raise a loan. Miss Hitchener's father forbade her from going off to become one of Shelley's 'mistresses', and William Godwin politely declined the offer, but said he might come down with his family for a holiday. On top of all these setbacks Shelley was worried about his wife's declining health. He was also growing increasingly worried over the fate of a case of his Irish pamphlets that was supposed to have been delivered to Miss Hitchener in Sussex. The case had in fact been opened at customs in Holyhead and the nature of its contents relayed to the Home Office. This was duly noted and added to Mr Shelley's file and a watch put on his 'acquaintance'.

Nantgwillt house C1900

In the end too many complications piled up on one another and sank the scheme - not only could Shelley find no-one to back him financially, but the value of the stock and chattels on the estate had been doubled, and anyway he would have been unable to sign the lease himself, as he was still a minor. On the 7th June the little party left Nantgwillt, temporarily staying with relatives in the locality before moving off south.

VESSELS OF RADICAL MEDICINE

They would settle next at the small Devon coastal village of Lynmouth taking a basic but somewhat rambling cottage, with enough rooms for Shelley to start to imagine trying to gather his friends around him. The arrival of such a party in the remote West Country was guaranteed to attract attention. Two and half months later a report landed on Lord Sidmouth's desk at the Home Office. Mr Shelley's whereabouts were noted and a watchful eye kept on him. The inhabitants of the embryonic commune were too busy to notice the watchful eye of the law; setting up house, unpacking books and writing copious correspon-

dence. ('So many as sixteen letters by the same post', Lord Sidmouth was informed.) This time they would get off to a better start. Miss Hitchener defied her father and came down to join them. On her arrival she and Shelley began radical propaganda work. Lynmouth would not seem the most strategic of places from which to try and disseminate propaganda, remote as it was from any centre of population and pretty much cut off from all communications.

Sketch portrait of Shelley

Shelley overcame these seeming obstacles in a manner befitting a radical romantic poet. Early in the morning or late at night, he and Miss Hitchener would pick their way along the rocky shore with arms and pockets full of bottles. When the tide turned and the wind was just right they would launch these little 'vessels of heavenly medicine', as Shelley called them in a sonnet, out into the sea destined to be washed up to Avonmouth or across to South Wales. Each bottle held a copy of *The Declaration of Rights* or a broadsheet ballad called *The Devil's Walk*. They also made small 'boats' - little waxed boxes with sticks attached to each end with a sail on to attract attention. One of these was picked up by a fisherman and its contents reported to the Home Office. Even more imaginative were the 'balloons of knowledge', handmade miniature silk hot-air balloons powered by a spirit-soaked wick. Despite difficulties in getting them to fly - they tended to catch fire - numerous copies of *The Declaration of Rights* sailed away into the evening sky out across the Bristol Channel. On a more down-to-earth level, Dan Healy was sent off round the local highways & byways to flypost broadsheets on any convenient wall or barn door when no one was looking.

During the long summer days Shelley worked on his long poem *Queen Mab*; a polemic attacking religious and political tyranny, war, commerce, marriage and prostitution, thinly disguised by a fairytale setting. Hoping to get round the censors by parading politics as poetry he wrote off to likely publishers. Events however were about to take a turn for the worse. On August 19th Dan Healy was caught putting up broadsheets in Barnstable. Interrogated by the local mayor he gave the pre-agreed cover story that he had met two travellers who had paid him to distribute the posters. However on finding that his master was already under suspicion, Healy was promptly tried and convicted of dispersing printed papers without the printer's name on them. Not being able to pay the £200 fine he faced 6 months imprisonment. The magistrate sat back and wait-

THE CHARTISTS BIBLE

Circulating in numerous cheap pirate editions *Queen Mab* was to be Shelleys' most widely read and influential work, finding its home not in the rarefied world of literature but as a basic text for the self-educated working class. Owenites and Chartists would take inspiration from its revolutionary message. Copies would reach radicals in America and on the continent and in 1848 a young Frederick Engels would begin a translation into German.

ed for Mr Shelley to appear. Shelley came the next day. To the authorities' surprise he neither admonished his servant nor paid the fine. After a brief conversation with Dan Healy, in which it appeared to the authorities that the two men already had an 'understanding on the matter', Shelley departed back to Lynmouth. By the time reports had been sent to London and instructions received back, the Shelleys would be far away. The Home Office now had 3 separate reports on the subversive activities of the young Mr Shelley. Due mainly to the fact that he was still a minor it was decided to continue with the policy of watch & wait.

WONDER OF WALES

Assuming that they were being followed Shelley and his small party hurried deep into Wales. Avoiding the area around Nantgwillt they pushed on into the northern mountains, hoping either to hide out in this remote region or head for one of the small ports and on to Ireland. As they skirted the coast along Cardigan Bay they came across the site of not only one of the great civil engineering projects of the early 19th century, but also one of the most advanced community and commercial experiments of the period. As far back as 1625 a scheme for the reclamation of the Treath Mawr tidal estuary had been put forward by a John Wym, but it wasn't until 1801, when the Irish Act of Union created the need for a clear route from London to Dublin that anything was done. There were two candidates for the route, up the A5, and then either along the north Welsh coast and on to Holyhead, or around Cardigan Bay and sail from the Llynn Peninsula. The northern route was blocked by the river crossing at Conwy and the Menai Straits and the southern route blocked by Treath Mawr. William Madocks hoped to create the southern route by building an embankment across Treath Mawr on which the main road could run and by building a harbour at Porth Dinllean. An initial 'cob' embankment had been built reclaiming 2000 acres of tidal estuary. Here Madocks laid out the settlement of Tremadoc under a dramatic cliff which rose several hundred feet above the village; neat stonebuilt houses, two chapels, several shops, a tavern and an imposing town hall were geometrically arranged on a T-shaped ground plan. It was hoped that the new township would become a centre of culture in North Wales. In 1808 work was started on the Grand Embankment, stretching for a mile across the mouth of the estuary. Its completion in 1811 was celebrated by the `Tremadoc Embankment Jubilee', complete with roast ox, Eistedfodd and horse races along the top of the 'Wonder of Wales'.

In February 1812 a near disaster was averted. High spring tides breached the central section of the embankment and the whole project was only saved by a massive effort from the locality, with no less than 892 men and 727 horses coming in response to the call for help. The effort however nearly bankrupted Maddocks and when Shelley arrived the scheme was in dire financial straits. He was immediately enthusiastic about the whole new town and land reclamation project, seeing it as a practical experiment in forming an ideal community and a chance to reform both man and his surroundings. Renting a local house, Tan-yr-allt, Shelley threw himself into fundraising on Maddocks's behalf. He spent six months chasing up the promises of funds from local farmers and businessmen with the zeal of a new convert. This did not endear him to some influential locals and neither did his vocal support for the Luddites, and local rioters. In his spare time Shelley busied himself with reading, trying to finish Queen Mab and distributing his political pamphlets to anyone he regarded as 'likely'.

Amidst stormy weather the following February Dan Healy arrived in Tremadoc fresh out of Barnstable gaol. Shelley welcomed him with open arms. What happened next has been open to wild speculation ever since. Seemingly expecting some sort of trouble Shelley retired that night with loaded pistols at his bedside. In the night the house was broken into and an apparent assassination attempt made on Shelley's life. Whether a Home Office spy had followed Healy from Barnstable, or it was an attempt by local businessmen to scare Shelley off was never discovered - it has even been suggested that the whole event was a fabrication or hallucination on Shelley's part. Whatever the truth Shelley and his companions left the next day never to return.

The building of Telford's suspension bridge over the Menai Straits would eventually swing things in favour of the northern route to Ireland with Holyhead as the port, leaving Tremadoc somewhat stranded in a backwater. However the redirecting of the river Glasyn had unexpectedly carved out a deep channel in the sands enabling the founding of the port of Porthmadoc, which would flourish, following the building of the Blaenau/Festiniog railway along the Great Embankment, as the major port of export for Welsh slate. Years later Shelley would make one last attempt to establish an egalitarian community. On the shores of the Mediterranean he would attempt to knit together a literary colony with his second wife Mary (the daughter of Mary Wollstencraft and William Godwin, & author of Frankenstein), Lord Byron and other friends - an attempt that would be cut short by his untimely death in a boating accident.

> 'I am the Fairy MAB: to me 'tis given
> The wonders of the human world to keep;
> The secrets of the immeasurable past,
> In the unfailing consciences of men,
> Those stern, unflattering chroniclers, I find;
> The future, from the causes which arise
> In each event, I gather; not the sting
> Which retributive memory implants
> In the hard bosom of the selfish man,
> Nor that ecstatic and exulting throb
> Which virtue's votary feels when he sums up
> The thoughts and actions of a well-spent day,
> Are unforeseen, unregistered by me;
> And it is yet permitted me to rend
> The veil of mortal frailty, that the spirit,
> Clothed in its changeless purity, may know
> How soonest to accomplish the great end
> For which it hath its being, and may taste
> That peace which in the end all life will share.
> This is the meed of virtue; happy Soul,.....'

Queen Mab

CIRCLES, SALONS, CLUBS, SCHOOLS, GUILDS, BROTHERHOODS AND COLONIES GALORE

Art schools seem to have been hotbeds of radicalism down the years, throwing up individuals who would not only try to change the face of art, but also the face of the world. In the crowd following the cart from Snigs End Chartist Colony, which was carrying the third great Chartist Petition to Parliament, were two young Academy students, John Everett Millais and William Holmann Hunt. As the demonstration was dispersed the two students faded away into the London streets to re-emerge years later as part of the Pre-Raphaelite Brotherhood. Other artists-to-be were affected by the Chartists. The young Edward Burne-Jones' nurse regaled him with scary stories of the violence out on the Birmingham streets, which his father patrolled as a special constable. Affected by these working-class agitations going on around them and the declining conditions in the new industrial cities these young men and their fellow students would become part of what amounts to a youth cult, when they reached Oxford.

Up at Oxford, in 1874, in the window of Shrimptons in the Broad, a caricature appeared under the title *President of the Amateur Landscape Gardening Society*. It showed the then Slade Professor of Fine Art wielding a pick and shovel in the act of resurfacing a stretch of road with his students. The professor in question was John Ruskin, perhaps the most influential figure of the Victorian art world. The project he had persuaded his students to take part in was part of a grand scheme of Ruskin's that went under the name of the St George's Guild. ......the students sweating away numbered among them a certain Oscar Wilde and Arnold Toynbee.

John Ruskin (1819-1900) perhaps best known for his defences of Turner and the Pre-Raphaelites and his home at Brantwood in the Lake District, produced an idiosyncratic monthly digest of his ideas entitled *Fors Clavigera*. This took the form of a series of letters to the workmen and labourers of Great Britain. Amongst the many personal anecdotes, Swiss folk stories, discourses on art and botany and promised recipes for a famous vegetable soup, Ruskin sketched out the framework for his own utopian world. It was a world where art and life were to merge as one. Money itself would be an object of beauty. Each trade and profession was to have its own distinctive costume. Work would be carried out by hand, without machines with their accompanying pollution. The mainly agricultural work would be interspersed withr folk festivals.

GUILD OF ST GEORGE

Ruskin conceived the Guild of St. George as a means of transforming the declining state of Britain into his utopian fantasy. "We will try to take some small piece of English ground, beautiful, peaceful and fruitful. We will have no steam-engines upon it, and no railroads; we will have no untended or unthought-of creatures on it; none wretched, but the sick; none idle, but the dead."

The Guild was to be a band of men of good will, giving a tithe of their income, and the best of their energies, to acquiring land, and developing it, in accordance with Ruskin's ideas and ideals. Membership would be in three categories:

(1)The Comites Ministrantes - Companions Servant - made up of a few men of independent income prepared to devote their main energies to the work of the Guild.

(2)The Comites Militantes - Companions Militant - comprising of persons occupied in agricultural labour, or other works directed by the master for the fulfilment of the Guild's aims.

(3) And the Comites Consilii - Companions Consular or Friends of the Guild: - who would form the majority of the members, giving a tithe of their income, and pledging themselves to live simply in accordance with the principles of the Guild.

The principles by which they were to live were laid out in *Fors Clavigera*. The supreme authority of the Guild would be vested in a popularly elected master - Ruskin only accepting the position until someone more suitable could be found. It was hoped that once enough Friends of the Guild had been recruited, that their example and sheer weight of numbers would "ultimately result in a change in the laws of the state." Ruskin poured a tenth of his fortune into the Guild to get it started. He persuaded two friends, Sir Thomas Dyke Acland and the Rt. Hon. William Cowper-Temple, to act as trustees, and waited patiently for both subscriptions and recruits to materialise. In April 1871, he received the sum of £30 from an anonymous donor that was to remain the total 'tithed' to the Guild for many years. On the membership front things were no better. In his annual report for the first 'official' year of the Guilds operation, in 1878, Ruskin bemoaned the fact that the membership still stood at the original 32.

Mr ruskin's teashop

This disappointing response did not stop Ruskin attempting to carry out small-scale experiments to put the Guild ideas into practice. Along with the amateur road building at Oxford he had carried out a road sweeping experiment in London to prove that "a bit of our London streets could be kept as clean as the deck of a ship" and opened Mr Ruskin's Tea Shop at 29 Paddington St. to sell high quality tea to working people.

A 7-acre woodland at Bewdley, Worcestershire was given to the Guild in 1871 by George Baker, a wealthy manufacturer and mayor of Birmingham. Despite plans to 'transform' the wood no work was actually carried out by the Guild. Over at Barmouth on the Welsh coast a group of cottages and an acre of rocky ground were gifted to the Guild by another benefactor. Here Auguste Guyard an exiled French social reformer, did go some way towards achieving Ruskin's vision of land

The Code of the Guild of St. George

I. I trust in the Living God, Father Almighty, Maker of heaven and earth, and of all things and creatures visible and invisible. I trust in the kindness of His law, and the goodness of His work. And I will strive to love Him, and keep His law, and see His work, while I live.

II. I trust in the nobleness of human nature, in the majesty of its faculties, the fulness of its mercy, and the joy of its love. And I will strive to love my neighbour as myself, and, even when I cannot, will act as if I did.

III. I will labour, with such strength and opportunity as God gives me, for my own daily bread; and all that my hand finds to do, I will do with my might.

IV. I will not deceive, or cause to be deceived, any human being for my gain or pleasure; nor hurt, or cause to be hurt, any human being for my gain or pleasure; nor rob, or cause to be robbed, any human being for my gain or pleasure.

V. I will not kill nor hurt any living creature needlessly, nor destroy any beautiful thing, but will strive to save and comfort all gentle life, and guard and perfect all natural beauty, upon the earth.

VI. I will strive to raise my own body and soul daily into higher powers of duty and happiness; not in rivalship or contention with others, but for the help, delight, and honour of others, and for the joy and peace of my own life.

VII. I will obey all the laws of my country faithfully; and the orders of its monarch, and of all persons appointed to be in authority under its monarch, so far as such laws or commands are consistent with what I suppose to be the law of God; and when they are not, or seem in any wise to need change, I will oppose them loyally and deliberately, not with malicious, concealed, or disorderly violence.

VIII. And with the same faithfulness, and under the limits of the same obedience, which I render to the laws of my country, and the commands of its rulers, I will obey the laws of the Society called of St. George, into which I am this day received; and the orders of its masters, and of all persons appointed to be in authority under its masters, so long as I remain a Companion, called of St. George.

Fors Clavigera, Letter 58

restoration cultivating rare herbs and trees on the hostile soil. At Cloughton, near Scarborough, a small plot of land was bought specifically for John Guy, a Companion of the Guild, who Ruskin admired for refusing to work a steam-driven machine. None of these small schemes were really what had been intended when Ruskin had sketched out his plans for the Guild. Rather than these little experiments which almost relied on some wealthy companion's whim, Ruskin had envisaged land-based colonies where 'Comites Militantes', housed in decent dwellings, would cultivate the land "in the most prudent and intensive manner," and would be offered leases to their own farms if they "proved suitable." The colonies would be provided with amenities such as libraries and schools, and the rents either lowered in proportion to the improvements made by the tenants or else invested in sponsoring other colonies.

St george's farm

The closest the Guild came to achieving this was at the Totley Colony near Sheffield.

"A small body - about a dozen - of men calling themselves Communists, mostly great talkers, had joined together with the idea of establishing themselves on the land somewhere; and I have understood that it was at their insistence that John Ruskin bought the small farm (of thirteen acres or so) at Totley near Sheffield, which he afterwards made over to St George's Guild, and which now, under the name of St George's Farm, has been put in the hands of another, less voluble and more practical, body of Communists -John Furniss, George Pearson, and Co. However that may be, it is certain that the first-mentioned set of men - of whom William Harrison Riley, formerly editor of the International Herald, was one of the most active, and among them our friend Joseph Sharpe - did for a short time occupy St George's Farm. Their idea was not (at any rate at first) to abandon their various occupations in and around Sheffield, but to give their spare time to communal work at the farm, and in some way to share its produce -

thescheme including as most Communistic schemes seem to do, some project for the establishment of a school on the place. Unfortunately the usual dissensions arose - usual, I would say, wherever work of this kind is ruled by theories instead of by practical human needs and immediate desire of fellowship. The promoters of this scheme knew next to nothing of agriculture - being chiefly bootmakers, ironworkers, opticians, and the like - and naturally were ready to dogmatise in proportion to their ignorance: and in a very short time they were hurling anathemas at each other's heads; peace and fraternity were turned into missiles and malice; the wives entered into the fray; and the would-be garden of Eden became such a scene of confusion that Ruskin had to send down an ancient retainer of his (with a pitchfork instead of a flaming sword) to bar them all out."

Edward Carpenter (quoted by Dennis Hardy.)

The scheme had caused dissension from the start, with some trustees of the Guild resigning when Ruskin announced the plans in 1876 to purchase the 13-acre farm at a cost of £1200 for the good workmen of Sheffield. However for some ten years it was the Guild's best attempt `to make some small piece of English ground, beautiful, peaceful and fruitful'. In a pattern that has repeated itself ever since in countless land settlement schemes the length & breadth of the country, the Totley Colonists struggled against the odds of poor quality land, lack of agricultural skills, crop failures due to the hostile climate and disagreement as to how best to run the Colony. Ruskin was blamed for not checking the quality of the land beforehand. It was described as a wasteland that had been neglected by the previous tenants. He was also blamed for not carrying out any selection of the colonists. That the colony lasted nearly ten years however, says something of the tenacity of those involved. One final attempt was made to salvage something from the project with Ruskin sending his head gardener from Brantwood to try and set up a Botanical Gardens to show `the best methods of managing fruit-trees in the climate of northern

England…..' This in turn was abandoned and the farm sold to the Pearson family who ran it as as a commercial nursery. It is known to this day as St George's Farm.

As much as his views on art, Ruskin's thoughts on social issues would affect a whole generation of artists and radicals alike. He was instrumental in starting the work of Octavia Hill, lending her the funds to buy her first house in London's East End. William Morris declared that art would have been impossible without him; Gandhi claimed that his life was changed by reading Ruskin; Proust would translate his works into French and Tolstoy would describe him as;

"One of those rare men who think with their hearts, and so he thought and said not only what he himself had seen and felt, but what everyone will think and say in future."

RUSKIN TENNESSE

In 1893 a socialist paper, The Coming Nation, appeared in Indiana, USA., closely modelled on Ruskins Fors Clavigera. It was the brainchild of Julius Wayland and soon had 50,000 subscribers. In a much more accessible style than Ruskin, Wayland promoted grassroots socialist ideas alongside adverts for books by Marx & Engels, as well as excerpts from Ruskin's writings. The paper also carried plans for Wayland's workers' utopia -

"a co-operative commonwealth colony, his town would have no rich, no poor, no judge, no saloon, no church, no idler; where labour would be king and where each was for all and all for each."

The Dickson Herald Fact Book 1994.

The colony was to be supported by sales of The Coming Nation and goods produced in the community. Wayland hoped to found the Ruskin Press at the colony to publish socialist books and pamphlets. Members would be expected to work a 9 hour day in exchange for a basic wage for everyone (including children) and the provision of free healthcare, food and shelter.

In 1894 inspired by Wayland's writings, people flocked to Ruskin, his community on 1,000 acres he had purchased near Tennessee City. The first colonists lived in tents whilst building 30 cottages and a 3 storey community building known as Commonwealth House - which housed a communal dining room, meeting rooms, a hotel, a theatre, nursery, bookstore, and library. The land at this site proved to be poor for agriculture and the community moved to the village of Cave Mills near Yellow Creek. Here they bought the entire village with houses, barns, a post office, blacksmith's shop, general store and grist mill, as well as outlying farms along with a large cave that gave the village its name, and which the colonists used as a natural cold store. To these basic buildings the community added a school, a bakery, a cafe, a steam laundry, a cannery and a number of workshops, where they produced a variety of household goods such as suspenders, leather belts, Ruskin chewing gum and a patent medicine called 'Ruskin Ready Remedy'.

For a number of years the community prospered with an economy based on agriculture, horticulture and small cottage industries. At its peak in 1897, Ruskin had some 250 members, some seventy-five buildings, 1,800 acres of land and assets totalling $100,000. The small town had a thriving cultural life with a town band and orchestra, theatrical group, lectures and art exhibitions. One contemporary observer remarked that Ruskin had all "the essential elements of a prosperous and thriving town (where) ostensibly, the principles of socialism were resoundingly successful." Built by ordinary working people without the help of an architect, or the benefit of wealthy patrons, the simple vernacular buildings of the town would have met with Ruskin's approval, but it is unlikely that he would have approved of the variety of machinery used by the colonists. Wayland invited Ruskin to visit his namesake town. Being too ill to travel Ruskin sent an autographed copy of his complete works in his place. The town's prosperity was not without its casualties and political divisions. Wayland himself had been forced to leave in 1895 accused of 'excessive individualism' and an argument over voting rights for the wives of new members eventually led to the break up of the colony in 1899.

LOOKING BACKWARDS FROM NOWHERE

In the late 19th century two visions of utopia did battle for the popular and particularly the socialist imagination, as illustrated in the two most widely read and influential utopian stories of the time, Looking Backward and News From Nowhere.

FROM CRADLE TO GRAVE

Looking Backward 2000-1887, by the American Edward Bellamy, published in 1888, depicted a state-managed capitalist utopia which through a bloodless and gradual revolution had transformed America. In the new model America, depicted by Bellamy, everyone is conscripted into the 'industrial army' until they retire at 45 to live a life of leisure until they are 80 or 90. Army recruits take care of all jobs including domestic work, freeing women from domestic slavery. Each family lives in elegant private rooms, and eats exquisite a la carte fare in communal dining-houses. Everything is paid for by credit card - cash having been abolished. Each year everyone's card is credited with his or her share of the nation's annual product. Goods are ordered from 'sample stores' - huge luxury malls with fountains, frescoes and statues where all goods are displayed. To purchase an item that you desire you simply fill in an order form and the goods are delivered directly from the warehouse to your apartment through 'electric tubes'. This consumer utopia has been made possible by advanced use of machinery, with such technical advances as 'music by telephone'. With each citizen having an equality of spending power, crime against property has been almost eradicated and along with it most of the legal profession.

Bellamy had abandoned a career in law to become a journalist & writer. He had a fascination with military discipline reflecting his upbringing in post-Civil War America and this and his lifelong struggle with ill health all come out in his vision. He gave voice to a collectivist vision where 'the nation guarantees the nurture, education and comfortable maintenance of every citizen from the cradle to the grave'. This was a reaction against the nineteenth-century individualism of Romantics. He preached instead a religion of solidarity, where `All men who do their best, do the same' and salvation is to be reached by becoming part of the egalitarian masses. Looking Backwards struck a chord with many people being widely read and translated into all major languages, including Russian, Bulgarian and Arabic. It became the manifesto of the Nationalist Movement in America, inspiring the formation of the People's Party, and was seen as an authoritative picture of what socialism would be like.

ORGANISED WITH A VENGEANCE

Some however did not greet Bellamy's vision with much enthusiasm. "(He) conceives of the change to socialism as taking place without any breakdown of (modern) Life, or indeed disturbance of it, by means of the final development of the great private monopolies which are such a feature of the present day. He supposes that these must necessarily be transformed into one great monopoly which will include the whole people and be worked for the benefit of the people . . …The great change having thus peaceably and fatalistically taken place, the author has put forward his scheme of the organisation of life; which is organised with a vengeance...."

William Morris Commonweal Jan 22 1889.

Morris's counterblast vision, News from Nowhere serialised in Commonweal used the same technique as Looking Backward, of the present day dreamer waking up in the future, but Morris's future was in sharp contrast to Bellamy's. Waking to find himself in London, some 150 years after a violent revolution had overthrown capitalism in 1952, Morris's hero is guided through the streets of a regenerated city to the house of the historian, old Hammond, who proceeds to answer his questions on the new life and how it was attained. London by now is a green city, Kensington is wooded, blackbirds sing in Piccadilly, salmon abound in the Thames and Trafalgar Square has become an apricot orchard. Hammond outlines how the Federation of Combined Workers took over after the ruling class had tried to cling to power through a military government. Following a popular uprising the country was re-organised through decentralised neighbourhood councils, or motes, with central government withering away, along with the law courts, police, military and prisons. All were no longer necessary following the abolition of private property.

THE CLEARING OF MISERY

The towns had been regenerated in a program known as 'The Clearing of Misery', an event that is still celebrated 150 years later. 'On that day we have music and dancing, and merry games and happy feasting on the site of some of the worst of the old slums, the traditional memory of which we have kept. On that occasion the custom is for the prettiest girls to sing some of the old revolutionary songs, and those which were the groans of the discontented once so hopeless, on the very spots where those terrible crimes of class-murder were committed day by day for so many years.'

The slums were replaced by neo-historical style buildings with ample gardens & surrounding green space, the best old buildings have been preserved or restored, except for the Houses of Parliament which have been turned into a 'Dung Market'. The slum dwellers repopulated the countryside, leading to the decentralisation of services and healing the age-old rift between town & country. Meanwhile the open spaces and 'wastes' have been protected for all to enjoy. In the new socialist society relations between the sexes have been transformed; marriage being a matter of choice and divorce disappearing along with other property disputes. Women's emancipation is taken for granted, though Morris seems to think that women given free choice would choose to stay at home in domestic bliss. Later however we do meet a female construction worker carving panels for a new house.

Contrary to later opinion Morris's utopia, whilst retro-medieval in appearance, was not anti-technology. Hammond points out that 'All work which it would be irksome to do by hand is done by immensely improved machinery'. 'Force' barges ply their way up and down the Thames carrying goods from small craft workshops and water powered mills that line the banks of the river. This shows Morris as being more concerned about the control of technology and its effects on the dignity of labour, rather than being simply anti-machine. The story recasts Morris's own experiences often with subtle jokes at his own expense, ending with a journey up the Thames to Morris's own house at Kelmscott, where during an idyllic harvest festival the dream fades and the hero finds himself back in the poverty & degradation of the 19th century.

"if others can see it as I have seen it, then it may be called a vision rather that a Dream."

Last line of *News from Nowhere.*

These two very different visions of a socialist future enthused their followers in turn; Bellamy's being embraced by the Fabians in Britain and informing the early Labour Party; Morris's altogether more romantic vision inspiring generations of artists, craftworkers and simple-life dreamers. And whilst few have heard of *Looking Backwards, News from Nowhere* is still in print a century later.

Endeavours towards

William Morris, (1834-1898) perhaps best known now for his wallpaper designs, though in his lifetime he was thought of most highly by the public as a poet who dabbled in other things - and dabble he did. His legendary work rate and breadth of interest and imagination led him to work in many fields; interior design, furniture making, tapestry work, dyeing, embroidery, architecture, stained glass, tiling, painting, illustration, book design, typography & printing. And although his writings and work inspired a whole generation of architects and craftsmen, not to say utopian dreamers and ordinary men & women, he himself never attempted to set up a community based on his ideals. He was tempted on a number of occasions. At The Red House at Bexleyheath, built for Morris by the architect Phillip Webb, he had planned to extend the house into a quadrangle and even commissioned drawings when it looked like fellow artist Edward Burne-Jones and his family would come and join him. Later when looking for a site to set up the workshops for Morris & Co he scouted the the half-deserted Cotswold village of Blockley with the view to setting up an Arts & Crafts based community at the abandoned silk mill there. He was persuaded against the move by his business partners, something he later regretted. He set up at Merton Abbey, near Wimbeoldon instead. Finally, in the later years of his life at Kelmscott, (the house he rented on the upper reaches of the Thames), he would hold gatherings of political and artistic colleagues who would plot the creation of a new world. Among those who gathered in the Thames-side drawing room was the elderly Owenite E.T. Craig, veteran of Ralahine and the Chartist agitation. At the end Morris proclaimed a sort of Marxist-based anarchism that ruled out setting up ideal communities until after the revolution.

Others saw no need to wait for the revolution and inspired by Morris set about reorganising existing society. The Guild of Handicraft which opened its doors in Whitechapel in 1888 was the brainchild of a young architect Charles Robert Ashbee. Whilst a trainee at the office of architect G.F.Bodley, and living at Toynbee Hall, Ashbee

Frontpiece to Ashbee's book on the Guild showing Essex House, Mile End Rd, London.

was influenced not only by the ideas of Morris & Ruskin, but also met Edward Carpenter, philosopher of the simple life and proponent of `homogenic love'. The Guild grew out of lectures Ashbee gave on Ruskin to the 'BWM', his shorthand for the British Working Man. Frustrated by the well-intentioned philanthropy of Toynbee Hall "neither a college, convent nor a club" he conceived of a more practical experiment, a craft 'co-operative' modelled on English Medieval Guilds, where skilled craftsmen working by the principles of Ruskin & Morris would not only produce hand-crafted goods, but also run a school for young apprentices. The idea was greeted with great enthusiasm by almost everyone except Morris himself, who was by now deeply involved in promoting revolutionary socialism. In an attempt to win his support Ashbee declared, "look I am going to forge a weapon for you;- and thus I too work for you in the overthrow of society", to which Morris replied, " The weapon is too small to be of any Value."

Ashbee, like Morris before him was a rich boy turned revolutionary. His mother came from a wealthy Jewish family in Hamburg and his father was a senior partner in a London law firm. Despite Morris's discouragement Ashbee pushed on with both the Guild & School of Handicrafts opening in rooms at Toynbee Hall on June 23rd 1888. The venture was a surprise success and shortly moved to larger premises on the top floor of a nearby warehouse and then onto a rather grand Georgian house in Mile End Road and open a shop in the West End to sell the Guild's goods. At Essex House the Guild carried out carpentry, carving, cabinet making and decorative painting. A smithy was built in the garden and metalwork, silverwork & jewellery were added to

the Guild trades. Ashbee's success in Whitechapel was based partly on his own developing architecture practice, with the guild providing the furniture, fixtures and fittings for a growing number of commissions. Other factors contributing to the success were no doubt the contact with the wealthy patrons of Toynbee Hall and the success of other young Arts & Crafts architects, supplied by the Guild. A lively social life was established at the Guild with programmes of lectures, and Guild suppers, where the men sang songs and acted in masques. An Essex House cricket XI was formed and a number of country cottages were acquired to which the guildsmen would cycle for weekend breaks and short holidays.

ARTS & CRAFTS INTERNATIONAL

Inspired by the Guilds example, and the British Arts & Crafts movement in general, others made attempts to emulate them throughout Europe and America. Following a visit to Morris's workshop at Merton Abbey in 1895 the American Elbert Hubbard founded the Roycroft community at East Aurora, New York. Hubbard was considered something of a conman. However his community survived until the depression of the 1930s producing an extensive line of crafts and providing its workers with decent housing and recreational facilities. Somewhat better thought of was the work of Gustav Stickley. Initially inspired by seeing Shaker furniture exhibited at the 1876 Centennial Show in Philadelphia, Stickley would go on to become one of the leading Arts & Crafts practitioners in the US, developing a distinctive America style known as 'Mission Furniture'. Stickley did not believe in a slavish adherence to handworking and used machines in an attempt to produce what he called 'democratic' furniture that was affordable to a wide range of customers. To a certain extent he was successful in this. Where others relied on rich patrons Stickley managed to reach a wide audience through his influential magazine, The Craftsman and through extensive use of mail-order catalogues. In 1898 he established workshops at Syracuse organised on Guild lines and renamed his company The United Craftsmen. Later plans to establish a community and model farm in New Jersey failed after the company went bankrupt following the purchase of a skyscraper in New York.

One of Ashbee's commissions led directly to the formation of a community at Darmstadt in Germany. Following work by Baille Scott & Ashbee to the palace of the Grand Duke of Hesse, the Duke sponsored the building of a series of artist studios and houses on his estate.

'Troy Type' used for publications by the Kelmscott Press. Designed by William Morris.

'Alphabet of Pinks' inspired by the flowers that grew in the garden of Essex House. Used in Essex House Press Publications. Designed by C.R.Ashbee.

Typeface designed by the Architect C.F.A Voysey from *A Book of Alphabets.* By E. Strange. 1906

Edward Johnston's Type face designed for the London Underground.

Meanwhile back in Britain Schools of Handicraft and Guilds were proliferating across the country. Schools had been set up in Birmingham, Glasgow, Edinburgh & Dublin. A friend of Ashbee, Godfrey Blount set up The Haslemere Peasant Industries in 1896 in Surrey. It was an umbrella organisation for a number of small craft workshops employing local skilled labour. Blount and his wife Ethel Hine were concerned with reviving local craft traditions and included weaving & embroidery alongside the by-now-standard crafts of woodwork, metalwork, bookbinding & handprinting. Their aim was; `the revival of a true country life where handicrafts and the arts of husbandry shall exercise body and mind and express the relation of man to earth and to the fruits of earth'.

WOMEN'S WORK

At the peak his success in Whitechapel in 1898 Ashbee married Janet Forbes, an accomplished musician who would bring a female dimension to the Guild's so-far-male, comradely atmosphere. Janet Ashbee would take an active role in the working of the guild; the Ashbee's marriage being a remarkably 'equal' partnership. Women were involved in the Arts & Crafts movement not only in traditional female crafts like weaving & embroidery, but also others such as bookbinding, with a Guild of Women Bookbinders being based in London. Mary Watts, wife of the painter G.F. Watts, directed a women's pottery guild at the Compton pottery. In the USA a successful women artists' community, Cogslea, was founded by Violet Oakley. At Ditchling in Sussex Ethel Mairet pioneered new weaving designs. Gertrude Jekyll, the garden designer & writer carried out much of her work in conjunction with Arts & Crafts architects. And May Morris, having worked alongside the old man himself, went on to produce original embroidery works of her own, becoming a figurehead for

---

TYPE FACE :

The tradition of the architect designing every last detail of a house was almost invented by the Arts & Crafts Movement - right down to the lettering on the nameplate. The Central School of Handicrafts in London ran an illumination and calligraphy class. The tutor was Edward Johnston who later designed the clear and precise type used by

craftswomen in England and leading to the setting up in 1907 of the Women's Art Guild.

In 1901 with a string of successful commissions behind it and an increasingly international reputation for its work the Guild of Handicrafts was facing the expiry of its lease on Essex House. A search was started for new premises conducive to 'good honest craftsmanship'. After looking for suitable properties close at hand in Bow, South Byfleet, Fulham, Chelsea, Ruislip & Harrow, Ashbee started to consider moving out to the country. A watermill at Sawbridge in Kent, possible buildings at Letchworth, the old silk mill at Blockley that Morris had looked at 20 years before were all considered. All were forgotten though on the 'discovery' of the run-down Cotswold market town of Chipping Campden. On offer in this sleepy agricultural backwater were empty buildings for workshops and schools, cottages available to let all in a picturesque quasi-medieval setting almost straight from the pages of News from Nowhere. Ashbee convinced himself that Chipping Campden offered an opportunity to fulfil his ambitions. However, whilst he was in effect the leader, the Guild had a democratic structure and the Guildsmen had to make the decision to move from the East End of London to the Cotswolds themselves. An 'official' visit by Ashbee and the foremen from each department of the Guild went well. A few of the men cycled over to see what they might be letting themselves in for. The craftsmen were by no means all in favour of the move, being split on workshop lines with the mainly-unionised carpenters and metal workers in favour and the un-unionised jewellers against. In the end the vote was 2 to 1 in favour of the move. On hearing the result of the vote Ashbee wrote in his journal;

" I am glad to think that the men themselves have decided on the whole it is better to leave Babylon and go home to the land."

Initial letter alphabet designed by Herbert Horne for the Century Guilds *Hobby Horse* magazine.

Perhaps the most widely used of the Utopian Fonts, 'Gill Sans', one of a number of typefaces designed by Eric Gill.

Decorative initials from The Prayer Book of King Edward VII Designed by C.R. Ashbee. for Essex House Press

Lettering designed by the Scottish architect Charles Rennie Mackintosh

the London Underground. One of the pupils there was the young Eric Gill whose later 'Gill Sans' typeface changed the face of modern printing. When first unveiled it was described as 'typological Bolshevism' but very quickly became popular, Gill most famously being commissioned to use it for the lettering on the Flying Scotsman. This book's body text is set in Gill Sans and the commentary sections in perpetua.

The Song of the Builders of the City of the Sun.

Comrades, our city of the sun!
A quest unfound, a joy unwon;
Ay, here in England shall it rise
Beneath her grey and solemn skies.
Far in her golden past, or far
Ahead where her Utopias are,
For hearts that feel and souls that find
Their inner life within the mind,
The inner life yet scarce begun,
Here stands our city of the sun!

C.R. Ashbee

Chipping Campden School of Handicrafts.
Woodcut by E.H. New. 1905

The journey from Mile End Road to Chipping Campden appeared to some of the men as a journey from the dawn of the 20th century back to the closing of the 16th century. What had been an affluent market town made prosperous by the wool merchants of the 1400s was by Ashbee's day a somewhat sleepy rural backwater, little changed since Sir Baptist Hicks had burnt down Campden House to stop it falling into Cromwell's hands during the Civil War. The picturesque stone buildings and air of semi-dereliction fitted the Guild's own mythology of a revival of a lost mediaeval England so well that they were unable to see their arrival as part of a ongoing cycle of rural depression and revival, the town not being quite as sleepy as was made out.

The arrival of some 150 Eastenders did however have a significant impact on the small town. The Guild moved out to the country over a number of months, workshop after workshop being installed one at a time into the Old Silk Mill now renamed Essex House. On the ground floor went the Essex House Press, set up with the presses from Kelmscott acquired on Wiliam Morris's death. Alongside the press were the drawing offices and showrooms. On the floor above went the jewellers and on the top floor the carpentry workshop, with the blacksmith's shop being set up in the yard. The mill was set in its own garden and orchard and had installed the first electric lighting in the town. A 'Hall of Residence' was established for the single men in Braithwaite House and various cottages were rented for those with families. Ashbee took a house in the centre of town renaming it somewhat grandly the Woolstaplers Hall.

Apart from a few of the men who grew homesick and returned to London the guildsmen thrived in the town. Almost as soon as they had settled in, visitors started to arrive curious to see this little island of utopia in the English countryside. The locals on the other hand didn't quite know what to make of this invasion from the metropolis: in the first place some were openly hostile with local shopkeepers overcharging the newcomers and others resentful at having been evicted from their homes to make way for higher-paying outsiders. The wages paid by the Guild were always more than the local agricultural wage. The local gentry in their turn didn't quite know what to make of the Ashbees. Were they the proprietors of this new enterprise on their doorstep or not? Relations would become easier as the years passed and the Guildsmen became involved with the life of the town. As in the East End a range of social activities were arranged by and for the men and their families. These were generally open to the local inhabitants, and ranged from the regular plays and lectures put on at Elm Tree House, to the Cotswold School of Handicraft which ran classes in cookery, woodwork, gardening, music and keep-fit. Much to the amazement of the town the 'lazy' village lads were organised by one of the men into a Harriers running club and later the Guild would build an open-air swimming pool for the town. And swimming would feature in the annual summer sports alongside football, hockey and cricket matches. Local people played in the townband set up and led by one of the Londoners.

Two of the numerous visitors to Campden during this time were none other than the grand architects of Fabian socialism Sidney & Beatrice Webb, who had taken a nearby cottage whilst engaged in writing their epic history of local government. The irony of the Webbs writing on municipal state-run socialism in the midst of his rural arcadia was not lost on Ashbee who was highly amused by their visit. Another visitor was Ashbee's old mentor Edward Carpenter who came to give a lecture on Small Holdings and Life on the Land. In many ways the comradeship of the Guild with its genial company of young men enjoying themselves together came close to achieving Carpenter's ideal of 'homogenic' love between men, which was based on Ashbee's own barely-concealed homosexuality, which both he and his wife Janet came to terms with remarkably well, given that these were the years after the Oscar Wilde trial.

ANGELS ARE CHEAP TODAY

Although the Guild produced some of its best work during the Campden years, financially some departments had been experiencing difficulties since they arrived. The jewellers and silversmith had been struggling against competition from semi-machine-made methods of other firms in London and Birmingham who produced goods much cheaper, and which to the customers' eyes were identical to the Guild's pieces. For the first time in its history the Guild as a whole recorded a loss in 1905. Trade had been low, with some men having been on short time during the year. There had been a general slump in trade that affected many independent craftsmen, not just the Guild, though the distance between Campden and the Guild customers was thought to have contributed to the loss of work. The Guild took the loss in its stride and carried on much as before, though belts were somewhat tightened and attempts made to be more competitive. The following year after poor sales of a hand-printed Bible the Essex House Press was forced to wind up: whilst the financial impact of closing the press was small, the symbolic loss of William Morris's printing machinery was great. The following years balance sheet, although not as bad as the previous showed

Guild workshops the Old Silk Mill
Chipping Campden 1904

another loss. The Guild was now on the brink of bankruptcy. Whilst it struggled on into the next year the measures to save it became increasingly desperate until finally it went into voluntary liquidation and was forced to sell its stock to pay its debts.

Critics pointed to its utopian idealism as the root of its demise, but the Guild was sunk largely by the competition of machine made replicas available in such shops as Heals and Liberty's. The Guild had lasted in one form or another for some 21 years: no mean achievement for an experiment in workplace democracy and community building. Many of the Guildsmen stayed on in the Cotswolds; some of them taking up the offer of American soap magnate Joseph Fels who bought 70 acres to be divided into small holdings in neighbouring Broad Campden. In 1909 a less formal and looser Guild was set up by those men still working in the area.

In the later part of his career Ashbee developed his ideas on Arts & Crafts, influenced by his friendship with the American architect Frank Lloyd Wright: ideas he expressed in his book, *Where the great city stands* published in 1917, in which he outlined his hopes for post war society. It contained plans for a co-operative Garden City at Ruislip. From 1917 to 1923 he worked in the Middle East, latterly in Palestine for the British Military Government, where he took over from Patrick Geddes the somewhat daunting task of quite literally building a new Jerusalem; an appointment that did not last, as Ashbee, though Jewish, was apparently stubbornly pro-Arab.

Others would establish craft-based communities but never on the scale achieved at Chipping Campden. Edward Barnsley and Earnest Gimson created a loose community of craftsmen around their workshop at Sapperton. Members of the Scottish Arts & Crafts Movement were intrumental in the founding of a homesteading scheme at Stirling in 1909. Craftwork and the revival of 'traditional' crafts has played a significant and continuing role in utopian experiments and back to the land movements right up to the present day. Chipping Campden still looks much the same as it did in the days of the Guild and the Old Silk Mill still houses craftworkers along with a small museum of the Guild of Handicrafts.

COTSWOLD CO-OPERATIVE HANDICRAFTS

Guest Article By
JOY THACKER

This article is reprinted from Joy's book: *Whiteway Colony*

'...........It was an interesting day. We found here people who seem to be 'back to the land' in grim earnest. 'Tis all very uncouth and experimental. In the cabins are pianos, books, machine made chairs and tables and other of the unearned incrementa of civilization, protesting as it were against this half-hearted return to barbarism.'

C.R. Ashbee on Whiteway

Whilst Ashbee's views of the Tolstoyian Anarchist Colony at Whiteway were unsympathetic. Some of the colonists were inspired to emulate the Arts & Crafts movement and establish their own Craft Guild. Joy Thacker a current member of Whiteway and community historian tells the tale.

Edward and Beatrice Adams were two of Whiteway's earliest settlers, coming in 1906. Bea originated from Hanley Staffordshire but moved to Leicester on her marriage to Ted. He was a dispensing chemist, owning a shop in Bradford, but decided to make the move to Whiteway after a visit. They came with their one-year-old daughter Irene, and stayed firstly at Whiteway House and then Woodcot with Walter and Mary, while they were building their home. It was a building with an upper storey, but known as The Bungalow.

They were still at Woodcot when their second daughter Winnifred was born. Ted was frequently away from home, due to his business commitments, and to supplement their income Bea joined the paying guest brigade. She became successful almost overnight, and soon her home was too small to accommodate all those who wished to stay with her. A year later another hut was built by Fred Foster in her garden for the overflow This was known as The Guest House. Later years it earned the names of The Wigwam, and Dear Old Place or DOP.

In 1921, Bea and her daughters visited the Holt Colony near Cromer in Norfolk, in order to learn leather work. While there an arrangement was made with some of its members, to form a Handicraft Guild, and several Holt Colonists agreed to come to live at Whiteway for this very purpose. Bea purchased a redundant hut from RAF Quedgeley and had it erected by the roadside, a few yards away from her house. This was to serve as the Guild's workshop. When the former Holt Colonists arrived, they were allocated plots of land and proceeded to build dwellings for themselves.

Stanley Randolph, whose craft was sandal making and Rose Rogers with family connections in Sheepscombe were granted an acre of Peter Howarth's land, near

Bea Adams weaving

Sinclair's cowshed. On this they put two circular corrugated irom huts connected by a covered way one was used for living and the other for sleeping.

Basil and Mary Robert also came equipped. On yet another of Peter's acres, near the road, they erected the hut which they had brought alomg with them, used as a weaving shed when at Holt. To this was added a canvas awning which served as their kitchen. Basil was an accounts clerk but worked at both weaving and leather craft. They were joined by other Whiteway craftsmen, each of whom brought their own particular skills to the Guild. A meeting was held at Bea's on 15 November to discuss the new venture, with Stanley taking the minutes. The main objective was, of working together in a mutually helpful manner, both to consolidate what degrees of efficiency and usefulness could be separately reached by common council and action to extend the same. The potential members were: Bea, Irene and Winifred Adams who worked in leather, Mary and Basil Robert also leather workers, Nellie Morand with knitting and her husband Marcel with his wrought iron and embossed metal work, together with Rose Rogers and Stanley Randolph, sandal makers. There was another leather worker, Kathleen Keene, and Kay contributed his craft of woodworking, which he did from his carpentry shop built to the end of the Adams' workshop.

A bank account was opened in the name of the Cotswold Handicrafts and note paper was printed. At another meeting a week later the pricing of completed articles was discussed, with the outcome that all members should provide their own materials and equipment, and ensure that all expenses, including time and labour, were taken into consideration in the selling price. A fund was also established. This was the Common Fund, from which expenses incurred by the guild as a whole could be drawn, including such things as advertising, writing paper, books and exhibitions. To set the ball rolling, everyone loaned ten shillings, but it was expected that when production began properly and the items were sold, this fund would be self-supporting, because two and a half percent of their sales would be fed into it. Nothing was to be sold privately, all was to be sold through the guild. In all it took over a year to get things in order. During that time, consideration was given to extending membership to enthusiastic unskilled applicants, and consequently Stormont was admitted as a trainee leather worker.

The pricing of goods and rates for labour were a problem at the start, as there was no previous experience to draw upon, but finally it was thought best to have a three-month trial to see how things progressed and then fix a rate. This proved a wise move, for when this period

Basil instructing Rosemary Randolf & Dedee Morand

was up, it was simplicity itself to divide the sales money by the combined hours worked, and so set the rate for all, everyone being treated equally. As the months passed it became clear that it might be more beneficial if each craft had a fund apart from that of the Common Fund, especially for its own needs, so that any costs involving their tools and materials would be covered. By completion of the first year of the Cotswold Co-operative Handicrafts Guild, the total sales of the leather workers amounted to £305.

All members had undertaken other essential duties within the Guild in addition to their normal ones, all vital to ensure smooth running. There was ordering, designing and pattern making, cutting and making up, packing and pricing, checking and dispatching, tooling and staining, stock taking, treasurer's and secretary's work, the rates, taxes and upkeep of the workshop to provide for, and exhibitions to arrange. These were held anywhere from Cheltenham to York, from Newcastle upon Tyne to The Draper's Hall in London.

When the exhibition was held in London, those visitors who came to view the crafts showed more interest in these strange Whiteway people they had heard about, than the crafts they exhibited, and reports appeared in the Daily Chronicle and other newspapers here and abroad. Headed 'How the Colony Began', the 11 November issue reports on an interview with Ray,

a sort of picturesque young giant you expect to meet only in childish fiction. He has long hair and a big beard; he wears sandals and homespun, and a blue shirt open at the neck. His appearance in the street of stockbrokers was sufficiently arresting to cause wonder. . . .He told me some things about the Cotswold Co-operative Handicrafts Colony - the free life, `free' marriages, the entire absence of law and authority - that made me yearn for fuller information. A description follows of a visit made later by the reporter to Whiteway with general background on its formation, Through avenues of beech and larch we drove to the roof of Gloucestershire, and then, on either side of a by-road, came suddenly upon bungalows and shacks, wonderfully variegated, and apparently dumped down haphazard over an area of 40 odd acres. It was like stumbling on a

No-Mans-Land of civilization. Gassy was chosen to be visited. The reporter states, I found another bearded, sandalled man of striking appearance. Books were open on the table, which was covered with a cloth of fine sacking . . . We sat for more than an hour in the room of that centrally heated frugally furnished shack, its walls lined with bookshelves and adorned by handicraft ornaments. Gassy explained to him how in the Guild and the Workshops, the people work together happily There is no boss. We call the workshops

The Randolph huts

Snip, Snap, Snob, Chip and Co. Snip is the tailor, Snap is the photographer, Snob is the sandal man, and Chip is the carpenter. We send our goods to art shops, and if a visitor wants a suit of clothes, the weavers weave the cloth, and Snip makes it up. Then he went to see Sudbury Protheroe `who lives next door to the Bakery over which he exercises a benevolent supervision: Sud was the one member of the colony he met who was not fantastically dressed. He was sitting by a log fire in dress shoes and smart riding breeches, and looked more like a MFH resting after a hard day with the hounds than a member of this strange colony. He told how few people leave Whiteway. `We try to be manuals and intellectuals, but we can realise that only in a certain measure.

This article caused countless people to write to Kathleen Keene, the colony secretary, enquiring about the possibility of coming to live on this small piece of land

where a few lucky people were living a simple uncompli-
cated idyllic life. Most stressed their love of their fellow
man, their conversion to vegetarianism and briefly, towards
the end, their lack of money and inability to work too hard
due to poor health. In June 1924, Stormont and Kathleen
withdrew from the Guild, Kathleen preferring instead to
devote her time to her Tea Shop business. Soon, Winnie and
Bea took up hand weaving instead of their customary
leather work, with Rene joining them a short while after.

Four years after its conception, in March 1926,
Basil and Rene were the only ones working full-time, with
Winnie, Mary and Fred Large's daughter Mabel working as
part-timers. Ibrahim Ismail from Somaliland or Salah, joined
the Art leather workers where he learned book binding
under Basil's capable wing, and Bert Mardell joined the Art
leather group as wholesale salesman. By 1927 it was felt
that a change should be made partly due to Bea needing
more space in the workshop for her own family's weaving,
so Basil built himself a workshop on his land by the road
for his leather work. Everyone who had used Bea's workshop over the years combined together to replace the
roofing, creosote the exterior walls and paint the windows,
so leaving it clean and tidy for the weavers to carry on their
work.

So ended the Co-operative Handicrafts Guild on
7 July 1930. In 15 Basil and Mary allowed their former
workshop to be converted into a home by Joy their daughter and her husband, Peter Evans. It became known as The
Makins. `Because it has the makin's of a fine home'. Peter is
a carpenter making fine furniture and Joy a carver. Alan
their son is an artist metalsmith, and has a forge next to his
father's carpentry shop. Marvellous examples of his work
can be viewed countrywide, with one of the earliest being
in our capital, when he designed and made the gates for St
Paul's Cathedral Treasury. He was awarded this commission
after winning the Crafts Council Competition. His early
years were influenced by Ernest Gimson and Sidney
Barnsley who were members of the Sapperton Arts and
Crafts Movement, close by. Alan's inspiration comes from
his emotional reaction to the area in which the job he is
commissioned to do is situated. As with the early craft
movement, his successes have been demonstrated in exhibitions and magazine articles. He also has the advantage of
television and wide media coverage unavailable to his predecessors.

Joy Robert carving

This article is an extract from:
WHITEWAY COLONY :The Social
History of a Tolstoyan Community.
By Joy Thacker. Sutton Publishing 1993.
Available from the Author:
Fairhaven, Whiteway. Glous.

Following blue arrows

If you walked through the Fontainebleau Forest 40 miles south of Paris in the late 1830s, every so often, painted on a tree you would come across a blue arrow. If you walked in the direction it pointed you would find another and so on and on, leading you deep into the old Royal Hunting Forest notorious for its bandits & snakes. No one knew what they were for. The Royal Foresters had seen a somewhat eccentric character wandering endlessly through the forest apparently doing no harm or committing any offence. Had they watched him at night they might have seen him venture out with paintpot and brush underneath his coat. He was Napoleonic War veteran, Claude Francois Denecourt, who having been finally invalided out of the army had (following a succession of odd jobs) ended up wandering through the forest following his particular vision. Single-handed he was inventing hiking. If you followed the arrows you would be led on a 10 kilometre woodland trail through the further reaches of the forest. A stunningly simple idea, but before Denecourt nobody had thought of it. He also published an *indicatuer,* a small guidebook to encourage visitors to the local chateau to venture out for a woodland promenade. As you made your way along the waymarked paths the guidebook would tell you of the folklore and myth of the forest and whilst guiding you to particular prominent trees, hidden caves and woodland glades tell you stories of the forests inhabitants and its historical connections. Not all these stories were necessarily based on fact. Not only did Denecourt fabricate some of the folklore, he also embellished the landscape itself, turning crevices into caves and caves into fabulous grottoes. The walks were an instant success - two years after their launch a second indicatuer was produced this time with Green, Orange & Yellow walks.

Artists had been drawn to Fontainebleau since the 1820s and Denecourt incorporated their painted views and later their studios into his walks. Theodore Rousseau was the first artist to settle in the forest at the small settlement of Barbizon in 1836 and others followed. In 1840 the railway reached Corbeil, an hour from the forest, and the whole enterprise took off. The trickle of 'open-air' tourists turned into a flood. Denecourt set up stall outside the station selling his guide books. The railway brought new artists down to paint the forest; the tourists bought their paintings and took them back to Paris, others saw the romantic views and booked their tickets .... a whole romantic forest enterprise was born; gift shops sold souvenirs, books, maps, juniper carvings, themed knickknacks and even 'scented forest water'. By the mid-1850s 150 kilometres of waymarked trail led to over a 1000 'explained' locations and by 1860 100,000 visitors a year were making their way along them.

By now known as the 'Barbizon school', the artists who had moved into the forest including American, Swiss and Belgian painters, had in effect become the first European artists' colony. In no small part, this had been made possible by the woodland walking industry that had grown up around them. They in turn considered Denecourt to have destroyed their romantic idyll by 'vulgarising' the forest.

In the 1870s a second generation of artists would venture to Fontainebleau amongst them a flamboyant Scotsman known to everyone as 'Bob'. Fairly typical, if a somewhat more colourful member of the new generation at Barbizon the young Scotsman was the archetypal aspiring Bohemian, eccentric in appearance and with a total disrespect for convention. He dressed in large striped socks, and wide brimmed hat, which along with his large black moustache gave him the appearance of a `Mexican vaquero'. He had studied in Paris before arriving in the forest and was an immediate hit with the circle of French & foreign artists who had settled there. Bob was joined by his younger cousin Robert Louis Stevenson who introduced himself to the painting colony as a 'writer chap'. Stevenson had been sent to France to convalesce by his Presbyterian family who were horrified when he fell in with his wayward cousin and feared the worse. But to the young writer the artists colony was a real taste of freedom after the repressive family background he grew up in and in the Bohemian atmosphere he would start to develop as a writer settling into a life of 'idle industriousness' and immersing himself in the daily life and drama of the colony that would provide material for his writing in years to come. In search of a place to swim the Stevensons and a few other English & American artists ventured to Grez-sur-Loing. An occasional artist had already settled in Grez and, taken by what they saw, the 'Anglais' decided to give the place a trial as their base. The pattern of life in the French artists' colonies centred around the inns where the artists lodged. Some took lodgings in the villages and rented studios, but all social life revolved around the inns, a number of whose matrons held legendary status among the artists and acted as surrogate mothers to some. At Grez the pattern of life also included women not just as matrons & models, but as artists. Robert Louis predicted that the entrance of women into their Eve-less paradise would be "the beginning of the end" and certainly for himself it proved to be true. 26 year old Louis fell in love with Fanny Osbourne, a Californian artist who had come to France with her 16 year old daughter and small son to escape an unhappy marriage. In a touch of romantic absurdity Fanny fell in love not with Louis but with Bob who was however infatuated by her daughter who was attracted to someone else. The romantic knot was eventually undone and Fanny became close to Louis.

By 1878 Louis was facing poverty having spent most of his advance from his family. Wanting to find a way to support Fanny & make her an 'honest woman', he broached his situation with his family. They were outraged - would their son never cease to shock? An American lover, with children, seeking divorce, whatever next? When the dust settled and little help was forthcoming Fanny felt she had no choice but to leave for America. The group that had turned Grez into a lively artists colony with the Stevenson cousins at its centre slowly broke up, some leaving through marriage, some like Bob just becoming bored with the place. Later Grez would become the haunt of a whole group of Scandinavian artists continuing as a colony up until the turn of the century.

Louis followed Fanny to America and they eventually married. As the writer of such books as *The Strange Case of Dr Jekyll & Mr Hyde* and *Kidnapped*, he would find acclaim, but he would never again find the freedom and joy

of life that he had found in the French forest.

The artists of Fontianebleau had established a new school of painting based on landscapes actually painted in the open air often with 'peasant' figures set in the landscape. This was in reaction to the previous dominant studio-based styles. This was part of a whole romanticising of the countryside that was going on at the time in reaction to the increasing industrialisation of life. Artists searched out idyllic landscapes populated with honest rural folk so they could capture a more 'truthful', but fading way of life. Ironically it was the advent of the railways that made these landscapes accessible, with most of the late 19th century artists' colonies being in easy reach by train.

THE WELSH ACADEMY

The LMNR Railway built a line along the Conwy Valley reaching Betws-y-Coed in 1868. Artists who had been working in the area during the previous 20 years viewed the approach of the age of steam into their quiet rural valley with some trepidation. They were about to become victims of their own successful vision. Back in 1856 Josiah Jenkins in a description of Betws had noted;

"English artists do not, like their brethren on the continent, form a class apart, and are not like them gregarious in their habits. English artists have no such places of rural rendezvous as the French meet with in the forest of Fontainebleau, at Barbizon. Perhaps the nearest approach to these continental assemblages which Great Britain affords, is at; Betwys, where "The Oak" occasionally shelters at one time ten or a dozen artists."

A generation of landscape painters, many from the North-West & the Midlands, had been drawn to the area after David Cox started to paint the rugged Welsh mountain scenery from 1844 on.

"What Walter Scott did for the Highlands, and Wordsworth for the Lake district, David Cox has done for Wales - attracting there not only the younger aspirants for artistic honours, but the admirers of wild, uncultivated, and picturesque scenery,....."

Josiah Jenkins

By the time the railway was built the village was a popular destination for summer painters and a number had already settled in the village. The advent of the train would bring artists, amateur and professional, in their droves. And hot on their heels followed the tourists seeking the picturesque scenery popularised by the paintings they had seen back in Manchester and Liverpool.

Artists arrive by train. Cartoon in The Graphic 1881

Artistic life in Betws developed along similar lines to that of the French colonies, and was centred on the pubs and inns in town, notably the Royal Oak. Later, artists would take lodgings with local farmers and rent local studios, finally building their own houses and forming their own club with clubhouse at Tal-y-bont. There is no record of what the Welsh inhabitants thought of these eccentric characters who had descended on them with their sombreros and beaver hats, but they were quick to see the opportunity afforded by the artistic immigrants and their tourist followers. Guesthouses sprang up throughout the village; all with English names, most with Welsh owners. Shops opened selling materials for artist and locals would hire themselves out as models. The artists would gather in the evenings or on rainy days around games of cards in the Royal Oak, where they would discuss art, life and the invasion of the tourists. They also organised concerts and dances for themselves and got together entertainments for charity.

The artists who came to Betws formed the core of what became the Royal Cambrian Academy of Art, which despite initially being made up of predominantly English artists was instrumental in fostering a distinctly Welsh artistic identity and Welsh art movement. A distinctive common

style or enveloping philosophy was never developed by the artists in the colony and by the 1890s they were geographically spread along the Conwy valley from Llandudno to Betws. This lack of a 'School' identity led to the eventual decline of the colony. Today Betws-y-Coed remains a tourist mecca, but little memory of the artists, to whom the area owes its original popularity, can be found among the mass-produced Welsh knick-knack souvenirs.

In contrast to the open-air painters were a group of painters that gathered in the small Kent town of Cranbrook. While their work was also a reaction to the increasing urbanisation and squalor of the industrial towns their portrayal of the countryside was much more romanticised than the open-air painters in part dictated by the views of the wealthy northern industrialists who bought their work. Once again it was the advent of the railway that opened up the countryside for the artists whilst still allowing easy access back to London. Cranbrook like Chipping Campden was a former prosperous wool town now in decline, presenting just the right image of the rural idyll for the painters and their clients. The first to arrive in 1853 was F.D. Hardy closely followed by his brother George and in succession Thomas Webster, J.C. Horsley, G.B. O'Neil and

A.E. Mulready. These six formed what became known as the Cranbrook Colony. They rented or purchased properties in the town to set up their studios and developed a loose and informal artistic community. They "were always paying and repaying social calls, dining and taking tea with one another, having large and noisy Christmas parties and, in hot Augusts and Septembers, endless games of croquet."

Andrew Greg.

Catalogue of the Cranbrook Colony Exhibition.

Using locals for models, and later each others families, although thy did not form their own particular style or school of painting their work is all of a recognisable genre, mostly staged portraits much influenced by earlier Dutch painting. Once they had found their niche in the Victorian art market they settled down to become a feature of the town for the later part of the 19th century and built up a body of work that mostly hangs now in municipal collections in the North and Midlands bequeathed by their wealthy benefactors.

Other enclaves of artists found the countryside in the South East conducive to their work, with small groups gathering around William Wells at Penshurst and Birket Foster at Witley in Surrey.

CIRCLES WITHIN CIRCLES

Not all gatherings of artists were in rural settings; the advantages of companionship of like minds, joint exhibitions and learning from each other were equally as true in London as in North Wales. As early as 1850 the Cosmopolitan Club was set up as a place where artists and writers could meet. Its members included painters George Fredrick Watts, Holman Hunt, John Millias & Frederic Leighton, actresses Kate & Terry Ellen and from the world of literature Ruskin, Trollope, Tennyson & Browning. This was followed by the Hogarth Club in 1858 which had more practical aims. Holman Hunt, one of the founders, describing it as 'a meeting place for artists and amateurs in sympathy with us', where they could 'use the walls for exhibiting our sketches and pictures to members and friendly visitors'. It organised four exhibitions, surviving until 1861 (first at 178 Piccadilly, then 6 Waterloo Place). Of its one hundred members, fifty had to be practising artists. Along with most of the members of the Cosmopolitan Club it attracted Ford Maddox Brown, Gabriel Rossetti, Edward Burne-Jones, William Morris and the architect William Burges, Val Prinsep, Stanhope Spencer, Robert Martineau, Michael Halliday and Clarence Whaite of the Betws-y-coed colony. Almost all were outside the Royal Academy and

THE ARTISTS RIFLES

One of the more surprising forms that these groupings of artists took was the formation of the Artists Rifle Volunteer Corps in 1860, formed along with numerous other volunteer battalions when the threat of invasion by Napoleon's forces seem imminent. The Corps' roll call sounds like a veritable Who's-Who of the Victorian art scene, including as it did; G.F. Watts, Frederic Leighton, John Everet Millais, Holman Hunt, Gabriel Rossetti, Walter Crane and William Morris. Drill took place in the gardens of Burlington House with volunteers expected to put in eight drills a month and to pay an annual membership fee of one guinea. Some quickly gave up attending, whilst others were quite simply incompetent, Hunt being notorious for losing the screws of his rifle, Rossetti disrupting proceedings by persistently querying orders and Morris, unable to tell his right from his left, apologising profusely on finding himself facing in the opposite direction to everyone else.

Not all the volunteers were well known artists. Walter Crane recalled a number of men signing up from the engraving firm where he worked and art lovers as well as artists joined in order to meet the artists socially on what might be termed 'a level battlefield'. The Artists Rifles did not see any active service until the Boer War, which given their level of competence was lucky for some. In 1947 when the Corps name was changed to the 21st SAS(Artists') Volunteers their reputed strength was put down to the 'Independence and irregularity' of its first volunteers.

would have regarded themselves as the avant-garde of the day. Out of the friendships made here grew the highly influential Pre-Raphaelite Brotherhood, and seven of its members went on to form Morris, Marshall, Faulkner & Co - later known simply as Morris & Co.

One of the wealthy patrons supporting this 'new wave' of artists was Sara Prinsep whose salon at her house in Holland Park would grow into a community of artists as Lady Holland released land on her estate for the building of a series of studio houses and studios. The first artist she supported was George Fredrick Watts who lived and worked from her own home, Little Holland House. Valentine Prinsep, Sara's son, was the first to build a studio house, I Holland Park Road, commissioned from the architect Phillip Webb shortly after he had finished building The Red House for William Morris. Even more than the house he built for Morris, Princep's house popularised Webb's work and the whole 'Queen Anne' style. With the interiors fitted out by Morris & Co it was featured in many of the style magazines of the day. 2 Holland Park Rd was built for Fredrick Leighton. It was Leighton's success and rise to eminence in the Victorian art world that sealed the success of the growing artistic community known since as the Holland Park Circle. Later when Melbury Road was built across the estate further studio houses were designed by the likes of William Burges and Norman Shaw.

"It is the funniest place in the world. Everybody is either a genius, or a poet, or a painter, or peculiar in some way; poor Miss Stephens says, 'Is there nobody commonplace?'"   Anne Thackery

By the late 1800s the Holland Park 'Avante Garde' had become the 'Old Guard', many having become members of the Royal Academy and Leighton himself being elevated to president. Surrounded by wealthy patrons the artists lived a comfortable life, their work in demand by the likes of William Lever of Port Sunlight fame, (who occasionally had their art turned into advertisements for his soap), and Henry Tate, the Sugar Baron, who was putting together his 'national' collection that would later form the basis of the Tate Gallery. In the twilight of their careers

Holland Park would become the quiet exclusive part of Kensington that it remains today.

"Melbury Road, Kensington, has for some years past been completely converted into a colony of eminent artists and sculptors in general, and R.A.s in particular. Pedestrians seldom pass by that way It is a corner of London which the birds seem to have singled out as a fitting place for early and impromptu concerts - a Kensington nook . . . altogether an ideal spot for the artist..... "   Strand Magazine6 1893

The art world of the Holland Park 'Old Guard' had been an insular one. They had all trained in England and met few foreign artists as few were attracted to come here and train. Members of the old Hogarth Club who did travel, like Ruskin & Morris, had vastly different careers to those who stayed in Holland Park. The background to the next generation of the 'Avante Garde' was very different. Many trained in France and had either seen or knew of the work of the Impressionists. They were also deeply affected by the work of the 'open-air' painting of the Fontainebleau and Breton artists' colonies were some of them stayed for short periods. Add to this a growing awareness of social justice and from the potent ideological mix a sort of loose school of open-air social realists was born who had a strong desire to live near their poor down-trodden subjects, preferably, in dramatic rural locations and with a nearby railway station. This led in the 1880s to the starting of a number of artists' colonies around the British Isles. In Scotland the painters known as the Glasgow Boys set up short-lived colonies at Brig o'Turk & Cockburnspath. Others from Glasgow settled in the small port of Kirkcudbright in SW Scotland. The Suffolk coastal village of Walberswick became the haunt of Charles Keene, Philip Wilson Steer and others, painting local fisher-girls and beach scenes and the Yorkshire coastal village of Staithes plaed host to its own gathering of artists. In London the "New English Artists" congregated in the then cheap and rundown riverside area of Chelsea, with Mansera Road in particular being known for its 'colony of artists'.

The artistic klondyke

" Struck Gold in the way of subjects."

Stanhope Forbes 1884

Turner & Constable had both taken their easels down to Cornwall in the early 19th century, but only when the railways opened the region up did the westward rush of artists really begin. By the 1880s artists who had worked

St Ives Art Club 1895

in the French colonies were making comparisons between Brittany and Cornwall - the landscape, language, and megaliths - all that was missing was a traditional peasants' costume. The railway had reached Penzance in 1852 helping it to develop into a prosperous 'modern' market town and tourist destination. This hardly presented the ideal subject for romantic rural painters. However 2 miles to the south was the small fishing village of Newlyn, almost untouched since the 1600s. Here on a hillside overlooking Mounts Bay were picturesque houses and fishermen at work.

The first artist to spend anytime in Newlyn was Slade student Caroline Yates. Others followed, spending summers painting the local fishermen and beach scenes. Walter Langley was the first to settle in Newlyn in 1882 when he was given a commission for a year's work there. By the following year he had been joined by others and a nucleus of ten or so had formed a colony.

By no means as grey as its painted

The artists took lodgings with local people and rented fishlofts as studios - sometimes having to share the space when the fishermen needed to mend their nets. The married artists rented houses in the village and it was in the front rooms of their homes that the social life of the colony went on. Unlike the French colonies Newlyn had no inns or pubs; in fact almost the whole village was teetotal Methodist when the artists arrived, and in the early years of the colony the liberal bohemian artists would come into conflict with the villagers. A particular point of conflict was Sunday painting; models refused to sit, landladies threatened eviction and there was at least one instance of a painter having his canvas slashed for painting on the sabbath. Stanhope Forbes considered himself to be living 'in a hotbed of narrow-minded bigotry' and in a letter to his father described the locals as 'a most disagreeable set of people, full of hypocrisy and cant.' Whilst this antagonism would fade in later years it made the relationships between the painters themselves all the more important; dinner parties were held to celebrate the sale of a painting, several artists played musical instruments and evenings would end with impromptu dancebands playing quadrilles, waltzes and polkas.

Stanhope Forbes became the central figure in the colony and it was his painting A Fishsale on a Cornish Beach exhibited at the Royal Academy in 1885 that started to bring the Newlyn group recognition and popularity, inducing more artists to make the excursion to the South West. Elizabeth Armstrong, a Canadian artist, and her mother arrived having seen Forbes' Fish Sale and Forbes fell hopelessly in love with her to the neglect of his painting. Liaisons between the colonists were common place and the influx in the summer months of students, known as the 'South Ken Girls', led to more than one of the older men making a fool of himself.

By 1887 there were upward of 30 or 40 resident artists at Newlyn, swollen in the summer months by students and amateurs. They concentrated on painting figures set in picturesque scenes and had a particular fondness for painting grey skies, so much so that a later artist, Frank

Richards had to point out that there was in fact a "good deal of Italian Blue in the summer" and that the place was "by no means as grey as it is painted".

DOWNALONG ST IVES

Across on the northern coast, only some 9 miles from Newlyn, St Ives was starting to attract a different grouping of artists. A series of prints by French painter & lithographer Emile Vernier had popularised it as a tourist destination. The tourists were attracted by the dramatic landscapes of the northern coast, as too were the artists who became known for their landscape painting. The artists drawn to St Ives were a much more cosmopolitan crowd than those at Newlyn - with a predominance of Americans, and few British artists. They set up their studios in a run-down end of the town known as Downalong utilising fishlofts as in Newlyn. Unlike Newlyn however, St Ives had hotels and inns in which artists stayed. Some individuals moved easily between the two colonies and a series of annual cricket matches cemented a friendly rivalry between the two.

As the artists matured so did the social life of the colonies. The St Ives Art Club was started in 1889. Firstly in the studio of Australian painter Louis Grier, transferring the following year to its own premises. The Newlyn Colony boasted a lively Amateur Dramatic Society that put on plays in Penzance and Falmouth. Both colonies established their own schools of art and a number of artists set up the Newlyn Industrial Class teaching locals various art, craft & design skills. In 1895 the Edward Passmore Gallery opened its doors in Newlyn, eExhibitions there replacing the previous annual open-air private view that had taken place each year on an open field prior to sending entries to the Royal Academy. Some of the older colonists bemoaned the passing of the private view and saw the 1890s as a period of decline as opposed to their memories of the early days of 20 years earlier. A second generation of artists came to Cornwall in the 1890s some setting up a satellite colony at Lamorna, south of Newlyn. Among those attracted down to Cornwall were Sir Leslie and Julia Stephen accompanied by their daughters Virginia(Woolf) and Vannessa(Bell) who would grow up in this Bohemia-by-the-sea. Also there at the same time was a young woman artist Edith Lees. Aready a 'veteran' of the French colonies and recently married to Havelock Ellis, she would later play a key role in the Fellowship of the New Life.

The coming of the war in 1914 could have marked the end of the Cornish colonies. A number of artists enlisted, one joined the Friends Ambulance Unit and another faced hostility as a conscientious objector. Older families lost sons and after the war a number moved away - leaving the others to carry on in a much more modest way than before.

The Cornish artist colonies of the late 19th century were considered to contain the most significant body of painters working in England at the time and as a body of work from a single location their work has yet to be surpassed. Their contribution to the local economy was significant and the sense of social justice held by some helped to influence local attitudes and conditions.

Sexual liberation

The idea of free love and communal living are inextricably linked in the popular imagination and, despite the protests of some modern day communards that love costs as much as it does anywhere else, the myth would not seem to be without justification. Communal history abounds with sexual adventurers from the individual highly active libidos of the likes of Eric Gill & Augustus John, through the sexual codes of whole communities, all the way to the abusive mix of sex, power and religion by Henry Prince & John Wroe.

Ranting about it

"I can....kiss and hug ladies, and love my neighbours' wife as myself, without sin."   Abiezer Coppe.

The English revolution of the 1640s was also a sexual revolution - women took part in civil life as never before, as preachers, printers, pamphleteers, but most of all they took part as equals, or at least they tried to. Historian Christopher Hill has suggested that the radical sects of the time gave a coherent voice to practices that had been common among the likes of vagabonds and squatter-cottagers. Groups such as the Baptists and the Quakers were able to practice openly what before only existed as underground custom. Marriage and divorce were carried out by simple declaration before the congregation with the Quakers also abandoning a wife's promise to obey her husband. The more libertarian Ranters preached and practised free love and the leader of the Diggers declared that;

'Every man and woman shall have the free liberty to marry whom they love, if they can obtain the love and liking of that party whom they would marry. And neither birth nor portion shall hinder the match, for we are all one family, mankind."

Gerard Winstanley

The Moravian Church who shared the same radical Christian roots as the civil war sects developed their own form of Protestant sacred sexuality in their communities in the 18th century, complete with their own style of sex education, marriage guidance and self-help counselling, making Moravian fringe meetings at Methodist conferences popular and well attended.

Even the strict celibacy of the Shakers could have it's liberating side, with many women joining the sect's communities as a socially acceptable way of getting out of an abusive marriage in the days before divorce.

Socialist sexuality

'Why should the sexual connexion be more fettered than hunger or thirst?........Mr Owen has often said we cannot pledge to love for twenty-four hours. If we cannot love as we like, why attempt to bind parties who do not mutually love? '

'Alice' a member of Manea Fen in The Working Bee

The words free and love came together again in the doctrines of the Owenite socialists. They were critical of the institution of marriage and devised their own marriage vows along with alternative babynaming and funeral ceremonies, a precursor of the later Humanist Society. Whilst the 'official' Owenite line might have been more reserved free love was certainly the order of the day at the unofficial Owenite communities at Manea Fen and Nashoba, playing its part in the notoriety and the demise of both groups. In the pages of The Working Bee a call was made for birth control to be studied and across the Atlantic Fanny Wright argued for the liberalisation of divorce laws in the Free Enquirer. After the demise of the Owenites it wasn't untill the anarchist colonies of the late 1800s that a philosophy of free love, or free union, would emerge again.

'The popular view of the anarchist belief in "free love" was that it meant constant orgies, and many visiting sightseers must have been disapointed. Although some anarchist men and a few women believed in having numbers of partners on the basis of sexual desire alone, for most free love meant something different: a (heterosexual) freely chosen monogamous commitment based on romantic love. If love died, in theory the partnership would end blamelessly. Unfortunatly, love did not always die for both partners at the same time."   Judy Greenaway.

Sex,Politics & Housework. D&D 94/95

HOMOGENIC LOVE

" ...you have made men to be not ashamed of the noblest instinct of their nature. Women are beautiful but to some, there is that which passes the love of women."

Edward Carpenter in Letter to Walt Whitman

Living an openly homosexual life on his small-holding in Derbyshire, where he ran a sort of open-house simple-life commune, Edward Carpenter influenced a whole generation of socialists through his writings and lectures. Few it seems were put off by his sexuality accepting it as part and parcel of the 'new life'. Carpenter was friends with numerous utopian experimenters giving support to both the St George Guild experiment at Totley and later to the Norton Anarchist Colony. His belief in what he called homogenic love between men was shared by C.R.Ashbee, and Carpenter considered the Guild of Handicrafts community at Chipping Campden to be "a fine bit of work altogether, and I wish there were more of the same kind."

Carpenter also advocated women's rights and numbered many feminists in his circle. He was close to Edith Lees who although married to the sexologist Havelock Ellis was a lesbian. Edith Lees was secretary of the Fellowship of the New Life and lived in a number of communal houses in London. She was also resident for a while at the artist colony in St Ives. Communal houses, particularly single sex ones, were places of refuge for gay men and lesbians at a time when it was extremely dangerous for them. The inherent secrecy surrounding gay history makes it hard to assess the extent of numbers living in communities in the late 19th and early 20th century, but certainly a number of the Women's Settlement Houses were home to lesbian communities and it is possible to historically 'out' the radical housing reformer Octavia Hill.

Sexual politics in communities mirrored that of the outside world with the chance of being surrounded by like minds rather than hostile ones. Still sexual freedom tended to be for men only whilst there was no effective birth control. Women had more to lose in defying sexual convention than men, but this did not stop many searching for a more equal relationship in communities than was on offer in society at large. Léonore Labilliére set off on her own personal quest for sexual liberation in 1847 visiting both the Abode of Love and the Onieda community in the USA. Finding both of them dominated by male-centred views of sexuality she return to France and set up her own free love commune in the Pyrenees.

"Freedom in Love means the freedom to rise above oneself. No religious community has made that possible. Freedom in Love means free love and therefore the freedom to love who one pleases without placing ridiculous obstacles in the way. But free love ought not to mean promiscuity, but merely a licence to find one's true partner by a process of experimentation."..."Such experimentation can be harsh and wounding as I have found to my cost."

L.Labilliére c1850
in *Eroticism in Religion.* by 'Seraph'.

THE KING OF BOHEMIA

Of all the larger than life characters that stalked the numerous schools, circles and salons of the literary and art world at the dawn of the 20th century the figure of Augustus John presents a towering archetype of the bohemian artist; wild, promiscuous, proto-type hippie, early new age traveller and commune patriarch - all on top of being the top portrait painter of his generation.

Born at Haverfordwest in 1878 into a somewhat Intimidating household - their Grandfather exhorted his grandchildren to " Talk! If you can't think of anything to say tell a lie!' and 'If you make a mistake make it with Authority!' - the John children were looked after by two aunts, Rose & Lily, who rode round the neighbourhood in a

wicker pony trap known as 'the Hallelujah Chariot'. The aunts held rank in the Salvation Army and variously followed the doctrines of the Quakers, Joanna Southcott and. Howell Harris. The John family moved to Tenby in 1884 and Augustus became a student at the Slade School of Art in 1894. In the summer between terms studying in London two incidents happened that would have a large influence in John's life - on a walking trip around Pembrokeshire he had his first encounter with Irish tinkers which would lead to a life long fascination with Romany culture and way of life. And in the

summer of 1897 he suffered a severe accident hitting his head on a rock whilst diving into the sea, this seemingly resulted in a radical change in character - later leading to the myth that he had dived into the sea, hit his head on a rock and emerged from the water a genius.

True or not - John returned to The Slade a different man. Gone was the 'methodical' student of the previous year to be replaced by the new bohemian student known for his mood swings, his womanising and his artistic talent. Sporting gypsy hat, silk scarf and gold earring that would become not only his trademark, but required dress for any would-be bohemian, John and his associates would frequent the Café Royal whenever their meagre student finances could afford - and John was a centre of attraction among the cosmopolitan crowd that gathered there. The café in the late 1890s was the haunt of artists, writers, circus people, magicians, aristocrats 'Celtic' gentlemen & politicos of numerous persuasions from anarchists of the Kropotkin school to Liberal capitalist 'Social Creditors'. Among the small group of fellow students wandering around sketching each other after classes and in and out of the anarchist clubs off Tottenham Court Rd were John's sister Gwen - later a considerable artist in her own right and mistress of Rodin, - and Ida Nettleship whom John would marry on leaving Slade to avoid being seen to 'live in sin'

Faced with the prospect of supporting a family John took a job as art instructor at Liverpool Art School which was attached to the University, but infact consisted of no more than a collection of wooden sheds. Here he met an older man, John Samson, university librarian and self-taught Romany scholar who opened the young artist's eyes to the richness of gypsy culture, language & lifestyle. For the rest of his life John would search out gypsy encampments wherever he went - often travelling in his own set of horse drawn vans. He had his own repertoire of Romany songs & dances. Joining them round their camp fires at night, penetrating behind the veneer of romantic glamour, John saw the gypsies as having true freedom, not compromised by the advance of industrialised society, - the supreme anti-capitalists whose belongings were always burnt at death. In turn the gypsies accepted John as an honorary gypsy. After Liverpool the young John family moved back to London - marriage did not stop John's womanising - he met and fell hopelessly in love with one of his sisters models and friend Dorothy McNeil, known as Dorelia or later affectionately as Dodo. Ida liked Dorelia and a tumultuous ménage-a-trois was formed. Despite numerous other affairs Ida & Dorelia would be the anchors round which John's world would revolve.

In the early years of the 20th Century John would make his reputation as an artist moving on the edges of a number of influential schools & salons of the time, exhibiting with the New English Art Club and the Camden School as well as being a regular visitor to Lady Gregory's Irish Salon at Coole Park. Critics by now were comparing his work with that of Matisse and Gaugin.

Tragedy struck the John clan in 1907 when shortly after the birth of her 5th child Ida died. With two other children by Dorelia, John, hardly the perfect father, had to struggle with Ida's family over who should bring up the children. In August 1911 John and Dorelia rented Alderney Manor, a strange fortified pink bungalow built by an eccentric Frenchman in 60 acres of heath and woodland on the Newton to Ringwood road outside Parkstone, Dorset. The property, actually quite a large low house with gothic windows and a castellated parapet with additional cottages and a round walled garden was owned by Winston Churchill's Liberal aunt, Lady Wimborne, who was "pleased to have a clever artist as a tenant." The John entourage arrived in a colourful caravan of carts & wagons with children singing as they came down the drive. They set to, turning it into the very picture of a bohemian commune - the coach house was converted into a studio, the cottage converted to accommodate the seemingly endless stream of visitors, some invited, some who just dropped in and would stay for days, months, even years. Others stayed in the blue & yellow gypsy caravans dotted around the grounds and when numbers swelled for weekend parties, in gypsy tents or alfresco in the orchard. The children played a natural part in the community joining in with chores. And, between private tutors for the girls and school for the boys, they ran wild over the heathland and through the woods & bathed naked

in the pond. The communal chaos was presided over by Dorelia in pre-Raphaelite robes looking as if she was constantly about to pose for a portrait - busy organising guests and making the house run smoothly, dressing everyone in handmade clothes - helped by her sister Edie who ran the kitchen. Over the years they acquired all the trappings of a back to the land community; cows, a breeding herd of saddleback pigs, various donkeys, New Forest ponies, carthorses, miscellaneous cats & dogs, 12 hives of bees that stung everyone, a dovecote from which all the doves flew away and a 'biteful' monkey.

Communal living did nothing to cramp John's style - the affairs continued, almost too numerous to mention - with Lady Ottoline Morrell, Mrs Strindberg, the actress Eileen Hawthorne & Mrs Fleming, Ian Fleming's mother, (a liaison which resulted in a daughter, Amaryliss, later an accomplished cellist.) John never seemed to deny any of his wayward offspring - taking some under his communal wing, paying maintenance to support others. Though the claim that he had fathered some 100 illegitimate offspring is probably an exaggeration - it being fashionable at one time to claim to have had a child with him. At Alderney John would spend his time painting and sketching the children and guests - taking part in afternoon jazz sessions - the tango was his speciality - and presiding over the many parties, bonfires & trips to local pubs. All the usual suspects from the Bohemian art scene would make their way down to Dorset; the Bloomsbury crowd; Brett, Carrington, Lytton-Strachey, Berty Russell, Wyndham Lewis........ Other more exotic characters would make it their home, amongst them Chilean painter Alvaro Guevara, wall paper designer Fanny Fletcher, Polish music doctor Jan Sliwinski and the Icelandic poet Haraldar Thorskinsson. At intervals John would leave for his studio in London or for a continental tour in search of gypsy camps or new lovers.

At the outbreak of the First World War John was perhaps the best-known artist in Britain. His friendship with Lord Beaverbrook enabled him to obtain a commission in the Canadian Army and he was given free rein to paint what he liked on the Western Front, but is only known to have completed one painting. He was also allowed to keep his facial hair and therefore became the only officer in the Allied forces, except for King George V, to have a beard. After two months in France, Lord Beaverbrook had to intervene to save John from a court-martial after he was arrested for taking part in a brawl.

The years at Alderney were the peak of John's artistic career. Everyone who was anyone seemingly wanted to have their portrait painted by the erstwhile King of Bohemia. Thomas Hardy on seeing his portrait painted by John in 1923 remarked "I don't know if that's how I look, but that's how I feel." As well a portraits of friends, like Ottoline Morrell and W.B. Yeats, he painted Lloyd George, Ramsay MacDonald & Winston Churchill. A controversial portrait of Lord Leverhulme, the founder of Port Sunlight, was returned to John minus its head, the soap millionaire having been offended by the artist's depiction of him. The resultant outcry at this insult to John's artistic integrity reverberated around the globe. A 24 hour art strike was called in Paris involving not only artists, but also models & picture framers. In Italy a huge soap effigy of Leverhulme was ceremoniously burnt and in Hyde Park art school students marched in protest bearing aloft a giant headless torso. (The portrait was later 'stitched' back together and hangs in the Lady Leverhulme Gallery at Port Sunlight.)

The Johns moved to Fryern Court, Fordingbridge - a 14th century friary turned farmhouse - in 1927. The house on the edge of the New Forest became a stopping-off point for artists travelling to the West Country from London and developed into more of an open house than bohemian commune. In the less hectic lifestyle at Fryern where he entered the twilight of his artistic career John became increasingly interested in politics. He was active in the National Campaign for the Abolition of Capital Punishment and perhaps somewhat ironically supported the Voluntary Contraception League. He pestered MPs on behalf of gypsy & travellers' rights, and was honoured to be elected president of the Gypsy Law Society in 1936. He was increasingly drawn to anarchism, both as a philosophy and a social system. He had come across the writings of the nineteenth-century French social reformer Charles Fourier, and was attracted to the heady mix of commutar-ian socialism and passion in the Frenchman's writing. John elaborated his own beliefs in the Delphic Review, a magazine edited in Fordingbridge and through a number of radio broadcasts. He argued for the breakdown of Nation States into small autonomous, self-supporting, communities - `Gigantism is a disease,' he declared, pointing out that 'Classical Athens was hardly bigger than Fordingbridge.' His attacks were elegantly argued, even if they did appear somewhat eccentric. He launched an attack on hedges. `Hedges are miniature frontiers when serving as bulk-heads, not windscreens. Hedges as bulkheads dividing up the Common Land should come down, for they represent and enclose stolen property. Frontiers are extended hedges, and divide the whole world into compartments as a result of aggression and legalised robbery. They too should disappear…'

Horrified by the rise of fascism across Europe he helped to form the Artists International Association along with the likes of Eric Gill, Henry Moore & Ben Nicolson. The association's aim was to establish an 'army of artists' to oppose the advance of 'philistine barbarism'. They organised a number of exhibitions 'Against Fascism & War'. John reserved a particular hatred for General Franco - and in the early years of WW2 he presented several of his pictures to war funds & used his influence to free German & Austrian refugee artists interned bythe British. During the war years he dabbled with the Greenshirts & the Social Credit Party and in 1945 joined with Benjamin Britten, E. M. Forster, George Orwell, Herbert Read and Osbert Sitwell in sponsoring the Freedom Defence Committee `to defend those who are persecuted for exercising their rights to freedom of speech, writing and action'. This was an alternative to the National Council for Civil Liberties that had temporarily become a Communist Front organisation refusing to help anarchists. John and Dorelia lived out the last years of their lives at Fryern, interspersed with occasional trips abroad or up to London - where John would proceed, even into his eighties, to out-drink, out-party and out-flirt his considerably younger companions.

THE 'MARRIED PRIEST' OF SCULPTURE

The sculptor Eric Gill was almost an exact contemporary of Augustus John. In his own field he enjoyed a comparable reputation, known mainly for his prolific sculptures - notably the Stations of the Cross in Westminster Abbey and the facade of Television House - and his work on typography. The two artists knew each other and were involved in a number of schemes together. Art had led them both to communal life, but where John was bohemian & anarchic, Gill was monastic & Catholic - where John was wild & flamboyant, Gill was obsessive & frugal and where John's sexual excesses were generally open & joyous, Gill's appear insular, manipulating and occasionally bordering on the abusive.

Born in 1882 into a large vicar's household, one of 13 children, Gill attended the local art school in Chichester and was then apprenticed to an ecclesiastical architectural practice in London where he came into contact with the burgeoning Arts & Crafts movement. He enrolled for an illumination and calligraphy class at the Central School of Handicrafts and came under the influence of Edward Johnston who awakened in him a life-long interest in print & typography. As well as moving in circles in London where the ideas of Ruskin and Morris were prevalent, young Eric joined the Fabian Socialists, offering to lecture at their meetings on 'Socialism and the Arts & Crafts' and even setting up the Fabian Arts and Philosophy group. The young architecture student spent his evenings attending numerous groups. He persuaded the utopian writer H.G.Wells to join the Housemakers Society with him - a group with early modernist leanings and ideas similar to the garden city architects and later Design & Industry Association. Along with these intensely serious pastimes he attended the Thursday night socials at the Morrell's house in Bloomsbury and the Club for Working Men in Hammersmith. In August 1904 he married Ethel Moore. They set up home first in Battersea but moved on to Hammersmith where a mini-colony of William Morris' associates were living. By this time Gill had taken up letter carving at the suggestion of W.R. Lethaby and continued to develop his skills, taking up wood engraving and making his first steps into business.

In 1907 the Gills moved to Sopers House at Ditchling, a small Sussex village near Lewes. Here they set up home and workshops with their 3 small children. By the time of the move Gill had become known in both the London art world and in radical-political circles. He initially commuted to London where he had kept on a studio. Other artists came and took up workshops in the village and a small artists' colony came into existence that would continue after the Gills had moved on. In 1913 they bought a nearby smallholding called Hopkins Crank on the edge of Ditchling Common. Here they could live a more self-sufficient way of life; keeping chickens & pigs, growing their own veg & making homebrewed beer.....and begin to gather a community of artists around them. A year before, Gill had converted to Catholicism following a revelatory visit to a monastery in France. This was a deeply unfashionable move to make at the time and lost him a number of friends and distanced him from many others. It did however bring him many commissions. Gill spent most of the First World War working on a major commission to carve a frieze of the *Stations of the Cross* for Westminster Abbey, avoiding conscription until the final days of the war and never seeing active service.

After the war the Gills were joined by two friends, Hilary Pepler, who had set up a printing press in the village, and the painter Desmond Chute and their families. Chute/Pepler bought the adjoining160 acre Fragbarrow Farm and the Guild of SS Joseph and Dominic was set up. New members came to live and work at the little Catholic artists' community; stonecarvers, printers, carpenters, farm labourers, monks & priests - some members came from the Guild of Handicrafts in Chipping Campden. The post war years were a prolific time for the new Guild. Gill & his assistants carved their way across southern England with a series of crosses, memorials and plaques that have a clarity & honesty of workmanship that sets then apart from other work of the time. Gill started figure sculpture at Ditchling, being one of the first, if not the first, sculptor to revive the technique of direct carving, to be followed later by the likes of Barbara Hepworth and Henry Moore and a whole new school of English sculpture.

Conrad Pepler, who grew up in the community, recalled it with affection; human eccentrics mingling with poultry, pigs, a goat, Guernsey cows & a pony, the excitements of sorting offal after a pigkilling, hot cakes from brick ovens, butter-making, wine-making, family prayers, harvesting, amateur dramatics and home-made music. Locals not quite knowing what to make of the semi-monastic community on their doorsteps referred to Mr Gill as 'The Married Monk'.

By 1924 Gill had become dissatisfied with the community at Ditchling, partly due to the nature of the growing community that was leading to a looser, less focused way of life and away from the ideals that had been there at the start. Also one or two of Gill's close friends had moved on. But there was also a further reason - his tangle of complicated relationships was starting to catch up with him. A remote 107-acre estate in the Black Mountains was available to lease from the Benedictine Monks on Caldey Island, complete with a quadrangle of accommodation somewhat in need of repair and its own semi-ruined monastery.

Gill escaped to Capel-y-ffin with his own family, two other families from Ditchling and an assorted menagerie of farm animals. For four years the little group of monastic artisans eked out a spartan existence on the bleak Welsh hillside; growing what food they could, making their own simple clothes and knitting through the long dark hours of the Welsh winter. Gill did some of his most well-known typography work during this period, designing the Gill Sans typeface for the Monotype Corporation and creating the perpetua font as an exercise in turning stone engraving into a print typeface. In all, Gill designed 11 new typefaces. However the monastic life was not to everyone's taste and particularly the women of the community were unhappy there.

`Personally I don't admire the things........... I know him personally. He carves well and succeeds in expressing one or two cut-and-dried philosophical ideas. He is much impressed by the importance of copulation ........ Gore calls him `the precious Cockney' and I call him `the artist of the urinal.'   Augustus John on Gill

John and Gill collaborated on a number of occasions; once in trying to set up a scheme for artists to bypass galleries and sell direct to the public and later as part of the Artists International Association. The two men were complete contrasts. The sculptor was a meticulous organiser and record keeper and thought of John as completely 'unmanageable'. While the Bohemian painter was wild and unorthodox in his social life, his painting was traditional and mainstream. On the other hand Gill's work was experimental, modernist and erotic, his art very much reflecting his life. There exists a large collection of erotic drawings & prints done by Gill throughout his life. Some under lock and key at the Victoria & Albert Museum, others in a collection at Texas University and in private collections - many are drawn on scraps of paper and show sexual acts in all forms from the sublime to the ridiculous, making Gill perhaps the only contender for illustrator of a particularly English form of sensuality and eroticism. Much of Gill's public work is openly sensual and erotic and had the ability to be beautiful and shocking at the same time with breast-feeding Madonnas and copulating suffragettes. In his life, as in his art, he spanned the two worlds of the Victorian and the modern. His own sex life was a strange mix of the patriarchal Victorian values where incest and affairs with maids were commonplace and accepted, and a modern liberated experimental attitude to sex. On top of this was a layer of belief in the sexual as spiritual and that sexual freedom was linked to political and artistic freedom.

Gill's third artistic community was in the heart of the Home Counties; a quadrangle of farmbuildings surrounded by 18 acres of orchard and pasture near the village of Speen in the Chilterns known as Piggots. Here once again the workshops and studios were set up, the printing press installed. This time separate households were set up and again an artist colony atmosphere grew up, this time containing Gill's extended family - with a school being set up, this time for Gill grandchildren.

A number of grand-scale works were carried out in the Piggots' years, consolidating his international reputation; for the League of Nations in Geneva, for the New Archaeological Museum in Jerusalem and perhaps his best-known work, a large figure of *Prospero and Ariel* over the entrance to Broadcasting House. The sculpture became notorious when the story leaked out that the BBC had had to ask Gill to reduce the size of Ariel's penis after a private preview of the carving had revealed that Ariel was "uncommonly well hung."

Whilst the little community situated in what felt like a small forest clearing continued the tradition of practical self-sufficiency, it was a case of the not-so simple life for some, with the older Gill enjoying creature comforts which others did not share. The set up at Piggots was less structured than at the previous communities - no talk of Guild organisation here - and Gill was the clearly acknowledged leader of the group. The air of communal chaos reflected Gill's by now chaotic web of relationships and a general despair at the chaos he saw in the world around him. Gill suffered a mystery illness, perhaps a minor breakdown; he was hospitalised for nearly a month. Some have suggested that it was a catching up of past experiences. Whatever it was, when he recovered he was reluctant to speak about it again. The accounts of Gill's later years have a sad, slightly seedy air to them, though at the same time somewhat comic, with Gill living in the middle of a somewhat neglected farmstead chasing his various lovers round like an ageing gigolo, as if played by Sid James in a version of Carry On Commune!

Eric Gill believed in the necessity of communal life to the end of his life; seeing the gathering of Christians into lay communities as the only was of saving the church from descending into 'the dust or the catacombs'. He died of lung cancer in 1940 and his coffin was taken from Piggots to the local Baptist graveyard on the back of a farmyard cart followed by friends and family, mirroring the simple funeral cortege 40 years before of William Morris.

"Above all things (I hope) that I have done something towards reintegrating bed and board, the small farm and the workshop, the home and the school, earth and heaven."

Eric Gill

Lady chatterley's salon

Of all the influences on the British art world at the turn of the 20th century perhaps the most often overlooked is that of the wealthy female patrons. Women's position changed faster than ever before in the 50 years from 1875 to 1925. Within this limited emancipation a number of new roles were seen as respectable; one was philanthropy the other was involvement in the arts. A number of wealthy women used their status and not inconsiderable resources to support the work of large numbers of artists. In Paris Mrs Chadbourne ran her influential salon in support of who Cézanne and Matisse. The Irish Lady Gregory became an influential figure in the Irish Nationalist revival. From her home at Coole Park she supported the work of such key figures in the Irish art world as W.B. Yeats, G.B. Shaw, J.M. Synge & Sean O'Casey, going on to make her own contribution as playwright, collector of folk tales and theatre manager at the Abbey Theatre in Dublin.

The most influential and notorious salon in England was the one that gathered around Ottoline Morrell, first in the Bloomsbury district of London and later at Garsington Manor in Oxfordshire. Born into the English aristocracy, she was a relative of the Queen Mother, and grew up at the eccentric Welbeck Abbey near Worksop, with its wondrous suites of underground rooms and endless tunnels including a subterranean ballroom and chapel. She married Phillip Morrell, a rather quiet unassuming young man who she discovered was like herself a secret Liberal hiding out in a Tory family. They moved into 44 Bedford Square in 1905 and in the pre-war years they both found their vocations. Phillip as a Liberal MP, first for South Oxford and then for the northern industrial town of Burnley and Ottoline as a patron of the arts.

'Thursdays' at the Morrell's would become legendary. Using her society connections wealthy patrons would be invited to dinner to be introduced later in the evening to a growing crowd of young artists. Lytton Strachy, E.M.Forster, Roger Fry, Maynard Keynes, Leonard Woolf, Clive Bell, Duncan Grant, Eric Gill, Walter Sickert, Ethel Sands, Vannessa & Virginia Stephen (later Bell & Woolf) who had grown up in the St Ives artists' colony, all became part of Ottoline's Circle. Some became lifelong friends, some drifted in and out, others Ottoline had intense affairs with; Augustus John, Henry Lamb, and most notoriously with Bertrand Russell.

Phillip meanwhile was something of a rising star in the Liberal Government becoming a friend of Herbert Asquith (who interestingly was educated at the Moravian School at Fulneck.) A great supporter of Ebeneezer Howard and the garden cities movement he may have influenced Burnley Boro Council to look into setting up a land settlement scheme for the unemployed that finally came to fruition after the war. Phillip Morrell was the only MP to speak out in parliament against Britain's involvement in the First World War, a courageous speech in the face of rampant jingoism that effectively ended his political career.

.

A STRONGHOLD OF FREEDOM

Ottoline's views were if anything more anti-war than her husband's and they became a rallying point for anti-war and pacifist sentiment if not actual protest - Thursday nights took on a different spirit. The guest list was pruned of 'warmongers' and a new crowd came in to dance the night away among them D.H. Lawrence and his wife Frieda. At the end of 1914 the Morrell's moved to Garsington Manor in Oxfordshire. The manor with its garden (carefully restored by Ottoline.), home farm and numerous cottages became a haven for conscientious objectors during the war years. Frieda Lawrence describing it in her autobiography as " a stronghold for freedom in those unfree days."

Phillip Morrell used his legal training and political influence to defend COs in the courts and offered alternative 'employment' on the home farm at Garsington. Few of the COs had any farming experience, some showed no aptitude for the work and others were physically unable to keep up. One or two managed to put in a full day's work alongside the local farm labourers. More than a few seemed ungrateful for their refuge from the killing fields of France, complaining that they were being used as cheap labour by the Morrells. This seems doubly ungrateful when it was their lack of competance that would almost ruin the farm as a going concern.

At Beaconsfield, Bucks. the Quakers were organising other schemes to assist COs. The Friends Ambulance Unit alongside its field ambulance units in France found places on sympathetic farms through its agricultural unit. Some of the placements were on ordinary farms; others were on community schemes such as the Women Co-operative farmers in East Sussex. At the Whiteway & Stapleton Colonies, members served prison sentences for their opposition to the war, and for its active involvement in opposing conscription and hiding COs Stapleton was raided 11 times. "Some arrests were avoided by using the 'manhole', then building a false wall in the manhole latterly by opening the wooden cover over the cellar steps. One man escaped altogether by means of these ruses."

A.G.Higgins *History of the Brotherhood Church.*

The work of these isolated groups and that of the No-Conscription Fellowship opened up the way for wider recognition of the rights of conscientious objectors during the Second World War.

THE GRUBBINESS AND DESPAIR OF OLD ENGLAND

At Garsington new visitors included Dorothy Brett Dora Carrington, Katherine Mansfield, John Middleton-Murry and Aldous Huxley. Both Seigfried Sassoon and Robert Graves made brief visits to the pacifist colony, as did the Asquiths and Ramsay MacDonald. Of all those who gathered at Garsington D.H. Lawrence saw in the embryonic community there, a possibility of a new way of living. As early as 1902, aged only 17, Lawrence had expressed a desire to 'have a big house' and 'gather all the people we like together.' After coming into contact with Ottoline he tried to persuade her that Garsington would be an ideal place to start such a community. He worked hard to convince friends to join him. Aldous Huxley said he would join the scheme, Middleton-Murry and Katherine Mansfield were enthusiastic, Bertrand Russell blew hot and cold, but crucially Ottoline herself was cool to the idea. Lawrence never really forgave her for not going along with his vision - going on to portray her somewhat cruelly as Lady Hermione Roddice in *Women in Love* and some have suggested even using her as a model for Lady Chatterley.

Calling his dream for a community of like minds, Rananim, Lawrence changed his tack. Deciding that the way forward was not among his close friends, but with fresh blood, he started a fortnightly magazine to promote it. The new community was to be one of primitive communism, "established on the assumption of goodness in the members;" a place away from the world of war and squalor where they could wash off the "oldness and grubbiness and despair" of England.

The Signature lasted for only three issues before collapsing amid violent argument. With mounting despair Lawrence turned his sights on America. Like Coleridge and Southey a century before he saw a possibility of hope for the future in America where in Europe all he saw was "only decomposition". Waiting for wartime permits to travel he escaped to a cottage at Zennor in Cornwall where along with Frieda, Mansfield and Murry he continued to dream of Rananim. Frieda recalled of the time in Cornwall -

"Lawrence thought of the new spirit of the life we would try to live there. Murry thought of the ship, and its equipment, that would take us to our island of Rananim. Katherine saw all the coloured bundles that we would have to take. By the hour we could talk Rananim."   *Not I, but the wind*

But it was not to be. Mansfield & Murry drifted away. The Lawrences were hounded out of Cornwall and followed by detectives for the rest of the war, thought to be German spies. After the war they left England travelling through Italy, Ceylon and Australia before ending up in New Mexico finding some sort of freedom and new life on a collection of desert ranches at Taos owned by Mabel Luchan and dubbed 'Mabeltown'. The end of the war was also the end of Garsington as a radical refuge. The artistic CO's went off to find fame and fortune, leaving Ottoline and Phillip to try and patch up the finances, farm and their relationship. The Manor was sold and the Morrells moved back to London in 1925.

COLONISING SARK

In 7 frantic weeks in 1933 E.S. Drake built a modernist art gallery, in shimmering pink and blue concrete complete with roof garden and veranda, on the Channel Island of Sark. It had always been Drake's ambition to establish an artist colony and he invited artists to come and stay with him, putting them up in holiday huts. One of the artists who responded to his call was the young Mervyn Peake who spent his time in the little colony painting and writing, supplementing his income by digging potatoes. Peake and other artists played for the Sark Football Club and an exhibition on the island led to work by the 'Sark Group' being exhibited at a gallery in New Bond St. in London.

Like August John before him, Peake worked as an official war artist being present at the relief of Auschwitz and covering the Nuremberg trials. He returned to Sark for a short while after the war where he wrote a children's story Captain Slaughterboard, illustrated Coleridge's Ancient Mariner and started work on his grand fantasy distopian Gormenghast trilogy.

ST IVES THE NEXT GENERATION

On the outbreak of WW2 two artists, Barbara Hepworth and Ben Nicholson, moved their family down to the relative safety of St Ives. They also tried to persuade other members of the small artists' colony that had grown up around their studios in Hampstead to join them. They knew of St Ives through the work of the naive/folk artist Alfred Wallis, a local Cornishman who had taken up painting late in life. They took a house in St Ives and Hepworth set up a children's nursery. They later found a house and studio space and from these small beginnings a whole new episode in the story of St Ives as an artists' colony began.

In St Ives at the time was the potter Bernard Leach whose work became central to the revival of craft pottery in the British Isles. Leach had been an artist in residence at Dartington Hall in Devon and links would grow between the new artists' enclave and Dartington with the Hepworth & Nicholson children attending Dartington School.

THE COMMITTEE OF 100 AND 1

"....you may count on me to follow your lead,..... it is up to all those of us above the idiot line to protest as vigorously as possible." So wrote the 84 year old Augustus John to Bertrand Russell during the build up to the mass anti-nuclear demonstrations of 1961. "...I cannot write, still less speak in public, but if my name is of any use you have it to dispose of." Recovering from an attack of thrombosis and suffering from what amounted to agoraphobia he made his way up to London on September 17th 1961, hiding himself, somewhat appropriately, inside the National Gallery until the demonstration started. At 5 o'clock he emerged, walked across the road to Trafalgar Square and sat down, joining the unprecedented numbers who had gathered to protest against the lunacy of atomic weapons - and declaring that he would " go to prison if necessary." Few there recognised the sick old man, but later when Bertrand Russell heard of John's attendance he described it as a "heroic gesture." A month later Augustus John was dead.

Commentary & Reflection.

ART WAS THE OLD ROCK'N'ROLL

How is it that so many 1960s rock'n'roll stars came out of the art schools? Did John Lennon ever meet the ghost of Augustus John walking the corridors of the Liverpool Art School and if so what did they say to each other - 'imagine there's no heaven, or Give peace a chance?' The older John's extravagant Bohemian life style in late 19th century student cafe society make him the Mick Jagger of his day, Dorelia his Jerry Hall - the comparison does not bear too much scrutiny, but has uncanny resonance's such as the women who queued up to claim that they had had John's love-child........

Augustus John was a non-conformist in everything but his art, but other artists managed to combine radical politics and lifestyles whilst pushing the boundaries of their art and in the process scandalising the respectable society of their day; the Stevenson cousins at Barbizon, Eric Gill's 'controversial' carving on the BBC building, the whole 'open-air' school(s) of painters - and I always did wonder what Mervyn Peake was taking when he wrote Gormenghast! It is hard now, when the images have become so familiar, to see their works as groundbreaking or in any way outrageous, but then to today's youth the Rolling Stones probably appear as a slightly embarrassing bunch of old rockers and Pink Floyd the besuited writers of advertising jingles not the cutting edge of the avant garde that they once were. We like to think that the 'counter-culture' came along in the 1960s not the 1860s, but all the elements were there then; the underground presses producing political tracts alongside beautifully-illustrated volumes of poetry, and next day cheap broadsheet ballads and political posters. The demonstrations, the riots, the long hair and beards, the sandals, even down to the fascination with Arthurian romances...........the remarkable likeness between Eric Gill's erotic drawings and the illustrations for *The Joy of Sex*. And instead of being set to a soundtrack of rock music it was accompanied by a colourscape of art - new art, shocking art, women's art, art that disturbed the status quo, revolutionary art. The connection between the one counter-culture and the other, if it is not one long continuous thread, may well lie in the art schools. No wonder they have all been closed down or de-radicalised - art was dangerous, art was revolutionary, art was rock'n'roll - and rock'n'roll was art.

The communities established by artistic visionaries show a variety of form comparable to those established by religious groups; varying from the loose supportive networks of individuals living close to each, through those gathered round a charismatic individual, to some (the Guild of Handicrafts for instance) that are verging on the institutional. The reasons for establishing them also bear comparison; escape from hostility, freedom to explore new practices & creeds, companionship, economy, co-operation, education. There is probably some sort of matrix of form and structure that would be applicable to all utopian communities, what ever the source of their foundation and raison d'être. A common set of community structures that get re-invented whenever people come together for whatever purpose.

'For our own England, she will not, I believe be blasted throughout with furnaces, nor will she be encumbered with palaces. I trust that she will keep her green fields, her cottages, amid her homes of middle life; but these ought to be, and I trust will be enriched with a useful, truthful, and substantial form of art.'

John Ruskin. *The Two Paths*.

Coleridge's Utopia Revisited. Clarke Garrett. In: The Family,Communes & Utopian Society. Harper & Row 1971

The early life of Robert Southey 1774 -1809. William Haller, New York, 1917.

Shelley the pursuit. Richard Holmes. Weidenfeld & Nicolson. 1974

The Shelleys at Nantgwillt. Diana Davenport. Privately published phamphlet. 1998

The letters of P.B.Shelley. Vol1 ed:F.L.Jones OUP 1964

The Betws-y-Coed Artists Colony: Clarence Whaite & The Welsh Art World. P.Lord National Library of Wales 1998.

Utopian Craftsmen. The Arts & Crafts Movement from the Cotswolds to Chicago. Lambourne.Astragal Books. 1980

The Guild of Handicraft. CR Ashbee. Essex house press 1909

An Endeavour towards the teaching of John Ruskin & William Morris. CR Ashbee. Essex house press 1901

Ernest Gimson His Life & Work. W.R.Lethaby Stratford on Avon. 1924)

Lawrence & Murry; A twofold Vision. FA Lea Brentham Press 1985

Barbara Hepworth. AM Hammacher,Thames & Hudson Revised ed.1987

Painting the Warmth of the Sun. Tom Cross. Penzance/Lutterworth Press. 1984)

Lady Gregory: The woman behind the Irish Renaissance. Mary Lou Kohfeldt. Andre Deutsch. 1985

Ottoline Morrell: Life on the Grand Scale. Miranda Seymour. Hodder & Stoughton. 1992.

Augustus John: The New Biography. Micheal Holroyd. Chatto & Windus. 1996

Eric Gill. Man of Flesh and Spirit. Malcolm Yorke. Constable & Co 1981.

Eric Gill. Fiona MacCarthy. Faber & Faber. 1989.

Robert Louis Stevenson: Dreams Of Exile. Ian Bell. Mainstream Publishing. 1992.

Mervyn Peake. John Watney. Micheal Joseph Ltd.1976.

Ruskin: The Great Victorian. Derrick Leon. Routledge & Kegan Paul. 1949.

The Holland Park Circle. Artists and Victorian Society. Caroline Dakers. Yale University Press.1999

Designing Utopia John Ruskin's Urban Vision for Britain & America. M.H.Lang Black Rose Books.1999 RECOMMENDED

Visions of Utopia: Nashoba,Rugby,Ruskin & the "New Communities" of Tennessee. J.Egerton. Uni of Tenn Press. 1977

William Morris. Fiona MacCarthy. Faber & Faber. 1994. RECOMMENDED

The Simple Life: CR Ashbee in the Cotswolds. Fiona MacCarthy. Lund Humphries. 1981 RECOMMENDED

The Good & Simple Life: Artist Colonies in Europe & America. Micheal Jacobs. Phiadon. 1985 RECOMMENDED

The Arts & Crafts Movement. E.Cumming & W Kaplin. Thames & Hudson. 1991.

Women in the Arts & Crafts Movement. 1870-1914. A.Callen.1979

Stone Upon Stone. The Story of Stanton Guildhouse. Mary Osborn. The Guildhouse Stanton. 1995

Stanhope Forbes and the Newlyn School Caroline Fox. David & Charles 1993. Brunel Ho Newton Abbot Devon

Landscape & Memory. Simon Schama. Fontan Press.1996

Designers Trade. Gordon Russell. Autobiography. Allen & Unwin 1968.

A Question of Conscience: Conscientious objection in the two world wars. F.Goodall. Sutton.1997 RECOMMENDED

Inspiration for embarking on the voyage to a better world came from many quarters. Utopians would latch on to ideas and theories that promised to underpin the foundations of their utopian beliefs. These might be part of a religious or spiritual quest or just as easily a theory from the frontiers of scientific thought. Phrenology was one such 'science'. Called "the only true science of mind" by its adherents. The basic tenets of Phrenology were worked out by a Viennese physician Franz Joseph Gall.

He put forward the theory that the brain was the organ of the mind and that each faculty of the mind had a corresponding seat or 'organ' in the brain. He went on to postulate that the size and shape of the brain determined the development of the 'organs' and their faculties, and that it was possible to accurately 'read' a person's psychological make-up from the shape of their brain as reflected in the shape of their skull.

Gall's lectures on phrenology in Vienna were banned by the government in 1802 as being hostile to religion. A commission of Parisian physicians investigated his system in 1807 and reported that it was worthless. Lectures demonstrating phrenology however attracted large audiences. At one given in 1817 in Edinburgh a lawyer named George Combe was totally converted, and set about spreading the phrenological gospel in Britain. Combe spent his time lecturing and writing and in 1834 was instrumental in founding the Phrenology Association. Between 1828 and 1860 his book, The Constitution of Man, sold an astounding 300,000 copies. Not a book on phrenology itself but a more general book on the philosophy of natural law, it had sections on crime and punishment, education, religious observance, and good government. Few books were more widely distributed or were so influential in changing the way people conceived of themselves and nature.

GIVING SOCIALISM A HEAD START

Combe's ideas fitted well with the theory of social environmentalism being developed by Robert Owen at New Lanark. George Combe and his older brother Abram visited Owen.

"On Saturday Mr John Buchanan and I went up to Lanark in a gig, where, Abram met us. I sent my compliments to Mr Owen, and begged to know when I might wait on him. He asked us all to breakfast on Sunday, We went; were kindly received; spent the whole day with him; dined with him, went to his chapel in the evening; were invited to breakfast with him on Monday, but stopped at the inn; met him at the mills at ten o'clock that morning; saw his system and everything else till two, when we left him and returned to Edinburgh. We were exceedingly delighted. The whole number of individuals at his mills is 2700, of whom 2400 reside in his own village of New Lanark, and 300 in Old Lanark. The number of children from two to ten years of age is 400. They are taken into the institution at two years. Three women watch them until they are four years old; they then go to school. The hour of meeting in winter is 10 A.M. A large hall receives the children assembling for school, and those who come early play there till the hour of meeting. We saw them romping and playing in great spirits. The noise was prodigious, but it was the full chorus of mirth and kindliness, and not the early growl of selfish passion."

A study was made of Owen's head -

"I believe I told you his development ?1 (Amativeness), 5 (Combativeness), 6 (Destructiveness), 7 (Constructive-ness), 8 (Coveticeness or Acquisitiveness), 9 (Secretive-ness), 12 (Cautiousness), 29 (Language), 31 (Causality), 32 (Wit), all small, especially those underlined; 2 (Phil oprogenitiveness), moderate; 4 (Adhesiveness), 11 (Love of Approbation), 13 (Benevolence), 14 (Veneration), 15 (Hope), 17 (Conscientiousness), 18 (Firmness), 30 (Comparison), large; 16 (Ideality), 10 (Self-Esteem), and 19 (Individuality), moderate. In short, he is a moral enthusiast, and his head is a key to his character."

Combe concluded however that Owen's head was on the whole rather a poor one, "the breadth both above and below, before and behind, being small, although the height and length are fair. The sentiments greatly predominate." He went on to explain Owen's later failures in terms of phrenology. Owen himself was taken with phrenology and after a successful demonstration on pupils at the New Lanark school he promptly ordered books and casts and booked the entire school in to have their bumps read and catalogued.

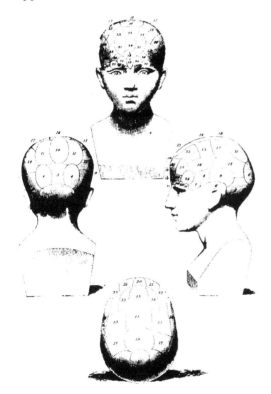

Frontpiece from George Combe's
Elements of Phrenology 1824

Whilst George Combe may have had his doubts about Owen's experiment, his brother Abram was converted and was only stopped from immediately moving to New Lanark by his family. Instead back in Edinburgh he proceeded to set up The Edinburgh Practical Society, a co-operative venture in his own tanyard and finally to be co-founder of the Orbiston Community the failure of which his brother put down to the lack of the use of phrenology in the selection of members. That phrenology should go on to have such widespread support in Owenite socialist circles is on the surface surprising with its seeming intrinsic support for innate psychological traits. But Gall had been an optimist at heart and his theory left room for the possibility that character traits could change. This in particular was stressed by British Phrenologists. It also tailored neatly with the Owenite ideas that a person's character was formed by their environment and that by changing a person's circumstances you could change the person. From these two ideas grew not only a whole socialist movement and ideology but also the basic premise of psychology and psychotherapy.

Charles Bray a Coventry ribbon manufacturer provided the most complete fusion of Owenism and phrenology in his work The Philosophy of Necessity (1841). Inspired by these ideas Bray founded The Coventry Labourers & Artisans Co-operative Soc. to provide gardens for working men along with a co-op store. He also drew up plans for a small community based on ribbon weavers 'cottage factories'. The scheme was never realised.

As Owenite scheme after scheme collapsed some Owenites seeing the need for some easy assessment of prospective members lent heavily on phrenology. This was given further credence by the thought that E.T. Craig's supposed success at Ralahine had in some way been due to his belief in and practice of phrenology.

Phrenology went on to become enormously popular. It featured on the lecture programs of Mechanics' Institutes up and down the country. It carried the warranty of famous names, numerous novelists inc: George Eliot, Charlotte Bronte, Charles Dickens, and Edgar Allen Poe. George Combe was even invited by Prince Albert to examine the royal children. In its first heyday of the 1820s and '30s, employers demanded character references from phrenologist to ensure that their prospective employees were honest and hard working. And in the later part of the century country fairs and seaside piers all had their resident phrenologist. When Charles Darwin published his Origin of Species in 1859 far from there being an entirely hostile reception there was a large readership already well-versed in doctrines of 'natural law' with which Darwin's views on natural selection easily meshed.

From the start phrenology had had it opponents from both sides of the religious / scientific divide. The Pope put Combes works on the index of books prohibited to the faithful and it never achieved the status of an accredited science so craved by Combe and his circle. However its ideas proved remarkably resilient and the British Phrenological Society was only disbanded in 1967.

"Ironically, most of phrenology has now been vindicated, though the particulars of reading character from the skull were greatly exaggerated. For example, the principle that many functions are indeed localized is now a commonplace (although many others are distributed). Also, areas of the brain that are more frequently used (as the hippocampi of London taxi drivers) become enlarged with use. Some personality disorders correlate to atrophied regions of the brain. Palaeontologists make endocasts of the skulls of early hominids to determine the shapes of their brains and have suggested that an enlarged node at Broca's region is evidence of language use. This is essentially phrenology in a new guise. Today we know that what was formerly called "the mind" is indeed a functioning human brain."

John van Wyhe, The History of Phrenology on the Web, (http://www.jmvanwyhe.freeserve.co.uk) 1.5.2001

SACRED SOCIALISM

Socialism in the early 1800s was a melting pot of overlapping ideas. Individuals moved easily between one group and another trying out all the ideologies of the new age. New ideas of social emancipation rubbed shoulders with older, less savoury, crusades such as the Jews Society for converting Jews to Christianity. The Owenite period also saw women becomiing increasingly involved in social issues. Mary Ann Greaves toured Europe in 1814 on behalf of the British and Foreign Bible Society. She visited the Moravian settlement at Herrnhut and the Pestalozzian school and community at Yverdun Switzerland. She bumped into the Pope in a church in Rome and also met the Quaker philanthropist William Allen who was on his own tour of European 'socialist' communities. May Ann's brother James Pierrepont Greaves had experienced a mystical revelation in 1817 and through his sister's contacts he visited Pestalozzi at Yverdun. Greaves was so taken by what he saw and heard at the experimental school there that he stayed for 3 years immersing himself in the ideas of the Great Swiss educator. Greaves was a prosperous London merchant whose business was ruined by the Berlin and Milan decrees of 1803. After being declared bankrupt he rebuilt his business, but then left it when he became interested in educational reform.

'I wish to wrest education from the outworn order of doddering old teaching hacks as well as from the new-fangled order of cheap, artificial teaching tricks, and entrust it to the eternal powers of nature herself, ...'

J.H.Pestalozzi

Pestalozzi developed a child-centred education based on the 'inner dignity of each individual'. He believed that as 'a little seed... contains the design of the tree', so each child holds the promise of his or her own potential. His 'system' was based on love for the child and education through doing rather than formal academic learning. He also abolished corporal punishment in his school and gave recognition to mothers for the role that they play in their child's education.

Greaves was at Yverdun when Robert Owen visited and acted as his translator. He spent another four years as a tutor in the Universities of Basel and Tilibingen where he came in contact with German pietist ideas and theology. He returned to England in 1825 where he was instrumental in the early years of the Infant School Society. Greaves' ideas were at odds with others in the society who saw the schools simply as 'Asylums for the Children of the Poor' whereas Greaves wanted them to be 'sacred schools' that would transform the lives of those who attended them. He was pushed out of the Infant School Society in 1827

Greaves continued to keep the fire of Pestalozzian ideas burning by issuing two small publications *Three Hundred Maxims for the Consideration of Parents* and *Physical and Metaphysical hints for everyone.* He also published on a weekly basis the *Contrasting Magazine* in which he contrasted the views of a well-known writer with his own under the heading, "Is this True? Or, is this True?" Quite how he supported himself during this time is not known. Upon his mystical revelation in 1817 he had adopted a simple vegetarian diet, partly out of frugality, and he survived by living simply and relying on the support of friends. Despite his poverty during these years he built up an extensive library of esoteric and mystical titles.

In December 1831 Greaves and his sister Mary Ann moved to Randwick, near Stroud in Gloustershire. Randwick was a declining woollen centre with a population of around a 1000 with a strong radical tradition. The Greaves' found the villagers suffering destitution with many weavers out of work and their cottage gardens unworked through lack of tools and seed. They devised a 'practical Christian plan' for the relief of the village and outlined it in a pamphlet issued to the unemployed. In an overtly moralistic tone it blamed the situation of the villagers on their own moral degradation, before going on to outline an elaborate scheme for their relief. The villagers were offered potatoes and clothes in return for carrying out work of benefit to the village as a whole. Tools and materials were provided and the scheme was overseen and administered by a couple of older men appointed by the Greaves.

Unskilled men were set to repairing roads and pathways in particular those to the church, Sunday school and village well. Men with skills in carpentry, stonemasonry, and gardening were asked to use them for the common good. A system of tokens was set up to pay for the work; the tokens could be redeemed for food and clothing or a variety of furniture, tools and religious books. A haircutter was 'paid' to visit every house in the village in recognition that self-respect and decency were as important as a full belly.

The Randwick experiment informed Greaves' formulation of his ideas on Sacred Socialism, which he developed in the few years following his return to London in 1833. He came to believe in three dimensions of man's existence - the external (or physical), the inward (or intellectual) and the spiritual (or moral), and that salvation lay in living in the spiritual dimension. Back in London Greaves worked at spreading his ideas and gathering a small group of followers around him. At his house at 49 Burton St on the edge of Bloomsbury he instigated the 'Aesthetic Institution' holding regular Wednesday night meetings to discuss theosophical questions. Out of this group grew the idea of founding a school and community to put Greaves' ideas into practice.

A HARMONIOUS INDUSTRIAL COLLEGE

In July 1838 a group of Greaves' followers, supported by two wealthy sisters, founded a community and school named Alcott House on Ham Common between Richmond and Kingston in Surrey.

'.........a Concordium, or a Primitive Home, which is about to be commenced by united individuals, who are desirous, under industrial and progressive education, with simplicity in diet, dress, lodging, &c., to retain the means for the harmonic development of their physical, intellectual, and moral natures. The institution is to be in the country, the inmates are to be of both sexes, they are to labor on the land, their drink is to be water, and their food chiefly uncooked by fire, and the habits of the members throughout of the same simplic-

ity. Their unity is to be based on their education in a religious love, which subordinates all persons, and perpetually invokes the presence of the spirit in every transaction.'

Ralph Waldo Emerson.
Uncollected Prose, Dial Essays 1842

Greaves himself did not initially move to Alcott House and the central figures at the community were Charles Lane, William Oldham and Henry Gardiner Wright The community, named after the American educator Amos Bronson Alcott, consisted of a plain brick building painted a stone colour and set in four acres of grounds. A second house was used as a communal dining room and sleeping accommodation. There was a large vegetable garden and fruit orchard and extensive recreational gardens with lawns, gravel walkways, arbours, a summerhouse and playground and swings for the children. The community also launched its own Pestalozzian school.

The Concordium was contemporary with the Owenite communities at Harmony Hall and Manea Fen and although very different attracted many Owenites to its ranks including the Owenite missionaries Alexander Campbell, Goodwyn Barmby, and William Galpin. During its first 2 years 32 people were recorded as living there. In 1841 the community reorganised and relaunched itself, Issuing; *A prospectus for the Establishment of a Concordium or an Industry Harmony College.*

PHYSICAL PURITANISM

`Pure air, simple food, exercise and cold water are much more beneficial to man, than any national doctrinal creeds, or any churches, chapels, or cathedrals'.

James Pierrepont Greaves

The Concordium acquired a reputation for a spartan puritanical regime and many members left because they could not adhere to the strictures imposed on them. Vegetarianism was central to the community's philosophy and in the pages of their magazine, The Healthian, they detailed a philosophy based on the tenet that we are what we eat. Alongside a general repugnance to the act of killing animals went the idea that to eat meat was to risk the physical arousal of dangerous passions, because beasts were by definition bestial. Heating the body might also arouse dangerous passions and therefore a diet of raw vegetables was promoted. They went on to maintain that flesh eaters, and butchers in particular, should be excluded from jury service on the basis that their 'moral coarseness' made them too ready to accept capital punishment. In 1843 the community established The British and Foreign Society for the Promotion of Humanity and the Abstinence of Animal Food. In July 1847 a great 'vegetable banquet' was held at Alcott house to promote vegetarianism and win converts. As a direct result of this 'Physiological Conference' a meeting the following autumn at Ramsgate founded the Vegetarian Society.

Greaves' dietary abstinence was closely allied to his belief in sexual abstinence. Taking an ultra puritanical stance he argued for celibacy and grafted onto his Pestalozzian educational ideas the reasoning that children needed to be saved from the sinful methods of their conception and birth.

The community became the first Hydropathic centre in the country in 1841 when C.Von Schlemmer brought his 'cold water cure' over from Germany. The cure entailed a combination of cold baths, being wrapped in wet sheets and drinking large quantities of cold water.

'The household averaging between 40 and 50 persons, were induced to bathe regularly once a day, early in the morning - a habit which was continued with delight to themselves during the whole winter months. Gentlemen, ladies and children of both sexes entered into the practice with enthusiasm, one lady having bathed, with wonderful advantage during the whole of her pregnancy, up to a period only a few hours before her delivery.'
C.Von Schlemmer
Hydropathy, the Cold Water Cure of Diseases. 1842

Numerous instances were cited of local people

James Pierrepont Greaves

cured by the method and members of the community took instruction from Schlemmer and continued the practice after he had departed. Greaves himself moved to Alcott House to partake of a water cure for his rheumatism and hernia. The cure was unfortunately unsuccessful and Greaves died shortly afterwards. The community continued to prosper after the death of its guru despite the spartan conditions and would outlive both Harmony Hall & Manea Fen. The community's namesake Amos Bronson Alcott visited shortly after Greaves' death and was impressed, setting off back to America in the company of Charles Lane, Henry Wright and a large collection of Greaves' books. In the States they would attempt to set up another 'Concordium' called Fruitlands.

The community on Ham Common recieved an influx of members on the collapse of Harmony Hall and the last few years of the community were lived under a less spartan regime - cooked food being allowed. The school would outlive the community finally closing in 1848. The achievements of the Concordists were perhaps better appreciated in their own time than anytime since, when they have either been portrayed as an eccentric side show to the more 'serious' Owenite communities or held up for sympathetic ridicule as in George Holyoake's *History of Co-operation.*

'The Concordium represented celibacy, mysticism, and long beards. One night, I and Maltus Questell Ryall walked from London to visit it. We found it by observing a tall patriarch's feet projecting through the window. It was a device of the Concordium to ensure ventilation and early rising. By a bastinado of the soles of the prophet with pebbles we obtained admission in the early morning. Salt, sugar, and tea were alike prohibited ; and my wife, who wished salt with the raw cabbage supplied at breakfast, was allowed to have it, ...

..........When the salt was conceded it was concealed in paper under the plate, lest the sight of it should deprave the weaker brethren.'   George Holyoake

The pioneering work of the Sacred Socialists in the introduction of infant education, vegetarianism and Hydrotherapy to England should really accord them a better place in the history books than that put forward by Holyoake and his successors.

The full story of Sacred Socialism is told in:
Search for a New Eden: James Pierrepont Greaves:The Sacred Socialist and his followers By J.Latham.
DickinsonUP1999

THE COMMUNIST CHURCH

Goodwyn Barmby and his sister Catherine were active 'communitarians' moving in both Owenite circles and among the Sacred Socialists. They both wrote for a whole array of radical publications of the time. Goodwyn devised grand schemes to transform the country into a communal commonwealth setting up groups like The Central Communist Propaganda Society to promote them, and publishing his own magazine, The Promethean, where he outlined the four ages of history; 'Paradisation, Barbarization, Civilization and Communisation'.

In 1843 they started the Moreville Communitorium at their house in Hanwell with themselves as 'archon' and 'archoness'. The community was advertised as open to all who wanted to put into practice the `Religion of Communism', described as a small villa with a beautiful flower garden, excellent kitchen garden and a pleasant meadow. The Barmbys had grand plans for the community with an aviary, a piggery, a hydropathy and a library with four hundred books. They claimed that there was plenty of room to extend the grounds if numbers made it necessary. The diet was only slightly less abstemious than that at the nearby Concordium. Raw vegetables were to be the staple diet for 3 months in the summer with cooked vegetables in the winter. Herb-teas were offered as a replacement for alcohol, which was banned (except for home-brewed wine) and sugar was only allowed in the form of honey.

The plans to extend the community proved unnecessary as 'few availed themselves of this opportunity and these were minds who were unprepared for the practice of the principles'. Undaunted by the failure of their community experiment the Barmbys concluded that further propaganda was needed 'before continuing with further practical proceedings'. Goodwyn launched The Communist Chronicle and Apostle of the Communist Church and promoted a scheme to turn the whole of the British Isles into a `Communarchy'.

THEOSOPIC FLAPDOODLE

'What Madame Blavatsky did was an immeasurably greater thing than the doubling of teacups. She made it possible for some of the most cultivated and skeptical men and women of this generation to believe-believe ardently, to an extent that made them proof against ridicule and disdainful of persecution-that not only does the invisible world that encompasses us contain Intelligences vastly superior to our own in knowledge of the Truth, but that it is possible for man to enter into communion with these hidden and silent ones, and to be taught of them the Divine mysteries of Time and of Eternity.'

William T. Stead. 1888, London

Helena Petrovna Blavatsky (HPB to her friends) can almost claim to have started the New Age on her own. She was the first of a subsequently long tradition of Gurus from the East claiming to bring the wisdom of the ancients to the West. Her early life is a convenient mystery (another tradition among gurus.) Born in Russian in 1831 to Russian-German nobility after a mildly dramatic childhood and disastrous marriage she claimed to have embarked on a series of exotic and mystical adventures in Egypt, India and Tibet, eventually turning up in America in the 1870s 'investigating' the recent spiritualist craze. Here she met Henry Olcot with whom in 1875 she formed the Theosophical Society for "the study of ancient and modern religions, philosophies and sciences", an aim which had wide appeal to inquiring minds of the time and somewhat disguises the quasi-religion that actually grew up around Madame Balvatsky. After a spiritual trek to India where she recieved 'letters from the Masters' HPB came to London where she set up the Blavatsky Lodge at 17,Lansdowne Road, Nottinghill.

'The household consists of six or seven persons, including a young doctor of medicine, a student of law and a Frenchman, an American (the friend of Edison), and a Swedish Countess. These are all particular disciples, who receive constant instructions from the lips of the priestess and who may be regarded as well on the way towards the attainment of the elongating principle....'

London Star. 1888

From this base the little group of Theosophists organised talks and made numerous converts to HPB's eclectic blend of spiritualism and Eastern mysticism; many attracted by the publication of The Secret Doctrine, a compilation of esoteric ideas from various sources that Madame B claimed to be her own.

GONE TO THEOSOPY

The most spectacular and influential convert to Theosophy at this time was Annie Besant who had been sent to interview Blavatsky for The National Reformer. A quite remarkable woman whose career encompassed leading roles in The Secular Society, Fabian Socialism and the Trade Unions - she was the organiser of the famous Bryant matchgirls' strike.

Her early radicalism had been awakened by contact with the lawyer William Prowting Roberts who as well as defending early trade unionists was the lawyer for Feargus O'Connor's Chartist Land Company. Her socialist friends were nonplussed and somewhat horrified at her conversion from secularism and socialism to the esoteric doctrines of Madame Blavatsky. A red line being struck through her name in the membership register of the Fabian Society and a note made by the secretary in the margin - "Gone to Theosophy."

In July 1890 HPB and the Lansdowne Road household moved "Headquarters" to Mrs. Besant's house in Avenue Road, St Johns Wood. 'It was a large house, standing in its own grounds, which formed a pleasant garden, with bits of lawn, shrubbery, and a few tall trees. Mounting the front steps, one entered a vestibule and short hall, from each side of which doors opened into rooms. The front one on the left was HPB's working room, and her small bedchamber adjoined it. From this inner room a short passage led into a rather spacious chamber, which was built for and occupied by the Esoteric Section. To the right of the hall on entering was an artistically furnished dining room, which was also used for the reception of visitors.............The meeting hall of the Blavatsky Lodge was of corrugated iron, the walls and ceiling sheathed with unpainted wood. Mr. R. Machell, the artist, had covered the two sloping halves of the ceiling with the symbolic representations of six great religions and of the zodiacal signs. At the south end was a low platform for the presiding officer and the lecturer of the evening. The hall had a seating capacity of about 200. On the opening night [July 3, 1890] the room was crammed, and many were unable to gain admission...........Avenue Road was a veritable beehive of workers, with no place for drones, HPB herself setting the example of tireless literary drudgery, while her strong auric influence enwrapped and stimulated all about her..'

Henry Olcott
Old Diary Leaves: The Only Authentic History of the Theosophical Society. 1931.

With her organisational and speaking skills Annie Besant quickly became a central figure in the London Theosophical world during this period and when Madame Blavatsky died In 1891 she was ideally placed to take over her mantle. Her succession to the role of Mother of

Theosophy wasn't without its opponents each eager to stake their own claim to HPB's spiritual inheritance. In the USA she was successfully challenged by Katherine Tingley leading to the breakaway of the American Theosophists and to the founding of the White City community at Point Loma California. Annie Besant decided to move the headquarters of the European Theosophists, exchanging a "barbaric England for a more civilized India." She set up on the estate at the mouth of the Adyar River bought by a well-wisher for HPB on her stay in India. From here she presided over a thriving Theosopical movement both in India and worldwide. She also became heavily involved in the India Independence movement using her Theosopical contacts in the ex-patriot community and her experience of the Irish struggle from her Socialist days to further the cause of Indian Nationalism. Mahatma Gandhi would say of her "I cannot forget, though it is many years ago, the inspiration I drew from her in my boyhood and then again in my experiences of political activity."

At the little spiritual colony at Adyar the Theosophists would 'discover' their very own home-grown master, variously known as the world teacher, Matrieya or Krishnamurti. The 'master' was in fact a 14-year-old boy who Besant and another Theosophist C.W. Leadbeater befriended. Criticism of this new messiah came from both within and without the movement. In spite of criticism, Krishnamurti and the Order of the Star of the East set up by 'Dr' Besant to support him gained support in India, Europe and the United States, claiming 12,000 members in 1913. Krishnamurti after schooling in England retreated to a ranch at Ojia in California where in 1929 he renounced any claim to be a messiah. This debacle demoralised the now aging Besant and the remains of the Theosophical Society. Annie Besant died, aged 86 in 1933. Krishnamurti, the non-messiah, built up a considerable following of his own almost despite himself.

Despite repeated exposes the ideas of Madame Blavatsky and the Theosophical Society proved remarkably persistent creating a distinctive neo-Hinduism that bears close resemblance to the teachings of the later Ramakrishna movement and Aurobindo. It introduced to an eager western audience Hindu ideas of karma and its own variant of reincarnation - past life trees. In doing so it paved the way for later gurus from the East such as the Maharishi Mahesh Yogi and his Transcendental Meditation movement. Through its introduction of Buddhist philosophy to a general audience it did much to prepare the ground for the resurgence of western Buddhism in the 1970s. In Germany Theosophy was transformed into Anthroposophy when after disagreeing with the increasing Indian bias of the movement the general secretary of the German Society, Rudolf Stiener, broke away in 1912 to form his own esoteric movement. Steiner's ideas have had their own far reaching influences particularly in the field of education through the Steiner Schools movement.

Not all of Madame Blavatsky's ideas have stood the test of time, in particular those on race. Somewhat surprisingly for someone who drew inspiration from the Asian sub-continent her views on race were consistent with the prevailing values of her time. In The Secret Doctrine she declared that the extinction of 'Redskins, Eskimos, Papuans, Australians, Polynesians, etc.' was a 'karmic necessity'. This strange take on Victorian racist views has returned to haunt Theosophy on numerous occasions with the Steiner movement still embroiled in controversy over the issue.

"was born a flapdoodle, lived a flapdoodle, and would die a flapdoodle." HPB about one of her disciples
[Flapdoodle was one of Mdme B's favourite insults.]

YOU CANNOT BE TOO SCEPTICAL

Another figure, whose career has parallels with that of Madame Blavatsky, though he was never resident in the UK, was George Ivanovitch Gurdjieff. Of Greek-Armenian decent, his early years in Eastern Europe are like HPB's conveniently hazy; he too went on exotic adventures where he met wisemen in the East - somewhat better documented than Madame B's. He brought back his own personal synthesis of Sufi mystical practices, music and dances known collectively as the Fourth Way or simply 'The Work'. After a period in Moscow developing a group of followers and a reputation as a dancemaster he moved to France in 1922 and founded the Institute for the Harmonious Development of Man at the Château du Prieuré in the Fontainebleau Forest.

'....... the only recorded institution with which Mr. Gurdjieff's school can at all plausibly be compared is the school which was established in southern Italy by Pythagoras about 550 B.C. The Pythagoreans lived in a colony and were subjected to all kinds of abstinences and physical exercises as a preparation for the extraordinary intellectual work which they accomplished. They were deeply concerned with rhythm, with movement, with the analysis of the octave, and with other apparently irrelevant subjects which are studied at Fontainebleau.' Clifford Sharpe. New Statesman, Mar 1923

At the Prieuré Gurdjieff gathered around him remnants of his family from Russia and a group of intriguing and influential followers including: P.D. Ouspensky, AR Orage, Katherine Mansfield, John Middleton-Murry, Frank Lloyd Wright, J.G. Bennett and a group of Parisian lesbian writers known as The Rope. The core of Gurdjieff's ideas was that people are spiritually "asleep" and all his techniques were aimed at acquiring true consciousness through "self remembering". These techniques included a whole range of shock tactics to the system to try and get people to live in the moment. Gurdjieff often referred to this as putting his followers "in galoshes."

'Imagine a big, black, smelly rubber boot-big enough so you can't see your way out, you are over your head. It's dark, unpleasant, unfamiliar, confusing, frightening, disorienting. Everything you were comfortable with is taken away. You don't feel at all happy in your own skin.'

Rob Baker
Gurdjieff and the Women of The Rope.
Gurdjieff International Review

He told one of his disciples, "I wish you be not like merde. So first I make you feel like merde. Only from there can one begin."

'TOO MUCH NIRVANA AND STRAWBERRY JAM'

Pyotr Demianovich Ouspensky was one of Gurdjieff's most devout and critical followers. He had been part of the group attracted to the ideas in Moscow - and like many followers of gurus believed in the ideas whilst losing faith in the master himself. Instead of moving to the Prieuré Ouspensky set up on his own in England in 1921 firstly working from a small flat in Warwick Gardens in London, then acquiring a house on the Great West Road at Hayes where he instructed pupils in The Work. Gurdjieff had given his blessing on Ouspensky's work and he attracted his own following many of them defectors from the Theosophical Society, fed up with the seemingly-endless internal arguments going on there. In 1935 a country house and farm were bought at Virginia Waters about 20 miles from London. Lyne Place was used for weekend gatherings of as many as 100 people on practical work of various kinds. Some of his older pupils lived there running the estate and setting up a small sawmill. In 1938 a large house was found at Hammersmith in London, with a studio with a capacity of over 300 people. At this time the Historico-Psychological Society was set up to give 'The Work' a respectable front and 'a brass plate on the door.' Ouspensky was at the time being watched by the home office as a possible Spy. The 'Objects' of the Historico-Psychological Society read like an update of the aims of the Theosophical Society;

'The study of problems of the evolution of man and particularly of the idea of psycho-transformism.

The study of psychological schools in different historical periods and in different countries, and the study of their influence on the moral and intellectual development of humanity.

Practical investigation of methods of self-study and self-development according to principles and methods of psychological schools.

Research work in the history of religions, of philosophy, of science, and of art with the object of establishing their common origin when it can be found and different psychological levels in each of them.'

At the London House one of the pupils set up a printing press in the basement of the house though none of Ouspensky's writing on 'The Work' appeared until after his death. Following the invasion of mainland Europe by Germany, Ouspensky decided to move to America for the duration of the war - somewhat reluctantly, having got quite used to the life of a country gentleman at Lyne Place, a comfortable life he found hard at times to square with the demands of 'The Work'. A few members of the London groups followed him across the Atlantic, but in New York he was able to tap into an existing network formed after Gurdjieff's occasional visits with his dance displays and sustained by the presence of A.R. Orage. Ouspensky held well

-attended meetings in New York whilst setting up base at Franklin Farms, a large house and estate in New Jersey, which was put at his disposal. By this time the 'Gurdjieff scene' was becoming somewhat confusing, certainly to any newcomer. Orage was a sort 'official' teacher in the USA, Ouspensky was preaching his own brand of 'The Work', with the blessing of the master whom he had rejected, Madame Ouspensky was doing her best to undermine her husband by teaching her own classes that still held faith with Gurdjieff, others were teaching the dance movements (shades of the splits in the Theosophical Society after Madame Blavatsky's death and Gurdjieff was still alive). In some ways the situation had been engineered by Gurdjieff himself who was after all preaching that everyone should find their own path to the truth.

After the war Ouspensky returned to England not to take up his old role of teacher, but in an action mirroring Krishnamurti's, to disown the works and "set free" his followers denying that there ever was a system of any sort.

He was at the time seriously ill and died at Lyne Place in 1947. Some held to the belief that Ouspensky had not really lost faith with the system and that his rejection of it was infact part of the teaching. Others carried on with 'The Work' in the post war years each with their own group of followers gathered together in small communities. Maurice Nicol at Great Amwell in Hertfordshire, Colin Rodney at Tlalpam in Mexico and AJ Bennett at Coombe Springs in Surrey. Like the Theosophical society before them these little beacons of spiritual light provided a bridge from one generation of seekers of wisdom in the East to the next.

Gurdjieff had stayed in Paris during the war emerging afterwards to wind up the Prieuré and give his pupils instructions on their lives - dying in 1949, having apparently outlived his own body! Scribbled on the study wall at the Institute for the Harmonious Development of Man was some French graffiti that when translated read "You cannot be too sceptical" and given his quixotic nature as likely as not written by Gurdjieff himself.

SGT MAGICK'S LONELY HEARTS CLUB

The 'Wickedest Man in the World' died in quiet obscurity in Hastings in December 1947, his reputation having been somewhat overtaken by one Adolf Hitler, and in quiet obscurity he might have stayed had he not appeared on the cover of one of the1960s iconic rock albums. When asked to draw up a list of names to appear on the cover of their forthcoming Sgt Pepper album John Lennon included that of Aleister Crowley thereby introducing 'the Beast' to a whole new generation. Crowley's diabolical reputation was based on press reports of his activities at the Abbey of Themela in Sicily in the early 1920s. The Abbey was to have been an 'ark of refuge' from the 'Aeon of a Dying God,' and an archetype of a new society based on ideas outlined in Crowley's The Book of the Law. In reality it appears to have been a rather squalid Mediterranean villa, with occult paintings covering the walls, where Crowley and a small band of followers carried out sex magick under the influence of drugs. Following the death of a disciple Raoul Loveday from gastro-enteritis at the Abbey the British Press had a field day with stories of drug induced 'bestial orgies' and 'satanic rituals' - not helped by Crowley's attempted to finance the community by publishing a fictionalised account of it under the title - The Diary of a Drug Fiend. Mussolini ordered the now notorious Crowley out of Italy and the community disbanded. Crowley had been born into a strict family of Plymouth Brethren. As a young man he was an adventurer on both the physical and the spiritual plane, firstly as a leading climber and mountaineer and secondly as a leading Edwardian occult magician, moving quickly through groups like The Hermetic Order of the Golden Dawn and the Ordo Templi Orientis, going on to try and form his own occult group based on his eclectic fusion of oriental and Masonic ideas. His personal mantra,' Do what thou wilt shall be the whole of the Law', his advocacy of the legalisation of drugs and liberal views on sexuality all chimed with a generation rediscovering him in the 1960s and has led to a rehabilitation of his reputation from the 'Beast' of the gutter press headlines to a key figure in the development of the occult.

THE CLOISTERS

'every fruit juice drinker, nudist, sandal wearer, sex-maniac, Quaker, nature cure quack, pacifist and feminist in England'

George Orwell, The Road to Wigan Pier **(1937),**

The Cloisters Letchworth

The new Garden City at Letchworth acted as a magnet for all manner of seekers for the new life. Here was the new world made in bricks and mortar waiting for its inhabitants. 'The Simple Life Hotel' was one focus of activity with its food reform restaurant and health food store. In the evening the good Letchworthian could enjoy a non-alcoholic beverage at The Skittles, the infamous pub with no beer, advertised as 'The Liberty Hall of the Letchworth worker'. And at the weekend, clad in rational dress and sandals, a talk on 'Progressive Religious Thought' given by the Alpha Union could be attended at The Cloisters in Barrington Road.

At its dedication ceremony in January 1907, founder Miss Annie Jane Lawrence dedicated The Cloisters

'To the unity, eternal reality, through all diverse, temporary and fragmentary seemings, the perfect inviolable whole, wherein sin and pain and death are not, and all contradictions are reconciled, all discords resolved, I dedicate this building, confident that, through progressive recognition of this unity, mankind will ascend to a full, harmonious and joyful expression of life, in soul, body and social organisation.'

Annie Lawrence, daughter of one of the promoters of the Garden City Baron Pethick-Lawrence, had moved to Letchworth in 1906 and leased an isolated three-acre plot where she built a house for herself 'Cloisters Lodge' and The Cloisters a fantastic towered building designed by William Harrison Cowlishaw intended as a Theosophical Meditation Centre and open-air school. The design reputedly came to Miss Lawrence in a dream and cost some £20,000. It consisted of; a large half-oval 'open-air room' called the 'Cloister Garth' with an open colonnade to the south and large glazed bays to the north, this was flanked by two wings, one housing the kitchen and store rooms and the other the cubicles & dressing rooms for an oval open-air swimming pool. Green veined Swedish marble columns supported the arcade of the Cloister Garth where at night men and women (strictly segregated by the expanse of the central hall) slept on hammocks that lowered from the ceiling on pulleys. A series of 'outdoor fireplaces' and canvas screens were provided in an, unsuccessful, attempt to ward of the winter nighttime chill. In the central hall of the garth there was an Art Nouveau fountain from which water flowed through a series of ceremonial hand washing basins and then on around the Cloisters in open channels.

'The outward expression of these functions was remarkable, with myriad symbolic overtones......... ....Cowlishaw was a gifted sculptor and modelled

The Cloisters Garth - open-air living room.

designs for the rainwater heads - doves represented guilelessness, bats were about to start their dusk patrols, bees built up honeycomb to provide food for the gods, and `butterflies dancing in the empyrean'.

Mervyn Miller. *Letchworth The First Garden City.*

THE GARDEN CITY PHILOSOPHY OF LIFE

A small permanent community grew up at the Cloisters augmented by people attending the numerous classes and summer schools. Communal meals were served on a great marble-faced dining table that stretched across a great bay window on a raised altar-like dais. Housework in the community was a male activity carried out by earnest young men in robes and sandals. Miss Lawrence was a believer in, and promoted the concept of a `Dual Day' whereby morning work was followed by a two-hour rest period and food and then re-assembly for communal recreation. Members of the community were encouraged to grow their own food, but seemed by all accounts to have preferred to spend their time philosophising, watching the sunset or stars from the rooftop promenade or partaking of nude bathing at dawn.

J. Bruce Wallace, one of the founders of the Garden City Association, found support for his Alpha Union at the Cloisters and between 1908 & 1911 organised an annual residential summer school. Bruce Wallace was for-merly a leading light in the Brotherhood Church who had by this time 'converted' to Theosophy and his summer school students joined with the community members in practical craft activities such as woodcarving and sandal making whilst pursuing their personal quests for psychic growth and personal freedom. Wallace's connection with the Cloisters ended in 1912 when he married Mary Tudor Pole and went off to become involved in the Glastonbury mysteries.

Four electric organs had been installed in the Cloisters entrance hall, and through a system of pipes and louvers the disembodied sound of organ music would waft around the building. After Wallace's departure the place became less of a commune and more of an adult education establishment with organist, Frank Merry, as the warden ,organising courses and lectures including one titled ' The Garden City Philosophy of Life'. The Letchworth Adult Educational Settlement took over arranging courses after

Hammocks that let down from the ceiling.

the First World War up until 1926.

Miss Lawrence, although somewhat deaf, was a great music lover. On one occasion she brought The London Concert Orchestra made up of 40 unemployed musicians to play at the Cloisters Garth. This was part of an ongoing series of concerts that she organised attended by audiences of 1,000 making organ recitals, band and choral concerts a regular part of the new town's cultural life. The last concert was given by the Brotherhood Orchestra in

1939 on the day the Second World War broke out. The building was commandeered during the War and suffered damage. The Cloisters became the North Herts. Masonic Lodge in 1948 when Miss Lawrence moved to St Catherine's Nursing Home where she died aged 90 in August 1953.

Whilst only a minority of Letchworth's residents subscribed to the more outlandish ideas of the new life The Cloisters was not the only place catering for 'Simple Lifers'. Amid the array of non-conformist chapels and recreation clubs Vasanta Hall, an odd flat roofed building in Gernon Walk, housed the local Theosophical society and The Mrs Howard Memorial Hall, the first public building in town modelled on the Folk Hall at New Earswick, and on the surface a civic extension of the activities that went on at the Cloisters.

'You will stroll into the Howard Hall one wintry day and find an artist . . . busy with decorating it . You will learn that there is to be a conversazione that night . . . or a gathering of new residents, or what not besides . . . There will be a scene from one of Tolstoy's plays or an impressive recitation ... discussions upon the Liquor Question, the Unemployed, Methods of Education. Political Organisations, Arts and Crafts, Science and Civilisation and so forth.'

The 'Borough' Pocket Guide to Letchworth 1902

GLASTONBURY FESTIVAL : 1914 - 1926

The English socialist classical composer Rutland Boughton and his librettist Lawrence Buckley dreamed of an English cultural revival, perhaps including the establishment of a 'national' theatre, certainly an annual festival in the countryside that might become an English Oberammergau or Bayreuth. Letchworth was considered as a venue given the potential support there, but Glastonbury with its Arthurian and spiritual associations was favourite from the start. Alongside the festival Boughton and Buckley envisaged a permanent group of artists who would share the running of a collective farm as a base for the festival. Encouraged by the likes of George Bernard Shaw and Edward Elgar and with financial support from the Clarks, Quaker shoe manufacturers at nearby Street, they set about trying to find a home for the festival and artists' colony.

A festival venue proved easier to find than a collective farm and in 1914 the first Glastonbury 'festival' kicked off with a summer school and a performance of Boughtons opera The Immortal Hour based on the book by 'Fiona Macleod'. Boughton's work was part English Romantic part Celtic revival, drawing heavily on Arthurian legend. From this beginning a series of festivals developed along with help from Alice Buckton's Guild of Glastonbury & Street festival players who performed their own series of masques and mystery plays. The festivals lasted with a wartime hiccup until 1925.

An opportunity presented itself to set up the dreamed of artists' colony when in 1919 Mount Avalon, a large house with extensive grounds, was purchased by a devotee as a base for the festival. This was however the year that Lawrence Buckley died and Mount Avalon failed through lack of income to pay back the benefactor. Boughton and his family moved to a smallholding at Kilcot, Glous. in 1926. The Glastonbury dream was over - for the time being!

The story of Glastonbury in the early 20th century is told in : The Avalonians. By Partick Benham. Gothic Image 1993. Rutland Boughton's Music is promoted by The Rutland Boughton Music Trust 526a Hitchin Rd. Stopsley. Luton Beds.

'The' new age

Of all of the seekers for a new life in the early 20th century perhaps the most influential in a roundabout way was Alfred Richard Orage. As the editor of the most important social, political and arts magazine of the Edwardian period, *The New Age,* he presided over and orchestrated through its pages all the discussions of the age. He was considered by contributors and readers alike to be editor supreme. Dogmatically undogmatic in his editorial policy he refused to let the paper be taken over by any particular faction or appear to have a party line. The breadth of opinion in its pages was as wide as its list of contributors was long and every argument on feminist, socialist, artistic and philosophical issue was allowed to play itself out to the full.

Orage's own ideas went through a series of transformations or developments. The first volume of the new age carried the banner "An Independent Socialist Review," with the emphasis on independent. He went on to support in turn a series of alternatives to the state-run socialism proposed by the Labour Party. Such as Guild Socialism that advocated a system of industrial self-government through national worker-controlled guilds. In 1915 the National Guilds League was created; it had a number of notable writers and speakers, including Bertrand Russell. After World War I several working guilds were formed. However, the most powerful of these, the National Building Guild, collapsed in 1922, and after that the movement faded. He was then taken by the economic theories of a Major C.H. Douglas. Known as Social Credit it was a sort of Consumer led socialism that Orage promoted through the pages of the magazine and which would eventually become popular not in Britain but in British Colombia.

After the war Orage became increasingly disillusioned with the search for an alternative to state controlled socialism. Feeling that there was 'something missing' he embarked on a spiritual quest and in 1922, at the age of forty-nine, he sold The New Age, cut all ties in England and went to join Gurdjieff at the Prieuré.

———

Carry on camping

In among the small ads in the left-wing papers of the day can be found notices for one of the odder forms of Edwardian utopian community - the Camp. This was the age when the masses discovered the great outdoors, with the formation of such groups as the National Trust, the Ramblers Association and the Youth Hostels Association. But more than anything it was through Baden-Powells Scouting movement that a whole generation would redefine its relationship with the countryside and nature. The Scouts were based on the ideas of American Ernest Thompson Seton, a lover of camping, the natural world and Native American culture. It all started from a small project set up to stop delinquents vandalising his land, where instead of chasing them he invited them in and taught them woodcraft skills and values of reverence for the land. An article in *The Ladies' Home Journal* led to the setting up of groups of `Seton Indians' all across the States and by 1906 they were holding annual camps and Seton had written the first of many books on the arts of woodcraft. Contact with Baden-Powell on a visit to England was the direct inspiration for the start of the Scouts. From the beginning there was a distinct difference between Seton's 'Tribes' and Baden-Powells 'Troops'. And although phenomenally successful by the First World War there was a rift in the scouting movement between the woodcrafters and the jingoistic military style leadership. This split lead to the break away of the woodcrafters in the 1920s under the leadership of John Hargraves who set up the Kindred of the Kibbo Kift.

Hargraves, a Quaker who had served in Royal Army Medical Corps during the war, was a charismatic figure who had played a key role in the early success of the Scouts. Fired by the anticipation of a better world following the war the Kibbo Kift was more overtly political in its aims.

'The Kibbo Kift was to be not merely a youth organisation but was to involve old and young, male and female. Hargraves called for Outdoor Education, Physical Training, the learning of hand crafts, the reintroduction of Ritual into modern life, World Peace and

the regeneration of urban man through the open air life. The new movement was to be nothing less than the 'human instrument' that would create a new World Civilisation.'
Professor LP Elwell-Sutton
A History of the Kibbo Kift.

Drawing on a combination of Seton's Native American lore and home-grown Saxon rituals they organised weekend Tribal Camps and a great annual 'Althing' where hiking and camping was elevated to the level of a spiritual exercise. Kift Kinsmen were organised into Clans and Tribes with each individual being given their own 'Red-Indian-style woodcraft name'. Each member was expected to not only make a 'habit' of Saxon hood, jerkin, shorts and long cloak, but to make their own lightweight one-man tents (the first seen in this country) and also design, carve and paint his or her own totem pole.

Hargraves, known among the Kin as White Fox, wrote what amounted to a manifesto for the Kift in 1927 entitled *The Confession of the Kibbo Kift,* deliberately named after the *Confession of the Brotherhood of the Rosy Cross*, one of the manifestos of the Rosicrucians. In it he outlined a set of beliefs known as the Noah's Ark policy that would help them "attempt to survive the flood of a disintegrating period of human association." He also sketched out a plan to establish a permanent home for the organisation called the Kin Garth.

'Kin Garth will be a tract of land which will form the Domus S. Spiritus of the Kindred throughout the world, and the regional core of the movement operating in these lands. It will be a place of research and experiment, as well as a retreat from the world without, and a living centre of all liberal Arts and Sciences. In the midst of green fields and wooded slopes we will build a university - monastery, lamasery, house of self-initiation? .... with a central Mote Hall open to the sky for the Socratic method of discussion. In this house there will be no place for sleeping nor eating, and no-one shall enter who is not intent upon some branch of the great work.

A great amount of the actual building of this house will be carried out by the Kin, even if this means some years of arduous toil..............in this place will be a bathing pool and a sungarth....handicraft sheds for the weavers, potters and workers in wood and metal etc will

Kibbo Kift Company of Archers

be situated away from the central building. On an open palin in front of the seats of council and the Great Standard of the Mark of the Kindred. Beyond this council circle shall be the place for the pitching of tents at such times as the Kindred assembles at the Garth....... ....Fields for tillage and pasture will be set aside, and sufficient food grown for the supply of so many. However, there will be no attempt to establish a colony of back to the land idealists - it will not be a Tolstoyian experiment. No plots will be let or sold to anyone, and it will not become a ramshackle, go-as-you-please huddle of odd folk with conflicting fads, putting up shanties and make shift bungalows of old railway carriages, broken down caravans and tarred felt................'
The Confession of the Kibbo Kift 1927

A permanent 'Kin Garth' was never established,

Greenshirts band

but the Kibbo Kift continued to hold its great annual 'Althing' gathering throughout the 20s. In 1923 Hargraves had been introduced to the Social Credit ideas of Major Douglas and these were gradually incorporated into the Kift's creed and by the early 1930s the Kibbo Kift, the Social Credit Movement and a Coventry based group known as the Crusader Legion merged and became the Green Shirt Movement of Social Credit named after their adopted paramilitary uniform. The Greenshirts organised numerous meetings and demonstrations in favour of Social Credit. On June 27th 1934 a green brick was thrown through the window of 11 Downing Street. In January 1937 the Public Order Act came into force banning the wearing of uniforms by political movements and although aimed primarily at the British Union of Fascists it conveniently dealt a blow against the Greenshirts as well. Not to be outdone, alternative forms of protest and propaganda were developed. Demonstrations were held with protestors carrying their shirts on poles, further green bricks were thrown, the Bank of England was daubed with the slogan "Britain Debt-Free!", 'Robin Hood' shot an arrow at 10 Downing Street and a protestor in a bright green crinoline dress marched up and down carrying a placard declaring, "Out-Of-Date - Like the Money System!"

At the height of the agitation in 1938 Hagreaves wrote the following utopian declaration;

What'll we do? What won't we do!
One time we'll build a new town: and if we don't like it
pull it down, and build another
you'd rather go fishing up the river? all right, then
what's to stop you? ... not me
we'll travel at 300 m.p.h. halfway round the earth
and the rest of the way on foot, just for fun
you'd rather stay at home and smoke a pipe,
... well, why not?
we'll turn every sound into its own colour-vibration
how's that?
you'd much rather have a garden to potter about in?
we'll show 'em how to print with light, instead of ink?
much prefer a round of golf?
We'll fit radiotelephones in every home?
you'd rather have no telephone at all?
right, we'll leave you out: that's easy ...
we'll take down all advertisement hoarding - good idea?
no one'll want 'em (they don't now)
you're too busy growing apples? ... well, that's all right
tell you what: we'll go for a walk, just anywhere
and not come back till we choose
you'd rather go on a luxury cruise? ... splendid
we'll use sun-energy direct for driving machines
not interested?
you'd rather go to a dancehall and dance?
we'll make a dancehall worth dancing in
in Xanadu did Kubla Khan
a stately pleasure-dome decree
You only want to dance in it? ... well, let me design it

The advent of the WW2 divided the members of the Kibbo Kift to the four corners of the earth and despite post-war efforts to revive the movement it was finally wound up in 1951. Never more than a few hundred strong the Kibbo Kift had an influence disproportionate to its size, partly through the space given to social credit in the pages of The New Age and partly through its influential mem-

179

bership list; suffragette leader Mrs Pethick Lawrence was a full Kinswoman and the Advisory Committee included such names as Havelock Ellis, Maurice Maeterlink, the Bengali poet Rabindranath Tagore, H.G. Wells and Professor Julian Huxley. In 1976 a rock opera, The Kibbo Kift, was performed at the Edinburgh Festival and subsequently repeated at the Crucible Theatre, Sheffield, where, when the cast was introduced to an aging Hargraves, such were his charisma and powers of persuasion that he could have formed a Clan of the Kibbo Kift right there and then in the dressing room. (For further info The Kibbo Kift Foundation have a website at : **www.enduser.co.uk/kibbokift/**)

THE DEMOCRATIC CAMP

A rift within the Kift in 1924 on the surface over the 'election of Kinsman Leslie A. Paul, Little Otter, as Thing Head Man of Brockleything' and 'the blackspotting of Eric C. Peake, Wanderwolf, of Eppingthing', but really about Hargraves' increasingly autocratic leadership lead to a breakaway of 'tribes' in South London and the formation of first, the 'The Wayfarers Fellowship' with recruits from the co-operative Junior Guild and then the Woodcraft Folk. The new group was to be a democratic working class pioneering fellowship based on the woodcraft methods of the Kibbo Kift but without its extravagance and more suited to the limited finances of city children. The small band of renegade tribes issued a declaration of aims in an attempt to get other dissident groups to join them.

"We declare that it is our desire:

(1) To develop In ourselves, for the service of the people, mental and physical health, and communal responsibility, by ; Camping out and living in close contact with nature; By using the creative faculty both of our minds and our hands; And by sincerity in all our dealings with our neighbours.

(2) To make ourselves familiar with the history of the world and the development of man in the slow march of evolution that we may understand and revere the Great Spirit that urges all things to perfect themselves. (3) We further declare that the welfare of the community can be assured only: when the instruments of production are owned by the community, and all things necessary for the good of the race are produced by common service for the common use: When the production of all things that directly or indirectly destroy human life ceases to be: And when man shall turn his labour from private greed to social service to increase the happiness of mankind, and when nations shall cease to suckle tribal enmities and unite In common fellowship".

Leslie Paul The Early Days of the Woodcraft Folk.

These remarkably utopian 'desires' attracted socialist interest and with the support of the Co-operative Union and the Labour Party the Woodcraft Folk went on to be the most successful of the woodcraft groups after the Scouts. Becoming in the 1930s a more overtly political and internationalist in its standpoint; marching against fascism and linking up with left wing youth organisations in Europe, such as the Red Falcons. The Woodcraft Folk exist today as a counterpoint to the militarism of the Scouts, with its history mirroring that of the wider Co-operative Movement and still eliciting among its members a passion for co-operation and the natural world that was implicit in its foundation.

'And there is the heart of the thing, the longing to live a kind of poetry, which so fulfilled the deep emotional hungers of the young people who joined it that some of them would speak of it as a new religion. Despite the socialist dressing we gave to everything, and believed we believed in, every kind of future reform or revolution paled beside our concern for the content of the actual life we were living at that moment. We were conscious that our youth was slipping away, and that unless we lived now the life we ought to live, the chance would soon be gone forever'

Leslie Paul. Angry Young Man .

CAMP CHIVALRY

In a clearing on the edge of the New Forest lie the remains of the leader of another branch of the woodcraft movement Ernest Westlake. He died in a car accident in 1922 and is buried not in a conventional grave but in a reproduction Bronze Age burial mound. The Order of Woodcraft Chivalry founded by Westlake in 1916 was the most overtly 'pagan' of the woodcraft organisations blending a mix of Ernest Seton's Native American lore with supposed Anglo-Saxon rites and the teachings of amongst others Edward Carpenter, Haverlock Ellis, Aleister Crowley, Nietzsche, Jane Ellen Harrison and Sir James Frazer.

Brought up a Quaker Westlake had, through reading widely, moved from being nominally Christian to a point where his wife Margaret could declare that the Order worshipped `the Great Spirit . . . under whatever manifestation or Name' On their estate at Sandy Balls in the New Forest the Westlake family drew up plans some time in 1919 for a forest park, which included the reintroduction of all the surviving animals of the Old Stone Age. Here bison would be hunted and young women 'attired like Artemis of old, would follow the deer on foot through the forests, tending and milking them'. The plans never got off the drawing board but by 1921 the order was strong enough to hold its first folkmoot ceremony on the old festival of Lammas. The opening ceremony bore a remarkable resemblance to the rites of modern pagan witchcraft with the lighting of a ritual fire within a sacred circle the blessing of the elements and the invocation of `Beloved Pan, and all ye other gods who haunt this place.' This and other similarities, namely the use of the term 'craft' to describe their work and the possible derivation of the word Wicca from the Anglo-Saxon Witan used as the name of the orders council, has lead to speculation that Woodcraft Chivalry was the forerunner of modern paganism and that the 'New Forest Coven' of Gerald Gardiner (the father of modern witchcraft) was none other than a meeting of the Order. The dates conveniently match up and further credence is given to this argument by the practice of gymnosophy, a form of naked dancing, by some members of the woodcrafters.

On the death of Ernest Westlake his son Aubrey took over the role of chief and the order continued to grow to a peak in the late 1920s of some 1200 members. The order became embroiled in internal conflicts as the pagan tendency fought against the Christian members leading to a decline in numbers and withdrawal of support from the Society of Friends. During the early 1930s a volunteer corps was set up called the Gryth Fryd (Saxon for Peace Army.) or Grith Volunteers and camps were held involving young unemployed men working on the land. A radical 'open-air' school known as the Forest School was also set up.

Aubrey Westlake resigned from the Order in 1934 depriving it of its base in the New Forest. The Order continued (and still continues) to hold weekend camps, social gatherings, and outings, discussion groups, and adventure expeditions including its annual Folkmoot. The Forest School closed, but was reborn as the Forest School Camps in 1948.

ORGANIC NATIONALISM

" We must plant ourselves again in the Universe."

D.H. Lawrence

Rolf Gardiner by Maxwell Armfield 1928

From far and wide they came bearing salt, earth, sulphur and lavender to the edge of Cranbourne Chase to dedicate 'a centre for the gathering and training of men and women for the weal of Wessex.' The Springhead Ring,

centred around the young blond Rolf Gardiner, wished to spark off a rural revival, 'from herb to the hymn', to restore England from the perilous state it had fallen in to since the end of the First World War. Springhead consisted of a group of mill buildings arranged around a courtyard on the edge of Gore Farm owned by Gardiner's uncle. This was no romantic rustic revival that was envisaged - this was hard-nosed pragmatism. The plan was to `rebuild a hill-and-vale economy along modern organic lines', restoring the ancient breeds of sheep to the Downs and reviving rural industries along with the traditional rural festivals.

From Austro-Hungarian/Jewish/Scandinavian background on his mother's side and with a British father, the young Rolf Gardiner was educated at the Bedales co-educational school in Derbyshire and as a young man became involved in the thriving Europe-wide youth movement of the time, having contact with the German Wandervogel and becoming something of a roving European ambassador for the Kibbo Kift. He saw hope for a renewed Europe in the "self-supporting communities" of young people that he saw "springing up all over Europe today." He met and corresponded with the novelist D.H. Lawrence.

'I'm sure you are doing the right thing, with hikes and dances and songs. But somehow it needs a central clue, or it will fizzle away again. There needs a centre of silence, and a heart of darkness--to borrow from Rider Haggard. We'll have to establish some spot on earth, that will be the fissure into the underworld, like the oracle at Delphos, where one can always come to. I will try to do it myself. I will try to come to England and make a place--some quiet house in the country--where one can begin--and from which the hiker, maybe, can branch out. Some place with a big barn and a bit of land--if one has enough money. Don't you think that is what it needs? And then one must set out and learn a deep discipline--and learn dances from all the world, and take whatsoever we can make into our own. And learn music the same.'

D.H. Lawrence

Letter To Rolf Gardiner. 3 December, 1926 .

ENGLISH SOCIAL LEADERSHIP

Gardiner set up the Gore Kinship and organised study groups and camps. This little group would turn into the Springhead Ring upon the purchase of Springhead Mill by his uncle and the work of building a movement for the revival of rural England could begin in earnest. Throughout the 1930s the Springhead Ring ran numerous camps with the aim of combating the effects of the depression years by creating a 'reinvigorated stock of countrymen' from the unused material of the towns. Gardiner wrote a report for

Springhead camp C1930's

the Minister of Labour on the camps in which he gave details of a 'Harvest Camp' at Springhead. Sixty-nine young men and women 'from different walks of life' spent a number of weeks gaining 'a direct experience of community by thinking, playing and working on the land'. The 'different walks' included; teachers and social workers, one farm girl, three public schoolboys, six university lecturers, two house painters, two miners, a brass engraver and a cinema operator. Also taking part were twelve members of the German Youth Movement. Quite what this cross section of the nations unemployed made of the heady mix of activities on offer at the camp we are not told. As they progressed the camps developed a regular pattern. Rising at 6.30 to 'the rhythmic beating of a mellow-toned gong' the campers would run barefoot behind the camp chiefs in sin-

gle file snaking in and out of the tents in 'circular evolutions' mimicking the twisting and turning rays of the rising sun coming to a rest around a central flagstaff where they sang a hymn to the dawn, whilst the Cross of St George with a Wessex Dragon emblazoned across it, flew above. After breakfast they worked on the farm, clearing neglected woodland, dredging the silted up millpond or planting willow for the revival of rural basket making. The afternoon was for quiet study and contemplation with singing or folk dancing at 4.30. An early evening lecture would be held on the subject chosen as a theme for the camp such as the Tradition of English Social Leadership or Land Settlement and Regional Reconstruction. The day would end by torchlight with everyone standing arm in arm singing:

The Earth has turned us from the sun,
And let us close our circle now to light,
But open it to darkness, and each one
Warm with this circle's warming,
Go in good darkness to good sleep
Good night.

At which point the camp herald would extinguish his torch and the members of the 'ring' would retire to their tents.

The camps were successful and attended by a wide variety of people including the comedian Jimmy Edwards and the composer Michael Tippet who provided music for some of the camps. Music and dance were important features of the camps with a strong emphasis on English folk songs. For a couple of years from 1932 the camps were extended to East Cleveland where Gardiner ran them for unemployed Ironstone miners creating allotments. Gardiner was highly critical of the other major example of rural revivalism of the time at Dartingon Hall where he himself had been educated in silviculture, bemoaning it's lack of soul and suggesting that it needed to "add an expert in social affection, an engineer in community joy" to its collection of experts on rural regeneration.

PHANTOM SWASTIKAS IN THE WOODS

Other more shadowy organisations were active in the Dorset countryside at the same time with similar aims as the Springhead Ring. The combative sounding Wessex Agricultural Defence Association and the much more overtly nationalistic English Array each with links to Oswald Moseley's British Union of Fascists. Each tried to woo Gardiner into their ranks. But whilst Gardiner was sympathetic with their talk of regenerating `English stock' and praise for unpasteurised milk and the cottage pig, he disagreed with the methods they chose to pursue their dream of an English revival and repeatedly distanced himself from their activities. This did not stop his name becoming associated with far-right politics and this along with his connections with the German Youth Movement, which he continued to support even after it was overrun by the Hitler Youth, mean't that he became the target of rumours and smears at the outbreak of the Second World War. The most persistent rumour was that he had planted trees in the shape of a swastika to guide German bombers. And perhaps because of his blond hair and Scandinavian good looks and fondness for wearing lederhosen it was reputed that Hitler had him marked out as a local dictator for Wessex following an invasion. The great irony in all these myths and rumours was of course that given his mother's Jewish heritage Gardiner would not have lasted long at all under Nazi rule. He himself considered the Nazis to be figures from some Wagnerian nightmare and later admitted he had been mistaken and misguided in his pre-war views of Germany.

Work camps continued at Springhead during the war years and groups of German prisoners came to work the farm. Gardiner inadvertently adding to the rumour mongering by greeting them in German when they arrived. The war also threw up an opportunity for a further venture in rural revival. In 1929 Gardiner became involved in developing the Wessex flax industry utilising a derelict flax mill at Slape in West Dorset. From this base Gardiner oversaw nearly 400 people as the government's agent for flax production in the West Country. With a core of experienced flax workers and a host of school children, Women's Land Army members and even troops drafted in at harvest time, he tried to create a thriving rural craft industry based on independent growers, processors, spinners and weavers with the aim of organising them into a regional guild under the slogan `Wessex fabrics from Wessex fields'. He tried to instigate flax feasts and harvest festivals with accompanying folk song and dance, but was thwarted in his attempts by the Home Flax Directorate who wanted to see a highly mechanised, centrally controlled flax industry and in the end left Gardiner no choice but to part company with them in 1942.

Rolf Gardiner's achievements on his uncle's farm were impressive. He had taken over the running of the farm in 1927 aged only 25 and carried out a mass reforestation programme planting in total some 3 million trees. He believed that upland planting would raise the falling water table even on the porous chalk downs: a belief borne out when in the 1970s drought years Gore farm remained green whilst all around turned brown. His forestry management was way ahead of its time with methods pioneered on the Dorset Downs in the 1920s only recently being taken up by the Forestry Commission as good practice. The farm was (and still is) managed on organic lines long before it was fashionable and Rolf Gardiner was a founding member of the Soil Association on its establishment in 1945. Springhead is now owned by the Springhead Trust, set up by Gardiner's widow with the help and encouragement of Fritz Schumacher after her husband's death in 1971 and is run as a conference centre hosting the like of the Other Economic Summit, the Soil association and Voluntary Services Overseas.

Rolf Gardiner never did manage to totally shake off the tag of being a Nazi sympathiser with Springhead visitors still asking, 'Is this where the Nazi lived?' He never planted a swastika in trees on the Dorset Downs. How could he have done? He had carried out his reforestation programme in the 1920s long before the rise of the Nazis. He did however plant a different symbol on a Wessex hillside, Balfour's Circle, a ring of evergreen trees, each one a different North European species, marking the site of his uncle Balfour Gardiner's interred ashes and perhaps marking in the circle of diversity a different vision of Europe.

COMMUNITY THERAPY

The idea that living in a community could have a therapeutic effect on an individual has its roots in the changes in British psychiatry in the early 1900's. When rather than seeing all mental illness as a result of physical degeneration it was recognised that a social dynamic was involved. Hospitals began to open their closed wards, admitting voluntary patients, and outside of hospital a wide range of private therapy was becoming available. This change would be felt firstly in educational experiments and later in the treatment of soldiers. Some therapist reached the conclusion that we are genetically equipped to live in small communities and that it is our large Western societies that are making us ill.

THE LITTLE COMMONWEALTH

The Junior Republic at Freeville and the Ford Republic at Farmington, both American radical educational experiments where self-government had been introduced into a residential school environment, attracted considerable attention from those looking for solutions to prison overcrowding and the treatment of 'delinquents'. In 1913 Homer Lane, who had worked at the Ford republic was invited to England to set up a similar experiment at Flowers Farm on the Earl of Sandwich's estate in Dorset and so The Little Commonwealth was born as a home for post school age adolescents referred by the Courts or their own parents.

'Flowers Farm was a place of breath-taking beauty, set in a narrow fold of the Dorset hills. The back of the farmhouse faced a large square courtyard, and the other three sides of which were farm buildings. The Committee's plan was to convert the back of the farmhouse so that it presented a `face' to the Great Court, and then convert the farm buildings into a workshop and laundry on the right, an executive building opposite, and a schoolroom on the left. .... North of this main group of buildings was to be a road with three cottages on each side, and perhaps, ultimately, a 'circle' at the end

of the road with three more cottages. To replace the farm buildings thus absorbed fresh ones were to be erected about half a mile away. All the cottages were to be given the names of local vegetation, and the original farmhouse was forthwith re-christened 'Bramble'.

David Wills *Homer Lane.*

Lane organised the 'citizens' that arrived from borstals and remand homes into family units that for many of them was their only experience of stable family life. Self-government was introduced through a Citizen's Court, which included all those over 14 years of age. Lane saw the court as 'an occasion for searching group analysis' where by dealing with complaints about their conduct and having to award punishment the citizens would start to take responsibility for their lives. For 5 years Lane carried out ground-breaking work with little but his own intuition to guide him. The Commonwealth was supported by an influential committee and Lane was much in demand as a speaker his influence and example spreading through both educational and penal reform groups. One visitor in 1917 for whom the experience would be a turning point in his life was a young Scottish teacher by the name of A.S. Neil, who would go on to found his own experiment in radical education in the 1920s known as Summerhill.

'The combination of self government and an inspiring personality has been the model for other pioneers of schools for the maladjusted. Lane used what we now call group therapy with shared responsibility 50 years ago.'

Malcolm Pines

Forgotten pioneers: The unwritten history of the therapeutic community movement.

In 1918, following allegations of sexual impropriety made against Lane by two girls, the Home Office withdrew is support and the Commonwealth was forced to close.

ALTERNATIVE TECHNOLOGIES

Yesterday's 'alternative' technology will one day be tomorrows mainstream industrial process. So it was in the past. All technology was once upon a time alternative. The social innovators who set up utopian experiments were often technical innovators as well, driving their visions of a new world with visionary new devices some of them fantastical flights of fancy, some remarkably practical.

THE MONEY BEHIND THE MACHINE

As far back as the1630s Dr Robert Fludd, a visionary Rosicrucian, designed and built a series of fantastical machines; a bellowing wooden bull, an 'automatic' dragon and a performing harp. But it was the Quakers who made the biggest impact on technological advance in the early industrial period. Denied access to universities and the professions because of their refusal to swear oaths they put their not inconsiderable talents and wealth into commerce and industry, where if they were not the actual inventors of new techniques and processes they appear time and time again as the money and quiet driving force behind them. At Nenthead the London Lead Mining Company pioneered new mining techniques. At Ironbridge the Darbys pushed forward advances in iron smelting, while in the North East the Pease family, prominent in the mining industry, provided finance for the development of Stevenson's Rocket and the Stockton to Tees Railway. The mechanisation of the weaving industry was pushed forward with Quaker backing, perhaps most significantly through the financing of Robert Owen at New Lanark. These advances were all carried out in a conventional business framework, but in each case the Quaker influence is discernible with in many cases money being spent on providing decent housing and social welfare for the workforce.

SHAKING TECHNOLOGY

Across the Atlantic the Shakers were innovators and inventors par excellence. They saw new technology as having social and moral benefits: `every improvement relieving human toil or facilitating labour [gives] time and opportunity for moral, mechanical, scientific and intellectual improvement and the cultivation of the finer and higher qualities of the human mind.'

Elisha Myrick. Harvard Shaker Community.

The Shakers are credited with a long list of inventions: a screw propeller, Babbitt metal, a rotary harrow, an automatic spring, a turbine water wheel, a threshing machine, the circular saw, cut nails, a pipe machine, a pea-sheller, a self-acting cheese press, a butter worker, the common clothes pin, the first one-horse wagon used in the US, a palm-leaf bonnet loom, a silkreeling machine, a revolving oven, a machine for paring, coring, and quartering apples, and the first metal pens. They patented none of their inventions, believing that patents smacked of monopoly.

SOLAR PARADISE

In 1836 a book was published by a J.A.Etzler entitled *The Paradise within the reach of all men, without labour, by powers of nature and machinery*. In it were plans for a community where solar, wind, tidal and wave energy would be harnessed. He declared that there were "powers in nature sufficient to effect in one year more than hitherto all men on earth could do in many thousands of years . . ." and the most profitable, shortest and easiest way to put them into operation for such great purposes, is, to form "associations". Etzler's remarkably prophetic vision included; huge prefabricated flat-roofed apartment blocks with `boxes that move up and down' to reach the upper floors and piped hot & cold water, gas and scents. Finding no takers for his solar paradise in his native America Etzler came to England in 1840 where he found, support for his ideas among English followers of the French visionary Charles Fourier. In a series of talks and demonstrations he presented a number of his inventions; among them a multipurpose plough-bulldozer and a wave-powered boat. After the automated boat sank on its maiden voyage and a brief speaking tour of West Yorkshire, where a number of Eztlerian groups were set up, Eztler set off for Venezuela with an invention for crystallising sugar without heat that he said would make slavery unnecessary.

STEAM CO-OPERATIVES

Many innovations in technology displaced as many, if not more, workers than they benefited leading to outbreaks of rioting and machine breaking by workers in last ditch attempts to prevent the destruction of their livelihoods. There is one instance of new technology being embraced in a co-operative form in an attempt to protect workers' jobs. In the ribbon-making industry in Coventry in the 1840's groups of independent ribbon weavers banded together and set up what became known as cottage factories in response to the introduction of steam powered looms. Living in rows of cottages with upper-storey workshops it was relatively simple for the weavers to run a continuous shaft through the entire row connected to a single steam engine at the end of the terrace and power each loom as it passed through the individual still independent workshop. These 'factories' varied from 2 or 3 houses up to a hundred and records show some 1250 looms were being powered this way by the 1850s. Whilst independent weavers set up most cottage factories a number were established by sympathetic manufacturers including the Quaker Cash brothers who were influenced by Owenite ideas. They planned a quadrangle of 100 'cottages' around a central steam engine and surrounded by allotment gardens. Only a small portion of the scheme was actually built. The cottage factory schemes lasted until the 1860's when cheap French imports undermined the whole Coventry ribbon industry.

A HUMANE REVOLUTION

Early 19th century utopians were mostly looking for a better, more humane, way of organising the industrial revolution and embraced the technological advances as the means to creating paradise on earth. Later in the century when the full effects of industrialisation started to bite, the same technology would be seen by the likes of John Ruskin and his Guild of St George as part of the old immoral world that they were fighting against, leading to the concentration on the hand-made and hand-crafted prevalent in the Arts & Crafts Movement. Occasionally technology was used to combat the ills of industrialisation as in the case of Titus Salt's mills at Saltaire.

The whole Saltaire model village was intended to alleviate the conditions of squalor caused by the industrialisation of Bradford. The great textile mill that dominates the village was equipped with a system of flues to provided ventilation. Great plate-glass windows let ample light into the building. Drive shafts for machinery were run between the floors to reduce dust, noise and the risk of accidents and the latest fire safety precautions were installed. Special conduits caught the rain-water and stored it in tanks, ready to be used by the factory. And perhaps most impressive of all the 250ft mill chimney was fitted with special smoke-burning appliances that meant that little if any of the smoke from the fifty tons of coal burnt each day ever reached the top.

'It is obvious that suspicion of the machine in the workplace is not a nineteenth century phenomenon; it continues with regard to the automation and computorization that characterize the present industrial revolution. Many of the contentious issues are similar and are concerned with control of the machine. And the issue of control is not, as some philosophers and historians would have us imagine. that of man versus machine. It is the much older conflict of man versus man.'

Witold Rybczynski. *Taming the Tiger.*

Q CAMPS

'There have been indications that a need exists for a camp community, that will especially cater for certain types of young men (camps for women may be started later) who, with a few exceptions, have been hitherto excluded. The category in mind is that of young men from 17 to 25 - that is, above the upper age limit for Juvenile Courts - who seem likely to respond to an unconventional but carefully thought out open air community life........'   *Q Camps Memorandum July 1935*

An invitation was sent out to a number of organisations and interested individuals to attend a meeting on May 3rd 1935 to discuss the proposal to set up Q Camps. The meeting was initiated by the council of Grith Pioneers, an organisation which offered camp life to young men at a time of massive unemployment and demoralisation. It was hoped that through living in a supportive community the men would regain their self-respect and experience 'improvement in self-control, social behaviour, physical health, mental alertness and general outlook.' The Q Camps Memorandum outlined the activities that would take place at the proposed camps;

'Gardening, elementary farm work, care of livestock and various handicrafts will be included. Among other activities within the scope of the camps will be

Camp staff, residents & friends outside a self-built hut.

games, folk dancing, drama, music, debates, reading and, when desired, instruction in academic subjects. The construction of the camp and much of the furnishing will be done by the campers themselves.'

THE EMOTIONAL VORTEX

Quaker David Wills had worked in a number of hostels for maladjusted boys and in the Settlement Houses sponsored by the Quakers in the Welsh Valleys. He was also the first British psychiatric social worker to have trained in America. Early in 1935 he wrote an article for *The Friend* calling for a bold experiment in the treatment of young offenders. He received a letter in response to his article from Dr Marjorie Franklin, a member of the Q Camps Committee inviting him to join them in setting up their first camp. Hawkspur Camp was established on a few acres of land on Hill Hall Common, near Great Bardfield, Essex in May1936 with David Wills as Camp Chief. Wills was an inspired choice; he knew of Homer Lane's work and became the lynchpin at the centre of the 'emotional vortex' that the camp became. The camp was set up on a self-governing basis with all decisions taken by a the Camp Committee. The camp consisted of an office; a two-storey wooden chalet-type building that stood at the top of the camp, the camp quad was further down the track, with cook and washhouses. At the bottom of the site was the

Hawkspur Camp Essex

accommodation with a long building used as the main bunkhouse and meeting/activities house. All of the buildings were built by the camp staff and residents, student helpers and Grith Fyrd volunteers.

'David Wills understood that the lads who came to the camp were profoundly dissatisfied with themselves; they were failures who hated themselves. Their protection was hating the world about them. On discovering that they were given freedom, not discipline, they had to begin to discipline themselves. .... In him the boys sought the loving parent they had not had and with great skill and understanding he lived through the 'corrective emotional experience 'they sought. They attached themselves to him and to his wife. Time and time again the lads would test his capacity to go on loving in the face of delinquency and bad behaviour.'

Malcolm Pines *Forgotten pioneers.*

In the front of the 2nd Edition of his account of the camp, *The Hawkspur Experiment,* David Wills catalogues a series of thumbnail biographies of the young men who came through the camp nearly all of them a testimony to the success of the community. The camp came to an end at the onset of the war. David Wills went on to create therapeutic communities for disturbed children at Barns House, near Peebles in Scotland, and at Bodenham Manor, in Herefordshire. Dr. Denis Carroll the young camp psychiatrist did pioneering work in the rehabilitation of disturbed soldiers at the Northfield Military Hospital and Psychiatric Training Centre in Birmingham using the experience he had gained at Hawkspur. Dr. Norman Glaister who had been a member of the original Grith Pioneer committee that had initiated the camp and a leading light in the Code of Woodcraft Chivalry joined The Commonwealth Party during the war and after was instrumental in founding the School of Integrative Social Research at Braziers Park in Oxfordshire to 'study the art and science of living in practical ways and explore the advantages and problems of living in a group'.

JUNGIAN COMMUNITY FOR THE HEALING ARTS

Irene and Gilbert Champernowne founded Withymead therapeutic community in Exeter in 1941 as an alternative to psychiatric hospitals. Intentionally small with a maximum of 45 patients so that the atmosphere could be kept informal and personal ' It aimed to be a sanctuary where self healing could take hold and regression could be understood, held and contained.'

Withymead had links the the Elmhirsts at Dartington Hall. The Champernowne family having sold the estate to them for their experiment in rural regeneration, the Elmhirsts became involved in supporting the Exeter community. The community revolved and evolved around Irene Champernowne, a woman of commanding personality and strong will, who had trained with Jung in Switzerland and had been influenced by contact with Alfred Adler in Vienna. At Withymead she created an 'anti-bureaucratic' spirit using a mix of psychotherapy and art therapy with painting, modelling, pottery, music, movement and dance all being used. The community admitted neurotic and psychotic patients and also others who came seeking help without an identifiable illness. The staff had all been in personal analysis, and all the therapists worked closely together.

'In the intimacy of its social organisation, Withymead resembled not only the extended family but a small tribal clan of the type that human beings have lived in since our species began. Withymead thus satisfied the archetypal nostalgia that all of us share for life in such small intimate associations of people, and this goes far to explain its compelling attractiveness.'

Anthony Stephens
Withymead. A Jungian community for the healing arts.

Although subsidised by the Elmhirsts the community ran into increasing financial difficulties and was forced to seek patients from the new National Health Service. Along with the patients came administrators and medical directors. The previous 'feminine' nature and traditions of the community were challenged by what the largely female staff saw as a 'masculine conspiracy'. The men in turn accused the women of allowing irrational prejudices to blind them to economic reality and the need for change.

'As the men increasingly took us over, imposing full medical cover, nurses, administrators, hospital routines and so on, the worse everything became, and the spiritual core of the community, which carried the despair and the sickness of the patients, was destroyed.'

Irene Champernowne

Withymead finally closed in 1954 having 'treated' 240 people over the 13 years of its existence. From these beginnings a whole therapeutic communities movement grew up during the 1960s & 70s with numerous small scale residential communities caring for the mentally handicapped and the mentally ill.

CURATIVE EDUCATION

As the Second World War began, a small group of refugees from Nazi-held Austria arrived in this country. Among them was Dr Karl König who had significant experience in working with children with a learning disability in a residential setting. Inspired by the work of a number of past utopian thinkers including Count Zinzendorf of the Moravian Church, Robert Owen and Rudolf Stiener, König argued that each of these three individuals had "imagined a new social order wherein a new social brotherhood could be established. They strove for a universal brotherhood among all men."

The Doctor and his group of young helpers settled at Aberdeen in Scotland and set about establishing a school to put their ideas into practice. All the men in the party were interned after Dunkirk, leaving the women to begin the project. They were released after six months and with a loan of £1,000 from the Scottish Council for Refugees Camphill House was able to open its doors to its first pupils. In the first year 19 pupils between 2 and 19 years old all with learning disabilities joined the 'school'. König claimed that the children were social refugees having been cast out of society in the same way that he and his co-workers had been cast out of his homeland.

At Camphill members lived and worked with the children in a community setting carrying out what König called 'Curative Education'. The work was based on three essential principles;

A regard for the spiritual nature of one's fellow man.

To endeavour to develop ones inner life.

The establishment of a true community.

Demand for places at Camphill house far exceeded the available space even with expansion and by 1950 there were 222 pupils with a further 156 on the waiting list. An H.M.I. Report compiled in the 1940s noted that the Camphill schools were the only form of education available for children with severe learning disabilities. Further Camphill schools were established across the British Isles.

Karl König still held out the hope of establishing true communities and in 1955 following requests from parents for Camphill to provide provision for adults The Camphill Village Trust was formed its aim being to 'establish and maintain villages (according to stated principles) for the development of working communities for mentally handicapped persons from school leaving age upwards.' Through the generosity of the Macmillan family, whose son had gone to the Aberdeen school, the first Camphill village community was formed at Botton Village in Yorkshire the first in a long line of such communities set up over the following decades. The International Camphill Movement now consists of more than 90 communities in 19 countries.

"I have no doubt that Camphill is an expression of a great intuitive thrust out of the deep heart of nature which has us in its keeping and knows that both we and it are in mortal peril."

Sir Laurens van der Post

Commentary
& Reflection.

HYPOCHONDRIACS OF THE SOUL.

Looked at close up the 'Old New Age' bears a remarkable resemblance to the present new age movement, complete with Mystic Magazines and Catalogues of the Cosmic, weekend courses in any subject you could care to imagine, dancecamps on organic farms, communes with strange diets or led by wise, or demonised gurus, take your pick. The whole scene a veritable supermarket of the esoteric.

It would be very easy, and it is very tempting, to ridicule many of the characters in the previous pages, which would largely be unfair both to the ideas of the leaders of the various 'fads and movements' and the desires of their followers. We should remember that yesterday's crank theory can easily turn into tomorrow's popular cult and today's quack scientist into tomorrow's Nobel prize winner. Ideas like phrenology are often referred to as 'quasi-sciences' but should really be seen as disproved sciences. After all much of what has been thought to be scientifically true has been later disproved. Just because phrenology ended its days as a seaside pier attraction should not detract from the seriousness of the intent of its originators. Neither should we take any less seriously the genuine search for spiritual meaning by the followers of the legions of teachers and gurus because some of their claims have been disproved, or that amongst their number there would appear to have been more than the occasional charlatan at work.

Originally magic and science were not separate but both part of a quest for understanding of the world; many early scientists being accused of witchcraft. Long before Darwin's theory of evolution started to undermine people's religious beliefs, the rise of science caused people to ask scientists if they could explain the unexplained. The rise in spiritualism came shortly after the invention of the telephone, (which as far as I am concerned is still as much magic as science.) People thought, with reasonable logic, that if you could talk to a living person hundreds of miles away by this new-fangled device, then it was not a huge leap to be able to get a direct line to heaven - maybe not Jesus on the mainline, but at least your nearest and dearest.

The communities in this thread were just the more visible tip of the various movements that they were part of. Many more individuals were involved in them either as believers or as intrigued onlookers. The communities, as with most other utopian experiments, can be seen as experiential, social and spiritual research & development departments for society as a whole - providing a supportive environment for the pushing of personal and social boundaries. Looked at in that way, the few esoteric blind alleys and potentially explosive social theories that were explored by their adherents seem inevitable and forgivable.

There is a sort of unspoken assumption that utopian experiments are somehow the province of those on the political left. Rolf Gardiner's experiment in Dorset shows how difficult untangling that assumption can be in reality and the experience of the Anthrosophical society in Germany under the Nazi regime would prove even more compromising. Even today intentional communities are not exclusively on the left - Some members of the British National Front, a small neo-Nazi group, sought solace on a 'back to the land' commune in France after they were driven off the streets by the Anti-Nazi League and other anti-racist organisations in the 1980s. And perhaps more ominously Front 14 in their magazine, The National-Socialist 41, and on their website talk of creating a new Ayran homeland through a trek or by founding a rural community.

Perhaps the New Age is not new at all, but with us all the time, just appearing to be new to each generation of seekers who come across it and mistake its novelty for newness. Ronald Hutton in his history of modern pagan witchcraft, The Triumph of the Moon, traces a convincing link, at least in form and role, from nineteenth century 'cunning folk' to present day 'alternative' health practitioners. Certainly the inheritors of the traditions of libertarian educators of the likes of Pierrepont Greaves and Homer Lane could be found in the membership list of Education Otherwise. And the speed with which Feng Shui went from obscure Chinese art to mainstream craze, either suggests a highly gullible,or cynical, popular press or a genuine mass interest in these thing bubbling away under the surface. Scratch that surface and how many of us would admit "there is probably something to it."

"Asked by Goldsworthy Lowes Dickenson how he related mysticism to socialism Carpenter replied that he liked to hang out his red flag from the ground floor and then go up above to see how it looked.. "

Edward Carpenter in appreciation ed. Gilbert Beith 1931

THE OLD NEW AGE : BIBLIOGRAPHY

The Dark Side of History. Subversive Magic & the Occult underground. Michael Edwardes. Corgi 1980

The cultural meaning of popular science. Roger Cooter. CUP 1984

Call No Man Master. Joyce Collin-Smith. Gateway Books. 1988.

The Village that Died for England. Patrick Wright. Jonathan Cape 1995.

The Life of George Combe. Charles Gibbon, 2 vols., Macmillan & Co., 1878.

Search for a New Eden: James Pierrepont Greaves:The Sacred Socialist and his followers J.Latham. DickinsonUP1999

California Utopia: Point Loma 1887-1942. E.A.Greenwalt. Point Loma Publications.1955 (Reprint 1978)

Madame Blavatsky's Baboon:Theosophy&the emergence of the Western Guru. P.WashingtonSecker&Warburg.'93 REC

Annie Besant. A Biography. Anne Taylor. Oxford University Press. 1992.

Gurdjieff. Fritz Peters. Wildwood House. 1976

G.I.Gurdjieff:The War Against Sleep. Colin Wilson. The Aquarian Press. 1986

Rudolf Stiener: The Man and his Vision. Colin Wilson. The Aquarian Press. 1986

The Strange Life of P.D.Oupensky. Colin Wilson. The Aquarian Press. 1993

The Order of Woodcraft Chivalry:1916-1944 2vols. Derek Edgell. Edwin Mellen Press 1993

Social Credit for Beginners. JS & JT Osbourne. Pulp Press. 1986

The Hawkspur Experiment. David Wills. Allen & Unwin 1967.

Homer Lane - a biography. David Wills. Allen & Unwin. 1964

The Triumph of the Moon: a history of modern pagan witchcraft. Ronald Hutton OUP 2000. RECOMMENDED

Social Movements and thier supporters. M.Drakefield. Macmillan. 1997

Socialism and the New Life. The personal & sexual politics of E Carenter & H Ellis. S. Rowbotham. Pluto Press.1977

The Avalonians. Patrick Benham. Gothic Image. 1993

Rutland Boughton and the Glastonbury festivals. Micheal Hurd. OUP. 1993.

Letchworth Garden City in old picture postcards. R.G.Lancaster. European Library 1994

Edward Carpenter in appreciation ed. Gilbert Beith Allen & Unwin 1931

Pioneer Work with Maladjusted Children. Maurice Bridgeland's 1971

Withymead. A Jungian community for the healing arts. A.Stevens Coventure. 1986

Guild Socialism Restated G. D. H. Cole,1920

The Confession of the Kibbo Kift. John Hargraves. Maclellan. 1927

Aleister Crowley: The Beast Demystified. R.Hutchinson. Mainstream Publishing. 1998

The Aleister Crowley Scrapbook. S.Robertson. W.Foulsham&Co. 1988

UTOPIA FOR EVERYONE

Land Fit For Heroes

PUBLIC LIBRARY

Land Settlement Association

SETTLEMENT HOUSE

PUBLIC BATHS

INFANT AND JUNIOR SCHOOL

As far back as Gerard Winstanley's address to Cromwell, The Law of Freedom on a Platform, in which he outlined what amounted to the first 'communist manifesto', plans have been issued with proposals to transform small practical utopian experiments into programmes for the country as a whole or at least for specific groups of citizens. The Civil War period produced a whole series of schemes for the reform of society as a whole. These detailed utopian programmes existed alongside a tradition of literary utopias, it being sometimes difficult to tell one from the other. Some fantasy utopias containing well-thought-out practical programmes as in James Harrington's The Common-Wealth of Oceana published in 1656. Harringtons book was dedicated to Oliver Cromwell who was given the task of turning England into Oceana. Cromwell appears in the book thinly disguised as the hero 'Olphaus Megalater'.

Underneath its allegorical trappings Oceana is a written constitution for a new model England with a series of proposals for solving the problems of the country that had occurred since the abolition of the monarchy. These included proposals for the conduct of elections, the carrying out of a national census, converting marriage into a civil rite, taxing bachelors & tax-relief for families with children and a scheme of compulsory free education. In 1659 the Levellers declared themselves in favour of Oceana and the book was influential in the adoption of secular constitutions by the founders of the American proprietary colonies in Carolina, New Jersey and Pennsylvania. Harrington tried to retire from public life after the restoration of the monarchy but was eventually imprisoned where he went mad.

The tradition of society wide utopian schemes would be continued by the likes of Quaker John Bellars, Thomas Spence, Robert Owen and John Minter Morgan. From the mid-19th century onwards in the wake of Owenite agitation and alongside the rise and fall of the Chartists others working more in the mainstream of English society put forward schemes to alleviate social ills.

NATIONAL EVILS AND PRACTICAL REMEDIES

James Silk Buckingham, seaman, writer & publisher, temperance and anti-slavery campaigner and the first Member of Parliament for Sheffield from 1832 to 1837, was the first person to attempt to introduce library legislation to parliament in 1834; a move that would eventually lead to The Public Libraries Act, with its concept of the provision of free access to libraries for the working class.

In 1849 he published a pamphlet entitled *National Evils and Practical Remedies, with a Plan of a Model Town.* which contained the blueprint for a new model town to be named Victoria in honour of the Queen. The name also signified a moral victory over the social ills of mid-19th century society. Buckingham declared that his design for Victoria was aimed at removing 'ignorance, intemperance, National prejudice, Commercial Mono-polies, war and competition.' as well as alleviating 'the helpless and hopeless condition of the Unfortunate.'

Buckingham had visited the American religious utopian communities of the Society of Separatists of Zoar in Ohio and Economy, the community set up by The Rappites in Pennsylvania after they had sold New Harmony to Robert Owen. He was influenced by the ideas of the Owenites and John Minter Morgan and the Church of England Self-Supporting Villages Society. Victoria however was on a scale far larger than Owen's Villages of Co-oper-

ation or anything envisaged by Minter Morgan.

The blueprint for Victoria outlined plans for a new town of 10,000 inhabitants to be built on the banks of a navigable river close to the coast. A site of 10,000 acres was to be purchased by a private development company, the Model Town Association, incorporated by Royal Charter through Act of Parliament. The company would raise 3 million pounds of capital to finance the scheme by issue of £20 shares; Each resident having to subscribe to at least one share. In the middle of the estate surrounded by farms the town would be laid out on a square plan with each side of the square a mile long. Eight concentric squares of buildings would end in the centre with a green park with the main public buildings grouped around it. Radiating out from the central park would be a series of avenues named; Faith, Hope, Charity, Fortitude, Justice, Unity, Peace and Concord. Alongside each 80ft wide main avenue was to be a 20ft glazed gothic colonnade to provide shelter from both the sun and the rain for people on their way to and from work. Every road was to lead somewhere as Buckingham deplored blind alleys that might lead the inhabitants to 'the morose defiance of public decency'.

'In the centre of the whole is an Octagonal Tower, of 100 feet diameter at the base, to be crowned with a spire of 300 feet elevation, and to contain an Electric Light for lighting the whole Town; a large illuminated clock; the bells for public worship....'

James Silk Buckingham.
National Evils and Practical Remedies.1849

Ground plan for Victoria
From: *National evils and practical remedies(1849)*

The plan for Victoria is similar to Christopher Wren's plans for the reconstruction of London after the Great Fire - which Buckingham acknowledged although he claimed not to have seen Wren's plan until after he had finished drawing up his own. It also bears a resemblance to William Penn's design for the city of Philadelphia, which Buckingham visited on his tour of America.

It was envisaged that the development company would not only build the new model town, but would continue to manage it once it was built retaining ownership of all buildings. It would also be the sole employer in the town operating a strict eight hour day, providing free medical services, nurseries, schools, public baths, kitchens and laundries. Doctors were to be paid to prevent disease rather than cure it. I million pounds of the original capital was to be used to finance industry and agriculture with 40 acres being set aside for factories and workshops. The Model Town Association would also lay down strict moral codes for the inhabitants. The town was to be teetotal and non-smoking, and free of pawnbrokers gambling-houses, and brothels. Freedom of worship would be guaranteed, however the Sabbath was to be strictly observed. Some of the moral codes were to be simply draconian. If a couple's marriage were to break down not only would they be expelled from the town, but the Minister who married them and all the wedding guests were to be expelled along with them.

Despite being an accomplished self-publicist producing a series of magazines *The Athenaeum, The Sphinx and The Oriental Herald and Colonial review*, nothing came of Buckingham's plans for Victoria during his lifetime.

THE HEALTHY CITY

As the 19th century progressed the issue of public health came more and more to the fore as the increasing environmental Impacts of Industrialisation and the accompanying concentrations of population in the cities were felt. public health reform would become another plank on which the foundations of town planning would be built. In 1876 a renowned doctor and public health reformer, Benjamin Ward Richardson, founder and editor of the *Journal of Public Health and Sanitary Review*, published a plan for a city which if built would result in the lowest mortality combined with the highest longevity. *Hygeia, a City of Health* put forward 'revolutionary solutions for abolishing the wretches of Victorian slums' in the form of a utopian novel. The hundred thousand inhabitants of the model city live in houses built of coloured glazed bricks arranged to each householders taste - the bricks are so attractive that the need for plaster & wall paper is eliminated thereby reducing damp. Each house is built over a solid brick 'subway' in which run all the services - drainage, water, gas. Each house has a system of air-conditioning whereby through the means of perforated bricks fresh air, which can be heated if required, is introduced to the house. Rubbish disposal is through shafts in the walls with access hatches on all floors. Each house had its own garden and many have roof gardens. All properties are subject to pollution controls. Every chimney has a secondary burner to burn off excess carbon. Areas are zoned with certain blocks reserved for artisans' and craftsmen's workshops. Water & gas are provided by the local authority who also run an ozone generator for use as a disinfectant. Public transport is provided by underground trains that run under each main road in the city where heavy traffic is prohibited. The population of Hygeia no longer suffer from infantile disease, typhoid, cholera and typhoid: all having been eradicated along with alcohol-related diseases. The city has 20 hospitals - one per 5000 people. The work of the hospitals are supplemented by homes for children & the aged which are built to resemble ordinary Hygeia homes. Cemeteries are situated on the outskirts of town. Burial grounds are of built up earth and quick growing plants. The dead are placed in wicker baskets or simply buried in shrouds in order to facilitate rapid & efficient decomposition. No individual gravestones are allowed but large memorial slabs are engraved with each individuals name. The Public Health Acts would eventually implement in the British Isles the measures previously only enjoyed by the residents of Hygeia.

His pamphlet would remain in circulation providing an inspiration for later town planners.

> 'The objects chiefly kept in view have been to unite the greatest degree of order, symmetry, space, and healthfulness, in the largest supply of air and light, and in the most perfect system of drainage, with the comfort and convenience of all classes; the due proportion of accommodation to the probable numbers and circumstances of various ranks; ready accessibility to all parts of the town, under continuous shelter from sun and rain, when necessary; with the disposition of the public buildings in such localities as to make them easy of approach from all quarters, and surrounded with space for numerous avenues of entrance and exit. And, in addition to all these, a large intermixture of grass lawn, garden ground, and flowers, and an abundant supply of water--the whole to be united with as much elegance and economy as may be found practicable. '

James Silk Buckingham.
National Evils and Practical Remedies. 1849

Robert Pemberton a contemporary of Buckingham put forward a similar vision though inspired by a different geometry. In *The Happy Colony* (1854) Pemberton gives details of Queen Victoria Town a new town to be established on an island in the Pacific. The layout of the town is based on a series of concentric circles. An inner 50-acre ring would house colleges, swimming baths, workshops and riding schools. An outer ring would contain factories, hospitals and gardens with the whole community encircled by a three mile long park. Pemberton went as far as to include a prospectus for the community in the book, but no-one seems to have taken him up on his offer to establish a 'happy colony'.

CO-OPERATIVE HOUSEKEEPING

The very scale of the undertaking of setting up a completely new town made the chances of any of these schemes actually happening relatively slim. Other more modest schemes were being put forward at the same time in the pages of the magazines of the Co-operative movement and in other more general housekeeping journals. The failure of the grand Owenite schemes for communal life had made some writers shy away from overtly communal schemes. Mary Gilles reassured the readers of *Howitt's Journal* in 1847 that her proposals for 'Associated Homes' were perfectly compatible with 'privacy, quiet and seclusion', and that all the benefits of cheaper housekeeping and better service could be had without compromising on personal privacy. Writing in the *Westminster Review* in 1849 under the title of *'Human Progress'* W.B. Adams lamented the inadequacies of housing design when compared to the desgn of factories. He suggested that 'social living' could be promoted by the erection of large blocks of flats with central kitchens, dining halls, baths, laundries, even libraries and schoolrooms. The whole building would be powered by a single steam engine driving grinding, chopping and cleaning equipment in the kitchens with a gas boiler to provide hot water and room heating.

The political writer Harriet Martineau advocated the formation of Associated Homes of 20 'Ladies' living together in a large house in an article titled *'Associated Homes for Poor Ladies'* in *The Leader* Oct 1950. Each woman would have her own rooms and share sitting room, library and communal meals together as an alternative to cheap lodgings for single women living in the city.

Both *The Co-Operator* and *Co-operative News* carried a number of articles on domestic co-operation in the 1860s & 70s. Several articles appeared giving details of an American experiment, the Cambridge Co-operative Housekeeping Society, which had been started by a Mrs Melusina Pierce in 1869. Using the British Co-operative Movement as an example she had devised a scheme for applying co-operative principles to the domestic economy. In a series of articles in the *Atlantic Monthly* Mrs Pierce put forward the suggestions for a group of 12 to 50 families living in small blocks of houses surrounded by gardens sited around a co-operative housekeeping centre where the women would share the household tasks as part of a sort of housekeeping co-op. Charges would be made for the services and any profits from the scheme would be returned to investors. The 'housekeeping centre' would include kitchen, laundry, sewing room and gymnasium. Meals would be delivered to individual homes by horse and cart. Mrs Pierce's main aim was to find a role for increasingly marginalized middle-class women and although she envisaged women-only meetings to organise the work, she made the mistake of making the highest decision-making authority a council of all the male heads of household who unanimously dissolved the Society in 1871.

The Atlantic Monthly was widely read in middle-class homes in England and Mrs Pierce's ideas were given a warm if somewhat muted reception in the pages of other Housekeeping magazines of the time. The idea of co-operative housekeeping was taken up by Mrs Elizabeth Moss King a prolific writer and speaker, member of the British Association for the Advancement of Science and founding secretary of the Rational Dress Society. She managed to get wide publicity for her ideas - The Times reported on a paper given to the annual meeting of the British Association entitled 'Confederated Homes & Co-operative Housekeeping' stating that Mrs King's paper was the chief attraction of the day. The Englishwoman's review and The Queen also carried reports on the lecture and the president of the meeting suggested at the end that the time had come for a practical experiment in co-operative housekeeping to be set up. Through Mrs King's advocacy the idea of shared forms of housekeeping circulated widely among middle-class circles being picked up by those women becoming involved in the growing women's suffrage movement. Mrs King went as far as to commission plans for a co-operative home from the architect Edward W Godwin which were printed in the April 1874 edition of Building News. They showed a block of flats for over 100 adults with a communal dining room, kitchen and play facilities for children. Designed to look as uninstitutional as possible it was 'neither a huge barrack - nor a flaunting hotel'.

Edward Vansittart Neale, a leading figure in the Co-operative Movement, had become an advocate of associated homes in the 1860s and in 1872 he detailed plans for a series of five storey blocks of flats with a separate building for various communal facilities. The article in Co-operative News in Jan 1872 listed the communal facilities as including a central kitchen & dining room, laundry, bathrooms, library, smoking & billiard rooms and a nursery, with the suggestion that schoolrooms and gardens could be added if desired by the residents. The response to proposals for model homes in blocks of flats was generally lukewarm. They smacked of tenement provision for the poor and were seen as a middle-class idea being foisted onto the working class when working class aspirations were for small individual houses.

A competition in the Aug 1887 issue of the monthly Work and Leisure magazine, to design a block of associated dwellings for single women earning between 20s & 90s a week, brought two poor responses from its readers. Undeterred the editor published her own proposals unremarkable in themselves were it not for the fact that the editor, Louisa M. Hubbard, followed up her suggestions by setting up the Ladies' Dwelling Company to make the plan a reality. After over 40 years of talk about associated homes and co-operative housekeeping there was 'suddenly' a flurry of activity. Another company, Ladies' Residential Chambers Ltd was registered and construction work started on two blocks of women's flats. The first to open was in Chenies St, Bloomsbury, built by Ladies' Residential Chambers Ltd in May 1889. The opening of the six storey, u-shaped block of self contained flats, complete with common dining room and kitchen, was attended by well known figures in the women's movement including Lydia Becker, Clementina Black and Elizabeth Garrett Anderson. Three months later Sloane Gardens House was opened by the Ladies' Dwelling Company just off Sloane Square. It catered for 106 women, providing a public restaurant, reception room, music rooms and studios. Single rooms and sets of rooms were for hire, a lady housekeeper was present and 4 shops at street level.

Social reform to social work

As the renegade Owenite community at Manea Fen was getting going in 1838, a daughter was born in Wisbech to the family of James Hill, Owenite and proprietor of the radical paper The Star in the East. Octavia Hill's whole background was steeped in traditions of social reform her mother championed a teaching method that involved both instructing and befriending students and her maternal grandfather was Dr. Thomas Southwood Smith, public health reform pioneer. Educated at home, in 1852 the young Octavia went to London to work at the Ladies' Guild, a Christian-Socialist co-operative association managed by her mother, where she met John Ruskin and Frederick Maurice. She became close friends with Ruskin working for him in her spare-time, becoming an accomplished illustrator. In 1856 she became secretary of the women's classes at Maurice's Working Men's College.

Houses for the poor

Her friendship with Ruskin would lead her to tread what was to prove to be an influential path in housing reform. In1864 Ruskin financed the purchase of a small group of derelict houses in Marlybone that Hill renovated and managed, developing a housing management style that was a combination of paternalistic philanthropy and solidarity with her tenants.

'Hill thought it better to renovate existing housing rather than build new accommodations because the latter would quickly deteriorate due to slovenly tenants. Habits of cleanliness and orderliness could only be learned over a period of time, during which gradual repairs to existing housing could be made. As tenants learned to respect their own units and common areas, further renovations could be made. Hill employed a team of visiting ladies to befriend tenants and inculcate house-keeping skills. She also set aside a fixed annual sum for routine repairs. Any unspent portion was returned to tenants to improve their own units, offering an incentive to care for housing and keep repair costs low."

Daniel T. Oliver
Helping Charities Succeed (Apr1998)
www.capitalresearch.org

With her lady rent collectors, Hill invented an entirely new role for women, an active participatory role in housing reform - doing a job of utmost importance - collecting the rent and at the same time acting as prototype social workers befriending and offering practical advice and help to their tenants. Steadily Hill built up a network of housing units, recruiting and training handpicked volunteers to manage the properties for their owners. Her excellent accounting practices and secure return on investments helped to ensure that she always had enough willing landlords and the necessary money to continue her work. She also organised social activities for the tenants - gardening, singing and drama, and outings to areas of natural beauty outside London.

Historic houses

Octavia Hill's influence was perhaps as great in the countryside as it was in the town - along with Ruskin she started the Commons Preservation Society (1865), which campaigned for the protection of the ancient commons, saving Hampstead Heath, Wimbledon Common and Epping Forest from development. In 1895 with Beatrix Potter, Canon Hardwicke Rawnsley and lawyer Sir Robert Hunter she helped to form The National Trust for Places of Historic Interest and Beauty. Again it was the ideas of John Ruskin that led to the founding of the Trust that has gone on to be the largest private landowner in the country and a major player in any debate about the countryside.

Hill's ideas on housing and social reform were unpopular at a time when either charitable giving or municipal interventions were seen as the main planks in the fight against poverty. Hill spoke out strongly against indiscriminate charity, or what she called "foolish almsgiving," arguing that "the lavish and sudden rush of ill-considered gifts. . . is deadly. It is the cause of a steady deterioration of character pitiable to watch." She also railed, somewhat prophetically, against municipal housing schemes. "Sinks and drains are stopped; yards provided for exercise must be closed because of misbehaviour...Staircases become the nightly haunt of the vicious... The yell of the drunkard echoes through the hollow passages; the stairs are blocked by dirty children - and the life of any decent hard-working family becomes intolerable."

Octavia Hill

At the time of her death, Hill was responsible for the management of nearly 2,000 houses and apartments for those on low-income.

SETTLEMENT HOUSES

" A Settlement is simply a means by which men and women may share themselves with their neighbours; a club house in an industrial district, where the condition of membership is the performance of a citizens duty; a house among the poor, where residents may make friends with the poor."

S. Barnet 1898

At the same time as Octavia Hill was feminising the world of housing reform, one man, a personal friend of Hill's was working to bring men back to philanthropy. He was Samuel Barnett custodian of Britain's first University Settlement at Toynbee Hall in the East End of London, who brought young men to the kind of philanthropic work that had been being pioneered by women. Toynbee Hall, started in 1884, turned out to be the first of many Settlement Houses aimed at bringing middle-class university students into direct contact with the working-class. Barnet saw his settlement as a "social laboratory" where "... university men might get to know workmen and their problems through contact and discussion, and through teaching, research, public service and sociability, contribute something in return...'. The idea was that residents came 'to learn as much as to teach, to receive as much as to give'.

Early work included adult education courses and university extension lectures, children's country holidays, after-school clubs, what we would now call special needs education, art exhibitions, literacy classes, literary and dramatic societies, assistance to Jewish immigrants, and the training of teachers and social workers.

Already in 1884 another Settlement, Oxford House, had opened in London and the idea of promoting social justice through Settlements in poor areas caught on fast. In the next two decades over 20 Settlements were established in the UK. In what was a significant move at the time, several Women's Settlements were established. In 1892 a National Federation of Settlements was formed. The University Settlements attracted a number of very able committed settlers, many of whom subsequently became deeply involved in the development of thinking and policy around the alleviation of poverty. The municipal socialists saw the possibility that through the education and participation of local residents the Settlement could provide civic leadership for the new Labour controlled local authorities.

The Settlement Movement grew to be an international phenomena with independent groups in America, France, Canada, Scandinavia, Japan, Holland, Germany Austria & Hungary and from around the turn of the century specific Jewish Settlements were set up in London and New York; Jewish people's homes in Berlin, Hamburg, Breslau and Vienna; and Jewish Toynbee Halls in Vienna and Prague. Octavia Hill's ideas were also taken up widely on an international stage with her methods being copied in Holland, Denmark, Germany, Russia, and the USA. However amid this expansions, and popularity, through a process of creeping professionalisation, the balance between personal commitment, scientific methods and direct experience that had been at the heart of the work of Octavia Hill and her co-workers somehow seemed to get lost.

Chocolate, soap and shoes

If any products can be said to have had a hand in the founding of utopias it is chocolate, soap and shoes that rank above any other, with fortunes founded on all three being used to fund model settlements. By the middle of the nineteenth century the necessity of creating housing for a completely new workforce, that had in many ways been the main driving force behind the very early model industrial settlements had gone. Leaving the more philanthropic motives to be the prime motivation for Victorian capitalists to improve conditions for their workers, though the adage that a happy worker was a more productive worker still played its part. Once again it was Quaker manufacturers that were to the fore.

Bournville

The two Quaker Cadbury brothers decided to move their factory producing cocoa and chocolate from the middle of Birmingham in 1879 to a site where they could find a guaranteed supply of fresh water, good communications and room for expansion. They chose an area known as Bournbrook to the south of city. During their years in the centre of Birmingham the brothers had been appalled by the living conditions there and George Cadbury vowed that if he had the opportunity he would do what he could to provide a community of decent homes for working-class families. Whilst the new Cadbury's factory was being built 16 cottages were also built alongside for key workers. This was to be the start of a scheme 'to make it easy for working men to own houses with large gardens secure from the danger of being spoilt either by.......factories or by interference with the enjoyment of sun, light and air'

George Cadbury
Bournville promotional pamphlet

In 1895 143 houses for sale, with mortgages provided by the company, were built on a 140-acre site adjacent to the factory. Further development was carried out including houses for rent and a quadrangle of almshouses, and by 1900 the village consisted of over 300 houses and cottages on some 330 acres of land. At this point The Bournville Village Trust was set up to take over the administration and future development. The trust quickly developed parks and open spaces, shops, schools, places of worship and an Arts & Crafts Institute. In contrast to other factory model villages, houses were available for people whether they worked for Cadbury's or not.

Semi-Detached houses Bournville

Port sunlight

Sunlight soap provided the financial foundation for a settlement that was almost the twin of Bournville. Built alongside the newly erected Lever Brothers factory on the Wirral, Port Sunlight was based on William Hesketh Lever's belief in 'prosperity sharing'. Following the same pattern of development as Bournville a number of cottages were built shortly after the factory was completed to be followed a few years later by further houses, a shop, allotments and Gladstone Hall - an assembly & recreation hall used as a canteen and concert hall. In 1910 a second phase of development was carried out to a new grand plan by Ernest Prestwich. The new plan included as its centre piece the Lady Lever Art Gallery. The houses in the village are in a variety of architectural styles, with almost no two blocks being the same, which again parallels the Cadbury's development, though the range of styles and number of architects used by Lever was far greater. The one major difference being that Port Sunlight was exclusively for Lever Bros. Workers.

Both Bournville and Port Sunlight attracted the attention and praise of housing reformers from around the world. Reproductions of Port Sunlight cottages were erected at international exhibitions in Paris, Glasgow & Brussels. The Lever village was also the inspiration for a musical comedy *The Sunshine Girl* set in a fictitious model village Port Sunshine.

The tradition of the model factory village would slowly be overtaken by model settlements set up by Public Utility companies and eventually by state provision of housing. The tradition would not die out completely though. The Clarks Quaker shoe manufactures at Street in Somerset developed what amounted to a company town carrying out various housing schemes and providing the town with social facilities.   During expansion in the 1920s Crittall's

International style housing Silver End Essex

carpet manufacturers commissioned a scheme for a brand-new company village at Silver End in Essex. The employees administered the village themselves through a company set up especially for the purpose. In the early stages the village consisting mostly of flat-roofed international-style housing. Other housing was plain neo-Georgian. There was also a village hall, hotel, bank, telephone exchange, surgery, dental clinic, shopping arcade, school and playing fields and a central public garden. Farms were established which sold pro-

duce direct to the villagers. Other factory villages were built in the 1920s by the London Brick Company at Stewartby in Bedfordshire and Bowaters paper manufacturers in Kent.

EAST TILBURY

In 1933 the British Bata Shoe Company established East Tilbury, a new model village around its new factory on the Thames estuary. Bata shoes had been founded in 1894 by Tomas Bata at Zlin in Czechoslovakia. The company had taken off when they supplied the armies of the Hapsburg Empire with boots during the First World War. Bata pioneered modern factory management techniques using continuous innovation, quality improvement, team self-management, profit-sharing and worker participation under the slogan, 'Thinking to the people, labour to the machines'. In the 1920s Bata had Le Corbusier design a new layout for Zlin, though he later decided to use a local architect Frantisek Lydia Gahura to carry out the plans. Simple, box like, redbrick houses were built to house Bata workers along with schools, research institutions, a film studio and hospital. The modernist designs make Zlin the only entire "constructivist" town in the world. Tomas Bata died in a plane crash in 1932 and his son took over the running of the company. In 1938 in the wake of the Nazi invasion the company moved its headquarters to Canada where it built another model community, Bataville, near Ottawa.

The village at East Tilbury is based on the company's designs for Zlin consisting mainly of flat roof-modernist houses, the first being built in 1933 in Bata Ave with all fixtures, fittings and materials imported from Czechoslovakia. The village grew to some 300 houses, a hotel, four dormitory buildings, shops, swimming pool, memorial garden, orchard, sports facilities, college, fire station, cinema and its own 300-acre farm. The village's social facilities were centred upon the area around the "Community House" or company hotel. The hotel itself provided accommodation for young unmarried factory workers with part of the top floor reserved as a private suite for Thomas Bata Junior. The building also housed shops, a French restaurant, a dance hall, social club & canteen seating up to 600 people.

ANARCHY IN THE UK

"It seems to me proved by evidence that, men being neither the angels nor the slaves they are supposed to be by the authoritarian utopians - Anarchist principles are the only ones under which a community has any chances to succeed. "

Peter Kropotkin

Open letter to comrades intending to start a Communist colony

Peter Kropotkin, a Russian émigré visited England a number of times finally settling here in 1886 after becoming persona non grata in other European countries. He was highly influential in the revival of anarchist and libertarian ideas through his theories and writing. He came to anarchism via biology having developed a critique of Darwinism. He had spent five years as a naturalist studying the geology and zoology of eastern Russia. During this period, he observed that living things coped with the harsh Siberian environment primarily through co-operative behaviour.

"During the journeys which I made in my youth in Eastern Siberia and Northern Manchuria . . . I failed to find--although I was eagerly looking for it--that bitter struggle for the means of existence among animals belonging to the same species, which was considered by most Darwinists as the dominant characteristic of struggle for life, and the main factor of evolution."

In his book *Mutual Aid* he laid out the arguments for a theory of evolution based on co-operation.

"If we . . . ask Nature: 'who are the fittest: those who are continually at war with each other, or those who support one another?' we at once see that those animals which acquire habits of mutual aid are undoubtedly the fittest. They have more chances to survive, and they attain, in their respective classes, the highest development of intelligence and bodily organisation."

Moving on from biology and evolution Kropotkin formulated anarchist theories of society, underpinned by his theory of mutual aid, which were in direct opposition to the theories of Social Darwinism that had grown out of the orthodox view of evolution and whose dictat 'the survival of the fittest' would be used to justify rampant capitalism and the atrocities of Nazi Germany.

When Kropotkin arrived in England he found a thriving anarchist and socialist underground made up of political refugees like himself and various groups of English anarchists. It was during the 1890s that his ideas were most popular inspiring some anarchists to try and put them into action. Kropotkin's most often cited book may have been titled *Fields, Factories and Workshops*, but it turned out to be mainly the fields that his readers were interested in.

"To the Anarchist, who places the happiness of men, women and children, above all other aims, the freedom of the human race not merely from authority, but also from bad surroundings, bad conditions, and hard and uncongenial work, there can be no cry more fascinating and so full of hope as "Back to the Land"!'   *Freedom*

FREE COMMUNIST AND CO-OPERATIVE COLONY

An advert appeared in the *Newcastle Daily Chronicle* in 1895 asking for 'about 40 acres with suitable farm buildings on Tyneside or Wearside'. What the advert didn't say was that it was wanted so that an Anarchist Land Colony could be set up. The two men behind the scheme William Key and Frank Kapper had been looking for a site for a colony for some time and when the advert brought an offer of 20 acres at Clousden Hill, after a quick inspection of the land, they signed a 20 year lease on the farm. Kapper and Key had already canvassed support for their venture, issuing a statement of aims for the community and even writing to Kropotkin inviting him to become the colony treasurer, an offer he declined.

Statement of objects and principles

1. The acquisition of a common and indivisible capital for the establishment of an Agricultural Colony.

2. The mutual assurance of its members against the

evils of poverty, sickness, infirmity and old age.

3. The attainment of a greater share of the comforts of life than the working classes now possess.

4. The mental and moral improvement of all its members.

5. The education of the children.

6. To promote or help any organisation to organise similar colonies.

7. To demonstrate the superiority of Free Communist Association as against Competitive production of today.

8. To demonstrate the productivity of land under intensive culture.

The plan at the colony was to run a co-operative market garden on intensive cultivation lines as promoted by Kropotkin. And while Kropotkin said that he had little confidence in schemes of communistic communities started under present conditions, warning of the dangers of insufficient capital, influxes of newcomers and members failing to see the need for hardwork, he wished the colonists well.

EACH ACCORDING TO HIS OR HER ABILITY

They took over from the previous tenant of the farm in July 1895, inheriting various quantities of hay, oats, potatoes, fruit bushes, vegetables, chickens and an assortment of agricultural tools for which they paid £100. Enthusiastically the new colonists set to transforming the smallholding into a Free Communist and Co-operative Colony based on anarcho-communist principles where `Every member works according to his or her ability and enjoys equally all the Colony can grant.' Putting in on average 19-hour days, including Sundays, and getting support from local ILP members and co-operators, their initial efforts met with success. Farm stock was increased by a cow, a goat, 2 pigs, 22 hens, 6 ducks, 65 geese, 8 turkeys and 2 pairs of rabbits. Milk sales were providing a steady source of income. There had been the odd set-back; the 100ft long glasshouses that were to be the centrepiece of the gardening scheme had blown down twice during erection

In 1897 the anarchist paper *Freedom* reported that there were fifteen men, two women and two children (with more women needed) at the Clousden Colony. They were receiving visits from many anarchist and labour movement activists. The likes of Tom Mann, Bruce Glasier, Katherine St. John Conway and Harry Snell came to see the progress of the Tyneside anarchists. The local ILP organised a mass picnic where over a hundred 'Visitors were shown round the farm and gardens by the colonists, and expressed their satisfaction and delight with what they saw, and with the greenhouses in particular, one of the latter containing upwards of 500 tomato plants.'

Behind the rosy picture of the successful colony the stress of trying to live out their ideals was starting to tell. One of the early colonists, a pitman named Miller thought having tried it, 'that Anarchism, pure and simple, would not do for agricultural or social life. It was not possible to get work done when any man might work or not, might work as he liked, might call to a halt to discuss the way in which others worked.......'

Freedom Mar 1896.

Miller was referring to a group of Tolstoyan anarchists who had been allowed to join the colony under the fairly open-house principle that anyone could join as long as they were willing to put 'Communist principles into practice'. The newcomers took this to mean that they were free to work where, when and how they pleased, leading to the planting of an orchard in a totally unsuitable place, the starting of a duck-breeding programme by one of them without the slightest idea what he was doing and another who believed that social salvation would be attained by rearing goats. Eventually relations with the Tolstoyans came to a head and they packed their bags and emigrated to Canada. The colony was also suffering from a shortage of capital and despite the picture of a thriving market garden, with peas, cauliflowers and cabbages, 120 apple trees, 25 cherry trees and some 2000 soft fruit bushes, which was presented to the outside world, the colony was struggling to keep going. Add to this an influx of large numbers of visitors from all over Europe in the summer of 1897, that the colony welcomed but could well have done without, and the colonists started to split into two camps those who wanted to turn it into a tighter, more disciplined organisation run on co-operative lines, and those who wanted to stick to the original out-and-out anarchist principles. Rule 32 of the colony's constitution stated that any change to the colony's principles could 'only be done by the unanimous consent of the members.' The attempt to reach consensus on the way ahead resulted in a seemingly endless round of increasingly acrimonious meetings, with the only thing that everyone could agree on being to ask visitors to give a week's notice of their arrival. In the end after a series of exoduses of frustrated members the colony was finally turned into the Clousden Hill Co-operative Nurseries that continued to trade until 1902. A number of the ex-members went on to set up the 'Whaggs Commune' on the Whaggs Lodge Estate west of Gateshead where they rented land from the Northern Allotments Society.

'there is no doubt that the existence of the Colony served a number of positive purposes. It offered a safe haven for victims of political persecution from all over Europe, and that should not be underestimated. It helped to shape the early ILP's notions of the form that might be taken by a socialist economy and community. It confronted the co-operative movement with the need to look again at it's own fundamental principles. It provided a focus for an Anarchist movement struggling to defend libertarian ideas against the deadening greyness of labour bureaucracy and the reduction of political philosophies to lifeless dogmas. And it made some people happy for at least part of their lives. All in all, it was not a bad balance sheet.'

Nigel Todd. *Roses & Revolutionists*

WE HAVE NO RULES

" Eventually the entire suppression of Capitalism and Government is looked forward to."

Associated Anarchists *Advert in Labour Annual 1897*

Other anarchists saw the establishment of land colonies as the way forward. Shortly after the Clousden Hill Colony had started a group was formed known as the Norton Community Colony on a rented smallholding at Norton Hall in Derbyshire. The impetus behind the scheme had come from Edward Carpenter whose example and encouragement from his smallholding at nearby Millthorpe had persuaded the men from Sheffield to launch out on their own venture. On a smaller scale than the Clousden Colony the group ran a successful anarchist market garden selling produce on a stall on Sheffield market and from door to door in neighbouring villages. 'Our little beginning here is strictly on communistic lines; we have no rules, all business is discussed and work arranged over the communal breakfast table.' Hugh Mapleton

Claiming that their aim was to `Return to Nature' they attempted to live a simple life practising vegetarianism and abstaining from alcohol, tobacco, salt, chemicals, drugs, minerals and all fermenting and decomposing foods. The group had plans to expand the community, but when the landowner refused to renew the lease the community disbanded in the spring of 1900.

Comrades of the Tolstoyan Anarchists who had so irritated the colonists at Clousden Hill were responsible for a series of land colonies in the late 1890s mainly on cheap land in Essex with colonies at Purleigh, Ashingdon and Wickford. In 1898 a breakaway group from the Purliegh colony formed what turned out to be the most enduring of the anarchist experiments on the edge of the Cotswolds at a place now known as Whiteway. Other groups have left little trace of their existence. The Edmonton Anarchist Group also active in 1898 announced the setting up of a Co-operative store to raise money for a co-operative colony. Whether they actually managed to start the colony is not known. Many individual anarchists were involved with projects that were not in themselves overtly anarchist, such as

[cont'd P 214]

ONE HUNDRED YEARS OF ANARCHY

In the summer of 1998 in the small Cotswold settlement of Whiteway a unique centenary was celebrated. As the crowd of intrigued onlookers followed the colony historian on a guided tour of the 40 acre site behind the veneer of late 20th century life the ghosts of anarchists past could be sensed hiding in old sheds and quiet corners of this mature anarchist arcadia. Long gone are the wide open fields of the Dry Ground and the Wet Ground, replaced by a patchwork of gardens and allotments set amongst a canopy of mature trees. Long gone are the heady days of Tolstoyan anarchism when all talk was of building a community free from restraint and injustice where everyone would share work, love and comradeship. Long gone also is the spartan simple life where the

'Most ideally minded they wouldn't use any money, just living from earth product, for instance for want of matches, they had to save time and light getting up therefore very early in the morning when the sun rises, and went to bed a sunset time. Lit the fire primitively helping themselves with two bricks and so. We never had bread, and used to eat raw wheat in the hollow of the hand. No salt, no sugar, nothing of this kind....'

Carmen Maurice C1914

In a hundred years the colony has seen it's share of comings and goings. Not just people; the early settlers, immigrant anarchists, Spanish refugees & wartime CO's, but with each decade the particular ideas and fads of the era; the no money period, vegetarianism, rational dress, naturism, free-love unions. Some of the 'fads' have endured mainly because the outside world has caught up with Whiteway and what once seemed extreme now passes without mention. Many of the early buildings have gone, the huts put up when 'individual living' started; William Sinclair's hand-made brick & thatch hut. Some of

Centenary guided tour in front of Whiteway House

the original timber clapboard houses have been extended and converted beyond recognition. Today houses have all the conveniences of modern living; piped water having arrived in 1949 and electricity in time for Christmas 1954.

On one level life at Whiteway seems little different today from that of other surrounding villages. But a rich vein of anarchism runs below the surface of modern day life. Present day colonists are aware of the stories and myths of the early days. The symbolic burning of the deeds spiked on the end of a pitchfork, the land tribunal case that upheld the principle of communal ownership of the land and the endless rumours of the 'nudist colony'. Anarchy is implicit in the jigsaw layout of the plots, the endlessly twisting and winding lanes that make no concession to the age of the car and in the patchwork of house styles; from modern brickbuilt bungalows to others still recognisably early 20th century DIY style. The governance of the community as a whole is still carried out through the general meeting, which oversees the communal facilities; the lanes and paths, the colony hall, the playing fields & swimming pool. And on our centenary-guided tour at least one house was proudly flying a black flag.

Two books have been written chronicling Whiteways history. *A Colony in the Cotswolds* in the

1930's by Nellie Shaw one of the original colonist and more recently an account by Joy Thacker a local woman who moved to the colony in the 1960's. In a century of colony life Whitewayans it would seem have been through the whole panoply of community activity practiced or dreamt of by communards before or since. As well as their smallholding and self-build activities there was; Protheroe's Bakery, the Cotswold Co-operative Handicraft guild, Whiteway Modern School, the Co-operative Gardening Group, the Whiteway Youth Club and the Whiteway Wanderers football team. On top of that various individual ventures; Lillian Woolf's wholefood shop, the temporary home for Freedom Press, numerous small businesses, craftworkers and artists…

The pattern of social life over its lifetime, from intense communality through to increasing individuality, could lead to the conclusion that Whiteway had failed the aspirations of its original settlers. It would be difficult for a penniless anarchist to find a way to join Whiteway today. But the sheer tenacity of the ideas that have underpinned its entire existence, and have arguably been responsible for its longevity, are an inspiration to all would be utopians everywhere. Today the Colony Hall has a new roof and coat of paint, 'Protheroe's' bakery has reopened and MI5 have just opened their files on the colony!

Whiteway Colony Hall 1998

Home Office sought to wipe out 'beastly' commune!

Home Office officials tried to shut down a prototype "free: love" hippy commune in the 1920s, according to official papers released yesterday. Files from the 1920's released to the Public Record Office showed that officials regarded the Whiteways Colony in Gloucestershire as a security risk. The commune had been created in the Cotswold Hills near Stroud around the turn of the century, attracting an assortment of socialists, pacifists, "free thinkers and refugees." "Manners had they none and their customs are beastly," wrote an official in 1925. Police paid a husband and wife £400 to infiltrate the commune in the hope of finding evidence of their unspeakable activities. The couple emerged claiming that "promiscuous fornication " was indeed a feature of life in the colony, but they were unable to produce proof. The Home Office could not even work up popular agitation against the commune, as local residents viewed members as cranks rather than as objects of fear.

Morning Star March 12 1999

'All this just goes to prove that having once lived here, those who find it suits them are reluctant to live anywhere else, and those who have left feel drawn to return when they can.'

Joy Thacker colony historian 1993

The full story of Whiteway is told in: *Whiteway Colony: The Social History of a Tolstoyan Community* By Joy Thacker. Self Published. Whiteway. 1993. Available from the Author: Fairhaven, Whiteway, Gloustershire.

W.C.Owen who went to live at 'The Sanctuary' near Storrington set up by Vera Pragnall in 1923. Some who set up communities for other reasons completely would later come to an understanding of anarchist ideas through the act of living in a small community as in the case of the painter Augustus John.

As it moved into the 20th century anarchy would move more into the mainstream of left-wing politics through the Anarcho-Syndicalists, finding allies in the likes of the Guild Socialists and amongst radical trade unionists. In doing so it would leave its communal wing behind in the quiet backwaters of Gloucestershire & Yorkshire. Anarchist ideas enjoyed a brief surge of popularity around the Spanish Civil War when through the Syndicalist CNT Union large parts of Spain were transformed into anarchist-run collectives with nearly 8 million people involved and British volunteers in the International Brigades fought alongside anarchist regiments against Franco's Fascists. Despite informing many of the wartime pacifist communities in Britain during WW2, following the defeat of the revolution in Spain anarchism once more became an underground movement kept enlivened by such groups as the International Situationists and the anarchist paper *Freedom*, to emerge two decades later to inform the 1960s counter-culture.

'In order to succeed, the Communist experiment, being an experiment in mutual accomodation among humans, ought to be made on a grand scale. A whole city of, at least, 20,000 inhabitants, ought to organise itself for self-managed consumption of the first necessities of life (houses and essential furniture, food and clothing), with a large development of free groupings for the satisfaction of the higher artistic, scientific, and literary needs and hobbies - before it be possible to say anything about the experimentally tested capacities, or incapacities, of our contemporaries for Communist life. (By the way, the experiment is not so unfeasible as it might seem at first sight.)'

Peter Kropotkin
To comrades intending to start a communist colony

THE ARCHITECTS OF UTOPIA

'In times of great movement in social matters, such as we are now passing through there are sure to be many experiments tried. I think we are sometimes too ready to believe that anything that does not quite agree with us is set going to deceive the people. Now I am more inclined to look upon all these experiments as our valuable allies, and am sure they will help to prepare for a more complete change when we are in a position to make one.'

Raymond Unwin
Early Communal Life & What it teaches.
Commonweal 1887.

Raymond Unwin, and his cousin Barry Parker, played a pivotal role in transforming utopian schemes from fiction to reality at the dawn of the 20th century. Unwin born in Rotherham, spent his childhood in Oxford educated at Magdalen College School and briefly considered holy orders & settlement work at Toynbee Hall before moving to Chesterfield as an apprentice engineer. In 1885 after moving on to Manchester he became secretary of the local branch of the Socialist League and spent his time lecturing and writing for *Commonweal*. He was personally acquainted with both Ruskin and Morris, and was a regular visitor to Edward Carpenter at his smallholding at Millthorpe. For a while he worked as an engineer for the Staveley Coal & Iron Co. laying out small housing estates for them. In his writings for *Commonweal* he explored many socialist themes including communal experiments and co-operative living. In one he fantasised that the empty Sutton Hall could become '....the centre of a happy communal life. Plenty of room in that large house for quite a small colony to live, each one having his own den upstairs where he could go to write,or sulk, or spend an evening with his lady-love or his boon companion; and downstairs would be large common dining halls, dancing halls, smoking rooms.....'

Raymond Unwin
Commonweal 1889.

After marrying Ethel Parker in 1893 he went into partnership with his brother-in-law and half-cousin Barry Parker in his Arts and Crafts based architecture practice in Buxton. They were both active members of The Northern Art Workers Guild based in Manchester and were commissioned to design a series of middle-class houses in the Midlands and north of England. Unwin more interested in the social purpose of design underlying the Arts & Crafts movement sketched designs for a block of 'co-operative dwellings' in Bradford later reproduced in their book The Art of Building a Home.

Unwin was invited to speak at the first conference of the Garden City Association held at the Cadbury's model village at Bournville in August 1901. The new Garden City movement was the result of one man's vision, Ebenezer Howard, put forward in his book Tomorrow: a peaceful path to real reform. Howard was an unlikely utopian. Born in 1850 the son of a shopkeeper, he worked as a clerk before spending five years in America where he tried his hand at farming and worked as a court reporter. Back in England in 1876 he worked as a shorthand clerk for Hansard whilst working on an experimental shorthand typewriter. He moved in middle-class radical circles where discussions on poverty and land reform drew his attention. A couple of his friends were involved in starting the Brotherhood Trust which proposed to open co-operative stores and workshops in London's East End. But it was a copy of Edward Bellamy's Looking Backwards, lent him by an American friend, which would set Howard on the path that would lead to the Garden City. Inspired by Bellamy's vision of a future based on co-operation rather than competition Howard was instrumental in getting Looking Backwards published in England and became a founder member of the Nationalisation of Labour Society. In the pages of its monthly paper, Nationalization News, proposals were put forward for experimental colonies based on Bellamy's ideas including one by Howard. This 'Home Colony' was to be a planned town surrounded by countryside, encircled by a railway with sites for libraries, schools, crèches, swimming pools and concert hall. It was to be built by a combination of central planning and individual initiative - a marked departure from Bellamy's total state control. By April 1893 a site at Hockley in Essex had been chosen for the establishment of a co-operative colony. Nothing came

Co-op city

Bradford Peck, a department store owner in Lewiston Maine USA, published the curiously titled The World, a Department Store. A story of Life under the Co-operative System, in Lewiston & London in 1900. Following the by then well worn utopian tradition of a traveller waking up in the future - this time after being in a coma for 25 years - Peck gives a glimpse of life as it might be in a city built by the Co-operative Association of America.

On waking Percy Branford declares that it is "Like coming from hell into heaven" as he views the neatly laid out city, with its apartment blocks arranged in a grid pattern with diagonal avenues leading to numerous parks and open spaces. Each apartment is designed so that every room has daylight. The whole city is run on a co-operative planned economy with every citizen given a guaranteed income through a system of 'coupon cheques' that have replaced money within the city. Health and Education services are provided by the Co-operative Association with all citizens undergoing regular medical examination. Children's health is supervised in school where every desk has flowers on it and there are never more than 25 pupils in a class. Cooking in the home has been done away with and people eat in a series of public restaurants which provide food eat in or take away. The purpose built restaurants have a range of facilities from cheap meals, through private dining rooms for families to banqueting suites for 400 guests. The city is served by a comprehensive public transport system of electric trains, taxis and a car pooling scheme - with drivers available if required. The availability of public transport has broken down the isolation of the surrounding rural areas.

Bradford Peck believed that his Co-operative City was a practical proposition and at the end of the novel includes an appeal for funds "that will enable us to perfect the enterprise, advertise it, and promote its growth."

of the scheme in Essex, but Howard continued to refine his ideas concentrating on the principles and mechanics of his model community rather than detailed designs. In his book, published in 1898, Howard acknowledged the work of James Silk Buckingham and Benjamin Ward Richardson, along with the likes of Thomas Spence as influences on his ideas. The book differs from its predecessors in that it lacks a detailed description of the layout and design of the proposed new city giving broad statistics for acreages (6000 acre site with 1000 acres in the centre reserved for the city) and populations (30,000 people) and concentrating on descriptions of the social and economic aspects of the project. Towards the end of the book it is proposed that 'a small Garden City must be built as a working model' whose example would then lead to further cities being built. Howard envisaged a development that would parallel that of the railways where after initial small scale developments by private companies the idea would spread across the country finally being taken up nationally by the government. The book received a mixed response with the Fabian socialists giving it a scathing review in their paper and The Times commenting that it was "an ingenious and rather entertaining attempt - the only difficulty is to create it." In spite of the critics and undaunted by the enormity of the task of building an ideal city that had defeated his utopian predecessors Howard with the help of the Nationalisation Society set up the Garden City Association (GCA) and set about promoting his ideas through a series of lectures up and down the country through which he won over a number of influential converts to the garden city cause including the proprietors of both Bournville and Port Sunlight.

'In the squares and quadrangles of our Garden City dwellings the spirit of co-operation will find congenial ground from which to spring, for there association in the enjoyment of open spaces or large gardens will replace the exclusiveness of the individual possession of backyards or petty garden-plots...'

Raymond Unwin
On the building of Houses in the Garden City
GCA Conference Report 1901

Raymond Unwin was not the only speaker at the GCA conference with an interest in co-operative housing schemes. A paper with the title 'The Advantages of Co-operative Dwellings' was presented by the architect Harold Clapham Lander. Lander was an old friend of Howard's and served on the executive committee of the GCA. Described as "the most aristocratic socialist I know" by one of his employees, he had his clothes made by co-operative labour and ran his practice on socialist principles. His ideas picked up from the co-operative housekeeping movement included a quadrangle of private apartments with communal facilities such as dining rooms, kitchen, laundry and recreation rooms provided. He pointed out a number of successful experimental homes already in existence, one in Stamford Hill North London which consisted of a block of flats with common billiard room, recreation room and gardens that had been going since the 1870s.

TENANT CO-PARTNERSHIP

The ideas of the Garden City Movement found enthusiastic support from the embryonic housing co-operative movement. Tenant Co-operators Ltd had been set up in 1887 with the idea of applying the principles of the co-operative retail movement to housing. It aimed to build or buy houses all over London to let to tenants at local rents, financed by a combination of Public Works loans, small investors and shares taken out by the tenants themselves. Rents would be set to cover maintenance, loan repayments with any surplus profit being credited to tenants as a dividend. It was hoped that in this way the tenant could build up a share account that would eventually be equivalent to the value of their house; in this way working people could own their own homes and instead of having to sell when they wanted to move they could simply transfer their shares to another co-operative housing scheme. They began by buying 6 houses at Upton Park and shortly after built 24 cottages at Penge. Known as a tenant co-partnership this form of organisation would become a favoured model of development in the Garden City movement.

Six members of the Ealing branch of a co-operative building venture, General Builders Ltd, decided to club together and buy plots to build nine houses each promising to invest £50 in the scheme. The group met at the Haven Arms and discussed their plans with the founder of the building co-op Henry Vivian, a carpenter and trade unionist with strong connections to the co-operative movement, (and later Liberal MP) who encouraged them not only to build houses, but also to form a tenant's co-partnership known as Ealing Tenants Ltd. At a meeting in the Ealing Public Rooms on 21 September 1901 Henry Vivian was able to announce that nearly £1,000 in share capital had been contributed and the roofs were being put on the first nine houses that were duly named Vivian Terrace. By 1905 the society had completed fifty houses and was negotiating to buy additional land on the Fowler's Hill estate. At this point the society thought it was necessary to look in detail at the overall design and layout of the estate and called on the services of Parker & Unwin, who by then had executed designs at both New Earswick and Letchworth. Based on the new 'garden village' plan 680 houses were eventually built and in 1911 the Brentham Club opened a newly built clubhouse and recreation centre where it offered a wide range of social activities with classes in art, needlework, cookery, first-aid, folk-dancing, horticulture and languages (including Esperanto). A nursery and kindergarten were started. The addition of recreation grounds made it possible to hold sports events. A cricket match between Brentham and Hampstead tenants was a special Whit Monday event for several years. The club produced a number of well-known sportsmen, of whom the most famous was the tennis champion Fred Perry.

'INDUSTRIAL' GARDEN VILLAGES

Mixing the traditions of the philanthropic industrial model village and the garden village Quaker Joseph Rowntree commissioned plans from Parker & Unwin for a village, for the workers at his cocoa and confectionery business in York, on 150 acres of land near the village of Earswick. In their scheme for New Earswick Unwin & Parker brought together for the first time elements of the model settlements at Bournville and Port Sunlight, Howard's Garden City ideas and the Arts & Crafts architectural tradition in a form that would influence the planning and design of settlements in Britain and beyond for the whole of the 20th century. Using the guidelines set out in their book, *The Art of Building a Home,* Parker and Unwin's plan created a classic new form of settlement. Today New Earswick's wide verges, low density housing, (12 to the acre) simple airy properties arranged in a variety of blocks, quadrangles and cul-de-sacs look like a 1001 other estates up and down the country what one has to remember is that it is in fact everywhere else that looks like New Earswick. Houses had gardens with fruit trees and enough ground to grow vegetables. Landscape features such as mature trees and streams were kept and enhanced. As at Bournville the village was not restricted to workers at the Rowntree factory and in 1904 the scheme was transferred to the Joseph Rowntree Village Trust. The Trust continued to develop the village building a 'Folk hall' in 1911 and to this day is involved in pioneering housing initiatives.

Folk Hall New Earswick

Mixing the same traditions the Vickers Shipyard at Barrow in Furness created a model settlement on Walney Island called Vickerstown. From 1901 onwards the company built an extensive housing estate complete with shops, parks & gardens, churches, institute, two community hotels and a home farm to supply the 'village' with produce.

211

Garden cities of tomorrow

None of these small estates came anywhere near Howard's vision for a great smokeless, slumless city. and work continued on the plan for establishing a full-scale garden city experiment. John Adams, the Garden City Association, secretary was an adept publicist for the cause attracting an expanding membership up to 1300 by 1902 and speaking at numerous meetings and conferences including the Manchester Co-operative Housing Conference where he delivered a paper on the subject of *'Municipal Bournvilles'.* Howard brought out a revised paperback edition of his book under the new title *Garden Cities of Tomorrow.* On June 2 1902 The Garden City Pioneer Company was formed with the express aim of finding a site *'to lay out, construct, manage, and carry on any such Garden City'.* A sub-committee drew up criteria for assessing a suitable site and a search began. Possible locations were looked at in Essex, Oxfordshire, and Worcestershire. The Chartley Castle Estate in Staffordshire appeared as a front-runner for the site of the first garden city meeting most of the committee's criteria and negotiations started to purchase the estate. However at the last minute plans were switched to a site based on the Letchworth Manor estate in Hertfordshire, where in 1903 3,818 acres were purchased for £155,587. In just five years Howard's plan had gone from paper dream to the reality of muddy Hertfordshire fields a remarkable achievement for a shorthand clerk with no resources of his own except his powers of persuasion. Over the next ten years the experiment only dreamt of by previous utopians would unfold in the English countryside.

The layout of utopia

Unwin & Parker, flushed with their progress at New Earswick, were appointed as the overall architects & 'planners' for the new garden city. The other layouts put forward were much more formal reflecting the geometric diagrams Howard used to illustrate his book, projected onto the landscape. The adopted plan in contrast blended both formal features and informal layouts following the contours of the landscape where possible and preserving most of the pre-existing trees and hedgerows. The plan drew heavily on the work at Bournville, Port Sunlight and introduced German ideas on land use zoning, defining the town centre, residential and industrial areas ringed by a belt of agricultural land where the farms meant to supply the city with produce would be located. First Garden City Ltd was set up as the overall development company with building being carried out by a combination of private companies, public utility companies, co-partnerships and private individuals. In 1905 a Cheap Cottage Exhibition was held and proved hugely successful both with architects - entrants almost amounting to a Who's Who of Arts & Crafts architecture - and with the public who flocked to see the new model housing for working people. When criticised that the cost of some of the houses put them beyond the pocket of working people Unwin replied that a rise in wages would be preferable to a drop in house standards. Garden City Tenants Ltd, Letchworth's own tenants' co-partnership carried out a number of schemes creating the Eastholm Green, Birds Hill and Pixmore Estates developing their layouts and designs along the way with the last being something of a pioneer planned neighbourhood complete with its own institute and recreation ground.

Sandals and scandals

A significant minority of the residents of the new garden city were drawn there by the utopian overtones of its founder and designers and though the 'simple lifers' were only ever a minority, their cult religions, vegetarianism, smocks and sandals became something of caricature of life at Letchworth being regularly lampooned not only by the press but also in the town itself at the annual pantomime. Among those drawn in by the magnet of Letchworth were those interested in co-operative housekeeping. Following a number of abortive proposals in 1906 in an illustrated article in the *Daily Mail,* Howard himself put forward a scheme designed by H.C. Lander for a leafy tree-strewn quadrangle of co-operative houses, each with its own sitting room, hall, scullery with gas stove, bathroom and from one to three bedrooms. From the common kitchen, dining room and administration block sited on one side of the quadrangle 'shared' servants' would service the houses. Howard suggested that this was of benefit to both the householders who would save money and enjoy greater privacy and the servants themselves who would enjoy greater freedom than if they worked for a single

Homesgarth Letchworth

household. A company, Letchworth Co-operative Houses, was formed in 1907 to take the project forward; on offer to prospective tenants were private gardens, the use of shared sports facilities and vegetarian meals. The scheme, named 'Homesgarth', as built, consisted of accommodation for 16 households on two sides of a quadrangle linked together by a covered walkway with a 3 storey accommodation block containing a dining room, seating up to 60 people on the ground floor, above it (to minimise cooking smells) was the central kitchen and staff accommodation. Built on a site facing Sollershot Circus, leased to the company by First Garden City Ltd for a nominal rent, Homesgarth ran as a co-operative housekeeping scheme for nearly 40 years. Howard and his second wife moved in in 1911 and lived there until 1921. Reaction to the scheme was mixed but generally supportive and in some instances downright enthusiastic. Lucy Carr Shaw, Bernard Shaw's sister, wrote to Howard in 1913 that after being "nearly worried to death by the cares of housekeeping and the intolerable incompetence of servants....One of your £64

houses presents itself to me as a paradise after the turmoil of private housekeeping". Co-op housekeeping continued at Homesgarth until after WW2 having changed its name to Sollershot Hall in the 1920s.

GARDEN VILLAGE BOOM

The development of Letchworth Garden City sparked a wave of enthusiasm for the development of new settlements on garden city lines, the best known being Hampstead Garden Suburb founded by Henrietta Barnet, the wife of Canon Barnet of Toynbee Hall. Hampstead's subsequent high profile has somewhat overshadowed the strength and breadth of developments in the rest of the country. Unwin & Parker's work at New Earswick had already established that Howard's garden city principles could be adapted and applied on a small scale either as independent 'Garden Villages' or as 'Garden Suburbs' to existing towns, though the two categories became interchangeable as more developments were carried out.

The co-partnership model pioneered at Brentham and used to develop parts of both Letchworth and Hampstead was used by many of the schemes; Manchester Tenants Ltd built Burnage Garden Village, 136 houses around a recreation ground & pavilion in 1906, and the Derwentwater Tenants Co-partnership developed 25 houses in Keswick in 1910. Other schemes were carried out at Fallings Park in Wolverhampton (1907), Westerton on the outskirts of Glasgow(1910) and at Penkhull in the Potteries where a group that had formed when Staffordshire was the preferred site for the first garden city, built an estate of 95 houses from 1910 onwards.

Industrialists building housing for their workers now saw the garden village as the favoured model for their developments, with the Woodlands garden village for miners at the Brodsworth Colliery near Doncaster being laid out in 1906, with assistance from the Garden City Association, and Pilkington Bros Glass manufacturers starting what proved to be the first of 3 workers garden suburbs at Ravenhead in St Helens in 1909.

Another device copied from Letchworth to try and kick start development was the Cheap Cottage

Exhibition. This was used at Cleveleys on the Lancashire coast to promote the establishment of a seaside garden village and again in Swansea in 1910 where a number of cottages were built as part of the exhibition and afterwards Raymond Unwin was asked to draw up plans for a garden suburb for the town. The suburb never materialised but the foundations were laid for an energetic Welsh Garden Cities movement whose influence would lead to numerous 'garden' developments mostly in South Wales, but others were built as far afield as Wrexham and Machynlleth.

Groups looking to provide their own housing also took the garden village as a model. Workers at the Anchor Boot and Shoe co-operative in Leicester built 96 houses, a block of shops and a meeting room at Humberstone on the edge of the city helped by loans from the local co-operative retail society. Miners' Unions in the Welsh Valleys were involved in a series of housing schemes on garden village lines for their members at Pengam, Hengoed and Aberaman. And perhaps most intriguingl,y a group of workmen who were renting allotments from the Fairfield Moravian Settlement at Droylsden formed Fairfield Tenants Ltd in 1912 and developed a garden suburb on land owned by the Moravians.

Brent Garden Village in Finchley developed from 1910 onwards was unique among garden villages in being conceived in its original plan as an entire village run on co-operative housekeeping lines. Built on the Brent Lodge estate under the guidance of co-op housekeeping enthusiast Alice Melvin the scheme didn't quite live up to its own high expectations. Still, a series of houses without kitchens and a block of flats were built with the lodge being used for the communal facilities, including dining room, kitchen, laundry and stables. By 1914 the village consisted of 33 households. Later housing on the estate was built on conventional lines. The term Garden Suburb or Village became so associated with good quality housing development that private developers started using it as a selling point for what amounted to fairly standard developments with gardens and a few trees. Other places were named Garden Suburbs in retrospect despite having been built before the term was coined. Bedford Park being called in some instances the 'first garden suburb' and the exclusive Birkdale Park at Southport being dubbed a seaside garden suburb despite being in many ways the complete antithesis of the garden city ethos.

The mushrooming of garden villages and suburbs in this period was facilitated by the availability of public works loans from central government. Much government action at this time was in reaction to pressure from the likes of the Garden City Association resulting in the 1909 Housing and Town Planning Act. Local Authorities also came under the influence of the promoters of the garden city ideal. The London County Council carried out two developments on their White Hart Lane and Old Oak estates that show an attempt to apply garden city ideas in design and layout within the financial constraints faced by the authority.

Unwin and Parker were by now the foremost proponents of the 'garden city style'. Their central involvement in the two most high profile schemes at Letchworth and Hampstead meant that their services were much sought after and they acted as advisors and planners to a number of schemes. Though, as part of the ethos was to provide a mix of housing types and styles, (as at Bournville and Port Sunlight before) a whole range of Arts & Crafts influenced architects became involved in designing 'model' cottages, individual houses for wealthy 'garden citizens' and public buildings, with both high-profile architects like Edwin Lutyens and M.H.Baille Scott and lesser known practices all getting commissions.

In *The Garden City Movement up to Date*(1914) E.G Culpin lists 54 schemes that had been started or planned 'on garden city lines' with some 11000 houses already completed. The clear contrast between these 'utopian' projects and those being built by private developers, both in terms of housing conditions and general environmental issues, attracted widespread interest and a steady stream of visitors from both at home and abroad. Development of many schemes was disrupted by the outbreak of the First World War.

CO-OPERATIVE HOUSEKEEPING BOOM

'The feminist flat is revolutionary, strikes at the root of the economic system, may involve vast adjustments of land tenure, communal building and taxation. But we are not afraid of revolution, for we are pioneers of a sex revolution.'
                                        Doris Neald Chew
                        Quoted in *One hand Tied behind us.*

Moving on from her role as secretary of Brent Garden Village Alice Melvin set up The Society for the Promotion of Co-operative Housekeeping and House service. In conjunction with the Co-operative Garden City Committee, whose secretary was H.C. Lander, an ambitious scheme for an entire co-operative Garden City to be built at Ruislip and called Melvin Park was proposed. Nothing came of Melvin Park, but a smaller scheme did come into being in 1912 at Golders Green. Known as Melvin Hall the 30 flats with communal kitchen & dining room carried on as a co-op housekeeping scheme until 1964 when it was demolished for a new block of flats. The seemingly indefatigable Mrs Melvin went on to set up a

Waterlow Court. Hampstead Garden Suburb

third scheme this time in Priory Rd, Hampstead. The Melvin Co-operative Residential Society consisted of 5 large town houses with about 10 tenants in each house. High repair bills and low profits forced the scheme to wind up in 1937.

Alice Melvin's work was covered by the feminist press of the time, *The Freewoman* carrying a number of features and letters on co-operative housekeeping. Others in the garden city movement were keen to experiment with shared housing. At Hampstead Garden Suburb a scheme for the elderly with shared baths, washhouses and baking ovens, the Orchards, was designed by Parker & Unwin for Hampstead Tenants ltd Co-partnership and a full blown co-operative housekeeping scheme for single women was built by the Improved Industrial Dwellings Company. Waterlow Court, designed by M.H. Baille Scott was made up of 50 flats arranged around a beautiful cloistered courtyard. Each flat had its own living room, bedroom or bed recess, bathroom and scullery. A central dining hall, common room and kitchen were serviced by a small group of servants. Many of the early residents at the court were feminists or suffragists and a strong communal spirit pervaded the place during the first few years.

Meadow Way Green. Letchworth.

Over in Letchworth Ruth Pym and Miss S.E. Dewe persuaded the Howard Cottage Society to build a co-op housekeeping scheme on Meadow Way Green. In all 9 cottages and a single flat were built around a communal garden with a (small) central dining room and kitchen. Housekeeping was truly co-operative with tenants taking it in fortnightly turns to be the tenant housekeeper with the only servant being a hired cook. Meadow Way Green was popular and successful continuing until after WW2 as a co-operative housekeeping venture.

GARDEN MUNITIONS

In the war years (1914-18) the government became involved in a massive programme to house workers in the rapidly expanding arms and armaments industry. The rise in numbers working in the munitions factories during the war was phenomenal. At the Royal Arsenal in Woolwich numbers rose from 10,866 at the outbreak of war to 74,467 by 1917 and in 1915 an entire new explosives factory intended to employ some 15,000 workers was started at the tiny village of Gretna on the Scottish border. The initial need for accommodation was met by providing temporary wooden huts on the grounds that this would be the most economic way to meet the need. As the supply of timber dried up this however proved to be something of a false economy and a switch was made to building permanent dwellings on 'the best garden city lines.'

That a cost-conscious government should have chosen the low-density garden city model to develop mass wartime housing seems on the surface surprising. But the Garden City Association had built up a head of steam for housing reform in the pre-war years and given the exceptional opportunity offered by the war some politicians opted to use it 'to secure a better and more humane standard of working conditions'. The presence of Seebohm Rowntree and none other than Raymond Unwin in the ranks of officials responsible for the housing and welfare of munitions workers pretty much sealed it. Unwin was in charge of the housing branch of the Department of Explosives Supply. From this position he oversaw the provision of housing for munitions workers, appointing Arts & Crafts based architects to carry out the detailed layout and design work on the estates. In all some 10,000 permanent houses were built in connection with munitions factories on 38 different estates in various parts of the country, many following modified garden city guidelines. A few were carried out by local authorities, others by the armaments manufacturers themselves with financial assistance from the War Office and a total of 13 schemes were carried out directly by central government departments, the most notable of the Ministry schemes being at Gretna and on the Well Hall Estate in Woolwich.

'A community which....is, from the architectural standpoint without equal in the world.'

E.G. Culpin
Sec.International Garden Cities & Town Planning Ass.

E.G. Culpin was not alone in his praise for the Well Hall Estate the first of the government's schemes. The architect for the scheme, Frank Baines, making virtue out of necessity at almost every turn, laid out a classic garden village development, using a variety of house types and due to wartime shortages an array of materials and finishes, in fact almost anything that came to hand - brick, stone, roughcast, half-timbering, tile & slate-hanging and weatherboarding - the effect created at Well Hall is almost 'picturesque old English village'. Baines had served his apprenticeship in the office of C.R.Ashbee in the 1890s and was steeped in the Arts & Crafts tradition but his work at Well Hall was in direct opposition to government demands for simplification in design and standardisation in materials.

Plan of Gretna Garden Village & Munitions Camp

At Gretna Unwin and resident architect Courtenay Crickner took on board the demands for the simple and the standard and alongside a vast temporary barracks built an estate of simple hipped-roof houses with 'neo-Georgian' features. The Gretna 'garden village', described by some as "depressing", was never the less praised for the high quality of the housing and provision of social facilities: shops, laundry, central kitchen, cinema, institute, churches and school. Simplification and standardisation was taken a step further by Patrick Abercrombie in his designs for the munitions village at Dormanstown and by the end of the war Baines was something of a lone voice arguing against the 'depressing fetish' of standardisation.

HOMES FIT FOR COUNTER REVOLUTIONARIES

'the money we are going to spend on housing is an insurance against Bolshevism and Revolution'

Parliamentary Secretary
to the Local Government Board 1919

At the end of the War Lloyd George's government displayed all the signs of revolutionary paranoia. They feared that demobilised soldiers might join together with militant trade unionist and form the military vanguard for a revolution. Maybe they were right. During the first half of 1919 alarming reports reached the government of discontent and radical tendencies among ex-servicemen's organisations culminating in their boycott of the July peace celebrations. In other parts of the country militant unions in the mines and shipyards flexed their muscles threatening strike action. A Home Office report warned that 'in the event of rioting, for the first time in history the rioters will be better trained than the troops.'

Faced with the spectre of Communist revolution the government looked to a raft of promises on social reform to distract the discontented masses and divert them off the road to revolution. Following the Armistice the government proposed a wide-ranging programme of reform that included unemployment protection, legislation on hours of work, industrial democracy and land settlement, but at the heart of its promises were 'Homes Fit for

Heroes'. The need for a mass house-building programme had been realised before the end of the war and Sir John Tudor Walters had been appointed to chair a committee to look into reconstruction housing standards. The committee's report published in the week of the Armistice was largely the work of Raymond Unwin. The Tudor Walters report became the most influential document on house design and layout ever issued by a government department. It was used as an international benchmark for housing standards and directly influenced the design of state provided housing in Britain for the following half century. It was in essence the distillation of Unwin's work in the Garden City movement and for the Ministry of Munitions translated into a set of recommendations and standards intended to replace the previous housing by-law regulations. Determined that its 'Homes for Heroes' campaign had to deliver something new to fulfil its counter revolutionary aims the government grasped the opportunity offered by the Tudor Walters report and turned to the Garden City movement to provide the required model housing.

'It was crucial for the ideological function of the housing programme that the houses be indisputably better than working-class houses of the past. Housing on garden city lines was not only unmistakably different ....but it had also been regarded as beyond the means of working-class incomes'.

Mark Swenarton. Homes Fit for Heroes

The immediate post-war years saw another mini-boom in garden village developments along co-partnership lines supported by public works loans. Existing schemes that had had their activities curtailed by the war carried out 'second phase' developments and many more were planned than were actually carried out. Very quickly it became obvious to the government that co-partnership schemes were never going to deliver enough new houses for propaganda purposes and they turned to local authorities to deliver the bulk of the 'Homes for Heroes'.

And so was born an uneasy marriage between political pragmatism and utopian ideology that resulted in the proliferation of that particularly British institution - the council estate. On the one hand politicians were busy propping up the status quo behind a smoke screen of change; almost calculating the size of gardens on the basis of the space required to keep a man busy after work and thus to tired to take part in political activity. On the other hand the garden city enthusiasts were grasping the opportunity to deliver the benefits of the garden city to the mass of the people. In all this, one aspect of the garden cities movement was coming full circle; the idea, originated by the industrial patrons of the movement, that by dramatically improving working peoples living standards they could be reconciled to a status quo that they had previously seen as against their own interests.

In 1921 against a background of economic slump which undermined the power of the unions the government abandoned its house building programme. Its insurance policy had paid off - revolution had been averted. In the following years whilst housing standards would be driven down the idea of municipal garden suburbs remained remarkably intact.

'...the 'homes for heroes' campaign had important lasting consequences for public housing in Britain. In terms of both scale and quality of municipal housing, it created a precedent to which subsequent reformers could refer and to some extent, a standard from which departure had to be justified.'

Mark Swenarton. *Homes Fit for Heroes*

BACKS TO THE LAND

The other major promise made to soldiers returning from the trenches was that those who wanted would be able to get smallholdings on the land. As a means of unemployment relief and rural regeneration, land settlement had a long history.

A number of wealthy men were promoters of land settlement experiments. Auberon Herbert, who had sheltered the New Forest Shakers when they had been evicted in 1878, proposed the formation of 'voluntary land companies' to encouraged the 'multiplication of landowners and those living on the land'. In 1885 he sponsored a series of smallholding schemes at Lambourne & Cottenham (Cambs), Foxham(Wilts) and Hay Farm in Essex. Holdings were offered for sale on instalments over 20 years with the down payment of a 10% deposit. The schemes continued until 1901 when the company set up to run them was wound up and presumably all the instalments paid. At Winterslow, near Salisbury, in 1892 a Major Poore divided up the 195 acre Cooper's Farm into 49 smallholdings to be run by a landholders' court and in 1915 the Smallholders Union was publicising the Sharnal Street Colony in Kent run by another ex-army officer.

Perhaps the most prolific wealthy supporter of land settlement was the American Jewish philanthropist Joseph Fels who had made his fortune out of the Fels Naptha Soap Company. Fels had been involved in utopian ventures in the USA before he got involved in schemes over here. He had supported the Arden and Rose Valley Arts & Crafts-based communities and as a supporter of Henry George's Single Land Tax campaign was involved with establishing the town of Fairhope, Alabama based on George's ideas. In 1904 Fels gave his support to two schemes being put forward by George Lansbury and the Poplar Board of Guardians. The Laindon Farm Colony in Essex and the Hollesley Bay Colony, near Felixstowe, were both training schemes for the unemployed, the Hollesley Bay scheme being much the larger in scale set on the 1300-acre estate of a former Agricultural Training College. The original plan was to train men and then place them on co-operative smallholdings but these were never set up and the schemes though intially succesfull ceased in 1911. Fels also bought 70 acres at Broad Campden in the Cotswolds as smallholdings for the craftsmen of the Guild of Handicrafts who wished to stay in the area after the Guild had ceased. He also threw himself into political campaigns in England, funding an English land tax campaign which culminating in the 'parliamentary revolution of 1909', which stripped the House of Lords of its power to veto tax bills.

It did not always take a weathly backer to make land settlement a reality. Schemes could be set up by individuals pooling their resources, especially in areas where land was cheap. The Methwold Fruit Farm Colony in Norfolk was started when a Mr Goodrich bought a couple of acres of land in1889 and proceeded to encourage others to join him, the colony eventually covering some 160 acres. Goodrich had been appalled ' to see large tracts of waste land about the country, and then to see in the towns so many people shuffling about without enough food and clothing' and had spent 3 or 4 years prior to moving to the country studying books on the land, fruit-farming, poultry and bee-keeping. The colonists sent any surplus produce direct, by rail, to consumers in London cutting out 'all those forty thieves' of middle men who stole growers profits on the way to market. Though Goodrich was the leading light of the scheme the colony had no formal organisation.

"There is no committee, and no form of self government. Any question affecting the interests of the Colonists generally is discussed amongst themselves in an informal sort of way, as they happen to meet over the labours of the day. This individualistic idea, grafted on to the socialistic system, seems to have been attended with singular success."

In his book entitled *Poverty and the State* Herbert Mills proposed self-supporting home colonies as the solution to the problem of unemployment. The colonies were to be totally co-operative in production, distribution and consumption. ".........we must grow our own wheat and oats, and potatoes and fruit; we must raise our own cattle, grow our own flax, spin and weave our own wool and linen, and grind our own corn."

In 1892 he started the Starnthwaite Home Colony, or Westmorland Commune centred on Starnthwaite Mill and the neighbouring Browhead Farm at Crosstwhaite on the edge of the Lake District. The colony got off to a good start recieving favourable comments from Robert Blatchford in *The Clarion*. Yet just a year later those attracted there by the promise of co-operative village life had fallen out with Mills. "...... we have been misled and unfairly treated; having been drawn into this place in the belief that it was a commune, whereas it is an outdoor workhouse conducted on more arbitrary lines than any known to Bumbledom."

Dan Irving . Burnley socialist.
`Trouble at Starnthwaite' letter to The Clarion 1893

The socialists were evicted and Mills carried on unrepentant directing operations undertaking mixed farming and fruit growing until he left in 1901, after which the colony continued as a training centre for the unemployed and as a home for epileptic boys.

SOCIALIST SETTLEMENT, OR SETTLEMENT OF SOCIALISTS?

Inspired by articles in *The Clarion* Manchester printer Thomas Smith bought 11 acres of land at Althorne in Essex. He built a house, the Homestead, and with his wife and two children set about cultivating the heavy clay soil whilst at the same time placing adverts in *The Labour Annual* offering `Individualist ownership, tempered by voluntary cooperation. Some more land can be had here, and Socialist settlers would find skilled advice and like-minded comrades.' Smith would become a skilled smallholder and despite hard going in the early days, when he had to take work back in Manchester to keep things going, the Mayland Colony grew; in the main it being city folk who were attracted to the colony. Smith gradually went over from mixed farming to glasshouse cultivation, growing tomatoes, lettuces and early strawberries. The colony also drifted away from its socialist roots going from calling itself `A settlement of Socialists rather than a Socialist settlement.' to being a group of `peasant proprietors'. Smiths reputation as a horticulturalist continued to grow and the publication of two books on French Gardening and The Profitable Culture of Vegetables attracted a stream of notable visitors to the site including Peter Kropotkin, Rider Haggard, Sidney & Beatrice Webb, Keir Hardie, George Lansbury - and Joseph Fels.

So impressed was Fels with Smiths achievements he bought the nearby 600-acre Nipsells Farm and created a series of 21 five to ten acre holdings each with its own dwelling and out-houses and partly planted up with fruit., and made them available to the unemployed as a long term opportunity rather than the short-term relief offered by the training schemes at Laindon & Hollesey. The rest of the farm was kept as a commercial venture. Smith became supervisor of the Fels Small Holdings, manager of the Fels Fruit Farm, the Windmill Nurseries and a demonstration 'French Garden'. Today Mayland is still predominantly an area of nurseries and smallholdings, the legacy of Smith and Fels' 'settlement of socialists'

THE NORTON CO-OPERATIVE SMALLHOLDINGS

The grand plan for a ring of municipal farms around the new garden city, that would supply all its needs never materialised at Letchworth., firstly because the site acquired was only about half the size that Howard had estimated would be required, and on top of that the soil was mostly clay or chalk resulting in poor crop yields. A number of tenant farms were set up, along with a sprinkling of individual smallholdings and in 1905 The Norton Co-operative Smallholdings Society established a 152-acre smallholdings centre at Norton Hall Farm. The co-operative sublet plots of up to 20-acres. 12 cottages were built at Norton Village as part of the scheme, some pig sties were constructed and 10-acres of fruit planted. The scheme however was not a success.

In the town itself the ample gardens provided with each house meant that it was possible for residents to grow large amounts of their own produce. Fruit trees were popular, the gardens of the new city having some 3500 apple, pear & plum trees growing in them. A thriving Allotment Cottage Garden Association was set up in response to the demand for additional growing space and by the time the call went out to 'Dig for Victory' during the Second World War there were some 600 allotments, plots covering an estimated 100-acres and many Letchworth families were able to be self-sufficient in fruit & veg during the war years.

COLONISING THE LAND

GUEST ARTICLE BY
COLIN WARD

This article first appeared in; *Diggers & Dreamers 94/94.*

If a single slogan had to be chosen to epitomise the hopes of utopian ventures in twentieth century Britain, the words would be "Back to the Land". This is as true of communities of production, where the intention was to practice the crafts in combination with food production, as of communities of spiritual endeavour or of pacifism where self-support depended on small-scale mixed farming. It was even true of the Garden City movement's aspirations, where the community is surrounded by market gardens and where the density of twelve houses to the acre gave "gardens of sufficient size to be of commercial value to the tenants ... and not too large to be worked by an ordinary labourer and his family".

In the late nineteenth century the `Land Question' had been one of primarily parliamentary politics rather than utopian hopes. The Drift from the Land', fuelled by the effects of the Enclosure Acts and the amalgamation of holdings, was a fact of British life. Britain was thought to be unique in Europe for having no peasants, and legislators promoted and protected the idea of the resettlement of the land or a century that ended only in 1982. All through the nineteenth century agitation for smallholding was linked with the campaign for allotments resulting in ineffective legislation, which empowered councils to provide both allotments and smallholdings for resale. But since most would-be smallholders were not in a position to enter into such commitments and simply wanted to rent, it was correctly described as window dressing.

Does the aim of the restoration of the peasantry belong to the world of utopian communities, or was it a matter of political expediency? Did the promoters of the ideal have different hopes from those of the people who experienced a whole series of policies towards land settlement? Were the settlers communitarians or rugged individualists? As long ago as 1845 it had been argued that the case for allotments was "moral rather than Economic".2 Historian Martin J Wiener observed: "The less practically important rural England became, the more easily could it come to stand simply for an alternative and complimentary set of values, a psychic balance wheel ". He cites the opinion of the sociologist O R McGregor that "the pathetic delusion that some sort of land settlement scheme contained the secret cure for the ills of industrial society had great survival value".3 It did not appear a pathetic delusion to the variety of charitable and propagandist organisations of a century ago advocating the recolonisation of rural England. Quite apart from the desire to stem the `drift from the land' there was a whole movement of revulsion against the horrors of Victorian industrial society and the hypocrisy of Victorian middle-class life reflected in the Tolstoyan, socialist and anarchist movements of the time and the cult of the `simple life'.

By 1908 the `window dressing Acts' had only provided 244 holdings. It was the Small Holdings and Allotments Act of 1908 which, at last, enabled county councils to provide small holdings for rent. It was in fact a very important piece of legislation. Eighty years later there are English counties where because of this Act the county council is the largest single landowner. County council small-holdings certainly met a long-felt need. They seldom addressed the aspirations that had surfaced unofficially for a community life on the land.

The First World War was a watershed in the aspirations for re-establishing a peasantry. Not only did it provide a short-lived viability for Britain's depressed agriculture and horticulture but it left an aftermath of desire for a life on the land. Lloyd George, as wartime Prime Minister declared in a speech which epitomised stimulated, and perhaps exploited the land settlement idea, that `There must be a scheme for settling the gallant soldiers and sailors on the land ... The vast majority will return to their old occupations, But I am told that a good many of those who have been living an open-air life do not want to return to the close atmosphere of workshop and factory. If that is the case they ought to have the opportunity of living on the land 4

ENGLAND CHANGES HANDS

In terms of aspirations this was certainly the case. Land came on to the market on a scale never known before. The pre-war introduction of death duties coupled with the slaughter of inheritors in the First World War resulted in a situation where, as Howard Newby put it "In four years between 1918 and 1922 England in the words of a famous Times leader of the day `changed hands'. One quarter of the area of England was bought and sold in this hectic period." Not very many of these transfers of ownership actually served the needs of the ex-soldiers for whom the Land Settlement (Facilities) Act of 1919 was intended. Its provisions had not had the anticipated effect even though these included farm colonies with central farms attached, profit-sharing farms and co-operative marketing.

Leah Leneman sought the recollections of settlers and their children in Fit for Heroes?5. "Those who had succeeded without previous agricultural experience," she found, "as characters of enormous grit and determination." In spite of the fact that their holdings were now supporting a third generation, to Robert Kirk and Bob Fraser, "the claim after World War I that ex-servicemen would be able to stand on their own two feet with just `five acres and a cow' was a terrible con. Not that they thought those who formulated the policy had been insincere but rather that it had been lunacy from the start although the ex-servicemen had believed what the government told them." The son of another responded that "It will be civil servants who dreamt that up, because they couldnae' have been practical men or they would never have gave anybody a holding of four acres say to make a living out of". Others of the second generation explained that their fathers survived with a second job, working at Parkhead or on the railway or for nearby farmers. "One holder with six acres was a stamp dealer and did well out of that." For others, how indeed did they manage? "There were two answers which applied to all the holdings of whatever size? Firstly, they managed by unremitting backbreaking work. The second answer was the crucial participation of the women and children."

In England and Wales the direct intervention by central government in the provision of smallholdings for ex-servicemen came to an end in 1926. This was also the year of the General Strike. The Religious: Society of Friends, popularly known as the Quakers in 1926, sought to find ways to alleviate the hardships endured by the miners. It found that some allotment gardens were going out of cultivation as plot-holders lacked even the money to buy seeds and fertilisers, and that men who did cultivate their allotments were penalised for unemployment pay because of the suspicion that they might be selling the produce. The Friends committee was enabled to get clear statements from the Ministry of Labour that he small amount of produce which a man could sell from his allotment would not affect the amount of his dole"s, and as a result of appeals the Friends were able to provide seeds, seed potatoes, tools, fertiliser and lime By the 1930s the Friends were exploring the possibilities of "Group Holdings" using a piece of land larger than an allotment but smaller than small holdings. This Group Holdings scheme began in county Durham in 1933 and within the next twelve months 16 groups were started in the North East, and "also took root in South Wales Monmouthshire, Yorkshire, Derbyshire Staffordshire Nottinghamshire Cumberland and Northumberland." The significance of this Quaker initiative is that it laid the foundations for the longest lasting government sponsored venture in collective horticulture, the

Land Settlement Association.

During the summer of 1933 a visitor called at Friends House to discuss a scheme which he had in mind. This was an experiment for moving unemployed industrial workers from Durham, providing them with full-time holdings of about five acres in another part of England: giving them training and providing marketing facilities, with a view to their becoming, in two or three years time, once more self supporting citizens. This Gentleman, Mr(now Sir)

Typical Land Settlement cottage Fen Drayton Cambs.

Malcolm Stewart, said he had £25,000 which he wished to devote to this purpose, and he asked if the Friends Committee or the Central Allotments Committee would consider such a scheme, provided the government were willing to give a similar amount. Consequently the Land Settlement Association (LSA) was formed in 1935 and at its first meeting the Minister of Agriculture announced "that money would be available up to £50,000 per year for three years." The founders were aware that behind their venture was a history of disappointments whether in "utopian" colonies, charitable enterprises or the experiment in settling ex-servicemen on the land. They adopted four fundamental principles:

1. Assistance would be given only to group settlements, not to individual smallholdings.
2. Co-operative methods would be adopted for the purchase of smallholders requisites, the marketing of their produce, and the general working of the scheme.
3. Settlers, both men and their wives, would be carefully selected. In General the Association proposed to select men who had successfully cultivated allotments.
4. Adequate training and supervision would be given.

FULFILLING DREAMS

The Association tended to acquire estates in areas with an established tradition of market gardening. A Characteristic LSA landscape emerged. There was a small home farm, usually the original farmstead, occupied by the supervisor or advisors, with central buildings for grading and packing of produce, and beyond it about forty holdings of around four to eight acres The tenants houses, each with a small front garden were built where possible on existing roads. Where necessary new access roads were laid out on a grid-iron layout. Close to the dwellings were glass-houses, pig sheds and chicken houses, followed by a patch for fruit and vegetable cultivation, and beyond that an area designed to be ploughed and harvested together with neighbouring plots, should this be necessary. Sometimes there was also a large-scale orchard.

It was not easy to assimilate a population of 150 to 200 newcomers with different habits and accents into the general life of quiet country districts, nor were the newcomers a ready-made community, since they were nearly all strangers to one another. Moreover physical facilities especially schools, were often quite inadequate. Nor were the problems only external. To be a successful smallholder a man must have ambition, enterprise, unremitting industry, and a love of the land for its own sake, qualities which his wife must share. They must be prepared to work

223

Port 'Fish' Light

Late on a Saturday night in June 1918 the inhabitants of Stornoway on the Outer Hebridean island of Lewis and Harris awaited the arrival of the new owner of the island. They had rigged a banner on the quay that read - 'Welcome to Your Island Home' and arranged for a pipe band to regale the new laird as he set foot on the quay. As the ferry pulled up to the quay just after midnight the Pipers and rest of the reception committee slipped away into the night in observance of the minute-old Sabbath leaving Lord Leverhulme the founder of Port Sunlight to arrive on his island in silence. At a hastily reconvened welcome ceremony a few days later Lever ended his speech in which he had put forward his plans for the revival of the island with the hope that 'We will be able to look each other in the face, and you will be able to say, "We thank you for nothing but the opportunity you have given us."

Lewis and Harris, joined by a narrow strip of land, are often spoken of as separate entities but are really one island covering an area of about a 1000 sq miles. In 1918 they had a population of about 40,000 who eked a precarious living from a combination of fishing, crofting and sheep farming. The history of the island in the 19th Century had been one of displacement of crofters by absentee landlords who replaced them with sheep, and later deer. This had led to a series of land campaigns by those crofters who had not been forced to emigrate, resulting in 'land grabs' and many crofts being occupied by squatters. A number of government measures had done little to help the crofters and the issue still gripped the island when Lever arrived.

Lever's grand plan for the island centred on reviving the fishing industry through the application of science and business skill. There would be an ice-making factory at Stornoway and refrigerated cargo ships to take fish to a depot at Fleetwood. To deal with gluts of fish, the herring curing facilities would be enlarged, a canning factory built and a plant installed to make fish-cakes, fish-paste, glue, animal feed and fertiliser from the offal. As McAlpines started work on the ambitious building programme; including

Houses at Stornoway built by Lever.

houses with bathrooms in Stornoway and a semi-self-build scheme to build new crofts, two companies were registered; MacLine to run the fishing fleet operation and MacFisheries to run a chain of shops. Lever then proceeded to buy 350 high street fresh fish shops throughout the British Isles as outlets for the produce of his new fisheries. Lever's grand scheme, whilst aimed at relieving the life of the crofters on the island, took no account of the reality of the crofters' lives. What the crofters most needed was casual work to supplement their subsistence farming; what was to be on offer was regular employment in an industrial process.

In 1918 the Scottish Office proposed that under the Small Landholders Act they should take over some of Lever's farms on Lewis and provide 150 crofts for returning servicemen as a start in the pledge to provide 'smallholdings fit for heroes'. In the spring of the following year, impatient with the lack of any action, ex-servicemen waiting for crofts invaded farms on the island driving off farmer's animals and staking out six-acre plots and erecting shelters for their families. They had expected support from Lever, who often railed at bureaucratic incompetence, but instead he condemned the squatters and ordered them off his land. Lever saw the croft system as a millstone around the islanders' necks and believed that once his streamlined commercial fisheries operation was up and running, the crofts would be deserted as men & women left the land for the better wages and conditions that would be on offer. Lever's arrogance made him enemies among local politicians, at the Scottish Office and among the crofters. Other islanders enthusiastically supported his reforms.

Two things conspired to undermine the schemes on the island. Firstly the finances of Lever Brothers went through a rocky patch and the source of money for developing the island became problematic leading to delays and setbacks. And the land settlement issue refused to go away. The 'illegal' crofters won the support of the Highland Land League and the newly elected MP for the island. When Lever moved to evict the squatters and have then imprisoned the Scottish Office made it known that it would let the men go free should this happen. When Lever backed down and offered to let the crofters stay, if the bureaucrats would leave him alone for ten years to implement his schemes, the Scottish Office declined the offer as it was government policy to push ahead with further crofts. This brought a threat from Lever to withdraw his scheme completely. At loggerheads with the authorities and the crofters Lever busied himself elsewhere letting the works on the island slowly drag to a halt.

On Sept 3 1923 Lever addressed the Stornoway and Lewis councils to announce that he intended to leave the island. What came next was a complete surprise to those present - he announced that he intended to give all the crofters a gift of the freehold of their land and that the rest of the island would be made over to a trust for each of the districts. He gave them a month to accept the offer. The Highland Land League and district councils took a long look at the implications of implementing the schemes they had been campaigning for and promptly turned the offer down, letting the island be sold back to absentee landlords instead of taking the risk of making their reforms work. Only Stornoway accepted setting up a trust and going on to make it work for the benefit of the town.

Lord Leverhulme died in May 1925 and the board of Lever Bros. ordered all work on the Lewis and Harris project to stop and so the Port Sunlight of Fishing finally ended. In 1948 when the Faroe Islands were granted independence from Denmark they implemented development policies with great effect that were similar to those that Lever had tried resulting in a remarkably successful island economy.

The Scottish Islands are a rotten deal,
Those Celts are terribly difficle.
We find them unwilling to pull their weight
When we let them in at the Golden Gate.

They've no team spirit, they wont take part
In our study circles and community art
And at garden parties they won't concur
In speaking English - which is de rigeur

So welcome now to the realm of the divine
And sign your name on the dotted line
You'll find life up here a spree
For Heaven is a joint-stock company.

But far below in the Western Seas
The moors were quiet in the Hebrides,
The crofters gossiped in Gaelic speech
And the waves crept over the lonely beach

From: *The Ballad of Lord Leverhulme* **Louis MacNeice**

The full story of Lord Leverhulme's scheme is told in: *Lord of the Isles.* **By N.Niclson 1960.**

225

for long hours for an uncertain and irregular income. A long term history of industrial unemployment hardly tended to bring out such qualities. Joe Chapman was a plasterer in Hayes, Middlesex, unemployed for eighteen months who applied for training at an LSA estate in Bedfordshire in 1938. His son explains that "When he went there he thought he was fulfilling his dream. He thought he was going to stay." But what was his dream? "I think that ultimately he was a romantic communist probably a utopian socialist before that What he read was books about *Island Farm* or *I Bought a Mountain.* He would really have liked to take over a deserted island." He was installed in an empty house on the LSA site and learned from the LSA advisers the secrets not only of horticulture but of goat culture. ` By the time we arrived four months later, he was very happy and had all sorts of things to show us, and it was all very exciting. We moved into no-man's-land where there were rows of houses that were empty still, and by the time we left the Land Settlement tractors were ploughing it all up. There were lots of advisors who he liked very much. There was a man who advised on pigs and a man who advised on glass-houses, and he enjoyed all that, but maybe he had a feeling that it was all going sour By the end of the year he had cycled over to Suffolk and decided this was the place and had the great good luck to find this farm where the whole family has been ever since. It seems to me that we lived on tomatoes and goats milk for years. I dare say that my father was almost unique, apart from his neighbour who was a Welsh miner in living out his dream of self-sufficiency on the LSA estate. I remember particularly the goats and the Angora rabbits. We all loved it.

Another was Ted Dunn, a veteran of the Friends Ambulance Unit in the Second World War who became an LSA tenant in Essex in 1948 and has been there ever since. His son is a member of the growers co-operative that took over since the closure of the Association in 1983. In spite of his pioneering experiments in organic growing, watched with scepticism by his neighbouring growers Ted Dunn is more readily associated with a whole series of books he has edited or written on the preconditions for world peace. Pinned down on the question of whether his LSA estate at Foxash was a community, he replied, "It was a community of individuals, as you might expect. The original settlers had everything against them. The organisation was very poor. The so 1 was poor The markets were against them ... My first main recollection from a community point of view was of harvesting ... because in those days you had twenty of us who would all join in together to stook, thrash and all the rest. It was a kind of community. That only lasted a few years actually, for then the combines came in ... There were also the monthly meetings, and through having a central store, that was a wonderful place to meet other people."10

THE BITTER END

By the early 1970s the average earnings of the Associations tenant's were well above the average agricultural wage. For some tenants, growing provided a good living. But this was subject to several qualifications. Some estates were more successful than others, and even on the same estate, some tenants were more skilful more hardworking, or just luckier than others, or had been able to invest more in glass-houses and equipment as encouraged by the Association's central office. In any case the income represented a `family' wage, for it usually resulted from the labour of the tenant and his wife, and often their children. Earnings which depended on being able to pick trim wash and package thousands of heads of celery in the early morning because one of the multiple stores was having a Celery Week, could not have been achieved otherwise.

The end of the Land Settlement Association was announced just as Parliament went into its Christmas recess in 1982. The, then, Minister of Agriculture Peter Walker told the House of Commons that tenants should take over responsibility for marketing their produce and that this should happen as quickly as possible. The decision covered the remaining ten estates comprising 3,900 acres, with about 530 tenants, as well as about 300 staff. Tenants were allowed to purchase their holdings at half the current market price. But the Ministry cut off any further short or long-term finance. Some of the growers cut adrift simply moved out and their homes and land were sold on behalf of the Ministry during the property boom of the 1980s. The plain little houses were expanded into ranch-style homes and the land was either neglected or flourished as paddocks for horse owners. But at two estates at least - Foxash Growers Ltd in Essex and Newbourn Growers Ltd in Suffolk - genuine co-operatives were formed. The members continue to produce in an extremely specialised way for the retail supermarkets, and at their behest the produce is picked in the early morning, washed, graded, trimmed, packaged and provided with the sellers label, bar-code and sell-by-date, ready for the truck. When questioned, the co-operative members, heavily dependant on bank loans, and at the mercy of the policies of a handful of big customers, as well as the ever present possibility of crop failures, claim that they are more content than in the days of their dependency on the LSA. But these survivors felt bitter about the abrupt closure in 1982 and started legal proceedings against the Ministry claiming the LSA had been falsely presented as a sound investment and had run tenants into debt by selling produce at too low a price The Ministry of Agriculture offered compensation of £6.5 million, cancellation of tenant's debts and all costs whilst continuing to deny liability.

This was the messy end of the longest-lasting, largest-scale venture in getting "back to the land" in Britain, as well as the only one, apart from its precursors in resettling ex-servicemen, to be sponsored and funded by government. Could it be called 'utopian" and could its estates be described as communities"? Undoubtedly its Quaker founders were seen as utopian even though they were conscious of experimenting, step-by-step with measures to relieve unemployment. In ordinary political circles very few alternatives other than Keynesian public spending programmes were being advocated in the 1930s. There is also some evidence that the men who were willing to commit themselves and their families to this leap into the country-side, far from home, were people who cherished the ideal of a return to the land. It is doubtful whether many were inspired by the concept of communal living. The Land Settlement Association was in retrospect, an attempt and the largest ever made in Britain, to accommodate utopian ideals of recolonising the land, with the harsh realities of ordinary life. For its tenants there were few alternative choices.

Parts of this article previously appeared in: The Raven:Anarchist Quaterly Mar 1992 and Freedom Press

Colin Ward is a veteran anarchist writer on land, planning and housing issues. Perhaps best known of his numerous publications are; The Child in the City and The Child in the Country. Colin has written widely on Utopian experiments introducing the subject to school children with his Utopia (Penguin Education 1974) He has also written many articles for planning & anarchist magazines and in Diggers & Dreamers. And along with Dennis Hardy he has written books on the plotlands settlements and a history of allotments.

Books available from: Freedom Press. 84 Whitechapel High Street. London E1.

REFERENCES:
1. Unwin,Raymond(1909) Town Planning in Practice.
2. The Penny Magazine. (1845)
3. McGregor,OR(1961)Introduction to Lord Ernie. English Farming Past And Present.5th ed.
4. Russel Smith, Newlin (1946) Land for the Small Man.Kings Crown Press.
5. Leneman, Leah Fit for Heroes? Aberdeen UP
6. Farmer, John (1980) "The Growing Years." in The Gardeners Compaion & Diary. Nat.Soc. of Leisure Gardeners.
7. Fry, Joan MAry (1947) Friends Lend a Hand in Alleviating Unemployment. Friends Book Centre.
8. Recollection kindly provided by Martin Chapman, Hitcham Suffolk. Nov 1991.
9. Dunn, Ted ed(1963) Alternatives to War and Violence. Clarke & Co.
10. Recollection Kindle Provided by Ted Dunn. Lawford Essex. Oct 1991.
11. Statement by the Minister of Agriculture Dec 1 1982

NEW TOWN FRIENDS

In 1917 a small group of Quakers had formed to discuss ideas for post-war reconstruction. This group evolved into the New Town Council. The secretary of the group was architect H.C.Lander and others on the council included members of the Fry's Quaker chocolate manufacturing family and the Welsh Garden City pioneer T. Alwyn Lloyd. In 1919 one of the council, William Ravenscroft Hughes, produced a book to promote the ideas that had come out of the adhoc group's discussions. *New Town: a proposal in agricultural, industrial, educational, civic and social reconstruction* was Garden Cities revisited, but this time with the emphasis on co-operative activity and communal facilities. Almost everything in New Town was to be run on a co-operative basis; housing, agriculture, health, education & industry. They hoped to draw on a wide range of experience seen to be already available from co-operative societies, trade unions, progressive local authorities and housing reformers. A development company, the Pioneer Trust Ltd, was formed to raise finance and take the idea forward. This mirrored the development process successfully used at Letchworth, which the New Town literature referred to frequently.

Much of the rhetoric regarding the proposed communal facilities came direct from the co-operative housekeeping movement. Emphasis was put on liberating women from household chores through radical domestic changes. This included a People's Kitchen and Restaurant that would serve food eat-in and take-away and lend out cooking utensils. Also a uniformed Household Auxiliary Corps would employ 'experts in household arts' to carry-out housework on a professional basis. Design would also reduce housework. Dust would be designed out by eliminating difficult-to-dust surfaces. It was assumed that a number of co-operative housekeeping schemes would be incorporated into the new city. No one would be forced to use the communal facilities; they would simply be there to 'promptly meet the demands' of residents as they arose.

The Pioneer Trust was successful in securing some finance for the scheme but no-where near enough for the projected 3000-acres that was needed. Rather than give up on the project completely, the group turned to the developers of the second garden city at Welwyn, where in 1921 after some negotiation the New Town group took over 500 acres of land and set up a co-operative Agricultural Guild to manage the land on a scientific basis. The guild was managed by a committee elected from the farm workers, the workers union, the local parish council and the New Town Trust, with the workers being in the majority. Paying 'fair wages' they produced food for the developing Garden City, concentrating on market gardening, milk production and chicken farming. Though they increased the size of the holding by another 500-acres during the first 2 years, and talked optimistically of high quality milk yields and producing food for the general good and not for profit, the guild was never a financial success and closed down after several years.

Other members of the New Town group involved themselves in educational activities at Welwyn and in encouraging the formation of worker co-operatives in various local industries. None of these ventures came to anything, but they were more successful in the field of co-operative housing. Guessens Court was designed by H.C Lander as a full blown co-operative housekeeping scheme with a mix of 20 detached & semi-detached houses surrounding a central block of 40 flats and a 3 storey communal services block with restaurant, kitchen and guest rooms. The central services were to be managed co-operatively by the residents. After much delay a revised scheme was opened in 1925 consisting of the communal block and the flats. Tenants were required to spend a minimum sum in the restaurant each week, (encouraged by discount coupons) maids could be hired at hourly rates along with boot cleaning & coal-carrying services. Rents covered; use of shared tennis courts and maintenance of the gardens & grounds. During the first 5 years the restaurant turned in a small profit and the scheme as a whole just about paid its way.

Elsewhere in the Garden Cities movement others were still showing interest in shared housing for single women. Elizabeth Cadbury, wife of the founder of Bournville, was instrumental in the formation of Residential Flats Ltd, which built St George's Court, 32 serviced flats with communal facilities, at Bournville in 1924.

AN EXPERIMENT IN RURAL REGENERATION

Where the aim of the Garden City was to bring the countryside into the town, an experiment got underway in the mid-1920s with the aim of taking the benefits of the town into the country. The Dartington Hall experiment by Leonard and Dorothy Elmhirst was in many ways the rural counterpart to the developments by industrial philanthropists of the likes of Lever & Cadbury. Leonard Elmhirst was a minor member of England's landed gentry, whilst his wife Dorothy, was a wealthy New York heiress. Between them they started and built up one of the best known and most enduring 'alternative communities'. What started off as little more than a radical management plan for a country estate became over time a highly successful experiment in rural regeneration proving that with enough investment a thriving rural culture and economy can be built up through decentralised facilities.

Not that any of this was apparent when the Elmhirsts bought the dilapidated Dartington estate in 1925. Then it was all a leap of faith & vision. Dartington's renown has been largely due to the reputation of the educational establishments that were established there. Firstly the experimental school under the headship of W.B. Curry (a close friend of A.S Neil from Summerhill) and later the Art College whose reputation in the early days was enhanced by the presence of the likes of Michael Chechov, Bernard Leach and Rudolph Von Laban. But the schools were only part of a wider rural regeneration project that touched all areas of rural life. As the arts were Dorothy's passion, Leonard's passion was the land. He busied himself with experiments on the estate in agriculture and forestry, trying out different 'scientific' methods to improve animal husbandry and crop yields. An attempt at intensive chicken farming gave a 'negative result' - Leonard believing that in an experiment there was no such thing as failure only positive or negative results. A more positive result was achieved when after a visit to the Soviet Union, where the only thing to impress him was the state of Russian agriculture, Leonard established a cattle-breeding centre from which developed the nation-wide artificial insemination programme for cattle. Leonard became head of the International Association of Agricultural Economists that was formed after a conference at Dartington.

An enormous amount of restoration work on the estate's historic buildings was financed by Dorothy's fortune and the Elmhirst's grand plans required much new building work. The surprise at Dartington is that this was not carried out in mock mediaeval style, or even the Arts & Crafts style favoured in the Garden Cities, but contains some gems of modernist international-style architecture carried out by some of the movements best-known architects: Walter Gropius, Louis de Soissons, and William Lescaze. Out of the building programme grew Staverton Builders that went on to be a successful building firm in its own right. The general manger A.E. Malbon who had previously worked for Welwyn Builders, building the second Garden City was later instrumental in the formation of the South West Co-operative Housing Society. Other business ventures were initiated from Dartington: a cider press, a retail outlets for rural crafts and perhaps best known, Dartington Glass.

With capital investment, undreamed of by previous utopians, the Elmhirst's have been criticised for not achieving more at Dartington. Despite, or because of, the inherent paradoxical nature of the project - a radical project to regenerate an essentially conservative rural culture, - landed gentry & Yankee tobacco dollars working alongside proponents of co-operation, democracy and libertarian education, Dartington has survived to be something of a beacon for rural regeneration. In 1931, as at Bournville and New Earswick before, a trust was set up to run the estate moving the control away from that of the founders and setting in motion a secure structure that could oversee the development of the estates in the future.

SUBSISTENCE PRODUCTION

Still sure as most changes take time in the making,
We'll build a new world in the midst of the old,
Where you'll do the milking and I'll do the baking,
Where goods will be bartered for goods and not gold.

Jim Forrester. Eastern Valleys SPS supervisor
SPS Bulletin

Other regeneration projects during the depression years of the 1920s & 30s may have been less enduring, and less well-funded than Dartington, but that did not make them any the less ambitious. Once again it was the Quakers who were heavily involved. In 1927 with the backing of the Friends Coalfield Distress Committee a Settlement House was set up at Maes-yr-haf in the Rhondda Valley as a base for relief work in the area. Working from this and eight other houses that were set up in the valleys some 52 'occupational clubs' with 9000 members were set up, some in specially designed self-build clubhouses funded by the Society of Friends. The clubs ran classes in a whole variety of subjects and the Workers Educational Association organised classes in allotment holding, pig and poultry keeping. Peter & Lillian Scott, two northern Quakers, came to work at a small 'family' house set up at Brynmawr. From here they distributed food & clothes, organised boot repairs and ran a soup kitchen for the unemployed. A group was organised to examine alternative futures for Brynmawr and a number of initiatives were started as a result. In 1931 Brynmawr & Clydach Valley Industries was registered as an umbrella co-operative for furniture, weaving and bootmaking activities. A District Poultry Association was started through which members could borrow the necessary cash to get set up and pay the loan off through surplus egg sales. The Scotts helped organise the first International Voluntary Service workcamp in this country, which colour-washed houses in the town and cleared a rubbish dump to form the site for an open-air swimming pool built later by unemployed volunteers from the town.

In 1934 the Scotts formed 'The Order of Friends' to push for "radical changes" in the way the unemployed were treated. Peter Scott put forward plans for setting up Subsistence Production Societies; where the unemployed would be able to work, take home the product of their labour, barter surplus goods amongst themselves and not have their dole reduced. Two trial projects were set up, one just outside Brynmawr and one outside Wigan in Lancashire at Up Holland.

Charles and Constance Wilkinson moved up from South Wales to start work in Wigan. 7 acres of land and some unused buildings were obtained on a short lease at Lawns Farm, Tontine, and 11 men and 2 women were selected from the local unemployed. Initially 100 poultry, 1 cow &10 pigs were aquired, using money provided by a local businessman. The farm produced tomatoes, potatoes, peas, beetroots, cabbages, onions, beans, turnips, carrots, soft fruit, honey, milk, bacon and eggs. A 'miniature factory' was set up in an adapted farm building where 2000 pots of jam were produced from soft fruit on a Primus stove! A workshop was set up in a barn repairing boots & clogs and

Brynmawr Pool. Under construction & in use

making clothes. Work started at 9am and you were expected to work a 6 hour day with 30 hours a week being regarded as 'fair'. Many worked much longer happy, to have work to do and keen to see the experiment succeed. Every member kept a 'bank' book recording their 'earnings' in hours & minutes. The price of goods was calculated in a combination of money and time, taking into account capital outlay, cost of production and estimated yields with the price of a jar of jam coming to 2d &15minutes. When anyone 'bought' goods from the on-site grocery store they paid the small amount of cash from their dole money and the minutes were taken off their labour credits. During the trial period a cash wage was paid at the same level as the dole as the project had not reached agreement that the labour credits would not affect anyone's entitlement to benefits.

The trial schemes were a great success and Lord Nuffield offered £30,000 for them to be extended. The Subsistence Production Society trials coincided with the Governments Special Areas Development and Improvement Act, which granted a commissioner powers to fund relief work in 'Special Areas'. The commissioner was persuaded by Peter Scott to provide funding to extend the scheme in South Wales on the conditions that:
1. Membership was voluntary.
2. Members were always available for work.
3. Members were not bound by hours of work.
4. There was not contract of service.
5. No products were be sold outside the membership.
6. Men must sign on at the Labour Exchange.
In Wigan which was not a 'special area' the Order of Friends expanded the scheme using the Nuffield money.

Suddenly from being a couple of small scale projects with a handful of members the Subsistence Production Society(SPS) expanded between 1934 & 1938 to a scale where the logistics, and the achievements, were quite breathtaking. In the Welsh valleys sites covering in total several hundreds of acres were acquired at Llandegveth, Beili Glas, Trevethin, Pontymoile, Griffithstown, Pontnewydd, Cwnbran & Cwnavon. In Lancashire the Wigan & District SPS grew to over 400 acres on 4 additional sites at Billinge, Parbold Hall, Stephens Farm Pemberton and Ashfield House at Standish. In both areas a wide variety of both agricultural and industrial activities took place, running through the whole range of animal husbandry and market gardening, and on the light industrial front including; tailoring, cob-bling, butchery, baking, woodworking, limestone, whitesand & coal extraction, a building team, furniture making, weaving, machine knitting and various handicrafts. Once up and running the production statistics for the schemes were staggering. In 1938 the Welsh Valleys SPS recorded production of: 242,590pints of milk, 38,500lbs of meat, 1,584lbs of blackcurrants, 9,578lbs of jam, 360yds of blankets, 90 suits, and 69,499 concrete bricks. The benefits to the unemployed and their families in terms of self-esteem, health and general well being were immeasurable. It was however estimated by one member that by participating in the SPS their dole money went "about half as far again."

"This shows the marvellous benefit the SPS was to the unemployed. As there were no wages the cash cost of production was low. Members who had no training in accounting watched the finances carefully and enthusiastically. In 1938 the agriculture and horticulture showed improvement; the cattle, pigs, sheep and poultry reared on the land owned by the society were largely self-supporting; very little fresh stock would be needed......."

Margaret.R.Pitt.
Our unemployed: Can the past teach the present.
Whilst some 900, mainly men, took part in the SPS schemes in Wales and Lancashire attracting considerable positive attention from the media and from social reformers, not everyone was sympathetic. In Wales the local Labour Party, Miners Unions and local shopkeepers were suspicious from the start and the men themselves were wary of the 'interfering BQs' (Bloody Quakers) and to begin with men joining up met with open hostility from their neighbours, some even being stoned on their way to work with a bus having to be provided for their safety. That the schemes were so successful was in no small part due to the combination of the careful Quaker organisation of the projects and the dedication of the unemployed who worked on them. The preparations for war in 1938 started to provide employment in the SPS areas and following the outbreak of war the schemes in both areas were wound up.

THE WAR FOR UTOPIA

"The choice is no longer between Utopia and the pleasant ordered world that our fathers knew; The choice is between Utopia and Hell."

W.Beveridge
Power and Influence 1953

On an ideological level the Second World War was a battle over the definition of utopia. Adolf Hitler's National Socialist creed was utopian in many ways and Germany had its own utopian past that the fascists were able to tap into and co-opt. Groups like the Wandervogel and Rudolph Stiener's Germanic theosophical movement had a large following and to a certain extent the 'old new age' was far more advanced in Germany than in Britain. The influence of mystical and green ideas was remarkably widespread through the ranks of the Nazi Party, right to the top. Hitler's vegetarianism and antipathy to smokers is well documented, less well known is that his deputy Rudolf Hess was a follower of Stiener and a homeopath who had a naturist hospital named after him. Through Hess, the regime supported intensive experimentation in bio-dynamic farming and 2000 bio-dynamic farmers were registered in the Nazi 'Battle for Production' lists. Experiments were carried out on feeding babies with organically grown food and an experimental organic farm at Dachau grew organic herbs for SS medicines. On the orders of Himmler anti-vivisection laws were passed and SS training included respect for animal life of near-Buddhist proportions.

The Weimar Constitution had contained a clause promising smallholdings to all applicants and the 'Blood and Soil' movement saw the creation of a yeoman peasantry all over Germany as a cure-all for social and moral ills. Nazi Germany was the first European country to establish nature reserves, the first country to insist that new tree plantations should include deciduous as well as conifers and passed laws in 1940 protecting hedgerows & smallwoods. The rise of the technocrats among the leadership of the fascist regime eventually led to open hostility towards the mystics and ecologists and after Hess's flight to England all such groups were tainted with treason in the eyes of the Gestapo, who started a campaign of harassment of organic farmers and other such groups.

RARE AND REFRESHING BEVERIDGE

In 1942 as the darkest days of the war were nearing an end, with the Germans occupying practically the whole of western Europe, Churchill ordered the church bells to ring out across the land as news came in of the Eighth Army's defeat of Rommel at El Alamein. The bells could equally have been rung 3 weeks later on the publication of, what turned out to be, Britain's secret utopian weapon, the Beveridge Report, the two events being arguably the turning points of the war.

The author of the report William Beveridge(1879-1963) was an academic civil servant who had been secretary at Toynbee Hall and editor of the Ruskinian paper St George, before he rose through the ranks of academia and the civil service. He had also helped the Salvation Army colonies at Hadleigh and worked for the Charity Organisation Society furthering the work of Octavia Hill. During WW1 he had worked in the Labour Dept. of the Ministry of Munitions and for the Ministry of Food concerned both with logistics and social policy. He was also the author of a number of reports on social welfare and insurance and from 1909 to 1916 he was director of Labour Exchanges, organising a national system of labour exchanges and a compulsory unemployment insurance scheme and later became director of the London School of Economics and master of University College, Oxford. In 1941 the wartime coalition government invited him to chair a committee to look into social insurance and allied subjects; he had wanted to work on manpower resources, but was happy to do 'anything that seemed useful'.

On publication of the committee's report a queue a mile long formed at the Government stationery office Such was the demand that it was continuously reprinted with well over half a million copies sold, giving rise to the

SLAYING THE FIVE GIANTS

Though there is no evidence that the committee drew directly on any of their utopian predecessors works, the Beveridge Report appears to be a sort of grand compilation utopian scheme drawn from elements of a myriad of proposals that had come and gone before, backed up by contemporary empirical evidence and argument.

The report identified what it called the five giants of poverty; Want, Disease, Ignorance, Squalor and Idleness, and laid out proposals for 'slaying' each one. A blow would be dealt against Want with a unified social insurance system that would provide unemployment benefit, a basic pension & Child Allowances. Disease would be combated by the implementation of a national Health Service; Ignorance through a comprehensive education system and Squalor through Town & Country planning and more & better housing. Idleness (unemployment) would be attacked through a commitment to full employment.

These cradle-to-grave provisions clearly carry echos of the voices of; Mary Cary, Gerrard Winstanley, Thomas Spence, Robert Owen, James Silk Buckingham, Edward Bellamy, Octavia Hill and Ebenezer Howard.

rumour that Beveridge was the author of a best seller and had made huge profits from it. *Time* magazine under the headline "Rare and refreshing Beveridge" reported that 'the London Times, traditionally the first newspaper on the breakfast tables of Britain's rulers.' saw the report as 'A momentous document which should and must exercise a profound and immediate influence on the direction of social change in Britain', whilst the mythical 'man in the street' was quoted as seeing it as "a bit of all right."

THE MOST POWERFUL WEAPON OF ALL

The popularity of the report in the country was not shared by conservatives in the coalition government who sat on it for months, made attempts to gag Beveridge and to prevent distribution of a publicly available document

to troops, on the reasoning that it might raise their hopes too high. Churchill would prevaricate on the plan right until the end of the war. The Nazis on the other hand clearly saw the use and effectiveness of the report. In a secret document retrieved from Hitler's bunker by a French journalist the Nazi regime's reaction to and plans for countering Beveridge are detailed:

'The following instructions are given for treating the Beveridge Plan in writing; Unnecessary dealing with the Beveridge Plan is to be avoided, as no indirect propaganda should be made for the plan............Detailed comparisons between our social system and the measures envisaged by the Beveridge Plan should be avoided.' it went on to say that the plan was '....... a product of the needs of war, designed to mislead the English public and the public of the world as to the real war aims of England........ It is the music of the future......'

Secret. Annexe to PLS-Nr.363/43g

It wasn't only in the bombed-out streets of Britain that Beveridge had given people hope. Copies of the report were parachuted into occupied Europe and translated by the resistance movements in Norway, Denmark, Belgium, Holland & France. Despite being handicapped by old typewriters, a lack of paper and English learnt through *"English by Radio"* classes broadcast by the BBC, underground translations of the report circulated widely, giving people something to fight for rather than against. After the war throughout Europe, everywhere Beveridge, went people came out to tell him that he had given them "the most powerful weapon of all to use against the enemy", a "silver lining in the dark clouds of war."

Giving people hope was one thing, delivering the utopian goods had always been another. How was it that the Beveridge Plan never went the way of all such plans before? How did the utopian experiment that was to become the Welfare State get up off the drawing board? A unique set of circumstances created by wartime conditions were the Welfare State's midwife. Not only had the coalition government given a generation of Labour politicians experience of running the country, but many of them were

RIGHT TURN

Contemporary cartoon. Reproduced from Beveridge and his plan

thinking 'minority' of up to 20% of the population believed that:

1. There must be work at a living wage for everyone who is capable of doing it.

2. Private profit must cease to be the major incentive to work; everyone must work primarily for the good of the community.

3. There must be financial security for everyone who is unable to work.

4 There must be decent homes for everyone at a cost which will not reduce people to poverty.

5. The same education must be available to everyone so that all will have an equal chance.

steeped in the traditions, however watered down, of their utopian forebears. Their leader Clement Attlee had himself been secretary at Toynbee Hall for a brief time. Their support for the plan, which was more a liberal creation than a socialist one, was crucial. The other legacy of the war time coalition was a consensus in British politics that was to last unbroken until Thatcherism in the 1980s. All parties were in general agreement on the plan, differing only on how far and how fast things should go, or how best to manage the new world ahead. Arguments that the country couldn't afford it, or that a planned economy wouldn't work had been patently undermined by the reality of the war effort - if the country could afford war it could certainly afford peace. And in the end the people wanted it. A Ministry of Information report as early as 1942 had observed that a

'........A landslide labour victory heralded a period in which utopian thinking, in a way, became Government policy. Commentators.........could sit back and assess the influence of utopian thought on state policy. For some it was a time to deride antiquated efforts of previous communalists; and for others to lament its passing. All in all however the road to utopia was concluded to be at an end for good or worse.'

Andy Wood
Diggers & Dreamers 96/97

Commentary & Reflection.

ANYONE FOR UTOPIA?

Today's environmental activists talk of greening the cities and restoring the land, largely unaware of the long heritage behind the cry to give us 'New Towns' and to get 'Back to the Land'. Ever since Gerrard Winstanley invoked the shaking off of the 'Norman Yoke' to justify the squatting of common land by the Diggers in 1649, ordinary people's access to land has been a burning issue. With an almost mythical resonance, the picture of a past populated by sturdy independent peasant farmers was used in the late 19th century to promote land settlement as a solution to the ills of industrial society. Cries of 'Back to the Land' were greeted with just as much enthusiasm in the 1890s as the Chartist Land Plan in the 1840s. Some members of the industrial workforce, for whom rural life was still a living memory, were willing to believe that salvation lay in returning to the land however unprepared they were for it in reality. In the 20th century, while politicians and planners have conjured up a new myth of England's green and pleasant land - located somewhere between a home fit for a heroes (& heroines) and the garden city, ordinary people have had their aspirations for more equitable forms of land ownership undermined and bought off with a sprinkling of land settlement schemes and a hearty dose of gardens & allotments, which while turning us into a nation of gardeners has done little to address the 'land issue'.

Two world wars simultaneously pushed utopian ideas and schemes two steps forwards and one step back. Without the wars there would have been no impetus for extending the work of the Garden Cities movement, no Land Settlement Scheme, quite probably no Welfare State. On the other hand post-war adoption of Garden City ideas as the way forward for state housing spelt the end for what might have continued to be a radical environmental movement. War put paid to the Subsistence Production Societies that might have offered a different model of poverty relief had they continued, one of self reliance rather than state reliance. Wartime conditions of enforced communality tainted schemes for communal facilities and co-operative living for almost a whole generation after 1945, curtailing the embryonic co-operative housekeeping movement before it had really got going and meaning that most post-war reconstruction plans that included communal facilities, like the Reilly plan, faded away into obscurity. And it is interesting to ponder what form the still ongoing utopian experiment of the Welfare State would have taken, if had not been born out of the necessity of post-war reconstruction.

The 20th century saw the democratisation of utopia. From being small pockets of a better world, inhabited by elite pioneers of a brave new life, utopian experiments became mass programmes for ordinary people. What was lost in the process is anybody's guess. But those who shepherded in the new utopian democracy were driven by an urgency that either couldn't wait for small-scale projects to evolve, or saw them as inappropriate models for delivering utopia to the masses.

And what would the originators of these ideas and programmes think of what has become of their blueprints? Perhaps Octavia Hill would rail against the stoney-faced indifference of our dependency-culture social services, prodding them to engage with real people in real communities, to give them genuine support and build self-esteem rather than undermine their independence, whilst finding praise for the many community-based social schemes that have appeared. Perhaps Canon Barnet would recognise in the current vogue for 'community capacity building' and 'public participation', the underlying ethos of the Settlement Movement writ large, and encourage the professionals that come to build our capacity and help us to participate, to actually come and live in our communities for a while and really engage with us, making the process one of mutual exchange. I hope Raymond Unwin would be able to find something to his liking, from out of the mess that architecture and planning got themselves into - maybe the community architecture movement, or the green building movement, or perhaps among the Agenda 21 environmental initiatives. And I would like to think that had Ebenezer Howard been faced with tree-housedwelling, tunnel-digging protesters as he embarked on covering the greenfields of Hertfordshire with his new Garden Cities, he would have donned harness and carabiners shinned up the nearest tree and amidst the dreadlocks & nose-rings sat down and had a serious discussion on the social and environmental implications of what he was doing. And found common cause with the protesters in contrast to the reaction of present day planners and developers who appear to have lost grasp of the historic thread amid the pressures of bureaucracy and big business.

1945 was seen as some kind of historical watershed. Some refer to the 'end of the road to utopia', but as we know the utopia tendency would continue into the second half of the 20th century. But that is another story.

Harrington and his Oceana. Russell Scott. Cambridge UP. 1914

Bedford Park The First Garden Suburb. T.A.Greaves. London 1975

The World, a Department Store. A story of life under the Cooperative System. Bradford Peck London1900Rpt1971

Ninety Years On. An Account of the Bournville Village Trust. P.Henslowe. Bournville Village Trust. 1991

A Guide to Port Sunlight Village. E.Hubbard & M.Shippobottom. Liverpool UP. 1988

The Slow Burning Fuse :The Lost History of British Anarchists. John Quail. Paladin books. 1978   RECOMMENDED

Roses & Revolutionists. The Story of Clousden Hill. Nigel Todd. Peoples Publications. 1986. RECOMMENDED

Anarchy A Grafic Guide. Clifford Harper. Camden Press. 1987

Demanding the Impossible : History of Anarchism. Peter Marshall. Fontana 1993.

Whiteway Colony :The Social History of a Tolstoyan Community. Joy Thacker. Whiteway. 1993. RECOMMENDED

Letchworth: The First Garden City. Mervyn Miller. Phillimore &Co 1989. RECOMMENDED

Hampstead Garden Suburb M.Miller & A.S.Gray.Phillimore &Co

A History of Welwyn Garden City. Roger Filler. Phillimore &Co

Wythenshawe: The Story of a Garden City. ed:Derick Deakin.Phillimore &Co

Homes fit for Heroes. Mark Swenarton. Heinemann. 1981

Home Front: Garden Suburbs for Munitions Workers.1915-18. Article in Architectural Review. June 1978

Lord of the Isles. N.Niclson 1960.

Fit for Heroes: Land Settlement in Scotland after WW1. Leah Leneman. Aberdeen UP 1989

Our Unemployed: Can the past teach the present? Margaret.R.Pitt. Friends Book Centre.1982.

The Architectural & Social History of Co-operative Living. Lynn Pearson. Macmillan. 1988. RECOMMENDED

The Road to 1945. Paul Addison. Quartet Books.1975.

Building Communities. The Co-operative Way. J.Birchall. Routledge & Kegan Paul. 1988. RECOMMENDED

Ecology in the 20th Century.A History.Anna Bramwell.Yale Uni.Press.1989.

The Elmhirsts of Dartington. Michael Young. Dartington Hall Trust. 1982.

Beveridge and his plan. Janet Beveridge. Hodder & Stoughton. 1954

The Up Holland Experiment. Alan & Mark Miller. In: Lancashire History Quarterly.Vol2 No4 Dec 1998.

Back to the Future. The history of the Settlement Movement. Ed. Jon Glasby. Univ.of Birmingham.

Octavia Hill and the Social Housing Debate: Essays and Lectures by Octavia Hill Inst.of Economic Affairs.1998

British Town Planning the Formative Years. Leics UP 1981.

The Garden City Movement up to Date E.G Culpin Garden Cities & Town Planning Ass. 1913/14

GAZETTEER OF UTOPIA

" all honour to those who have fought to establish
these little communities. They have kept the sacred
fire alight through a long and dark night."

Edward Carpenter

BEDFORDSHIRE

DUNSTABLE DIGGERS COLONY
1649-50?
One of a series of 'other' Diggers colonies. (See St George's Hill, Surrey for more details)
GRID REF: Location Unknown
REF : World Turned Upside down

MORAVIAN COMMUNITY HOUSE
C1740
Five newly-wed couples from the Bedford Moravian Congregation lived together in one community house.
GRID REF: Location Unknown
REF : Moravian Pamphlet

CARDINGTON   1763-4
FOUNDER/ LEADER : John Howard.
Cottages built around a green by prison reformer John Howard.
GRID REF: TL089477
REF Villages of Vision

SHORTSTOWN   1917
Garden Village development by Short Bros. aircraft-makers - later became RAF property.
GRID REF: TL 064452
REF : Villages of Vision

CHAWSTON LAND
SETTLEMENT SCHEME 1935 - 82?
Government sponsored experiment in Land Settlement. Schemes were set up throughout the country providing group smallholdings for the unemployed. Each scheme was planned on a similar layout, leading to an identifiable Land Settlement scheme landscape.

The plots are usually laid out on a grid pattern with small cottages and vast acres of greenhouses. Success of the schemes was patchy; depending on quality of the land, proximity to markets and experience of the smallholders. Some schemes had joint marketing and distribution set-ups. The whole Land Settlement programme was wound up by the Thatcher government in the 1980s with holders forced to buy their leases or leave. Some of the schemes have thriving horticultural businesses still operating from them, but more than a few have derelict holdings on them.
GRID REF: TL 153559
REF: Colin Ward D&D 94/95

STEWARTBY   1927
Model factory village built by London Brick company.
GRID REF: TL020424
REF : Villages of Vision

POTTON   1935 - 82?
Land Settlement Association smallholding scheme. (See Chawston Beds.)
GRID REF:
REF: Colin Ward D&D 94/95 / Utopian England

Gazetteer Notes:

DATES:
Dates can be assumed to be accurate. C1850 means that I have not found accurate date information. No second date for an entry signifies either that the community is still in existence or a lack of information as to the date of its demise.

FOUNDER/ LEADER:
Name of key figure in the formation of the community.

GRID REF:
The location grid references are as accurate as I could make them. In the the case of sites I have personally visited they are almost spot on. Others only give an approximate location. Location Unknown means either I don't know the location, or nobody knows where they were.

REF:
The text reference is to the best source(s) for information on the community that I have come across - details if not shown are in the relevant bibliography section.

When visiting any of the places listed please respect peoples privacy many are private homes.
Information on museums was accurate at time of going to press. Please ring for confirmation of opening times.

BERKSHIRE

BRADFIELD   1649 -1654 /1665-

FOUNDER/ LEADER : 'Father Abraham' John Pordage.

Pordage, radical rector of Bradfield, kept open house or 'family communion'. Other members included; Diggers' leader William Everard, Ranter Abeizer Coppe, vegetarian ascetic Roger Crab & Millenarian Tomas Tany. Pordage went on to set up the Phildelphians with Jane Leade.

GRID REF: SU 605724

REF *Heavens Below p32/ World Turned Upside Down*

BUCKING HAMSHIRE

IVER DIGGERS COLONY

C1649-50?

Issued their own pamphlet, may have been behind the *Light Shining in Buckinghamshire* pamphlets. (See St George's Hill, Surrey for more details)

GRIDREF: Location Unknown

REF : *World Turned Upside Down*

OWENITE COMMUNITY.   1832

A four hundred acre estate inspected by the first Co-operative Congress as a possible site for a community.

GRID REF: Location Unknown Aylesbury

REF : *The History of Co-operation.*

CHOLESBURY   Late 1840s

Possible allotment scheme mentioned in parliamentary enquiry into Chartist Land schemes.

GRID REF: SP 933070

REF : *The Chartist land Company P58*

JORDANS   1919 -

Garden village development built by Quaker Trust. Brick cottages with Tudor detailing set around green designed by Fred Rowntree.

GRID REF: SU 975915

REF *Villages of Vision*

PIGOTTS   1928-40

FOUNDER/ LEADER: Eric Gill

Loose artists colony and farmstead. Centred initially around Eric Gill's extended family. The colony survived after Gill's death in 1940.

GRID REF: SU857982

REF: *Eric Gill F.McCarthy/Utopian England*

KINGSTON COMMUNITY FARM

1939-45

3 acre smallholding set up by a group of pacifists from Kingston on Thames.

GRID REF:Rectory Farm.Charney Basset

REF: *Andrew Rigby/D&D*

CAMBRIDGESHIRE

THORNEY COLONY   1630-1727

Colony of Walloon / Hugenot Protestant refugees set up to drain the fens.

GRID REF: TF282042

REF: *The River Makers. T. Bevis*

NEWMARKET DIGGERS COLONY   C1650

Site of planned Diggers Colony.(See St George's Hill Surrey for details.)

REF: *World Turned Upside Down*

The United Advancement Societies   C1830s

Allotment societies set up with the support of James Hill. The societies supported the Manea Fen community,
GRID REF: Location unknown
REF : *Heavens Below*

Wretton   1837

FOUNDER/ LEADER: James Hill
Estate was chosen by the National Community Friendly Society for its first Owenite community. They abandoned the scheme due to Hill's insistence on directing the project himself.
GRID REF: TL 690998
REF: *Heavens Below p142*

Manea Fen   1838-41

FOUNDER/LEADER: William Hodson
'Unofficial' Owenite community on 200 acre fenland estate. Built cottages, school, pavilion and their own windmill. Was the most radical and notorious of the Owenite communities in the UK. Issued its own paper *The Working Bee* and had a 'uniform' of Lincoln green suits which gave the men the appearance of being part of Robin Hood's merry men. Failed to find markets for its goods and collapsed after Hodson lost money following the failure of a local bank. 'Colony Farm' marks the site of the community and there is a scale model of the community at the Octavia Hill Birthplace Museum at Wisbech.
GRID REF: TL515920
REF: *Alt Com 19th Cent Eng/Eve & the New Jerusalem /Heavens Below*

Thorney Model Village
1856/7

FOUNDER/LEADER: Duke of Bedford
Model Village built for the Duke of Bedford by Samuel Sanders Tuelon who was a descendent of one of the original Huguenot colonists.
GRID REF: TF 282042
REF: *Personal visit.*

THORNEY HERITAGE MUSEUM

The Tankyard
Station Road
Thorney
Peterborough
website: www.thorney-museum.org
Open Easter to the end of Sept,
2-5pm, Saturdays and Sundays,
and by appointment

Tours of the village and talks may be arranged, with refreshments. Free entry to the museum on general opening days, or a small charge for special arrangements.
Please write to the above address with any queries.

Lambourne   1885 - 1901

FOUNDER/LEADER: A. Herbert
In *The Right and Wrong of Compulsion by the State* Herbert argued for the setting up of voluntary land companies. He proceeded to set up a number of experiments buying estates and selling them as smallholdings. Others at Foxham (Wilts), Hay Farm(Essex) and Cottenham (Camb).
GRID REF: TL 450674
REF: *Heavens Below p285*

Cottenham   1885 - 1901

FOUNDER/LEADER: A. Herbert
Part of a multi-site smallholding scheme. Other schemes at Foxham(Wilts),Hay Farm(Essex) and for details see Lambourne(Camb).
GRID REF: TL 452678
REF: *Heavens Below p285*

Fen Drayton   1935 - 82?

Land Settlement Association smallholding scheme. (See Chawston Beds.)
GRID REF: TL 339682
REF: *Colin Ward D&D 94/95*

CHANNEL ISLANDS

Caxton's Communitorium

Community proposed by Goodwyn Barmby in The Communist Chronicle.
REF: *Alt Com 19th Cent Eng p35*

Sark Artists Colony   C1933

FOUNDER/ LEADER: E.S Drake
Small colony of artists lived in holiday huts around a purpose-built modernist gallery of pink & blue concrete. Mervyn Peake became the most famous of 'the Sark Group.'
REF: *Mervyn Peake. Biography.*

241

CHESHIRE

BOLLINGTON   1832- 46

FOUNDER/LEADER:Samuel Greg Jnr
Model village around mill - cottages with gardens, educational & recreational facilities provided to "elevate the position of the working class." Owner Samuel Greg's faith in the scheme was shaken when his supposedly contented workers went on strike causing him a nervous breakdown and the scheme to collapse.
GRID REF: SJ941778
REF: Industrial Colonies & Communities. ed.S.Jackson.Fingerpoint 1988.

BROMBOROUGH POOL   1853-8

FOUNDER/LEADE:Wilson Brothers
Factory Village created by the enlightened owners of Price's candle factory. Cottages with large gardens & indoor toilets, along with a social club and playing fields. The Wilsons also set up a branch of the Belmont Mutual Improvement Society 'for their workers instruction and intellectual recreation' and to promote "intellectual, moral and social advancement".
GRID REF: SJ356828
REF: Villages of Vision

PORT SUNLIGHT   1888 - present

FOUNDER/ LEADER : W.H. Lever
Influential model village named after the soap whose fortunes it was based on. Built round the Lever Bros. factory that was moved from Bolton to a marshy site on the south side of the Mersey in 1888. The first phase of the scheme was completeted by 1897. A second phase of building was carried out in 1911after further drainage works had been carried out. 30 different architects created a variety of picturesque & romantic stlye houses. Also a grand boulevard and art gallery along with schools, hospital, gym, social clubs, church and theatre. The village

like its contemporary at Bournville was a model for the Garden City & Suburbs movement with W.H.Lever (later Lord Leverhulme.) being a key member of the Garden Cities Association. Also developed model housing on company estates in the Congo and attempted to revive the fishing industry on the Scottish island of Lewis & Harris. Port Sunlight is now a conservation area.
GRID REF: SJ 335340
REF: Villages of Vision / A Guide to Port Sunlight Village.

'REILLY GREENS'   1946

The Reilly Plan was an alternative report on post war reconstruction based on Sir Charles Reilly's post-war plan for Birkenhead. Reilly had been Professor of Architecture at the University of Liverpool (a post created by Lord Leverhulme of Port Sunlight fame.) The plan included Reilly Greens, small village greens which most houses adjoined. With groups of 3 to 5 greens around a community centre containing a restaurant, bar, sports and hobbies areas, library and hall. Family houses around the greens would not have kitchens, as the community centre's restaurant was to provide a low cost catering service to be managed by residents. Houses would be provided with small electric cookers for emergencies. This would leave women free to undertake paid work. Only Bilston and Dudley councils showed any interest in implementing the plan. Dudley beginning an estate on modified 'Reilly Green' lines in 1950.
GRID REF: 'Birkenhead'
REF: The Architectural & Social History of Co-operative Living. L.F.Pearson

CORNWALL

NEWLYN ARTISTS COLONY
1883-C1914

Artists settled in Newlyn after a series of summer painting seasons. Some had been at the French artists colonies. Lived in lodgings and used fishermen's huts as studios. An art school and gallery were set up. The artists ran an Amateur Dramatic Society and played an annual cricket match with the colony at St Ives.
GRID REF: SW463285
REF: Stanhope Forbes & the Newlyn School / The Good & Simple Life.

LAMORNA ARTISTS COLONY
C1890

Satellite of the Newlyn Artists Colony set up in a number of cottages in a small wooded valley by S.J. 'Lamorna' Birch and others of the 2nd generation of Newlyn artists.

GRID REF: SW449246

REF: Stanhope Forbes & the Newlyn School.

ST IVES ARTISTS COLONY 1885 -

The best known of the English artists colonies. Originally known for its mainly foreign landscape painters. Was always more cosmopolitan than its sister colony at Newlyn. Enjoyed a renaissance when discovered by a new generation of modern artists in WW2, becoming home to Barbara Hepworth & Ben Nicholson. Still a magnet for the art world with the recent opening of the new Tate Gallery there.

GRID REF: SW515404

REF: Stanhope Forbes & the Newlyn School / The Good & Simple Life.

TREGERTHEN   C1916

Cottages rented by D.H. Lawrence, his wife Frieda, John Middlton-Murry & Katherine Mansfield. Here they planned their utopia 'Ranamin' whilst being watched by detectives who thought they were German spies.

GRID REF: SW454385 Nr Zennor.

REF: Heavens Below

PACIFIST COMMUNITY   C1939

Community of pacifists that grew from a single smallholding to a number of households farming 42 acres.

GRID REF: Nr Penzance.

REF: Utopian England.

CUMBRIA

NENTHEAD   1692 - 1905

Entire village built 1400ft up on the Pennines to provide accommodation and facilities for miners by the Quaker owned London Lead Mining Company. The company also provided small holdings and carried out experiments in upland farming. Other developments carried out in surrounding villages and at Middleton-in-Teesdale.

GRID REF: NY 782436

REF: Two Centuries of Industrial Welfare. (TCIW) A.Rastrick.

GARRIGILL   1798 - 1905

In 1798 London Lead Mining Company purchased the cornmill, 140 acres of ground, two houses, and sundry cottages were built.

Experiments were made with small-holding, small cottages being built with up to six acres of enclosed land attached, with additional rights on a fifty-acre pasture. Money and a site were provided for a girls' school, a parsonage, a Wesleyan Chapel and a Primitive Methodist Chapel. A library was built and the salary provided for a curate. Drainage and adequate water supply were provided to the village, and all old property was either pulled down and replaced, or renovated.

GRID REF: NY 746415

REF: (TCIW) A.Rastrick.

KESWICK RESIDENTIAL PARADISE   C1819

Proposal put forward by writer of Lakeland Guidebooks William Green for an "ideal residential paradise stretching from Castlehead to the shores of Derwentwater. To have

NENTHEAD MINES

Heritage Centre based at the centre of the Quaker London Lead Mining Company's operations on Alston Moor. As well as exhibitions and displays they also look after a 200 acre site full of mining remains which are undergoing excavation and restoration. As part of the experience they have re-opened an authentic lead mine for visitors. Also tea room and gift shop.

Nenthead Mine Heritage Centre, Nenthead, Alston, Cumbria. CA9 3PD
Tel: 01434 382037. Web site : **www.npht.com**

2001 Opening: every day from 7th April to 31st October, 10.30am to 4.30pm,
Adults £4.95, Child £2.95, Over 60 £3.95, Family (2Adults+2 Children) £12.95
For those not wishing to go underground:
Adult £2.95, Child £1.50, Over 60 £2.50, Family £7.50
Group discounts available.

consisted of 300 houses, church, tavern, concert hall assembly rooms surrounded by trees, parkland and "cascades". The whole scheme was to be patrolled by its own wardens.

REF: *Keswick : The Story of a Lake District Town. G.Bott. 1994*

DUFTON   1825 - 1905

Land purchased by the London Lead Mining Company. An agent's house and smelters' houses were built. Old cottages pulled down and new ones built with running water and gardens. Contributions were made by the company to local schools & churches.

GRID REF: NY 691250
REF: *(TCIW) A.Rastrick.*

HILTON   1825 - 1905

Hamlet where London Lead Mining Company built cottages with running

water and gardens and made contributions to local schools & churches.

GRID REF: NY 733206
REF: *(TCIW) A.Rastrick.*

CONISTON   1872 -

After 'retiring' to nearby Brantwood John Ruskin involved himself in the life of the local village. He established The Coniston Working Men's Institute and Literary Society, The Coniston School of Wood Carving and inspired the setting up of the Langdale Linen Industry

GRID REF: NY////////
REF: *Ruskin Museum Coniston.*

STARNTHWAITE HOME COLONY
1892-1901

FOUNDER/LEADER: Herbert V. Mills. Community based on Starnthwaite mill and the neighbouring 127 acre Browhead Farm. Mills made extravagant claims for his 'co-operative' village, but came into conflict with socialist members early on who disputed his autocratic leadership. Had a good reputation in land reform circles and was known for the quality of its fruit. Quaker craftsman A.W. Simpson from Kendal was involved with the colony after Mills left when it was used for training men sent from workhouses and as a home for epileptic boys.

GRID REF: SD 435922
REF: *Alt Com 19th Cent Eng*

DERWENTWATER TENANTS
CO-PARTNERSHIP   1910

Twenty-five houses built as a Garden Village known as Greta Hamlet. Tenants were encouraged to take shares & take part in the management

of the estate. Largely the idea of local Quaker A.B. Wilson.

GRID REF: NY 265237 Keswick
REF: *Villages of Vision/And Sometime Upon the Hills/Keswick . G.Bott. 1994*

MARYPORT EDUCATIONAL
SETTLEMENT.   C1930s

Set up by the Cumberland Friends' Quarterly Meeting to provide cultural and educational services to the unemployed - continues as an adult education centre.

GRID REF: (High St above museum)
REF: *And Sometime Upon the Hills*

Brantwood

Brantwood is the most beautifully situated house in the Lake District. It enjoys the finest lake and mountain views in England and there is no other house in the district with such a diversity of cultural associations. The home of John Ruskin from 1872 until his death in 1900, Brantwood became an intellectual powerhouse and one of the greatest literary and artistic centres in Europe. Tolstoy, Mahatma Gandhi, Marcel Proust & Frank Lloyd Wright can all be numbered amongst Ruskin's disciples.

Open all year
March - Novemher 11.00am - 5.30pm
Winter Season
Wednesday - Sunday 11.00am - 4.30pm
Open every day during school holidays.
Closed Christmas Day and Boxing Day

Coniston Cumbria LA21 8AD
Telephone: 015394 41396
website: **www.ruskin.org.uk**

DALSTON   1935 - 82?
Land Settlement Association small-holding scheme. (See Chawston Beds.)
GRID REF: NY 360500
REF: *Colin Ward D&D 94/95*

BROADWATH   1935 - 82?
Land Settlement Association small-holding scheme. (See Chawston Beds.)
GRID REF: NY479548
REF: *Colin Ward D&D 94/95*

CROFTON   1935 - 82?
Land Settlement Association small-holding scheme. (See Chawston Beds.)
GRID REF: NY301499
REF: *Colin Ward D&D 94/95*

DERBYSHIRE

OCKBROOK   1751/2 -
Moravian settlement consisting of 'Choir' houses, workshops, school and farm, chapel & burial ground set around an open green. Due to its central location was for a while the national co-ordinating point for the Moravian Church.
GRID REF: SK 426365
REF: *Villages of Vision*

TOTLEY COLONY   1876 - 188?
FOUNDER/LEADER: John Ruskin
13-acre farm purchased by Ruskin's St George's Guild for a group of Sheffield workmen. Run initially as an allotment scheme, then as a land colony with around 12 members. There were numerous arguments and disagreement that finally sank the scheme. Still known as St George's Farm. Referred to variously, even by Ruskin himself, as Abbeyfield Allotments, Mickley Botanical Gardens & Totley Colony.
GRID REF: SK303801
REF: *Alt Com 19th Cent Eng / Heavens Below/Designing Utopia.*

MILLTHORPE   1883-?
FOUNDER/LEADER: E.Carpenter
7acre smallholding where socialist philosopher Edward Carpenter and his gay partner George Merrill kept open house whilst living the 'simple life'.
GRID REF: Location unknown
REF: *My days and dreams. E.Carpenter.*

RADBOURNE CO-OPERATIVE FARM   C1894
Experiment in co-operative agriculture carried out by Bolton King, secretary to the Mansion House Ctte.
GRID REF: SK284360 Radbourne
REF: *Heavens Below p325*

NORTON COLONY   1896 - 1900
Simple life anarchist land colony inspired by Edward Carpenter. Ran a small market garden in the grounds of Norton Hall.
GRID REF: Location Unkown
REF: *Alt Com 19th Cent Eng*

THE SETTLEMENT   C1905
Women's University Settlement.
GRID REF: Church Lane Chesterfield
REF: *Listed in Labour Annual 1905*

OXCROFT   1935 - 82?
Land Settlement Association small-holding scheme. (See Chawston Beds.)
GRID REF: SK482734?(Nr Bolsover?)
REF: *Colin Ward D&D 94/95*

DEVON

DEVON & EXETER CO-OP SOC.
1826
37 acre estate taken on by members of the Devon & Exeter Co-op Soc. They had originally proposed an ambitious Owenite community of 2000 people. 12 cottages were built but the scheme collapsed after its backer Jasper Veysey withdrew his support for domestic reasons. Some of the "communitarians" moved on to form the Dowlands Devon Community.
GRID REF: SY024948 Rockbeare.
REF: Alt Com 19th Cent Eng

DOWLANDS COMMUNITY 1827
Community set up after the collapse of the Devon & Exeter Co-op Soc. community. They grew crops through the summer of 1827 and had plans to set up their own school. Lack of capital and new members caused the community to fold by the end of the year.
GRID REF: Location Unknown
REF: Alt Com 19th Cent Eng

BUCKFAST ABBEY 1882-present
New monastic order originally set up by French monks fleeing persecution. The self-sufficient community rebuilt the original Abbey church and produced their own successful tonic wine.
GRID REF: SX ???????
REF: Utopian England.

DARTINGTON HALL 1925 - present
FOUNDER/ LEADER: Leonard & Dorothy Elmhirst

Successful experiment in rural regeneration financed by New York heiress's fortune. Inc: 800 acres of farms & forestry, experimental school, art college & open-air theatre, cider press, glassworks and various research projects. Became a series of trusts in 1931 and managed to maintain its radical edge beyond the death of its founders.
GRID REF: SX 800626
REF: The Elmhirsts of Dartington.

SOUTH WEST CO-OPERATIVE HOUSING SOCIETY 1944 -
Pioneer housing association set up by L.Elmhirst of Dartington Hall, A.E. Malbon of Staverton Builders and Dr A. Mansbridge a leading figure in the WEA and Co-operative Movement. Carried out developments at Yate, Totnes & Bridgewater.
REF: Brick Upon Brick. Eric Stafford 1994

PACIFIST COMMUNITY 1939-45
FOUNDER/LEADER : R.Duncan
Pacifist land colony
GRID REF: North Devon?
REF: All Men are Islands .R.Duncan.

WITHYMEAD 1941 - 54
FOUNDER/LEADER : Irene Champernowne.
'The Jungian Community for the Healing Arts', a pioneer therapeutic community, treated 240 adults between 1942 and 1954 in a residential setting supported by the Elmhurst's of Dartington Hall.
GRID REF: Exeter
REF: website.

HIGH CROSS HOUSE
A superb example of the International Modernist style designed in 1932, by the Swiss American architect William Lescaze, High Cross House stands within the grounds of Dartington Hall, an 800 acre mediaeval estate. Its bright blue and white exterior contrasts sharply with the ancient buildings of the crown of the estate. High Cross has been renovated and specially adapted by the Dartington Hall Trust as an exhibition and study centre. The house is listed Grade II.

Opening Hours: 14.00 - 16.30
1 May - 26 Oct. Tues to Friday
Admission £2.50 (Con.£1.50)
High Cross House. Dartington Hall.
Totnes. Devon. TQ9 6ED
Tel: 01803 864114

DORSET

TALBOT VILLAGE 1850 -
FOUNDER/LEADER: Georgina & Mary Talbot
22 houses, 17 cottages with an acre of land attached, 5 farms, church, school and almshouses set up by two wealthy

sisters following a unemployment relief scheme. 150 acres of heath was left uncultivated. Inspired in part by the writings of Robert Owen it was described by the sisters as an institute for the industrious working man. No lodgers were allowed and no business was to be carried out except smallholding. A trust was set up to administer the estate which still exists.

GRID REF: SZ 066945 Bournemouth
REF: Villages of Vision/ The History of Talbot Village. M.Talbot. 1873.

COOPER'S FARM   1892

FOUNDER/ LEADER : Major Poore 195-acre farm sold in lots of varying sizes either for cash or by instalments. From the 49 smallholdings a landholders' court (registered as a limited company) was set up to collect rents. The court had £1,500 at its disposal to advance as working capital. Some of the small plots were used as building sites, and 33 of the holders built houses. A Rechabite Hall and a Mission Hall were built on land belonging to the land court.

GRID REF: Winterslow.Nr Salisbury
REF: Heavens Below P324

ALDERNEY MANOR   1911-1927

FOUNDER/ LEADER : Augustus John Strange large house with the appearance of a 'fortified bungalow' set in 60acres of woodland outside Bournemouth. Artist Augustus John set up house here with his entourage of women, children, fellow artists and hangers-on. The house was demol-

ished shortly after John left.

GRID REF: SZ046942
REF: Augustus John. M.Holroyd 1996

LITTLE COMMONWEALTH
1913-18

FOUNDER/ LEADER : Homer Lane Experimental therapeutic/educational community based at Flowers Farm on the Earl of Sandwich's estate. In 'family' groups in farm cottages the community offered delinquent teenage girls & boys a stable home environment. A Montessori school catered for young children. The scheme closed after allegations of sexual abuse were made against Lane.

GRID REF: ST580042 Nr Evershot
REF: Homer Lane. D.Wills.

ANGLICAN COMMUNITY
OF ST FRANCIS   1921 -

FOUNDER/ LEADER : Brother Giles / Brother Douglas
Anglican community set up to provide shelter for unemployed & homeless 'wayfarers'. Based on vows of poverty, chastity & obedience. In the 30's depression they set up other centres. In 1931 attracted by the simple life, single people and married couples set up a third order to support the Brothers' work. They established schools for maladjusted children, missions for lepers and Friaries scattered over the country. During WW2 took Jewish refugees & evacuated children.

GRID REF: ST665011 Cerne Abbas
REF: Stone upon Stone. M.Osborn.

FRYERN COURT   1927 - 1969

FOUNDER/ LEADER : Augustus John

Second 'communal' household of the John clan. More open house than commune. John and his partner Dorelia lived here until their deaths. A statue to John is in a corner of the village.

GRID REF: SU153140
REF: Augustus John. M.Holroyd 1996

SPRINGHEAD   1933 -

FOUNDER/ LEADER : Rolf Gardiner Base of the Springhead Ring founded to promote the revival of rural life. Pioneered work in organic farming and reforestation alongside reviving countryside festivals and traditional song and dance. Became target of rumour of Nazi sympathys during WW2. Is now run by the Springhead Trust as a conference centre.

GRID REF: Gore Farm Melbury Abbas
REF: The Village that Died for England.

DURHAM

NEW MIDDLETON   1815 - 1905

The second largest estate of the London Lead Company, purchased and built in 1815, on similar lines to Nent Head. During the first fifty years over 100 cottages were built and many houses and farms rebuilt. Like Nent Head, offices, school, chapels, baths, a clock tower, etc., in fact all the social amenities that the old village did not possess were provided. After 1880 Middleton became the head office of the Company and the residence of the agent and general manager.

GRID REF: NY952251

REF: *Two Centuries of Industrial Welfare.*

Stockton Provident Soc.

1865 -

In 1904 the Stockton on Tees Co-operative Society expanded its operations into house building for its members Land was purchased for the erection of 200 or more houses.

GRID REF: Location Unknown

REF: *The History of Co-operation.*

Heartbreak hill   C1930s

Land colonisation scheme set up for Cleveland ironstone workers by Rolf Gardiner.

GRID REF: Location Unknown

REF: *Journal of the Oral History Soc.*

ESSEX

Greensted   1838 - 1845

Two farms leased by the Dorchester Labourers Farm Tribute for the Tollpuddle Matyrs on their return from transportation. George Loveless, James Brine and the Standfield family farmed New House Farm and a farm at High Laver until they emigrated to Canada. The farms became centres for union and chartist activity in the area.

GRID REF: TL 526031

REF: *The Book of the Tollpuddle Martyrs 1834-1934 TUC*

Barkingside   1873

Dr Barnardo's 'Village Home'. Cottages and chapel opened in 1873. Hospital added later.

GRID REF: TQ445898

REF: *Villages of Vision*

Hay Farm   1885-1901

FOUNDER/LEADER: A. Herbert

Part of a multi-site smallholding scheme. Other schemes at Foxham (Wilts), Cottenham(Camb)and for details see Lambourne(Camb).

GRID REF: Location Unknown

REF: *Heavens Below p285*

Hadleigh Farm Colony

1891- Present.

FOUNDER/LEADER: William Booth

Highly successful scheme for training the poor and destitute and resettling them on the land run by the Salvation Army. Consisted of 3,200 acres with arable, dairy and chicken farms, market gardens, workshops, brickworks, pottery and its own wharf. Resettled over 7'000 colonists up to WW1 when it went into decline, any social aspects ending in the 1960s. The farm is now run on a commercial basis and the rest of the colony either built on, or part of Hadleigh Country Park.

GRID REF: TQ 802862

REF: *The Poor & the Land. Ryder Haggard. 1905./ Hadliegh Past.*

Co-operative Land Soc. 1892

Organisation set up to promote common ownership home colonies with the involvement of Ebeneezer Howard. Looked at land in Essex but nothing came of it.

REF: *Utopian England*

Looking Backward   1893

Site chosen for a co-operative colony to be set up on the basis outlined in Edward Bellamy's *Looking Backward*. Never carried out.

GRID REF: Hockley Nr Southend

REF: *The Architectural & Social History of Co-operative Living. L.F.Pearson*

Mayland Colony   1896

FOUNDER/LEADER: Thomas Smith

Inspired by articles in *The Clarion* Thomas Smith bought an 11 acre plot for his family and advertised for "socialist settlers" to come and join him. Impressed by Smith's efforts the soap manufacturer Joseph Fels purchased the neighbouring 600acre Nipsells farm and made it available as smallholdings.

GRID REF: TQ910990 Althorne

REF: *Alt Com 19th Cent Eng*

Purleigh Colony   1896 - 99

Tolstoyan Anarchist colony that grew out of the Croydon Brotherhood Church. Some members had lived in, or visited Russia and were personally acquainted with Tolstoy. Initially based on a 10-acre plot, as the group grew the colony rented local cottages with land attached. They worked the poor land using intensive methods which impressed visitors;

"Various buildings have been put up - a tool shed, a 100-foot green house (thirty feet fitted with heating apparatus), a workshop with carpenter's bench, a stable to accommodate a horse and pony, some fowl houses, a cow shed large enough to hold six cows, a coal shed and a six-roomed

brick cottage. The cottage is occupied by the family and one of the single men, and most of the colonists come in to dinner every day." Hubert Hammond Colonist. The colony ran a printing press, publishing translations of Tolstoy and for a while *The New Order* magazine. For a time the colony sheltered some of the Russian Doukhobors, members of the sect forced to leave Russia to avoid political persecution. Some of the colonists went with the Doukhobors to Canada, and a small group went to form the colony at Whiteway after a disagreement with others over membership policy. This exodus seems to have resulted in the closure of the colony.
GRID REF: TL 812046 Cocks Clark.
REF: *Alt Com 19th Cent Eng*

LONGLEY 'TRAINING FARM' 1896
28 acre farm set up as training scheme for the unemployed by printer Walter Hazell. Moved to Chesham in Beccles.
GRID REF: Longley
REF: *Heavens Below p324*

ASHINGDON COLONY 1897
Small Tolstoyan Anarchist smallholdings colony started by James Evans.
GRID REF: The Chase, Ashingdon.
REF: *Alt Com 19th Cent Eng*

WICKFORD COLONY 1898
29 acres divided into plots of 1 to 3 acres by a group of 'socialists' inspired by the writings of Tolstoy. The group had links with the Croydon brotherhood and the colony at Purliegh. Known as the 'Colony for City Men'

because of good rail access to London where colonists continued to work.
GRID REF: TQ729958 Downham
REF: *Alt Com 19th Cent Eng*

LAINDON FARM COLONY 1904-11
FOUNDER/ LEADER : Joseph Fels / George Lansbury
The Poplar Guardians were given 3 years free use of the 100acre Sumpners Farm by soap magnate Joseph Fels. A hundred men from the Poplar workhouse, many of them young ex-soldiers, were housed in corrugated iron huts and set to digging reservoirs and building chicken huts. The plan to turn the site into co-operative smallholdings was not carried out by the Local Government Board.
GRID REF: TQ681881 Laindon
REF: *Heavens Below / Utopian England*

BOXTED 1906 - 1916
Large estate divided into eighty plots, of up to six acres as a Salvation Army Land Colony. A scheme for co-operative distribution of produce was organised through a central grading store. The scheme appeared to be so successful that the Army decided to form a company called 'Land for the People Ltd.' However the smallholders were unhappy with the administration and it was wound up in 1916 with many holdings bought by the County Council to resettle ex-servicemen.
GRID REF: TL 995319 Nr Colchester
REF: *A Short History of Boxted.*

SILVER END 1926
FOUNDER/ LEADER : F.H.Critall
During expansion in the 1920s Crittalls

carpet manufacturers commissioned a scheme for a brand-new company village. The employees administered the village themselves through a company set up specially for the purpose. In the early stages the village consisted mostly of flat-roofed International Modern housing. Other housing was plain neo-Georgian. There was also a village hall, hotel, bank, telephone exchange, surgery, dental clinic, shopping arcade, school & playing fields and a public garden. Farms were established which sold produce direct to the villagers.
GRID REF: TL 808196
REF: *Villages of Vision*

BATA INTERNATIONAL C1930s
The company, founded by Thomas Bata in 1900 in Czechoslovakia with ten employees, by 1938 claimed to have a workforce of 27,000 through out the world - with model settlements including 7 towns in Czechoslovakia and others in Europe, Canada and India. East Tilbury followed the pattern of the other settlements with the separation of the factory and housing by a green belt and the use of advanced building techniques for its cottages in the International Modern style.
GRID REF: TQ 679705 East Tilbury
REF: *Villages of Vision*

ADELPHI CENTRE 1934-37
FOUNDER/ LEADER : John M.Murry
Socialist comunitarian 'training centre' set up by John Middleton-Murry at 'The Oaks'. A market garden was set up in the old kitchen garden & paddocks. The house was used during

WW2 for East End evacuees.
GRID REF: TM 029316 Langham
REF: Utopian England

FOXASH 1935 - 82
Land Settlement Association small-holding scheme. (See Chawston Beds.)
GRID REF: TM068298
REF: Colin Ward D&D 94/95

YELDHAM 1935 - 82?
Land Settlement Association small-holding scheme. (See Chawston Beds.)
GRID REF: Location Unknown
REF : Colin Ward D&D 94/95

LANGENHOE ? -1935
FOUNDER/LEADER: John Hawkswell
A group of 30 or so worked a 1500 acre estate bought by a Mrs Judges. Part of the Catholic Land Movement.
GRID REF: TM009185
REF: Heavens Below

HAWKSPUR EXPERIMENT
1936-40
Hawkspur Camp was sponsored by the Q-Camp Committee,(Q for quest) set up in 1935 with the aim of creating a series of therapeutic camps or communities for young men. Hawkspur was the first of these. Camp Chief was David Wills a Quaker who had worked before in the South Wales Settlement Houses. At Hawkspur disturbed and delinquent young men lived communally in tents and buildings that they constructed themselves. It was one of the earliest intentional therapeutic communities in Britain exploring what became known as Planned Environment Therapy. The camp ended

at the outbreak of war.
GRID REF: TL677305 Hill Hall Common, Great Bardfield,
REF: The Hawkspur Experiment. D.Wills.

SOUTHEND COMMUNITY 1939
Wartime community listed in the journal *Community Life* issued by the British Llano Circle.
GRID REF: 34 Retreat Rd.Westcliffe-on-sea / Oakwood Brook Hill.Wickford.
REF: Heavens Below p415

MOORE PLACE 1939-45
15 acre holding worked by 12 pacifists during WW2.
GRID REF: TQ685819 Stanford le Hope
REF: Andrew Rigby/D&D

GLOUCESTER SHIRE

DIGGERS COLONY 1649-50?
One of a series of 'other' Diggers colonies. (See St George's Hill, Surrey for more details)
GRID REF: Poss Slimbridge Waste.
REF: World Turned Upside down

FRIENDS WORKHOUSE 1696-1720
Quaker poor relief scheme that provided housing and work for unemployed Quakers.
GRID REF: Location Unknown Bristol
REF: Quakerism & Industry before 1800

WARMLEY 1760's
FOUNDER/LEADER: W.Champion
Cottages, shops & clock tower built by Quaker industrialist. Cottages built of basalt slag. (brass foundry waste). Also built housing at Bitton(Glos.) and Kelston(Somerset).
GRID REF: ST673729
REF: Quakers in Science and Industry

RANDWICK EXPERIMENT 1831-3
FOUNDER/ LEADER : Mary Ann Greaves & James Pierrepont Greaves
'Social service' scheme to relieve distressed weavers set up by the 'sacred socialist' & his sister. Food and clothes were given in exchange for 'community work' around the village. Tools were supplied and an overseer and record keeper appointed. Roads were improved by unskilled men, and women taught to make clothes. A local currency was introduced whereby tokens were issued for work and were exchangeable for food, clothes, tools, furniture & books.
GRID REF: SO809076
REF: Search for a New Eden.

LOWBANDS 1846 - 51
FOUNDER/LEADER: F. O'Connor
Second Chartist estate consisting of 23 smallholdings with model cottages laid out on a network of lanes around a schoolhouse and 10 acre common water meadow. 22 working horses and rows of fruit trees were provided along with firewood, manure and seeds. Each cottage had its own water supply and privy.
GRID REF: SO 775314
REF: The Chartist Land Company

SNIGS END 1847 - 51
FOUNDER/LEADER: F. O'Connor
81 plot Chartist estate laid out on 268 acres around the village of Staunton with model cottages, schoolhouse, roads and pathways. As on other estates settlers who had won their plots were provided with supplies of manure, firewood and seed. The third National Chartist petition was taken to parliament in 1848 on a cart made at Snigs End & pulled by estate horses.
GRID REF: SO 792288 Staunton
REF: *The Chartist Land Company*

KELMSCOTT MANOR 1871- 1896
FOUNDER/LEADER : William Morris
Part-time home of William Morris, inspiration for a whole movement in architexcture and final destination of the utopian traveller in *News from Nowhere*. Morris is buried with his wife & daughters in the graveyard of the small chapel in Kelmscott village.
GRID REF: SU253987
REF: *William Morris. Fiona McCarthy*

BLOCKLEY C1878
FOUNDER/LEADER : William Morris
Half-deserted Cotswold village with abandoned silk mill, that William Morris surveyed for an Arts & Crafts based community. Morris regretted being persuaded not to move there by his business partners, setting up at Merton Abbey instead. (Rock Cottage, Blockley was the last home of the Prophetess Joanna Southcott.)
GRID REF: SP165349
REF: *Designing Utopia. M.H.Lang.*

CHIPPING CAMDEN 1902-1909
FOUNDER/ LEADER : C.R. Ashbee
Sleepy Cotswold town that became the home for the Guild of Handicrafts. Some 150 East End craftsmen moved into the town setting up workshops in the old silkmill just off the centre of town and renting accomodation throughout the town. The Guild had a major impact on the town both economically and socially, setting up a band, sports club, drama society and allotment association and building a swimming pool. Cheap mass produced imitations of their work led to the end of the Guild.
GRID REF: SP151388
REF: *The Simple Life. Fiona McCarthy*

BROAD CAMPDEN 1908-1914
70 acres bought by soap magnate Joseph Fels as smallholdings for the craftsmen of the Guild of Handicrafts after the Guild had ceased.
GRID REF: SP158378
REF: *The Simple Life. Fiona McCarthy*

WHITEWAY 1898 - Present
42acre holding taken by a breakaway from the Tolstoyan colony at Purleigh. Originally a communal group in Whiteway House surrounded by open fields the colony became a thriving anarchist community over the years developing into a patchwork of smallholdings with people living in a variety of homemade sheds, huts, houses and railway carriages etc. In 1924 a colony hall was erected to house social activities and a school house and in 1969 the colony swiming pool was opened. Still operating under their original constitution they are the longest surviving secular community in the country.
GRID REF: S0 919105
REF: *Whiteway Colony.Joy Thacker*

SAPPERTON WORKSHOPS 1901 -
FOUNDER/LEADER : Ernest Gimson / Sidney Barnsley.
Loose Arts & Crafts based community that grew up around workshops of Gimson & Barnsley. Rented Daneway house and built 3 houses.
GRID REF: SO946032
REF: *The Arts & Crafts Movement. E.Cumming & W.Kaplan*

SNOWSHIL MANOR C1920s?
FOUNDER/ LEADER : Charles Wade
Arts & Crafts 'Utopia' set up by Raymond Unwin's assistant.
GRID REF: Location Unknown
REF: *Hampstead Garden Suburb*

KELMSCOTT MANOR

Country home of William Morris - poet, craftsman and socialist. The house contains a collection of Morris' possessions and works. He is buried in the village nearby.
Open April - Sept. Weds and occasional Saturdays Contact for details:
Kelmscott Manor. Kelmscott
Nr Lechlade. Glous. GL7 3HJ
Tel: 01367 252486
Website: www.kelmscottmanor.co.uk

THE GUILD OF HANDICRAFT TRUST

Small museum set in the mill used by C.R. Ashbee's Guild of Handicrafts. Exhibits include work of the Guild and other local craft workers. Contact for opening times and admission charges.

The Silk Mill. Sheep St.
Chipping Campden. Glous. GL55 6DS
Tel: 01386 841417

NATIONAL HOMECROFT ASS.
1926-37
FOUNDER/LEADER: Prof. J.W.Scott
Public utility company inspired by working-class housing schemes in California. Built ten houses at Cheltenam with smallholdings attached. The families kept poultry &

pigs and grew potatoes and fruit. It was hoped to replace individual holding with group homecrofts. As the depression worsened the scheme was used to teach groups of unemployed to grow food. A market was set up where the members could buy and sell their produce using their own local currency. The scheme had close links with Cardiff university from where student came to help. By 1934 The Times reported, in a favourable article, that light handlooms were in use.
GRID REF: Cheltenam
REF: Self-subsistence for the Unemployed. Prof. J.W.Scott / Utopian England

PRINKNASH ABBEY   1928 -
The 20th Earl of Rothes gave Prinknash house and 28 acres to the Benedictine Monks from Caldey Island. The monks converted the building and acquired more land creating a self-contained community that was given abbey status in 1937. Further communities were founded in 1947 at Farnborough & Pluscarden(Scotland).
GRID REF: SO869141
REF: Utopian England

NEWENT   1935 - 82?
Land Settlement Association smallholding scheme. (See Chawston Beds.)
GRID REF: SO723258
REF : Colin Ward D&D 94/95

GLOUCESTER LAND SCHEME
1939-45
Land loaned by local Quaker for a pacifist land scheme. Half a dozen or so COs lived in an old sports pavilion whilst growing vegetables and dream-

ing of self-sufficiency.
GRID REF: SO811169 Nr Hempsted
REF: Andrew Rigby/D&D

RICHMOND COMMUNITY   C1940
Wartime pacifist land settlement community.
GRID REF: Nr Ross-on-Wye
REF : Utopian England

BROMSASH   C1941
Small community that took some Bruderhof members when others went to Paraguay.
GRID REF: SO650241 Ross on Wye
REF: Heavens Below

TAENA FARM   1942-51
FOUNDER/ LEADER : George Ineson
Small pacifist based community on 55 acre wooded farm on sloping rocky site. Intially highly organised with consensus decision making, communal meals and plans for home education. Later became more informal. When the lease ran out they moved to Whitley Court, nr Prinknash Abbey.
GRID REF: Forest of Dean
REF: Utopian England

HAMPSHIRE

HARMONY HALL   1839 - 45
FOUNDER/ LEADER : Robert Owen
The official Owenite community sponsored by the Universal Community Society of Rational Religionists. Concieved on a grand scale it consisted of a series of farms around an

impressive 3 storey communal house. The scheme was beset with problems almost from the start, the only sucesses being on the farming side. Much of the failure of the community must be blamed on Owen's mismanagement, despite attempts by others to save the project. The failure of Harmony Hall marked the end of Owenite socialism as a movement.

GRID REF: SU298304 East Tythersley
REF: Alt Com 19th Cent.Eng/Robert Owen & the Owenites in Britain & America. JFC Harrison.

LITTLE BENTLEY   1845-6
FOUNDER/ LEADER :
William Galpin / Isaac Ironside
Ex-General Secertary of the Owenite Rational Society William Galpin on the collapse of Harmony Hall set up a small community of 'sacred socialists' on an adjoining farm - where the mainly ex-Harmony Hall colonists lived a spartan vegetarian life.

GRID REF: SU298304
REF: Robert Owen & the Owenites in Britian & America. JFC Harrison.

NEW FOREST SHAKERS 1872 - 86
FOUNDER/LEADER: MaryAnnGirling
160 'Shakers' lived at New Forest Lodge. They were followers of Mrs Girling a female messiah. They were evicted from the Lodge in 1875 and moved to a farm at Tiptoe. New Forest Lodge is now a nursing home.

GRID REF: SZ274952 Vaggs Lane, Hordle
REF: Alt Com 19th Cent.Eng

'OLD HOUSE'   1907
House given to the theosophists by Nan Ino Herbert to turn into the British version of the Theosophists community at Point Loma California. The site however was deemed unsuitable.Herbert Auberon sheltered & supported the New Forest Shakers.

GRID REF: New Forest
REF: Heavens Below p285

SANDY BALLS   1919-34
FOUNDER/LEADER :Ernest Westlake Estate on the northern edge of the New Forest bought as a base for the Code of Woodcraft Chivalry. Westlake & his family drew up a plan for a forest park stocked with the surviving fauna of the Old Stone Age. Annual folkmoots were held here until 1934 and Westlake is buried there in a replica Bronze Age burial mound.

GRID REF: SU169151
REF: The Triumph of the Moon.

LITTLE PARK   1935 - 82?
Land Settlement Association smallholding scheme. (See Chawston Beds.)
GRID REF: SU365457 Abbotts Ann
REF : Colin Ward D&D 94/95

PEACE SERVICE COMMUNITY
C1940
Wartime pacifist land settlement.
GRID REF: SU646349 Ropley
REF : Utopian England

TRISTAN CLOSE   1961-2
Home of the Tristan Da Cunha Islanders during attempt to resettle them in this country following the volcanic eruption on the island.
GRID REF: SU 480012 Calshot

REF: Crisis in Utopia. P.Munch.

HEREFORDSHIRE

BRAMPTON BRYAN CO-OPERATIVE FARMING SOCIETY   C1870
FOUNDER/ LEADER : Walter Morris
Profit sharing co-operative farm.
GRID REF: SO372722
REF: The History of Co-operation.

HERTFORDSHIRE

BARNET DIGGERS COLONY
1649-50?
One of a series of 'other' Diggers colonies. (See St George's Hill, Surrey for more details)
GRID REF: Location Unknown
REF :World Turned Upside down

FRIENDS BOARDING SCHOOL
Quaker school that derived from a school at Islington Rd which was the descendant of the Clerkenwell workhouse set up from John Bellars' plans for a College of Industry of all Useful Trades and Husbandry.
GRID REF: TL538381 Saffron Walden
REF: The Second Period of Quakerism / Quakerism & Industry before 1800

O'CONNORVILLE (Heronsgate)
1846 - 58
FOUNDER/LEADER: F. O'Connor
103 acre estate divided into 35, two, three and four-acre plots. Model cot-

tages were built and each plot was laid out with roads and paths between. The first season's crops were planted and two year's supply of firewood and manure awaited the smallholders who had won a draw for places on the scheme. A schoolhouse was provided and a beerhouse built on adjacent land. - now the Land of Liberty, Peace & Plenty Public House.

GRID REF: TQ011936

REF: *The Chartist Land Company*

CARPENDER'S PARK 1846

130 acre estate bought for a Chartist Land Colony sold after a month.

GRID REF: TQ123920 Nr Pinner

REF : *The Chartist Land Company*

LETCHWORTH GARDEN CITY

1903 - present

Completely new city based on the ideas in Ebenezer Howard's book, *Tomorrow: a peaceful path to real reform*. Became the flagship of an international Garden Cities movement

GRID REF: TL220326

REF: **www.letchworthgardencity. net/heritage /index-3.htm**

NORTON CO-OPERATIVE SMALL-HOLDING SOCIETY. 1905

A 152-acre smallholding centre established at Norton Hall Farm The Society paid the Garden City Company 25s. an acre and sub-let smallholdings of up to 20 acres. 12 cottages were built, pigsties were constructed and 10 acres planted with fruit. It was planned to set up a local farm credit bank and co-operative

marketing scheme but the experiment was unsuccessful.

REF: *Letchworth: The First Garden City*

'Co-operative Dwellings' 1905

FOUNDER/LEADER: Walter Crane

Scheme put forward by Walter Crane, first president of the Arts & Crafts Exhibition Society, in the July 1905 issue of *The Garden City* magazine. It consisted of 16 cottages arranged around a courtyard with shared kitchen, dining/recreation room and meeting room accessed by means of a covered walkway. Plans were drawn up by Cranes' son, scheme never built.

REF: *The Architectural & Social History of Co-operative Living. L.F.Pearson*

The Cloisters 1906-

FOUNDER/LEADER: Miss Lawrence.

On an isolated three-acre plot Miss Lawrence built "The Cloisters", with a house for herself, `Cloisters Lodge' alongside. W.Harrison Cowlishaw was her architect. £20,000 was spent on the project intended as an open-air school. The design included an open colonnade to the south for open air sleeping. Two wings: one for kitchen and store rooms, the other with cubicles and dressing rooms leading to an oval open-air swimming bath. A small community developed dedicated to Theosophy. It became the base for the Alpha Union set up by J.Bruce Wallace of the Brotherhood Church, who organised summer schools and residential courses. After WW2 it became the local Masonic Lodge.

REF: *Letchworth: The First Garden City / Utopian England / Heavens Below.*

Garden City Tenants Ltd 1907-9

Tenant Co-Partnership that built the pioneering Pixmore estate of 164 houses with recreational facilities and institute designed by Raymond Unwin.

REF: *Letchworth: The First Garden City*

Howard Cottage Soc. 1909

Developed over 300 'cottages' between 1911 and 1914. Became international renowned for thier design of decent affordable housing. George Bernard Shaw was a shareholder, Ebenezer Howard a director and Fredrick Osbourn secretary.

REF: *Letchworth: The First Garden City*

Homesgarth 1911-

FOUNDER/LEADER: E.Howard

32 flats set out around a quadrangle on a 4 acre site as a co-operative housekeeping scheme. All flats were serviced with meals from a central kitchen, taken either in your flat or in a communal dining room. Ebenezer Howard was a prime mover in the scheme and lived here till moving to Welwyn. Designed by H.C.Lander the scheme aimed to provide co-operative living for professional people.

REF: *Letchworth: The First Garden City*

Meadow Way Green 1914 - 1960s

FOUNDER/LEADER: Ruth Pym and Miss S. Dewe.

Co-operative housekeeping scheme.

GRID REF: Meadow Way Green

REF: *The Architectural & Social History of Co-operative Living. L.F.Pearson*

The Pearsall Group C1920

FOUNDER/LEADER: Ellen Pearsall.

Proposed group of co-operative houses for clerical, managerial and professional workers, put forward by Ellen

Pearsall. The plan was for 20 four-bedroom houses, with no kitchens, arranged as a half quadrangle facing a large central block containing the central kitchen and staff accommodation. Two meals a day were to be delivered to each house, and all washing up would be done centrally. The plan included gas fires, central heating, electric lighting and a children's playground. Never built.

REF: *The Architectural & Social History of Co-operative Living. L.F.Pearson*

Welwyn Garden City

1919 - Present

Second garden city on a modest scale conpared to Letchworth and with modest aspirations to utopian ideals. Was the forerunner of the series of satelite new towns built after WW2.

GRID REF: TL238124

REF: *A History of Welwyn Garden City. Roger Filler. Phillimore &Co*

New Town

Quaker sponsored proposal for a co-operative new town on garden city lines. The group teamed up with the Welwyn development company and ran a 500-acre co-operative agricultural guild and promoted co-operation in the garden city. Members were involved in setting up Guessens Court.

REF : *Utopian England.*

Dailymail   1922

Model village built as part of the Daily Mail Ideal Home Exhibition at Welwyn. 41 houses were built using in all 16 different 'modern' construction methods. On one side of the village was a fruit tree belt. After the exhibition the houses were sold off, one of them being occupied by the Canossian Daughters of Charity, who held meetings in the living room and consecrated one of the bedrooms as a chapel. The same house was later the international headquarters of the Youth Hostel Association.

REF: *The Ideal Home. D.S.Ryan*

Guessens Court   1925

Co-operative Housekeeping scheme of 40 flats on 3 sides of a quadrangle. On the 4th side a 3 storey block of communal facilities inc: restaurant, kitchen & guest rooms. Designed by H.C. Lander. Later the communal block was converted into a hotel with the flat currently used as sheltered accomodation for the elderly.

REF: *The Architectural & Social History of Co-operative Living. L.F.Pearson*

SPIELPLATZ   1929 -

FOUNDER/LEADER: C. Macaskie

Residential nudist camp. Up to 35 families rented plots in an area of woodland. Grew out of the Gymnosphy Society.

GRID REF: TL131012 Bricket Wood

REF: *As Nature Intended: A pictorial history of the nudist. Clapham & Constable. Elysium Growth Press 1986*

GREAT AMWELL   1935-53

FOUNDER/LEADER: Dr M.Nicoll

Community set up by Harley St psychologist who reinterpreted 'The Work' of G.I.Gurdjieff in the light of psychoanalysis.

GRID REF: TL373125

REF: *Madame Blavatsky's Baboon/ Venture with Ideas. K.Walker. Cape 1951.*

HUNTINGDON SHIRE

LITTLE GIDDING 1625 - 1657
FOUNDER/LEADER: Nicolas Ferrar
Small religous community with connections to Charles1. Broken up by Cromwell's Roundheads. Featured in poem by T.S.Eliot and today the home of a small Christian community.
GRID REF: TL133818
REF: Villages of Vision

ISLE OF WIGHT

QUARR MONASTERY 1908
Established by French Benedictines fleeing persecution. As well as farming the monks are known for their music, painting, weaving, and carpentry.
GRID REF: SZ573925
REF : Utopian England.

KENT

COX HALL DIGGERS COLONY C1649
One of a series of 'other' Diggers colonies. (See St George's Hill, Surrey for more details)
GRID REF: Poss. NW of Dover or Cox Heath Nr Linton or Cock Hill Nr Maidstone or even Coggeshall, Essex.
REF: World Turned Upside down

THE RED HOUSE C1860's
FOUNDER/LEADER: William Morris
Innovative early Arts & Crafts House designed by Phillip Webb for William Morris. Morris planned to establish a working community of artists at the house going as far as having Webb draw up designs for extending the house to a quadrangle so Burne Jones and his family could join. The house was sold when Morris moved to London.
GRID REF: SU874430
REF: Designing Utopia. M.H.Lang./ William Morris. F.MacCarthy

CRANBROOK COLONY 1853-1900
Small artists colony based around the artists homes at 2 Waterloo Terrace, 'the old studio', High St and a building known as the Willseley Hotel.
GRID REF: TQ776359
REF: Catalogue of the Cranbrook Colony Exhibition.Wolverhampton. 1977 A. Greg.

NEW & LATER HOUSE OF ISRAEL 1875 - 1905
FOUNDER/LEADER: Clarissa Rogers & James White
Breakaway group from John Wroe's Christian Israelites. Known as the Jezreelites they set about building a great temple on Chatham Hill. The Temple was never completed and was demolished in 1961.
GRID REF: Nr Gillingham
REF: Alt Com 19th Cent.Eng p150

CRAYFORD GARDEN VILLAGE 1915
Built by Vickers to house munitions workers with a grant from the War Office. Designed by Gordon Allen.
GRID REF: TQ516754 Barns Cray
REF : Homes Fit For Heroes.

DURLOCKS 1919
FOUNDER/LEADER: Phillip Sassoon
Garden Suburb development
GRID REF: TR270565 Folkstone
REF: Villages of Vision.

BRITISH LEGION VILLAGE C1923
Bungalows with verandas & Gardens - reminiscent of Chartist cottages.
GRID REF: Nr Maidstone
REF: Villages of Vision

KEMSLEY C1923
Model factory village built by Bowaters paper manufacturers.
GRID REF: TQ896657
REF: Villages of Vision

LANCASHIRE

TOXTETH PARK PURITAN COLONY C1600's
Settlement of puritans from Bolton on the disemparked royal deer park. 25 farms were laid out on land that had the advantage of not coming under Church of England jurisdiction. Built the 'Ancient Chapel' of Toxteth. Remembered in names in the area - Jericho farm, River Jordan & Holyland.
GRID REF: SJ361884
REF: The History of the Royal & Ancient Park of Toxteth. R. Griffiths.

SHAKING QUAKERS 1747-74

FOUNDER/LEADER: Jane & James Wardley (or Warlaw)

Group of Quakers influenced by the mystical ideas of the 'French prophets' or Camisards. Were joined & later lead by 'Mother' Ann Lee. Emigrated to America where they set up a series of 22 highly successful communal villages. Known in USA as the Shakers.

GRID REF: Bolton on the Moors

REF: *The People Called Shakers.*

DUKINFIELD MORAVIAN SETTLEMENT 1743 - 1779

Started with `choirs' in private houses, reorganised in 1757 when a house for single brethren was obtained, and houses for the single brethren and single sisters were built, then enlarged A trombone band was formed, a school for girls built in 1760, and another for boys in 1766. Due to lack of space for expansion the community moved to Fairfield.

GRID REF: SJ 943972Manchester

REF: *Heavens Below.*

FAIRFIELD MORAVIAN SETTLEMENT 1779 -

Settlement of the Church of the United Brethren, an early Protestant sect from Moravia, now part of Czech Republic. Houses, communal 'choirs for men & women, workshops and farm. Also chapel, school and burial ground. Success of the settlements inspired Robert Owen. Later became known for the quality of their schools.

GRID REF: SJ 895977 Droylsden

REF: *Villages of Vision / Heavens Below.*

QUAKER FARM COLONY C1800s

FOUNDER/LEADER: James Cropper

GRID REF: Nr Warrington

REF: *Quakerism & Industry before 1800.*

CHRISTIAN ISRAELITES 1824-30

FOUNDER/LEADER: John Wroe

Headquarters of the Southcottians, or Christian Israelites, under the leadership of John Wroe. An elaborate sanctuary was built for the sect and, convinced that Ashton was to become the New Jerusalem, they proceeded to build four gateways to the town. Wroe

Fairfield Moravian Settlement Droylsden

lived in a Doric mansion west of County Bridge on the River Tame. Wroe forced to leave Ashton after a sex scandal went to set up a community in Wakefield. The site of the sanctuary was later the Star Theatre - named after the symbol of the sect. Their were Southcottians in Ashton into the 1950s running a co-operative shop called the Israelite Stores.

GRID REF: SJ 940991

REF: *England in Ashton-Under-Lyne. W.M.Bowman. Sherrat & Son. 1960*

CHAT MOSS 1827-32

Co-operative smallholding scheme on Chat Moss a large area of drained 'waste' to the west of Manchester.

GRID REF: SJ 702958

REF: *William Thompson biog./co-operative msc.May 1830 / Heavens Below.*

BIRKACRE 1831-33

Co-operative community set up by the Calico Block Printers Union based at Birkacre Mill, with 54 acres of land, a large house converted into 'apartments' and 11 acres of reservoirs. They had 150 employees & 300 members. The site is now a country park.

GRID REF: SD572149 Nr Chorley

REF: *Co-operation & Owenite Socialist Communities.*

BARROW BRIDGE 1831

FOUNDER/LEADER: R.Gardiner

Model industrial village built around Dean Mills. Cottages with gas lighting, running water & a washhouse at the end of every row. An educational institute was added in 1846. Workplace facilities were well in advance of those in most other mills and factories. A canteen was provided along with daily newspapers. Hot water was available all day for tea and coffee, and hot baths and showers were provided for all. The factory ovens baked 150 loaves a day for the workers and a Sickness & Burial Club was organised. Disraeli's novel *Coningsby* is thought to be based on Barrowbridge and may have also have inspired Port Sunlight.

GRID REF: SD688115 Bolton

REF *Barrow Bridge,Bolton. Deanmills Estate - A Victorian Model Achievement. D.O'Connor.*

OLDHAM SPINNERS UNION

1830s

8 acre market garden run by the union for its unemployed members.

GRID REF: Location Unknown

REF: *The Peoples Farm.*

CALDER VALE/OAKENCLOUGH

1835

Model village built by Quaker brothers Richard & Jonathan Jackson. Terraced houses built around textile mill in wooded Pennine valley. Also school and village hall.

GRID REF: SD533457

REF: *And Sometime Upon the Hills.*

SELF-HELP CO-OPERATIVE

SOC. C1838 / 1848 / 1858

A series of attempts by factory workers to set up land based co-operative schemes - first an allotment scheme run by a group of young men, then a 'cow co-operative', whereby a cow was bought direct from a farm , butchered and divided up amongst the group, and finally under the name of The Self-Help Co-operative Society a few people took a nine acre farm with 2 cows, half a dozen pigs, ducks & rabbits and grew wheat & veg, the scheme

failed when one of the cows died.

GRID REF: SD892012 Failsworth

REF: *The History of Co-operation.*

BANK TOP   1817- 1945

FOUNDER/LEADER: Ashworth Bros. Basic cottages and detached house built around mill by the Ashworth Bros. enlightened employers. Library & School provided - In 1833 all but 7 out of 532 workers could read. Continued as 'private' village till WW2.

GRID REF: SD729118 Bolton

REF: *A Study of Model Villages: Bank Top, Eagley & Egerton. P.J.Smalley.*

PENDLE HILL CHARTISTS   1842

Following a visit to Burnley by Chartist leader Feargus O'Connor some unemployed went out to Pendle Hill and staked their claims.

GRID REF: SD800414

REF: *The History of Burnley.Bennett P292*

EGERTON   1844

FOUNDER/LEADER: Ashworth Bros. 100 cottages & school built for millworkers.

GRID REF: SD710148 Bolton

REF: *A Study of Model Villages: Bank Top,Eagley & Egerton. P.J.Smalley.*

BIRKDALE PARK   1848 - 1912

Exclusive seaside suburb developed for the Merseyside 'nouveax riche' by the Birkdale Park Land Co. Private schools became something of a local cottage industry. Working class banished to beyond railway line.Described in retrospect as a garden suburb,

GRID REF: SD321157 Southport

REF: *New Birkdale - The Growth of a Lancashire Seaside Suburb. H.Foster.*

EAGLEY VILLAGE   1850-1932

FOUNDER/LEADER: James Chadwick Cottages, school, library, reading room, park, bowling green and cricket field built by James Chadwick & Bros Ltd.

GRID REF: SD717141 Bolton

REF: *A Study of Model Villages:*

OLDHAM FREEHOLD LAND SOC.

C1850-55

52 acre 'Votingham' estate divided into 363 plots. 109 houses were built.

GRID REF: Location unknown

REF: *Land Reform & working class experience in Britain and the US 1800/1862. J.L.Bernstein. .Stanford UP 1999.*

FREEHOLD PARK   1852 -

38 acre 'Votingham' estate promoted by local Liberals to the east of Lancaster consisting of Ullswater, Grasmere, Windermere, Rydal, Dalton & Borrowdale Rds. Plots were just big enough for freeholders to qualify for the vote. Development of the estate was sporadic resulting in a variety of stone terraces all with large gardens.

GRID REF: SD485616 Lancaster

REF: *The Story of Freehold. Centre for NW Regional Studies. Bulletin 4 1990.*

DALTON HALL 'COMMUNITY'

1876 - 1957

Hall of residence for students of Owens College set up by Manchester Friends. Held up as a pioneer example of student accommodation. Linked to the University Settlement Movement.

GRID REF: Manchester

REF: *Dalton Hall*

BLACKBURN BROTHERHOOD

1899

Group of about ten Tolstoyan christian anarchists who ran an electrical repair business on `non-commercial' lines. They tried to live their lives based on the teachings of the Sermon on the Mount. Connected with the Brotherhood workshop in Leeds.

GRID REF: 35, Victoria St. Blackburn
REF: *Slow Burning Fuse / A History of the Brotherhood Church. A.G.Higgins*

DAISY COLONY   C1902

Land colony at Poulton-le-Fylde set up by Bolton socialist Allan Clark.

GRID REF: Location unknown
REF: *Getting Back to the Land: The Daisy Colony Experiment. P.Salveson. - In Labour's Turning Point in the North West 1000-1914. NW Labour History Soc. 1984*

VICKERSTOWN   1901- 4

'Marine' garden village built by Vickers Shipbuilders on Walney Island for their workers. 900 houses with shops, churches, institute, public house and school modelled on Port Sunlight.

GRID REF: SD182688 Barrow in Furness
REF: *Villages of Vision*

BLACKLEY ESTATE   1902

Manchester Corporation estate built on 'Bournville / Port Sunlight lines' consisting of 150 houses, co-op store and shops run from houses, 13 acres open space & 30 acres of smallholdings

GRID REF: SD855036
REF: *British Town Planning the Formative Years. Leics UP 1981.*

VICTORIA SETTLEMENT C1905

Womens University Settlement.

GRID REF: 322 Netherfield Rd Liverpool
REF: *Listed in Labour Annual 1905*

LANCS. COLLEGE SETTLEMENT C1905

Womens University Settlement.

GRID REF: Embden Rd Hulme Mancs.
REF: *Listed in Labour Annual 1905*

HOLLINS GREEN   1906-13

156 house early garden suburb. Ebenezer Howard came to opening in1909.

GRID REF: SD921027 Oldham
REF: *Villages of Vision*

BURNAGE GARDEN VILLAGE

1906-10

136 houses built by Manchester Tenants Ltd as a Co-partnership housing scheme. Designed by J.Horner Hargreaves. Built around recreation area and 'Pavilion'.

GRID REF: SJ 869923
REF: *Villages of Vision*

BROAD GREEN GARDEN SUBURB   C1906

Garden Village development

GRID REF: Liverpool
REF: *Heavens Below*

CLEVELEYS   C1906

Seaside Garden Village development.

GRID REF: SD317431
REF: *Lancaster Library*

ALKRINGTON GARDEN VILLAGE

Garden Village development.

GRID REF: SD872041 Manchester
REF: *A.Taylor*

TOWNLEY SMALLHOLDINGS

1909 - 70?

Early land settlement scheme set up by local council for the unemployed known as Townley smallholdings. After WWI extended to include returning servicemen. Wound up in the early 1970s. Two plant nurseries remain the rest has become part of local park.

GRID REF: SD 865315
REF: *Heavens Below*

RAVENHEAD GARDEN SUBURB

1909 - 1915

Development by Pilkington Bros Glass works SW of company's headquarters. Original plans were extensive covering 45 acres inc: 500 'cottages' shops and recreation area. Only a small part of the plan was built.

GRID REF: St Helens
REF: *Pilkington Bros Garden Village Ventures.*

FAIRFIELD TENANTS LTD   1912

Garden suburb scheme that grew out of successful allotment project on land owned by the Moravian settlement. In 1912 a group of local men made an approach to the Moravians to develop 22acres of land next to the settlement.

GRID REF: SJ895977
REF: *British Town Planning the Formative Years. Leics UP 1981.*

ECCLESTON HALL GARDEN VILLAGE   1919-20

A Pilkington Glass development that superceded the scheme at Ravenhead. Advised by Prof Abercrombie plans were drawn up for "a scheme to rival Port Sunlight" covering some 700

acres. Rising costs meant that the scheme was never carried out in full.
GRID REF: St Helens
REF: *Pilkington Bros Garden Village Ventures.*

WYTHENSHAW   C1930's

Large Garden Suburb development built by Manchester City Council. Clear example of evolution of Garden Suburbs into council estate. Lack of community facilities resulted in 'centre' being tacked on later.
GRID REF: SJ 825867 Manchester
REF: *A History of Welwyn Garden City. Roger Filler. Phillimore &Co*

FAZAKERLY NEW HALL   1930s?

Self-sufficient colony built by Poor Law Guardians. Cottages and central dining hall.
GRID REF: SJ365965 Liverpool
REF: *Villages of Vision*

WIGAN & DISTRICT SUBSISTENCE PRODUCTION SOCIETY   1934-39

Smallholding scheme for the unemployed sponsored by a group of Quakers. Originally based on 12 acres at Lawns Farm, UpHolland where 40-50 men worked on a smallholding whilst still living in their own homes. Cobblers', tailors' and joiners' workshops were set up. The men could take home produce from the scheme equal to the time they put in, without it affecting their dole. The scheme was later expanded taking in 300 acres of dairy farm at Parbold Hall, 18 acres at Billinge, 54 acres of poultry, pigs & greenhouses at Stephens Farm,

Pemberton, and 60 acres at Ashfield House, Standish, where along with a bakery were joiners', tailors', butchers', jam-makers' and bacon-curing workshops. The scheme was made redundant by the onset of WW2.
GRID REF: SD512106/SD571095/ SD508039
REF: *Heavens Below / Lancashire History Qtrly Vol 2, No 4. Dec98*

THE STONE BOWER FELLOWSHIP   C1939

FOUNDER/LEADER: Fred Hellowell
Peace Pledge Union sponsored communal scheme for elderly WW2 evacuees supported by Canadian Red Cross and Mennonites at Stone Bower House, Burton in Lonsdale. After the war became independent old peoples home, becoming a housing society in 1949 and moving to the Cove, Silverdale in 1950. Merged with large housing association in 1995.
GRID REF: SD464750
REF: *The Stone Bower Fellowship. R.Douglas Young*

YEALAND MANOR   C1939

Experiment in communal living for evacuated children set up by the Manchester Friends' monthly meeting. Up to 50 children lived together in 'an atmosphere of service, love & peace.'
GRID REF: Location unknown
REF: *Pacifism in Lancashire. Pat Starky*

LEICESTERSHIRE

BOSWORTH DIGGERS COLONY C1650

One of a series of 'other' Diggers colonies. (See St George's Hill, Surrey for more details)
GRID REF: Location Unknown
REF : *World Turned Upside down*

EQUITY SHOES   C1890's

Shoe co-operative made loans to members to build 60 houses - some built by a builders co-operative.
GRID REF: Location Unknown
REF: *Building Communities*

LEICESTER TOLSTOYANS   1899

Land society formed by 5 Tolstoyan vegetarians. They had half an acre in Braunstone and hoped to eventually live 'a communal life on the land'.
GRID REF: SK529032
REF: *Heavens Below / Labour Annual 1900*

HUMBERSTONE GARDEN VILLAGE   1906

96 houses built by members of the Anchor Boot and Shoe co-operative with money loaned by the co-op. Also shops, meeting and recreation room. Scheme was a Co-partnership. Still in existence today.
GRID REF: SK 634060
REF: *Building Communities*

RIVERSIDE   1914-18

FOUNDER/LEADER: Russell Hoare
Riverside village - experimental educational community - Hoare insisted that the children should do whatever seemed good to them. Gave talk to the Friends Guild of Teachers.

"I am not out to make good little citizens. I am out to make rebels."

GRIDREF: MeltonMowbray? Lincolnshire?
REF: Heavens Below / The Hawkspur Experiment.

ELMSTHORPE   1935 - 82?

Land Settlement Association smallholding scheme. (See Chawston Beds.)
GRID REF: SP462961
REF: Colin Ward D&D 94/95

LINCOLNSHIRE

SANDTOFT COLONY   1626-1650

Colony of Walloon Protestants set up to drain Hadfield Chase. Driven out by locals whose livelihoods were threatend by the drainage works.
GRID REF: SE 744079
REF: The River Makers. T. Bevis

RED HALL   1848

FOUNDER/LEADER: Thomas Allsop
London Stockbrokers private estate divided into smallholdings on the Chartist Land Plan model.
GRID REF: Nr Lincoln
REF: The Chartist Land Company

WOLDSEA   C1909

Proposed coastal garden village.
GRID REF: TF???????
REF: The Architectural & Social History of Co-operative Living. L.F.Pearson

FULNEY   1935 - 82?

Land Settlement Association smallholding scheme. (See Chawston Beds.)
GRID REF: TF255225Nr Spalding
REF: Colin Ward D&D 94/95

HARROWBY   1935 - 82?

Land Settlement Association smallholding scheme. (See Chawston Beds.)
GRID REF: Location Unknown
REF: Colin Ward D&D 94/95

HOLTON BECKERING C1941

Wartime pacifist land settlement set up by Max Plowman on a 300 acre farm under the auspices of the Community Land Training Association.
GRID REF: TF118813
REF: Heavens Below

LONDON

FAMILISTS   1552 - 1645

Kent/Cambridge/Essex/Devon/London
FOUNDER/ LEADER: Henry Niclaes
Niclaes was an Anabaptist from Munster. He inspired a group known as the Familists who lived communally and tried to establish 'heaven on earth'. As their message spread they were persecuted by the authorities.
GRID REF: Exact Locations Unknown
REF: Heavens Below / World Turned Upside down

HAMPSTEAD DIGGERS COLONY
C1650

Site of planned Digger Colony. (See St George's Hill Surrey for details.)
Ref: World Turned Upside down

HOUNSLOW HEATH DIGGERS
COLONY   C1650

Site of planned Digger Colony. (See St George's Hill Surrey for details.)
Ref: World Turned Upside down

LING ALLEY   1651

FOUNDER/LEADER : John Robbins
John Robbins planned to lead 144,000 people to the Holy Land, sustained on a diet of dry bread, raw vegetables and water. His wife was to mother a Messiah and he claimed to have appeared on earth before Adam. The Ling Alley community was raided in May 1651 and the ten people found there locked up in Clerkenwell Prison.
GRID REF: Moorfields
REF: Heavens Below p16

CLERKENWELL WORKHOUSE
1701
FOUNDER/ LEADER: John Bellars
Attempt by London Friends Meeting to put into practice John Bellars proposal for *Raising a College of Industry of all Useful Trades and Husbandry*. Starting off as a small workhouse factory with 30 'inmates', making yarn and mops it later became a hospital & nursery and finally a school.
GRID REF: Location Unknown
REF: *Heavens Below p30*

PHILADELPHIAN SOCIETY C1703
FOUNDER/ LEADER: Jane Leade
London base of the mystical group.
GRID REF: Location Unknown
REF: *Heavens Below p34*

THE FETTER LANE SOCIETY
1741
Early 'Methodist' group converted to the Moravian church - when leaders arrived from Bohemia they set up a 'Pilgrims House' near the chapel and a series of community houses for members to live in.
GRID REF: Location Unknown
REF: *The Moravian Church in England. 1728-1760. Colin Podmore.*

MORAVIAN CHURCH   C1750
Houses bought by Count Zinzendorf in an attempt to 'settle' the London Moravian Congregation. A chapel and a minister's house were built, the mansion itself renovated, and a cemetery laid out. Plans were made to establish a settlement with choir houses and other dwellings, but these were never realised. (234 years before the

Moravians acquired it, Beaufort House had belonged to Sir Thomas More, the author of *Utopia*.)
GRIDREF: LindseyHouse/Beaufort House
REF: *Heavens Below p50*

SPA FIELDS CONGREGATIONAL FAMILIES   1821-24
FOUNDER/LEADER: George Mundie
First community set up on Owenite principles by a group of printers. Housed in a number of rented properties 21 families had their own private apartments with communal facilities inc: meals, all domestic services & childcare. They pooled wages from community businesses and outside jobs. Ran a printing press, a community 'heath centre' and planned to open a Fellenbergian school.
GRID REF: Guildford St East, Bagnigge Wells Rd & Spa Fields. Islington
REF: *Eve & Jerusalem/Alt Com 19th Cent.Eng/Heavens Below p92.*

WEST HAM   1825
FOUNDER/ LEADER: Samuel Gurney
7 acres of land divided into allotments.
GRID REF: Location Unknown.
REF: *Heavens Below p88*

LONDON CO-OPERATIVE SOCIETY   1826
Owenite Society registered with the aim of forming a communty within 50 miles of London. There would be `community of croperty' and `equal means of enjoyment', self-government by majority vote, and `to women, forming half the human race-freedom from domestic drudgery of

cooking, washing, and of heating apartments, which will be performed on scientific principles on a large economical scale'. Labour was not to exceed eight hours daily. There would be a system of mutual instruction, and all community dwellers were to undertake some tasks in both agriculture and industry: any unhealthy occupations that could not be done by `machinery, chemical or scientific means, or modified, or by rota, will be banished'. The society envisaged a community consisting of a number of adjoining farms up to 2000 acres in size. The scheme was never realised.
REF: *Co-operation & Owenite Socialist Communities / The History Of Co-operation / The Peoples Farm.*

BRITISH ASSOCIATION FOR PROMOTING CO-OPERATIVE KNOWLEDGE (BAPCK) 1828-30s
Originally set up in frustration at the lack of progress by the London Co-operative Society (see above) and known as London Co-operative Society Trading Association it changed its name to BAPCK when it too failed to set up a land based community and became a propaganda organisation. Members were almost a roll call of London's radical artisans of the time.
REF: *The Peoples farm.*

CO-OPERATIVE CENTRE   1827 - ?
Centre of Owenite co-operative activity where publications could be bought and regular meeting were held.
GRID REF: 19, Greville st Hatton Gardens
REF: *The History of Co-operation.*

BARNSBURY PARK COMMUNITY C1830s

14 acres of 'Experimental Gardens' owned by the somewhat eccentric Mr Baume who proposed setting up a co-operative college and community on the site. Known locally as the 'Frenchmans Island,', the furze-covered wasteland was dotted with 'mysterious' cottages. Here a group of radical tailors & shoemakers and thier families worked the land co-operatively.

GRID REF: New North Rd, Holloway (now the site of Pentonville Prison.)
REF : *The History of Co-operation / The Peoples Farm.*

INDUSTRIAL / AGRICULTURAL SCHOOL 1830s

FOUNDER/LEADER: LadyNoel Byron
School set up to train people in the skills needed to live in a co-operative community. Run by E.T.Craig the manager of Ralahine Community. When enough people had been trained the plan was to form a community within 8 miles of London.

GRID REF: Ealing Grove
REF: *The History Of Co-operation.*

WESTMINSTER CO-OPERATIVE SOCIETY 1830s

Largest of the London Co-op Societys at the time acquired land for unemployed members to work on.

GRID REF: Addington.Nr Croydon.
REF: *The Peoples Farm.*

LAMBETH CO-OPERATIVE TRADING UNION 1830s

Promoted a Bakery-cum-land society, with plans for a school & library

GRID REF: Location Unknown
REF: *The Peoples Farm.*

SPADE HUSBANDRY COLONY 1830s

Scheme promoted by Edward Lance, surveyor & agricultral lecturer, who advertised for Owenites impatient for the communitarian life to join him.

GRID REF: Lewisham
REF: *The Peoples Farm.*

1ST LONDON MANUFACTURING COMMUNITY 1830

Small community making boots, shoes, brushes etc for sale in it's own store planned to expand into cultivation.

GRID REF: Old St. Skene.
REF: *The Peoples Farm.*

PHILOSOPHIC LAND ASSOCIATION 1832 - 36

'Interim' community set up by 32 members of the Land Ass. They rented premises including a chapel & school room. The group's leader, William Cameron, a Scottish tailor, was a communal enthusiast: he had been a member of The Edinburgh Practical Soc. & the Spa Fields Community, he wrote his own proposal for a community entitled *The First Trumpet*, went on to support the Chartist Land Plan.

GRID REF: Cromer St. Off Grays Inn Rd
REF: *The Peoples Farm.*

HALFPENNY A WEEK LAND CLUB 1834 -

A scheme developed by the Builders Union to settle unemployed members on the land. In 1835 they offered a cottage and smallholding to one of the Tollpuddle Martyrs next of kin.

GRID REF: Location Unknown
REF: *The Peoples Farm.*

AESTHETIC INSTITUTION 1839-42

FOUNDER/LEADER: J. P. Greaves.
Greaves developed his ideas on sacred socialism here whilst gathering a group of followers together through meetings at his house and writing articles for the *Monthly Magazine.*

GRID REF: 49 Burton St. Bloomsbury
REF: *Search for a New Eden.*

'CHILDREN OF GOD' 1870-72

FOUNDER/LEADER: MaryAnnGirling
Original home of group that went on to become the New Forest Shakers.

GRID REF: 107 Bridge Rd Battersea.
REF: *Alt Com 19th Cent. Eng*

STAMFORD HILL COOPERATIVE HOMES 1870

Early Co-operative Housekeeping scheme.

GRID REF: Stamford Hill.
REF: *The Architectural & Social History of Co-operative Living. L.F.Pearson*

THE PROGRESSIVE LITERARY & SPIRITUAL INSTITUTION C1871

London recruiting office of the American Shaker communities set up by FW Evans an Owenite who joined the Shakers at Mount Lebanon and became an elder there.

GRID REF: 15,Southhampton rd.WC
REF: *Heavens Below*

Chelsea Artists Colony
C1880s
Group of artists living in the rundown riverside area. Mostly members of the New English Art Club.
GRID REF: Manresa Rd.
REF: *The Good & Simple Life.*

Tite Street
Late 1800s?
FOUNDER/LEADER: Edward Godwin / Ellen Terry
Loose artistic community revolving around Godwin the Architect of Bedford Park and the Actress Ellen Terry.
GRID REF: Tite Street
REF: *Villages of Vision*

Toynbee Hall
1888
First of the University Settlement houses. Set up by Canon Barnet to bring middle-class students in touch with working class communities and carry out social relief work. Among the students to pass through its doors were C.R. Ashbee. Willaim Beveridge and Clement Attlee.
GRID REF: Whitechapel
REF: *Heavens Below*

Wyldes Farm
1884 -
FOUNDER/LEADER: Charlotte Wilson
Gathering place firstly for Fabian Socialists then assorted Anarchists. Later architect & planner Raymond Unwin lived here whilst working on the nearby Garden Suburb.
GRID REF: Hampstead Heath
REF: *Hampstead Garden Suburb.*

Royal Arsenal Co-operative Society.
1885
The Society purchased Bostall Farm and in 1900 bought the Bostall estate where during 1903-4 they built 250 houses for sale to members.
GRID REF: TQ468777
REF: *The History of Co-operation.*

Tenant Cooperators Ltd
1887
First housing co-operative. Planned to buy houses all over London to let to members at 'local rents' to be financed through nominal £1 shares from members, a loan from the Public Works Loans Board and small investors. Started by buying 6 houses at Upton Park, followed by building 24 cottages in Penge. Grew to have 210 dwelling on 5 sites.
GRID REF: Upton Park, Penge, East Ham, Epsom
REF: *Building Communities*

'Blavatsky Lodge'
1888
FOUNDER/LEADER: Mdme Blavatsky
"The household consists of six or seven persons, including a young doctor of medicine, a student of law and a Frenchman, an American (the friend of Edison), and a Swedish Countess. These are all particular disciples, who receive constant instructions from the lips of the priestess...." *London Star Dec 1888*
GRID REF: 17, Lansdowne Rd, NottingHill
REF: **http://www.theosophical.org**

Essex House
1888-1902
FOUNDER/LEADER : C.R. Ashbee
Home of the Guild of Handicrafts set up by C.R. Ashbee as - *An Endeavour towards the teaching of John Ruskin & William Morris.* The Guild was a cooperative community based on the crafts of metalwork, woodwork and decorative painting. They ran a shop in central London at 16a Brook St. and by 1900 had grown to 150 members. The community moved en-masse to Chipping Campden in 1902.
GRID REF: Mile End Rd
REF: *Designing Utopia MH Lang/ The Simple Life F.MacCarthy*

Sloane Gardens House
1889
Block of self-contained small flats for 106 women with public restuarant, studios and music rooms. Built by the Ladies Dwelling company.
GRID REF: Sloane Gardens. Sloane Sq .
REF: *The Architectural & Social History of Co-operative Living. L.F.Pearson*

'City Colony'
1889
FOUNDER/ LEADER: William Booth.
Trial 'City Colony' - part of the Salvation Army's grand plan - outlined in Booth's book *Darkest England & the Way Out.* Hostel & workshop, making benches and matting for S.Army meeting houses. The unemployed and homeless worked there on the basis of a days work for food & lodgings. Residents could move on the the 'Farm Colony' at Hadliegh, Essex and eventually to Oversea's Colonies. The plan was to open a 'City Colony'

Ladies Residential Chambers Chenies St.

in every town in the country. In fact these became the nationwide network of S.Army Hostels.
GRID REF: Whitechapel
REF: Darkest England & the Way Out W.Booth / Blood & Fire. R. Hattersley.

LADIES RESIDENTIAL CHAMBERS 1889 - 1945

Six-storey block of self-contained flats built by the Ladies Residential Chambers Ltd for single women. Designed by J.M.Brydon the chambers had a common dining room & kitchen. 18 residents carried out cooking on a co-operative housekeeping system.
GRID REF: Chenies St. Bloomsbury.
REF: The Architectural & Social History of Co-operative Living. L.F.Pearson

THEOSOPHIST 'COLONY' 1890 -

FOUNDER/LEADER: Mdme Blavatsky House and grounds rented by Annie Besant. Became a 'colony' of like-minded "earnest, loyal, self-sacrificing and studious" Theosphists upon the arrival of Mdme Blavatsky.
GRID REF: 19 Avenue Rd
REF: Annie Besant. A Taylor

BROTHERHOOD CHURCH 1891

FOUNDER/LEADER: J.Bruce Wallace. In 1895 the Brotherhood Co-operative Tust was registered and opened a North London store, a 'Mutual Service Circle' was set up using barter notes as an alternative to money. Legal difficulties were encountered over the issue of barter notes as wages. Also a coalmine was acquired at Swadlincote in Derbyshire & run as a co-operative.
GRID REF: Southgate Rd.
REF: A History of the Brotherhood Church. A.G.Higgins

YORK STREET CHAMBERS 1892

Block of 50 flats for single women: artists, authors, nurses and other working women. Common dining room and kitchen in the basement.
GRID REF: York St. Marylebone
REF The Architectural & Social History of Co-operative Living. L.F.Pearson

MECKLEBURGH SQUARE 1890s

Communal house of the Fellowship of the New Life.
GRID REF: Bloomsbury
REF: E.Carpenter Biog

MANSFIELD HOUSE UNIVERSITY SETTLEMENT 1895-6

Settlement house at which J.Bruce Wallace was warden.
GRID REF: Location Unknown
REF: A History of the Brotherhood Church. A.G.Higgins

DOUGHTY ST ASS.HOME 1895

Associated Home advertising for residents in Seed Time Magazine.
GRID REF: 29 Doughty St WC.
REF: Seed Time Oct 1896

BROTHERHOOD HOUSE 1896

Associated home run "on very free lines for young men interested in the movement" by Mary & Walter Order. Centre for the Brotherhood Church & the Fellowship of New Life. A tailors and dressmaking business and a store were run from the house. Taken over by Edgar Bottle who opened it as a socialist home called Morris House.
GRID REF: Waddon Hotel. Stafford rd Croydon
REF: Colony in the Cotswolds. N. Shaw.

MORRIS HOUSE 1897/8

Advert in Seed Time Magazine - "Morris House has been opened as a home for advanced thinkers and socialists of all kinds and both sexes. The house is opposite the railway station and is within easy reach of

the country. The rooms are large and the household arrangements are described as "middle-class, but democratic" - members of the family taking a share of the domestic work. Board and residence costs from 14/- to 18/- a week......"
GRID REF: (as above)
REF: Seed Time July 1897

DOUKHOBOUR COMMUNITY 1896
House next to Brotherhood House used by Doukhobour refugees.
GRID REF: Duppas Hill, Croydon
REF: A Peculiar People . Aylmer Mandea

FOREST GATE COMMUNITY 1897
Group listed in the Labour Annual as making preparations for settling on the land in Essex.
GRID REF: 14 Leonard Rd. Forest Gate.
REF: Labour Annual 1897

EDMONTON ANARCHIST GROUP 1898
Co-operative store set up by local Anarchists to raise money to finance a co-operative colony.
GRID REF: Location Unkown
REF: The Slow Burning Fuse.

LINEN & WOOL DRAPERS COTTAGE HOMES 1898
FOUNDER: James Marshall (son of founder of Marshall & Snelgrove.)
An enclave of 1 and 2 storey cottage homes, ranged around a garden and a central institute.
GRID REF: Mill Hill
REF: Villages of Vision.

SESAME CHILD GARDEN & HOUSE FOR HOME LIFE TRAINING 1898 - ?
Institute closely modeled on the Pestalozzi-Froebel Haus in Berlin. Had 65 students in 1902 and ran classes in gardening, household management, diet and the welfare of children. One

of the committee members was Alice Buckton who went on to play an active part in establishing Glastonbury as a cultural centre.
GRID REF: Acacia Rd. St Johns Wood.
REF: The Avalonians. P.Benham

FABIAN CO-OP. HOME 1899
Co-operative home advertised in the May 1899 issue of Fabian News.
GRID REF: 87,Barking Rd.Canning Town
REF: The Architectural & Social History of Co-operative Living. L.F.Pearson

HAMMERSMITH ARTS & CRAFTS 'COLONY' C1900
Loose circle of Arts & Crafts practitioners living in West London. Inc:Arthur Penny, Romney Green, Emery Walker, Cobden-Sanderson & May Morris. Also from 1905 E. Johnston and Eric Gill.
GRID REF: Hammersmith
REF: The Arts & Crafts Movement. E.Cumings/W.Kaplan.

BRENTHAM GARDEN SUBURB 1901 - Present
FOUNDER/ LEADER: Henry Vivian. Pioneer Tenants Co-Partnerships scheme started by memebers of a building co-op with help from Liberal MP Henry Vivian. In all 680 houses and a social club and recreation ground 60.5 acres in all were built. Parker & Unwin oversaw the design and layout from 1905 onwards. Was taken over by Bradford Property Trust Ltd in the 1940's & run as a comercial concern. Became a conservation area in 1969.
GRID REF: TQ184793 Ealing
REF: //home.clara.net/sender/brentham

BEDFORD SQUARE 1905 - 1915
Home of Ottoline & Phillip Morrell. Ottoline gathered around her a group of young radical artists whom she supported. Arguably the start of the Bloomsbury set. They moved to Garsington Oxfordshire in 1915.
GRID REF: 44 Bedford Sq. Bloomsbury.
REF: Ottoline Morrell. LIfe on a Grand Scale.

WHITE HART LANE ESTATE C1905
Early council estate built by the LCC with some garden city influence.
GRID REF: ?????
REF: Homes fit for Heroes. M.Swenarton.

Waterlow Court Hampstead

LONDON VACANT LAND CULTIVATION SOC. 1907

FOUNDER/ LEADER: Joseph Fels
Proposed scheme to utilise the 10,000 acres of cultivable land said to be within a tram ride of the Bank of England as smallholdings. Launched at Toynbee Hall by Joseph Fels.
REF: Heavens Below p379

HAMPSTEAD GARDEN SUBURB

Best known of the Garden suburbs. Built by Henrietta Barnet. Laid out to a plan by Raymond Unwin. Was originally to have housed a broad cross section of people, but quickly became an exclusive suburb.
GRID REF: TQ255882
REF: Hampstead Garden Suburb M.Miller & A.S.Gray. Phillimore &Co

WATERLOW COURT 1909 -1960s

50 flats arranged as a cloistered quadrangle designed by M.H.Baille Scott as a women's home for the Improved Industrial Dwellings Co. Run on Co-op Housekeeping lines until the1960s.
REF: The Architectural & Social History of Co-operative Living. L.F.Pearson

THE ORCHARD 1909

57 flats for elderly residents with shared baths, washhouses and baking ovens designed by Parker & Unwin for Hampstead Tenants Ltd.
REF: The Architectural & Social History of Co-operative Living. L.F.Pearson

BRENT GARDEN VILLAGE 1910

FOUNDER/ LEADER: Alice Melvin
Garden Village set up on co-operative housekeeping lines. 33 households shared communal facilities and servants housed in Brent Lodge.
GRID REF: Finchley
REF: The Architectural & Social History of Co-operative Living. L.F.Pearson

GREAT WESTERN GARDEN VILLAGE SOCIETY C1910

Developed the Coldharbour Lane Estate at Hayes and at West Acton.
GRID REF: Ruislip
REF: //home.clara.net/sender/brentham/

UPMINSTER GARDEN SUBURB

Garden Suburb development.
GRID REF: Location Unknown
REF: Upminster the Story of a Garden Suburb. T. Benton & A. Parish . 1996

OLD OAK ESTATE C1911-

Early council estate built by the LCC with influenced by garden city ideas.
GRID REF: ?????
REF: Homes Fit for Heroes. M.Swenarton.

MELVIN PARK 1911

FOUNDER/ LEADER: Alice Melvin
Unbuilt co-operative garden city.
GRID REF: Ruislip
REF: The Architectural & Social History of Co-operative Living. L.F.Pearson

MELVIN HALL 1912 - 1964

FOUNDER/LEADER: Alice Melvin
Co-operative Housekeeping scheme consisting of 30 flats with communal dining room & kitchen.
GRID REF: Golders Green
REF: The Architectural & Social History of Co-operative Living. L.F.Pearson

MELVIN CO-OPERATIVE RESIDENTIAL SOCIETY 1912- 37

FOUNDER/ LEADER: Alice Melvin
5 houses run as a Co-operative Housekeeping scheme.
GRID REF: Priory Rd.South Hampstead
REF: The Architectural & Social History of Co-operative Living. L.F.Pearson

NINE ELMS SETTLEMENT   1914

Womens Freedom League Settlement where children were served dinners of vegetarian soup and large slices of pudding, which they could either eat at the settlement or take home. The settlement also distributed free milk.

GRID REF: I Everett St. Nine Elms Lane.
REF: The Architectural & Social History of Co-operative Living. L.F.Pearson

WEMBLEY HILL GARDEN SUBURB   1914 -

Garden suburb built on Sir Audley Neeld's 220 acre Tokyngton estate by Wembley Hill Estates Limited.

GRID REF: Wembley
REF: www2.brent.gov.uk/planning

KINGSLEY HALL SETTLEMENT 1915

Kingsley House was a mixed sex settlement where residents agreed to the communal sharing of all income, housework, and responsibilities. When Gandhi visited London in 1931, he insisted upon staying at Kingsley Hall rather than in a hotel.

GRID REF: Location unknown
REF: Independent Women

FERN ST SCHOOL SETTLEMENT

FOUNDER/ LEADER: Clara Grant
Small women's settlement begun in Clara Grant's flat from where she served children's breakfasts, a friend ran a clinic, and a small food cooperative was started. On Saturday mornings "farthing bundles" containing; a toy, cheap candy, yarn, bits of cloth, and other oddments were distributed to

children below a certain height.
GRID REF: Location unknown
REF: Independent Women

NUTFORD HOUSE   1916

Residential Club for single women. Single rooms with common dining room & kitchen, social room, library and lounge.

GRID REF: Off Hyde Park
REF: The Architectural & Social History of Co-operative Living. L.F.Pearson

THE SMALLEST GARDEN 'CITY'

Commercial attempt to cash in on garden city movement

GRID REF: Warminster Rd. S Norwood
REF Semi-Detached London. A.Jackson.

WELL HALL ESTATE   1915

Estate of 1298 houses built on modified Garden Suburb lines by the government for First World War munitions workers. Estate was designed by Frank Baines who had trained with C.R.Ashbee. Some rented property on the estate was managed by the Royal Arsenal Co-operative Retail Society.

GRID REF: Eltham
REF: Homes Fit for Heroes. M.Swenarton

DEVONSHIRE HOUSE   1923

Design by C. F. A.Voysey for three 30-storey blocks of flats with communal dining rooms, shops and other services. The 'medieval style' tower blocks would have stood opposite Green Park underground station. The design was not built.

GRID REF: Piccadilly, London,
REF: The Architectural & Social History of Co-operative Living. L.F.Pearson

DEWDROP INN   1931

FOUNDER/LEADER: Mary Hughes
Social centre set up by Quaker daughter of Judge Hughes - author of Tom Brown's Schooldays. Mary lived a simple life devoted to helping the poor. The 'Inn' window displayed an array of posters on vivisection, vegetarianism, the effects of alcohol & smoking.

GRID REF: Vallance rd. Whitechapel.
REF: Stone Upon Stone. M.Osborn.

HAYES   1933-36

FOUNDER/LEADER: P.D.Ouspensky
House used by followers of Ouspensky's 'fourth way' who sought 'self-observation' through physical work including gardening, woodwork amd housekeeping.

GRID REF: (Great West Rd?)
REF: The Strange Life of PD Ouspensky. C.Wilson / Madame Blavatsky's Baboon.

'THE GORGONS'   C1930s

Group of neo-pagan feminists mentioned by Elliot O'Donnell in Strange Cults and Secret Societies of Modern London(1934) who reputedly lived in a large house on the Thames above London and 'love open-air life and cocktails but have no liking for men'.

GRID REF: Location Unknown (O'Donnell unreliable source.)
REF: The Triumph of the Moon.

HAMPSTEAD ARTISTS COLONY C1930s

Loose group of artists & sculptors. Inc: Barbara Hepworth, Henry Moore, Paul Nash & Ben Nicholson. (formed a group known as UNIT ONE) In mid 30's following the closure of the

Buahaus in Germany the enclave was joined by Moholy-Nagy, Walter Gropuis and Mondrian.

GRID REF: 7 Mall Studios, 11a Parkhill rd, 3 Eldon Lane. Plus others.
REF: Hepworth Biog.

'MINIMUM FLATS' 1934

Flats designed by Wells Coates with a bedsitting room, kitchenette and bathroom plus communal services; including bed-making, shoe-cleaning, laundry collection and window-cleaning, and in its early years meals could be obtained from the staff kitchen.
GRID REF: Highgate
REF: The Architectural & Social History of Co-operative Living. L.F.Pearson

ARTISTS REFUGE 1936

Refuge set up for artists fleeing persicution in Nazi Germany.
GRID REF: 47 Devonshire Hill Hampstead
REF: Phiadon Companion of Art.

HIGHPOINT 1 1936

Lubetkin's block of flats called Highpoint 1 in north London, built in 1936, were described by Le Corbusier as 'a vertical garden city', residents having the use of a communal tea room, tennis courts, a swimming pool and a garden.
GRID REF: Highgate
REF: The Architectural & Social History of Co-operative Living. L.F.Pearson

HISTORICO - PSYCHOLOGICAL SOCIETY 1936 - ?

FOUNDER/LEADER: P.D.Ouspensky
London house of Ouspensky's followers. Had meeting room for 300.

GRID REF: Hammersmith
REF: The Strange Life of PD Ouspensky. C.Wilson / Madame Blavatsky's baboon.

COMMUNITY OF THE WAY 1930s

Small community set up in house owned by Doris Lester of Kingsley Hall. A Christian spiritual community they spent their time spinning, weaving, dyeing, making wooden toys, printing and doing shoe repairs. Bartered their goods for vegetables grown by the unemployed in Kent.
GRID REF: Whitechapel
REF: Stone Upon Stone. M.Osborn

KENSAL HOUSE. 1937

Housing association flats built including a social club and nursery school.
GRID REF: W.London
REF: The Architectural & Social History of Co-operative Living. L.F.Pearson

HACKNEY FLATS 1938-40

585 flats built by Hackney Borough Council. Each quadrangle of flats had its own community centre with a hall, clubroom and washhouse provided with individual washing cubicles and electric washing machines.
GRID REF: Hackney
REF: The Architectural & Social History of Co-operative Living. L.F.Pearson

ONSLOW SQ 1941- 42

House of Primrose Cordington with almost an acre of ground from where a group of J.G. Bennet's pupils grew veg & kept chickens in bombed out gardens prior to Coombe Springs.
GRID REF: Location Unknown
REF: Madame Blavatsky's Baboon

MIDDLESEX

ENFIELD DIGGERS COLONY C1650

One of a series of 'other' Diggers colonies. (See St George's Hill, Surrey for more details)
GRID REF: Location Unknown
REF : World Turned Upside down

ENFIELD CHASE 1659

FOUNDER/LEADER: William Covell
Following riots sparked by enclosure of the Chase, Covell published a scheme for setting up collective farms. Digger influenced .
REF: World Turned Upside down/ Essex the Rebel.

MOREVILLE COMMUNITORIUM 1843

FOUNDER/LEADER: Goodwyn & Catherine Barmby
Shortlived community of the Communist Church at the Barmby's house,
GRID REF: Hanwell
REF: Alt Com 19th Cent.Eng/ Eve & the New Jerusalem/Heavens Below.

BEDFORD PARK 1880 -

Early planned suburb became known in retrospect as the 'first' garden suburb.
GRID REF: Chiswick
REF: Villages of Vision

NORFOLK

MOUSEHOLD COMMONWEALTH
1549
FOUNDER/LEADER: Robert Kett
Shortlived community formed by rebels taking part in Kett's rebellion. 20,000 rebels set up a mini-commonwealth on Mousehold Heath for six weeks.
GRID REF: Location unkown
REF: *The English Rebels. C.Poulsen*

METHWOLD FRUIT FARM COLONY
1889 -
FOUNDER/LEADER: Mr Goodrich
160 acre smallholding scheme. Plots averaged 4 acres each, with little brick-built or wooden cottages. Land was used intensively, with a wide variety of fruit, flowers and vegetables, together with chickens and bees. Diet was primarily vegetarian. Goods not consumed within the colony were sent directly to consumers in London.
GRID REF: TL736946
REF: *Alt Com 19thCent Eng*

NORTHAMPTON SHIRE

WELLINGBOROUGH DIGGERS
1650
Issued a declaration in 1650 saying they had begun to 'dig up, manure and sow corn upon the common waste ground called Bareshank.' (See St George's Hill for details of Diggers.)
GRID REF: Wellingborough.
REF: *World Turned Upside down*

THE NORTHAMPTON TOWN & COUNTY BENEFIT BUILDING & FREEHOLD LAND SOCIETY
1848
Land club set up to enable working men to buy enough land to gain the right to vote. First development was in Freehold St, Primrose Hill, Elysium Terrace, St George's Place & Terrace. The Society went on through amalgamations to become the Nationwide - the world largest building society.
GRID REF: SP751604
REF:**www.kingsthorpe.demon.co.uk / bcrapage.html**

KETTERING BOOT & SHOE SOC.
C1880's
100 houses for rent to members built by shoemaking co-op. Also bought land to sell as plots.
GRID REF: SP870787
REF: *Building Communities*

ABINGTON
1935 - 82?
Land Settlement Association smallholding scheme. (See Chawston Beds.)
GRID REF: SP775606
REF : *Colin Ward D&D 94/95*

LAXTON
1935 - ?
FOUNDER/LEADER:John Hawkswell
Catholic land community where 5 families worked the land together on a 77 acre holding attempting the 'restoration of Christian rural life.'
GRID REF: SP950961

REF: *Utopian England*

NORTHUMBER LAND

WALLSEND CO-OPERATIVE SOC.
1860s
Small estate built by Co-operative Retail Society - Rochdale St, Provident Terrace, Mutual St & Equitable St.
GRID REF: NZ285663
REF: *Industrial Colonies & Communities. ed.S.Jackson. Fingerpoint 1988.*

ANNFIELD PLAIN SOCIETY
1888
134 houses built by Co-operative retail society in local villages.
GRID REF: NZ174513
REF: *Industrial Colonies & Communities. ed.S.Jackson. Fingerpoint 1988.*

BISHOP AUCKLAND INDUSTRIAL CO-OPERATIVE SOCIETY
1888
Co-operative retail Society provided houses for employees and from 1897 onwards helped members to buy their own homes.
GRID REF: Location Unknown
REF: *Industrial Colonies & Communities. ed.S.Jackson. Fingerpoint 1988.*

NORTHERN ALLOTMENTS SOC.
C1890s
Society formed to provide land and assistance to working men who wanted to become smallholders. In 1892 bought the Whaggs Lodge Estate west of Gateshead. Had up to 100 resident members.
GRID REF: Location unknown
REF: *Roses & Revolutionists. Nigel Todd. Peoples Publications 1986*

WINDY NOOK & DISTRICT INDUSTRIAL CO-OP.SOC.C1890s

Co-operative Retail Society built houses for sale to members. Also built a street of rented properties.
GRID REF: NZ270599
REF: Industrial Colonies & Communities. ed.S.Jackson. Fingerpoint 1988.

CLOUSDEN HILL FREE COMMUNIST & CO-OPERATIVE COLONY   1895 - 1902

Anarchist Land Colony inspired by the ideas of Kropotkin, ran an intensive market garden on 20 acres at Clousden Hill Farm with local support from the ILP and Co-operative movement. The colony came to an end in 1898 due to 'internal dissension' with on ex-member commenting that 'Angels might have lived the Life, flesh and blood could not.' Frank Starr. Was taken over by two members who ran it as the Clousden Hill Co-operative nurseries until it went bankrupt in 1902.
GRID REF: NZ271684 Forest Hill
REF: Roses & Revolutionists. Nigel Todd. Peoples Publications 1986

WHAGGS COMMUNE   1898 - ?

Anarchist commune set up after the end of the Clousden Hill community, on land owned by the Northern Allotments Society at Whickham.
GRID REF: Location Unknown
REF: Roses & Revolutionists. Nigel Todd.

THE LADIES SETTLEMENT C1905

Womens University Settlement.
GRID REF: Darlington
REF: Listed in Labour Annual 1905

CONGREGATIONAL HO.   C1905

Womens University Settlement.
GRID REF: Middlesboro
REF: Listed in Labour Annual 1905

SHILBOTTLE   1916 - ?

Small colliery and cottages bought by Co-operative Wholesale Society following war time coal shortage. Society built semi-detached houses with gardens and gave land for a co-op store, chapel and Aged Miners' Homes.
GRID REF: NU197088
REF: The New History of CWS.P.Redfern. 1938 Dent & Sons

STANINGTON   1935 - 82?

Land Settlement Association smallholding scheme. (See Chawston Beds.)
GRID REF: NZ212793
REF: Colln Ward D&D 94/95

NOTTINGHAM SHIRE

SCROOBY   1606

A group of dissenters known as the Scrooby Seperatists formed, after attempts to settle in Boston, Lincs and at Immingham on the Humber. They emigrated to Leiden in Holland. (Later they emigrated again to America becoming the Pilgrim Fathers.)
GRID REF: SK 654907
REF:www.plimoth.org/library/scrooby.htm

'DIGGERS COLONY'   1649-50?

One of a series of 'other' Diggers colonies. (See St George's Hill, Surrey for more details)
GRID REF: Location unknown.
REF: World Turned Upside down

OXFORDSHIRE

CHARTERVILLE   1847 - 52

FOUNDER/LEADER: F.O'Connor
Third and largest of the Chartist estates. 300 acres divided into 80 smallholdings with model cottages. 40 oxen and 18 pigs were provided to the 'winners' of the plots, along with manure, firewood and seed. Area still known as Charterville allotments.
GRID REF: SP 314104 Minster Lovell.
REF: The Chartist Land Company

WATERSIDE COTTAGES   C1880s

FOUNDER/LEADER : C.R.Ashbee
Holiday cottages run by the Guild of Handicraft for its workers.
GRID REF:SU596963DraytonSt Leonard.
REF: The Simple Life. Fiona McCarthy

COMMUNITY OF THE RESURRECTION   1882-87

Foundation of an Anglican monastic group by Charles Gore. Group later moved to Mirfield (Yorks.)
GRID REF: Pusey House. Oxford.
REF : Utopian England

Chartist cottage Minster Lovell

GARSINGTON MANOR 1915-1925
FOUNDER/LEADER: Ottoline Morrell

Artistic salon and wartime refuge for artistic COs,. including: D.H. Lawrence, Aldous Huxley, Lytton Strachey, Bertrand Russell, Katherine Mansfield, John Middleton-Murry and Virginia Woolf among countless others.
GRID REF: SP586016
REF: Ottoline Morrell. M Seymour

TYLTHROP HOUSE AGRICULTURAL ESTABLISHMENT 1939 -
Formed by Jewish refugees. Listed in the journal Community Life.
GRID REF: SP 745068 Kingsey
REF: Heavens Below

SHROPSHIRE

COALBROOKDALE 1780s
FOUNDER/LEADER: Abraham Darby
Housing, schools and landscaping carried out by Quakers Ironmasters. The company lso provided food at cost-price in times of shortages
GRID REF: SJ658034
REF: Quakers in Science and Industry

WHEATHILL BRUDERHOF 1942 - 1960
Farm bought by the Bruderhof for their English members when the main German group went to Paraguay. Served as a refuge for pacifists and had grown to 200 members by 1950.
GRID REF: Lower Bromden, nr Ludlow
REF: Utopian England

SOMERSET

AGAPEMONE (ABODE OF LOVE) 1856 - 1958
FOUNDER/LEADER: Henry Prince.
19th Century cult centred around defrocked clergyman who built extensive house and cottages surrounded by high wall on estate bought with money given by wealthy converts. Became the scandal of Victorian society when news of the Rev Princes sexual antics got out. The Reverend John Hugh Smyth-Pigott took over as leader and 'heavenly bridegroom' on Prince's death in 1899. Community ended as a sort of liberal finishing school for young ladies. Wound up after the death of Smyth-Pigott's chief 'soul bride'.
GRID REF: ST234367 Spaxton
REF: The Rev.Prince and his Abode of Love. Charles Mander. EP publishing.

STREET 1829 - Present
Street almost developed as a company town around the works of Clarks Quaker shoe manufacturers. The Clark family carried out a number of housing schemes and provided a town institute and outdoor swimming pool. The Clarks were also sponsors of the first Glastonbury Festival in 1914.
GRID REF: ST485365
REF: Clarks Guidebook.

BRAD PLAIN HOUSE C1905
Men's University Settlement House.
GRID REF: St Phillips Bristol
REF: Listed in Labour Annual 1905

MOUNT AVALON 1919
FOUNDER/LEADER: Rutland Boughton
House and grounds bought as a base for the Glastonbury festival by a devotee. Failed due to lack of finances. This was the closest Boughton came to his dream of a community of artists living on the land and supporting the festival.
GRID REF: ST505389 Glastonbury
REF: The Avalonians. P Benham.

STAFFORDSHIRE

POTTERSVILLE
C1845 - 1851
FOUNDER/LEADER: William Evans
Emigration scheme set up by the Trade Union of Operative Potters in response to the introduction of new technology. 134 people were settled on 1600 acre in Wisconsin. The scheme collapsed amid accusations of mismanagement and almost bankrupted the union.
GRID REF: Stoke on Trent / USA
REF: The Staffordshire Potter. H. Owen

CHARTLEY ESTATE 1902
5000 acre estate, proposed site for the first Garden City. Project was abandoned in favour of Letchwoth.
GRID REF: SE of Stoke on Trent
REF: A.Taylor

FENTON HOUSE C1905
Womens University Settlement.
GRID REF: Stoke-on-Trent
REF: Listed in Labour Annual 1905

PARK VILLAGE 1907 - present
A Co-partnership Garden Village built by Sir Arthur Paget on the Old Fallings Estate. Work began in 1907, with a model housing exhibition being held the following year. By 1915 75 houses had been completed. A 2nd phase of building was carried out in the 1920s with the village being later engulfed by the expansion of Wolverhampton.
GRID REF: SJ930009. Wolverhampton
REF: Villages of Vision

PENKHULL GARDEN VILLAGE
1910 -
95 houses built by Stoke on Trent Tenant Ltd a Co-partnership housing society. Was to have been the first of 4 garden suburbs ringing Stoke. Barry Parker oversaw early designs with the houses being designed by a local firm of architects. Houses are arranged in clusters around greens. Some social provision was made through a small institute and tennis courts and bowling green along with allotments. A further phase of development was carried out in 1939. In 1964 the scheme was bought by Bradford Properties Trust who also own property at Hull Garden Village, Saltaire & Brentham.
GRID REF: SJ 869443 Stoke on Trent
REF: The Garden Cities Movement in a Local Context: The development & decline of Penkhull Garden Village Estate. A.Taylor,. The Local Historian Feb 1997.

THE WOODLANDS 1941- present
Hostel run by the Friends War Victims Relief Committee for elderly bombed out evacuees. In 1945 became a home for the elderly with a quarter of the residents Quakers. Has its own Quakers Meetings - The Penn Meeting.
GRID REF: Penn Rd. Wolverhampton
REF: Wolverhampton Quakers 1704-1988. C.Jones et al. Clark&Howard Books.

SUFFOLK

ASSINGTON HALL 1829
Co-operative Farm.
GRID REF: Location Unknown
REF: Co-operation & Owenite Socialist Communities / The Land and the Labourers. C.W.Stubbs. 1884

CHURCH ARMY COLONY 1882
Early smallholding scheme.
GRID REF: TM015783 Thelnetham.
REF: Heavens Below p324

WALBERSWICK ARTISTS COLONY C1880
'Seaside' artists colony. Early residents inc: Charles Keene, Phillip Wilson Steer. Charles Rennie Mackintosh & his wife lived here(1914/15), they were forced to return to London suspected of espionage after letters were found in therr house from the Austrian Successionist painters.
GRID REF: TM494744
REF: The Good & Simple Life.

HOLLESLEY BAY COLONY
1904-11
FOUNDER/ LEADER : Joseph Fels
1300 acre site of former Agricultural Training College acuired by Joseph Fels for the Central Unemployment

Committee. The college could accommodate for 355 men. There were eight glasshouses and 200 acres of gardens, thirty cottages, four groups of farm buildings, an open-air swimming bath, workshops, a warehouse on the river front, a wharf and a tramway connecting the wharf to the farmers' gardens. 300 unemployed men worked there. George Lansbury, and others from Toynbee Hall used to come down at week-ends to organize classes and recreation. In the end the Local Government Board turned it back into a deterrent workhouse.
GRID REF: TM370449 Nr Felixstowe
REF: *Heavens Below p378*

SOCIAL SETTLEMENT   C1905
Mens University Settlement house.
GRID REF: 133-35 Fore St. Ipswich
REF: *Listed in Labour Annual 1905*

WISSET LODGE   C1914-18
Fruit farming scheme that took COs in WW1 - inc: Bloomsbury artists Duncan Grant & Vannesa Bell.
GRID REF: TM 366792
REF: *Ottoline Morrell Biog.*

NEWBOURNE   1935-82?
Land Settlement Scheme to assist out-of-work miners.
GRID REF: TM 270249
REF: *Villages of Vision*

DENHAM   1935 - 82?
Land Settlement Association small-holding scheme. (See Chawston Beds.)
GRID REF: TL 755615
REF : *Colin Ward D&D 94/95*

THELNETHAM   1942-45
FOUNDER/LEADER: J.M.Murry
Run down Lodge Farm was bought as Murry's last attempt at forming a community. Was a refuge for COs, but as a community was beholden to Murry who owned the property and was editor of *Peace News* at the time.
GRID REF: TM015783
REF: *Villages of Vision/ Heavens Below / Community Farm.J.M.Murry 1952*

ELMSET COMMUNITY   1939-45
FOUNDER/LEADER: E.Cocksedge
Ambitious wartime venture in practical Christian based community based on 41 acre mixed farm. Aim was to "lay the foundations of a new order" whilst restoring buildings, running study groups, setting up a community library, holding peace Pledge Union meetings, sunday services and selling *Peace News* in Ipswich market each saturday. All decisions were made by consensus, links were made with neighbours and the local retail co-op. The group hoped that by example they could demonstrate "the soundness of community as a new order of voluntary and non-violent communism."
GRID REF: TM059463 Nr Ipswich
REF: *Andrew Rigby D&D / Heavens Below*

SURREY

ST GEORGES HILL DIGGERS COLONY   1649 - 50
LEADER/FOUNDER: Gerard Winstanley
On April 1st 1649 half a dozen men began to dig common land at St George's Hill - the best documented 'Diggers Colony'. Soon joined by others, they attempted to tend the heath as a "common treasury for all", building huts, grazing livestock and cutting firewood. Continually harassed & attacked by local landowners the Diggers, or True Levellers as they called themselves, were forced off St George's Hill and moved to Cobham a few miles away. Through Winstanley's writing others were inspired throughout England to take up their spades and start to cultivate the commons.
GRID REF: TQ125664
REF: *World Turned Upside down*
WEBSITES:
www.tlio.demon.co.uk/diggers.htm
www.users.globalnet.co.uk/~royhan/film/
FILM: *Winstanley. British Film Institute*

COBHAM HEATH   1650
LEADER/FOUNDER: G.Winstanley
Diggers from St George's Hill moved here after eviction. Here they built seven houses and cultivated 11 acres. Finally driven out of the area after their huts and furniture were burnt in April 1650.
GRID REF: TQ114602
REF: *World Turned Upside down*

CONCORDIUM
1842 - 48

FOUNDER/ LEADER : J.P.Greaves
Community and school set up by followers of Sacred Socialism at Alcott House on four acres of land with extensive gardens planted with fruit-trees. Also a playground, lawns, walkways, arbours and summerhouse. The residents lived a spartan life of Physical Puritanism, eating a raw vegetarian diet and subscribing to a whole range of 'new' ideologies, including phrenology, hydropathy, mesmerism and celibacy. They promoted their ideas through printing *The Heathian* and *New Age* magazines. They established The British and Foreign Society for the Promotion of Humanity and the Abstinence of Animal Food, a forerunner of the Vegetarian Society. In 1848 the community disbanded, and the building was used as a cholera orphanage for girls, later known as `The National Orphan Home'. The building was replaced in 1862, and its use was subsequently changed to a private residence, `South Lodge' and more recently into luxury flats.
GRID REF: Ham Common Richmond.
REF: *Search for a New Eden.*

CONCORDIUM 2
C1843

Community set up by the Owenite Missionary Alexander Campbell after he left the Ham Common Concordium.
GRID REF: Hampton Wick
REF: *Search for a New Eden.*

THE COKELERS
1850 - Late 1800s
Followers of John Sirgood lived in the area. Called The Society of Dependants, or Cokelers they ran a series of co-operative shops and built a number of small chapels - numbered 2000 at their peak in 1885.
GRID REF: TQ044434 Loxwood, Northchapel, Warnham & Shamley Green
REF: *Alt.Com 19thCent Eng*

MERTON PARK ESTATE
1870s
Model estate developed in the wake of Bedford Park by John Innes.
GRID REF: TQ263694
REF: *Villages of Vision*

MERTON ABBEY
1881- ?
FOUNDER/LEADER: William Morris
Collection of buildings set in some 7acres of grounds on the banks of the river Wandle 7 miles from the centre of London where Morris set up the workshops for Morris & Co.
REF: *Designing Utopia*

JEZREELITES
1881-1905
FOUNDER/LEADER: Clarissa Rogers and James White
An offshoot of the Christian Israelites built 'Jezreel Tower', a great temple on Chatham Hill near Gillingham. A remarkable building that would have housed the sect if it had ever been completed. It was demolished in 1961.
GRID REF: New Brompton
REF: *Alt.Com 19thCent Eng*

CRAIG FARM
C1880s
FOUNDER/LEADER: Harold Cox
Co-operative farm set up by Harold Cox, a disciple of Edward Carpenter to whom he sent his first pair of hand made sandles from Kashmir. Bernard Shaw reported that the only succesful crop grown was radishes which were made into jam! The farm appears as 'Crankie Farm' in the book by Goldsworthy Lowes Dickinson.
GRID REF: SU874430 Tilford
REF: *Heavens Below / The Simple Life.*

WITLEY ARTISTS COLONY
C1880s
FOUNDER/LEADER: Birket Foster
Enclave of artists gathered around watercolourist Birket Foster. Foster started in a cottage and ended building himself a great half-timbered mansion.
GRID REF: SU955394
REF: *Villages of Vision*

THE HASLEMERE PEASANT INDUSTRIES
1896 - ?
FOUNDER/LEADER: Godfrey Blount.
The Haslemere Peasant Industries, set up by Godfrey Blount and his wife Ethel was an artistic community with the aim of integrating work, leisure and the country life and the philanthropic principles of the home industries movement. The Peasant Industries was an umbrella organisation of small workshops that employed local craft-workers. It also ran a shop in London. Along with C.R.Ashbee's wife Janet the Blounts were prominent members of the Healthy and Artistic Dress Union(1890) which promoted the wearing of "unusually comfortable, loose-fitting clothes made of hand-woven cloth."
GRID REF: SU904328 Haslemere
REF: *The Arts & Crafts Movement. E.Cumming & W.Kaplan*

WOODCOTE VILLAGE   1901
FOUNDER/LEADER: William Webb
Garden Suburb development.
GRID REF:
REF: Garden First. W.Webb.

WHITELEY VILLAGE   1907
Cottage homes village.
GRID REF: TQ094623
REF: Villages of Vision

ONSLOW GARDEN VILLAGE 1921
Original plans for the village included a number of blocks of flats to be run as Co-operative Housekeeping schemes, an institute & recreation grounds. The Co-partnership ran out of finance after building 300 houses and the flats were never built.
GRID REF: SU 971499 Nr Guildford
REF: The Architectural & Social History of Co-operative Living. L.F.Pearson

LYNE PLACE   1935-41& 45-47
FOUNDER/LEADER: P.D.Ouspensky
Country house and farm set up as a base for the Historico-Psychological Society by P.D. Ouspensky a follower of GI Gurdjieff.
GRID REF: TQ010669 Virginia waters.
REF: The Strange Life of PD Ouspensky / Madame Blavatsky's Baboon.

SUSSEX

BRIGHTON CO-OPERATIVE TRADING ASS.   C1819
FOUNDER/LEADER: Dr William King
Dr King was an early advocate of using the profits of small retail co-operatives to set up communities. A group of working people inspired by his ideas set up a society and after successfully running a grocery business took a lease on 28 acres of land some 9 miles from Brighton, where they ran a garden/nursery employing 4 or 5 of their members who lived on site and took their meals communally.
GRID REF: Location unknown
REF: British Co-operative Movement

LINDFIELD COLONY   1823-1833
FOUNDER/LEADER: William Allen
Land colony set up on the 100 acre Graveley estate by Quaker William Allen. The estate was divided into plots provided with a cottage, wood-house, wash-house, bakehouse and piggery. The colony also had its own school, workshops and printing press on which it produced its own newspaper. Allen's school still survives as a private house, and the colony is remembered in the names of Allen Road, America Lane & Hanbury Park.
GRID REF: TQ363253
REF: Villages of Vision / Heavens Below

SUSSEX GENERAL TRADING ASS   1828
Owenite co-operative society set up to accumulated profits for the purchase of land to set up a community.
GRID REF: Location Unknown
REF: Co-operation & Owenite Socialist Communities.

'ABODE OF LOVE'   C1844
Large house where the Rev Prince gathered together a small band of followers prior to moving to Spaxton.
GRIDREF: Location Unknown Weymouth
REF: The Reverend Prince and his Abode of Love. C. Mander. EP Publishing.1976.

SMALLHOLDING COLONY   1896
'Projected' co-operative smallholding scheme announced by J.Kenworthy at a conference on 'Land Co-operation and the Unemployed' at Holborn Town Hall. The scheme was to supply a co-operative centre in Croydon.
GRID REF: Horeham Rd Sussex?
REF: Roses & Revolutionists. N.Todd.

HERITAGE CRAFT SCHOOL 1903
A spin off from the Bermondsey Settlement, set up by Grace Kimmins under the banner of the "Guild of the Brave Poor Things". The Heritage Craft Schools and Hospitals for Cripples believed that disabled children could not be trained to their full capacity in city slums and so set up residential schools in the country. The Guild motto was "Happy in My Lot."
GRID REF: TQ393194 Chailey
REF: Independent Women

DITCHLING ARTISTS COLONY 1907-24?
FOUNDER/LEADER: Eric Gill
Starting with the Gill family house, Sopers, a small colony of artists grew

up in the village. Following WWI Gill set up a distinct community - a sort of self-sufficent monastic Craft Guild. The looser artists' colony continued after Gill moved to Wales.

GRID REF: TQ326151
REF: Eric Gill F.MacCarthy/Utopian England

WOMENS CO-OPERATIVE FARMERS LTD   1916 - 1918?

Farm divided into smallholdings. Took in COs during WWI.

GRID REF: LocationUnknownEast Sussex
REF: A Question of Concience

'THE SANCTUARY'   1923- 30s?

FOUNDER/LEADER: Miss V. Pagnall
Community started by Miss Pagnell a mystical Christian socialist (inspired by Edward Carpenter), who bought land using her inheritance and gave away plots to anyone who cared to live there. One resident was anarchist W.C.Owen, another was Dion Byngham ex-leading light in the Order of Woodcraft Chivalry. Miss Pagnell tolerated ("but did not encourage") naturism, `free love' and paganism.

GRID REF: Nr Storrington
REF: Freedom:A Hundred Years. Freedom Press/The Triumph of the Moon.

SIDLESHAM   1935 - 82?

Land Settlement Association smallholding scheme. (See Chawston Beds.)

GRID REF: SZ857982
REF: Colin Ward D&D 94/95

WARWICKSHIRE

BIRMINGHAM CO-OP.SOC.   1828

Owenite society set up with the aim of `mutual protection against poverty' and `independence through growth of common capital' by means of weekly subscriptions, trading and manufacturing operations, and community settlement.

GRID REF: Location Unknown
REF: Co-operation & Owenite Socialist Communities.

'COMMUNITY COTTAGE'   C1830

The `inmates' of Community Cottage sent narcissus bulbs, trees and seeds as gifts to Harmony Hall. Possibly the home of William Pare.

GRID REF: Vauxhall Rd. Birmingham.
REF: Co-operation & Owenite Socialist Communities.

STUDENT COMMUNITY   C1830s

FOUNDER/LEADER: G.J.Holyoake
Whilst a student at Birmingham Mechanics Institute Holyoake discovered Owenism and set up a small community house with three fellow students. Holyoake went on to become a radical journalist, champion of the co-operative movement and founding father of the secular movement.

GRID REF: Location Unknown (poss. Community Cottage. See above.)
REF: Robert Owen & the Owenites in Britain & America.

COTTAGE FACTORIES   1857 - 60

FOUNDER/LEADER: J&J Cash
Steam-powered cottage industries

with a shared steam engine placed at the end of a row of independent ribbon-weavers' cottages with a drive shaft running through the party wall of each house along the whole row. 48 cottages out of a planned 100 were built surrounded by vegetable plots by the Quaker Cash Bros.

GRID REF: Radford Coventry
REF: Taming the Tiger/ Villages of Vision.

COTTAGE FACTORIES   1858 - 60

FOUNDER/LEADER: Eli Green
67 ribbon-workers 'steam powered' cottages. (see above) built by benevolent manufacturer.

GRID REF: Location Unknown Coventry
REF: Taming the Tiger

THE COVENTRY LABOURERS & ARTISANS CO-OPERATIVE SOC. C1840-60

FOUNDER/LEADER: Charles Bray
Ribbon manufacturer Charles Bray was a leading light in the Coventry intelligentsia. A friend of George Elliot & Ralph Waldo Emerson. He helped to found a co-operative society which provide gardens for working men and a co-op store. Inspired by the cottage factories in Coventry he drew up a plan for a small community based on the same system - squares of 3-400 houses, each with their own steam engine to provide power would be surrounded by enough land for each house to have its own allotment. The scheme was never realised.

GRID REF: Location Unknown
REF: Robert Owen & the Owenites in Britian & America. / The Industrial Revolution in Coventry. J Prest 1960

St George's Court Co-operative Housekeeping Scheme

BOURNVILLE VILLAGE TRUST

1879 - Present

FOUNDER/LEADER: G. Cadbury.

Influential model village founded by the Quaker Cadbury Brothers after moving their Cocoa & Chocolate factory to a site just south of Birmingham. Started with a few cottages provided alongside the factory, it grew into a whole planned village that was turned into a charitable trust in 1900 at which time it consisted of 330acres and 313 dwellings. Became a model for the Garden City & Suburbs movement with the First Garden City conference being held there in 1901 and George Cadbury was one of the first vice-presidents of the Garden City Association. The village is laid out with ample open space, shops, public buildings and each house has a large garden attached. Tenancies were open to anybody, not just Cadbury employees. During the 1930s the trust developed what were known as 'Ten shilling houses. The trust has continued to managed the village and be involved in housing development up to the present day. In the 1930s the trust acquired a series of farms as a 'greenbelt' on the southern side of Birmingham and now manage some 2770 acres of open or farm land.

GRID REF: SP046809 Birmingham
REF: Villages of Vision / Ninety Years On.

BIRMINGHAM WOMENS SETTLEMENT   C1905

Womens university settlement.
GRID REF: 318 Sumer Lane
REF: Listed in Labour Annual 1905

BOURNVILLE TENANTS LTD 1906

Co-partnership scheme that developed part of the Bournville village.
GRID REF: SP046809 Birmingham
REF: Ninety Years On.

ST GEORGES COURT   1923/4

FOUNDER/LEADER: E.Cadbury.

Block of 32 flats for single professional women developed by Residential Flats Ltd at Bournville model village along Co-operative Housekeeping lines. The flats were arranged as an open quadrangle. Communal facilities included a communal dining room, kitchen and 'shared servants', with groups of flats sharing bathrooms and living rooms. The communal facilities declined and were wound up in 1957.
GRID REF: SP046809 Bournville
REF: The Architectural & Social History of Co-operative Living. L.F.Pearson

DUDLEY   1950

Dudley council estate based on modified 'Reilly Green' lines.
(See 'Birkenhead' for details)
REF: The Architectural & Social History of Co-operative Living. L.F.Pearson

WILTSHIRE

FOXHAM   1885-1901

FOUNDER/LEADER: A.Herbert

Part of a multi-site smallholding scheme. Other schemes at Hay Farm (Essex), Cottenham(Camb) and for details see Lambourne(Camb).
GRID REF: ST977770
REF: Heavens Below

ASHTON KEYNES   1936 -1940

Bruderhof community set up on the 200 acre Ashton Felds Farm after the sect was forced to leave Europe by Nazi persecution. Grew to some 250 members attracting English followers. The group developed the farm, renovating buildings and cultivating the land; adding 103 adjoining acres in 1937 and running a successful mixed farm & large market garden. They also set up craft and publishing ventures. Following anti-German harrassment at the outset of the War they sold up and moved to Paraguay.
GRID REF: SU051937
REF: Utopian England

OAKSEY   1938 - 1940

320 estate bought by the Bruderhof as their community at Ashton Keynes expanded. The purchase was referred to the Home Office when local landowners complained about the sale of land to Germans. The Home Office supported the Bruderhof, but following further harrasment the community decided to move to Parguay.
GRID REF: ST993935
REF: Utopian England

WORCESTER SHIRE

KIDDERMINSTER CO-OPERATIVE INDEPENDANT LAND ASS.
1847

The Kidderminster Co-operative Independant Land Association was reported by the *Worcestershire Chronicle* in October 1847 as meeting at the Fish Inn in Orchard Street. It was reported that they had purchased the Hoboro or Hooborough Estate near Castle Hill in the parish of Wolverley. It was their intention to locate 25 or 30 families on the "O'Connor system". It is also reported a short time later that they had made a purchase of an estate in the Wyre Forest.
GRID REF: Location Unknown
REF: Kidderminster Rebels website

MATHON   1848
FOUNDER/LEADER: F. O'Connor

The Mathon estate was surveyed and an offer made for it by O'Connor for Chartist smallholdings, but the purchase was never completed
GRID REF: SO 730453
REF: The Chartist Land Company.

GREAT DODFORD   1848 - 51
FOUNDER/LEADER: F. O'Connor

Last of the Chartist estates set up almost in defiance as the Land Company fell apart.. The 40 smallholdings were allocated by auction, rather than lottery. No school was provided as on other estates and supplies of seeds were restricted due to lack of funds. After the end of the Chartist Land company the smallholdings were more successful than elsewhere due to their closeness to markets in Birmingham
GRID REF: SO 931730
REF: The Chartist Land Company

Rosedene cottage at Great Dodford has been purchased by the National Trust who intend to retore it to its original condition.

BEWDLEY   1871

7 acres of woodland gifted to John Ruskin's Guild of St George by Birmingham mayor and manufacturer George Baker. The wood was not 'transformed' by the Guild.
GRID REF: Location Unknown
REF: Alt.Com 19thC Eng p80 / The Wider Sea -A Life of John Ruskin. J.D.Hunt.

YORKSHIRE

SMITH HOUSE 1739-44
Small Moravian community house. Base for Moravian activity prior to founding of Fulneck.
GRID REF: Location unknown Wyke
REF: *The Moravian Church in England. 1728-1760. Colin Podmore.*

FULNECK 1744 -
Moravian settlement with chapel choir houses, shop, bakehouse and work-shops, set on dramatic hillside at Pudsey Nr. Bradford. The Moravian school now on site numbers among it's past pupils; Herbert Asquith PM & Diana Rigg.
GRID REF: SE225319
REF: *The Moravians at Fulneck. R.Strong.*

ABBEYDALE HAMLET 1785
FOUNDER/LEADER: Earl Fitzwilliam
Model industrial community.
GRID REF: SK325818
REF: *Villages of Vision*

LOYAL GEORGIAN SOCIETY 1779
Early Land Club - Mutual benefit society of mainly small business men that lent money to members to build houses - out of this group grew the Halifax Building Society.
GRID REF: Location Unknown Halifax
REF: *Workers Housing in W. Yorkshire. 1750-1920. HMSO 1986*

OLD TOWN C1820
'Club Houses' built by local Land Club.
GRID REF: Location Unknown
REF: *Workers Housing in W. Yorkshire.*

GOLDEN FLEECE FRIENDLY SOC. 1822
Small cottages built by Land Club.
GRID REF: 1-7Strike Lane Skelmanthorpe
REF: *Workers Housing in W. Yorkshire.*

THE MORAVIAN MUSEUM

Small museum housed in one of the settlement cottages. Contains artifacts and displays on the history of Fulneck and the Moravian Church.

55/57 Fulneck.Pudsey. LS28 8NT
Contact for opening details.

COPLEY 1847 - 53
FOUNDER/LEADER: Col. Ackroyd
Model village of 112 simple stone houses built next to mill. With canteen, school, library and allotments.
GRID REF: SE084223
REF: *Villages of Vision*

WINCOBANK LAND COLONY 1848
Sixty-eight acre farm acquired by the Sheffield Edge Tool Grinders Union with the aim of setting up a Land Colony after meetings in the town by Owenite Frances Wright and Chartist leader Feargus O'Connor.
GRID REF: SE380909?Nr Sheffield
REF: *Heavens Below p246*

GLEADLESS COMMON SIDE LAND COLONY 1848
A dozen men and a manager ran the 11acre farm for The Sheffield Brittania Metal Smiths supplying a shop in town.
GRID REF: SK377836? Nr Sheffield
REF: *Heavens Below*

'FILE HARDENERS' LAND COLONY 1848
Land Colony set up by Sheffield File Hardeners Union.
GRID REF: Nr Sheffield
REF: *Heavens Below*

HOLLOW MEADOWS FAR 1848/54
Following a revolt over conditions in thier flour mills the Sheffield Board of Guardians acquired the 48 acre moorland Hollow Meadows Farm with the aim of reclaiming moorland and setting up a Land Colony using workhouse labour. Dormitories and a dining hall were built using local stone. 22 acres were reclaimed and planted with root crops. Instead of setting up small holdings for the unemployed as planned the land was let to private farmers.
GRID REF: SK285866 Rivelin Valley.
REF : *Heavens Below*

SALTAIRE 1851 -
FOUNDER/LEADER: Titus Salt
Extensive model village built around Salt's textile mills. Included housing, shops, institute, hospital, alms houses, park and mausoleum. Declined along with the textile industry revived in the 1990s by a combination of hi-tech industry, heritage and art.
GRID REF: SE138379 Shipley.
REF *Villages of Vision / Salt & Silver*

LEEDS REDEMPTION SOC. 1851

Outlet for the produce of the Garnlwyd Community. Main item for sale was blackberry jam.

GRID REF: 5 Trinity St. Leeds.
REF: *Heavens Below / Social Reform in Victorian Leeds JFC Harison 1954*

LEEDS MODEL COTTAGE SOC. C1850s

Non-profit group set up to enable 'Artisans' to build their own homes by acting as guarantor for loans. Tried to ensure good quality and design by providing 'improved plans'.

GRID REF: *Locations Unknown*
REF: *Workers Housing in W. Yorkshire.*

CHRISTIAN ISRAELITE INSTITUTE 1857 - 63

FOUNDER/LEADER: John Wroe
Wrenthorpe House was built as the headquarters of the Christian Israelites after Wroe was kicked out of Ashton-Under-Lyme by the Southcottians. Here he waited for the second coming whilst building up a following in Austrailia and the US.

GRID REF: SE306221 Nr Wakefield
REF: *Alt.Com 19thC Eng.*

ACKROYDON 1859

FOUNDER/LEADER: Col Ackroyd
Second and larger model village built by Edward Ackroyd (also see Copley) Houses laid out round large green with market cross. Scheme carried out with encouragement of Halifax Building Society.

GRID REF: SE091261 Halifax
REF: *Villages of Vision*

WEST HILL PARK 1863-68

Model housing estate built by Crossleys carpet manufacturers.

GRID REF: SE084328 Halfax
REF: *Villages of vision*

SHARLSTON C1860's?

The New Sharlston Colliery Company supported by the Crossley's of Halifax built miners housing along with a chapel,school, Penny Bank,literary institute, reading room, library, coffee room and co-op store. Francis Crossley even bought out a beer shop to keep the village alcohol free.

GRID REF: SE393188
REF: *Workers Housing in W. Yorkshire.*

ROCHDALE PIONEERS MUSEUM

Regonised as the birthplace of the Co-operative movement. The original Pioneers shop houses displays and memorabilia of 150 years of Co-op History. Inc: Co-operative stamps, Commemorative china and rare dividend coins.

Open: Tues-Sat 10am to 4pm
Sun 2pm to 4pm
31 Toad Lane Rochdale
Tel: 0161 832 4300

BRIGHOUSE CO-OPERATIVE SOC. 1865-1890

Co-op Retail Society founded in 1856, started building housing for sale to members on a small scale in 1865. Built 12 houses next to a new store at Bailiff Bridge in 1877 and a cresent of 16 houses in Brighouse in 1880. Built a further 45 houses in Raymer Rd & Harriet St." The society has not sought to make money on its cottage building schemes. The houses have been sold to members at the cost price and the result is so gratifying that further schemes of this character may well be developed."

Society report 1890

GRID REF: *Locations unknown*
REF: *Workers Housing in W. Yorkshire.*

LEEDS INDUSTRIAL DWELLINGS CO. 1867

Model Dwelling Society built a block of galleried tenements. Each with 2-3 bedrooms, living room & coal cupboard. Communal washhouse and basement refuse collection system also provided.

GRID REF: Sharman St Leeds
REF: *Workers Housing in W. Yorkshire.*

CLOUGHTON C1870s

A small plot of land bought specifically for John Guy, a Companion of the Guild of St George, whom John Ruskin admired for refusing to work a steam-driven machine. Guy worked the difficult ground for five years as a tenant of the Guild.

GRID REF: TA010944 Nr Scarborough
REF: *Alt.Com 19thCent Eng.*

G.W THOMPSON & CO C1886

Inspired by the teaching of John Ruskin George Thompson registered his woollen company as a friendly society and introduced welfare provisions,

pensions and a profit sharing scheme for his employees.
GRID REF: Huddersfield
REF: Designing Utopia. M.H. Lang

WILSHAW 1873
Small courtyard of model dwellings.
GRID REF: St Mary's Court. Wilshaw.
REF: Workers Housing in W. Yorkshire.

STAITHES ARTISTS' COLONY C1880
Small artists' colony
GRID REF: NZ782184
REF: The Good & Simple Life

THE QUARRY 1887 - ?
The Community of the Resurrection set up by Charles Gore in Oxford moved here in 1887. The monks were actively involved in Christian Socialism. Kier Hardie visited and spoke at a meeting in the grounds.
GRID REF: SE201194 Mirfield
REF: Utopian England/Possible Dreams

THE BROTHERHOOD WORKSHOP
Group of Christian anarchists formed around an electrician's workshop after an engineers strike. They had links with the Tolstoyans in Croyden and became a northern outpost of the Brotherhood Church. Became involved in machine knitting to earn an income. Moved in 1921 to set up a land based colony at Stapleton.
GRID REF: Victoria Road, Leeds
REF: A History of the Brotherhood Church. A.G.Higgins / Slow Burning Fuse / Utopian England

NEIGHBOURHOOD GUILD C1897
Sheffield University Settlement .
GRID REF: 282 Granville Rd.
REF: Listed in Labour Annual 1905

NEW EARSWICK 1901- Present
FOUNDER/LEADER: Joseph & Seebohm Rowntree
Model village for workers at the Rowntree chocolate factory where Parker & Unwin developed their Garden City design ideas. The village was built from the very ground it stands on: the bricks were made in the brickworks on the outskirts of New Earswick. From 1950 the brickyard, which closed down in the 1930s, was developed into a nature reserve.
GRID REF: SE626549 York
REF: Villages of Vision

BRADFORD CO-OPERATIVE DWELLINGS C1901
Quadrangle of flats with common room & communal kitchen designed by Parker & Unwin. Published in The Art of Building a Home. Never built.
REF : The Architectural & Social History of Co-operative Living. L.F.Pearson

WHITWOOD 1904
Housing designed by Voysey for colliery owners Henry Briggs & Son. The Briggs's also provided a workmens institute.(Now the Rising Sun.)
GRID REF: SE421242
REF: Workers Housing in W. Yorkshire.

CROFT HOUSE C1905
UniversitySettlement house.
GRID REF: Sheffield
REF: Listed in Labour Annual 1905

WOODLANDS C1906
Garden Village for miners at the Brodsworth Colliery laid out with advice from the Garden City Ass.
GRID REF: SE519063 Nr Doncaster
REF: Heavens Below

'RESURRECTION' HOSTEL C1908
Elegant Gothic hostel built by the Community of the Resurrection at Mirfield to house members who were taking art degrees at the university. The Community's links with the university contributed to several generations of radical theological scholars inc. Trevor Huddleston and David Jenkins.
GRID REF: Location Unknown. Leeds.
REF: Alfred Orage & The Leeds Art Club.

HULL GARDEN SUBURB 1908
Garden Suburb development.
GRID REF: Location Unknown
REF: Villages of Vision

BRADFORD 1917
Proposals for ten Garden Suburbs to be situated on the outskirts of Bradford. The Bradford Health Committee suggested 'the provision of an efficiently staffed communal laundry and cooking kitchen for each village'. Other facilities were to include a school, baths and allotments.
GRID REF: Locations Unknown
REF: The Architectural & Social History of Co-operative Living. L.F.Pearson

PAINTED FABRIC LTD 1918-1959

FOUNDER/LEADER: Mrs A.Carter

Small community of disabled ex-servicemen based on the old Women's Auxiliary Army Corps camp. They made high quality fabric goods whilst living in converted huts & 10 houses. Also worked gardens & allotments.

GRID REF: SK349820 Norton Woodseats.

REF: Exhibition Leaflet

MARSDEN   C1920s

Garden Suburb development proposed by S & C Firth of Cellar Clough Mills. 169 houses for mill employees with allotments, parkland and playgrounds. Scheme never built.

REF: Workers Housing in W. Yorkshire.

BROTHERHOOD CHURCH STAPLETON COLONY

1921 - present

Christian anarchist land colony set up by group from Leeds. They live by the precepts of the Sermon on the Mount, recognising no authority other than that of God, a stance that has brought them into repeated conflicts with the authorities, for erecting dwellings without permission (the group rebuilt the houses everytime time the council demolished them!), failing to register children's births, keeping their children out of state schools, refusing to fill in census forms & to pay the poll tax. They have close links with the Peace Pledge Union (PPU) & War Resisters International holding a 'Strawberry Teaparty' each summer to raise funds for them. During the 1960s they ran a film van for the PPU, showing back-projection peace films in town centres up & down the country. The colony consists of a series of small cottages dotted about a large smallholding. Over the years they have run a market garden, carried out knitting, sold honey and Christmas trees to support themselves as well as running their own small printing business publishing booklets, recipe books and calendars. Over the years the community has developed into a network of extended 'families' that extend beyond the geographic bounds of the colony.

GRID REF: SE517192 Stapleton

REF: A History of the Brotherhood Church. A.G.Higgins/ D&D94/5 / Slow Burning Fuse / Utopian England.

CUBLEY GARDEN VILLAGE

1921-2

Garden Village development.

GRID REF: SE246025 Penistone

REF: Villages of Vision

KIRK SANDALL GARDEN VILLAGE   1922

258 houses built for workers of Pilkington Glass under the direction of Prof Abercrombie. Shops were in wooden huts inc; Co-op shop.

GRID REF: SE621072 Nr Doncaster

REF: Pilkington Bros Garden Village Ventures.

THE BROTHERHOOD CHURCH

INTERNATIONAL WOMEN'S DAY

MILITARISM & PROSTITUTION GO HAND IN HAND THE POVERTY CAUSED BY WAR & THE PRESENCE OF FOREIGN TROOPS IN CAMBODIA & FORMER YUGOSLAVIA, EVEN UN TROOPS ONLY WORDS IN ONE LANGUAGE WERE HOW MUCH & WHERE

SAY NO! TO ALL WAR

QUARRY HILL FLATS   1935-40

938 flats modelled on Karl Marx Hof flats in Vienna, built by Leeds City Council. Was the largest housing scheme in the country at the time and aimed to incorporate the latest housing ideas and techniques. Flats had solid fuel ranges, electric lighting and non-drip window boxes. A suction powered refuse disposal system sucked rubbish to a plant that provided heat for the communal laundry. Other communal facilities included a communal hall, welfare centre, shops, playgrounds, tennis courts & bowling greens. A planned social centre and sports complex were never built. The 'revolutionary' steel frame and concrete clad construction was to prove disastrous and within 35 yrs the whole complex had been demolished.

GRID REF: Leeds

REF: Workers Housing in W. Yorkshire.

SNAITHE   1935 - 82?

Land Settlement Association small-holding scheme. (See Chawston Beds.)

GRID REF: SE641219

REF : Colin Ward D&D 94/95

WALES

Utopian communites in Wales are a mix of indigenous Welsh communities and those set up by English settlers drawn by the romance of the Welsh landscape, or simply it's remoteness.

INDUSTRIAL/RELIGOUS
SETTLEMENT   C1620

Settlement begun by a Rowland Vaughan - ended by 1620.

GRID REF: Golden Valley.

REF: Howell Harris & the Trevecka Family. A.W.Owen. MA Thesis Uni N.Wales 1957

HOWELL HARRIS MUSEUM

A small museum dedicated to the work of Howell Harris and the Methodist community that he founded. Collection includes books, prints and furniture from the time of the community.

For information on opening times contact: The Warden.
Coleg Trefeca.
Trefeca. Brecon. Powys. LD3 0PP
Tel: 01874 711423
www.ebcpcw.org.uk/pcwtrefeca.ht

COLEG TREFECA   1750 - C1847

FOUNDER/LEADER: Howell Harris Methodist community known as The Family (Y Teulu) partly inspired by the Moravians. Up to 100 members lived in the main house or on surrounding farms supporting themselves through agriculture & a variety of trades. The Presbyterian Church of Wales now run the house as a training centre and it houses a small museum.

GRID REF: SO146320

REF: Howell Harris & the Trevecka Family. A.W.Owen. MA Thesis Uni N.Wales 1957 www.ebcpcw.org.uk/pcwtrefeca.htm

MELINGRIFFITH   C1780s

Quaker ironworks which provided welfare provision for its workers through a benefit club and school. A small number of houses also built.

GRID REF: Glamorgan

REF: Quakers in Science and Industry.

MILFORD HAVEN   1793-1843

'Whaling colony' established by Quakers from Nantucket. Built a number of houses and meeting house. Most returned to America when the whale oil industry declined.

GRID REF: SM900058

REF: Quakers in Wales Today. Pub. Meeting of Friends in Wales.

NANTGWILLT   1812

Large country house with 200 acre farm and extensive woodlands where the radical romantic poet Percy Bysshe Shelley and his first wife tried to set up a 'rendez-vous for the friends of liberty and truth'. The scheme to set up a radical rural commune failed as Shelley could not secure the necessary

finances. The estate was flooded by the Caban Coch reservoir in 1903.
GRID REF: SN916629
REF: *The Shelleys at Nantgwillt. D. Davenport. / Shelley the Pursuit. R. Holmes*

TREMADOC   1805 -
FOUNDER/LEADER: W. Madock
Model village built after the reclaimation of 2000 acres of Treath Mawr. Neat stone village laid out round a square with town hall and market. A 'great embankment' was built across the mouth of the river Glasyn nearly bankrupting Madock. The poet Shelley lived for a while at Tan-yr-allt whilst trying to help raise funds for the scheme. Tradition has it that Tremadoc was the starting point of Prince Madog's 12th century voyage to America. The villages name has recently been changed to Tremadog.
GRID REF: SH561402
REF: *Villages of Vision/Shelley the Pursuit. R. Holmes/History of the Llynn Peninsula*

BLACKWOOD   1820
FOUNDER/LEADER: John Moggridge
Successfull 'Owenite' inspired community set up by local industrialist on self-help/self-build basis. Small plots were let on long leases to local miners who built their own cottages. Also shops, workshops, a school & market house. Became the small town of Blackwood.
GRID REF: ST180973
REF: *Villages of Vision*

YNYSDDU   C1820s
FOUNDER/LEADER: John Moggridge
Village on same lines as Blackwood.
GRID REF: ST182933
REF: *Villages of Vision*

TRELYN   C1820s
FOUNDER/LEADER: John Moggridge
50 houses built as a spin off from the commnity at Blackwood.
REF: *Villages of Vision*

PANT GLAS   1840
FOUNDER/ LEADER: John Moncas
'Unofficial' Owenite group farmed 1000 acre Welsh mountain estate under the name: The Community of United Friends.
GRID REF: SH473478?
REF: *Heavens Below*

ROBERT OWEN

MUSEUM

Museum telling the remarkable story of Owen's life from his birth in Newtown to international fame.
The Cross, Broad St.
Newtown. SY16 2BB
Tel: 01686 626345

GARNLWYD   1847-55
Early Christian Socialist community set up on 90 acres by the Leeds Redemption Society. 14 members attempted to set up a scheme based on a Christian version of Owenism & Fourierism. The society issued it's own paper the *Herald of Redemption*. Sent shoes and farm produce back to Leeds for sale in their own shop.
GRID REF: Nr Carmarthen
REF: *Heavens Below*

BETWS-Y-COED ARTISTS'
COLONY   C1850 - 1914
Artists' colony that grew up in the late 19th century after the area was first 'discovered' by the landscape painter David Cox. Large numbers of artists & tourists flocked to the area on the new railway. Liverpool artist Clarence Whaite was a central figure & although no Betws school of art formed the colony was part of the forming of a distinct Welsh artistic identity.
GRID REF: SH794566
REF: *The Betws-y-coed Artists' Colony.*

BARMOUTH   1874
FOUNDER/LEADER: John Ruskin.
An acre of rocky ground together with some cottages given to the St Georges Guild. One of the residents, Auguste Guyard, an exiled French social reformer, cultivated rare herbs and trees on the hostile soil, and went some way towards achieving Ruskin's vision of land restoration. A combination of legal difficulties and Ruskin's poor health left the scheme under the effective management of the donor rather than the Guild.
GRID REF: Location Unknown
REF: *Alt. Com 19th Cent Eng.*

CARDIFF SETTLEMENT   C1905
Welsh University Association for the furtherance of social work.
GRID REF: Grove Ho. Richmond Cres.
REF: *Listed in Labour Annual 1905*

CALDEY ISLAND
1906 -
Set up as an Anglican community, the reformed order of Benedictines, who converted to Catholism in 1913. The island was sold to Cisterian monks in 1928 and the original community moved to Prinknash.
GRID REF: SS142965
REF: Utopian England

SWANSEA GARDEN 'SUBURB' C1910
Following the Cheap Cottage Exhibition at Swansea in 1910 Raymond Unwin was asked to design a Garden Suburb for the town. The suburb was never built but the original exhibition cottages still stand.
GRID REF: Mayhill Swansea.
REF:www.swanseahistoryweb.org.uk/history/houses/gsuburb.htm

MERTHYR TAFF GARDEN VILLAGE
Small mining Garden Village.
GRID REF: ST980105
REF: O/S Map.

GORSEINON GARDEN VILLAGE
Garden Village development.
GRID REF: SS 599967
REF: O/S Map.

PENGAM GARDEN VILLAGE
Garden Suburb development carried out in co-operation with local mining union.
GRID REF: ST149171 Rhymney Valley
REF: A.Taylor

Friends Coalfield Distress committee clubhouse

HENGOED GARDEN VILLAGE
Garden Suburb development carried out in co-operation with local mining union.
GRID REF: ST115519 Rhymney Valley
REF: A.Taylor

ABERAMAN GARDEN VILLAGE
Garden Suburb development carried out in co-operatition with local mining union.
GRID REF: ST011008 Nr Aberdare
REF: A.Taylor

WREXHAM GARDEN VILLAGE C1917
Co-partnership Garden Village scheme sey up for local miners by the Welsh Garden Cities movement.
GRID REF: SJ366523
REF: The Arcitectural & Social History of Co-operative Living. L.F.Pearson

BARRY GARDEN VILLAGE C1917
Seaside Garden Village built on hillside overlooking Barry.
GRID REF: ST103668
REF: Garden Cities Upto Date.

SEALAND ESTATE
C1917
Garden Village development
GRID REF: SJ328692
Queensferry
REF: The Architectural & Social History of Co-operative Living. L.F.Pearson

MACHYNLLETH GARDEN VILLAGE C1920s
Very small Garden 'Village' on the edge of Machynlleth. A handful of house arrange around a small square.
GRID REF: SH754008
REF: Garden cities upto Date.

CAPEL-LE-FFIN 1924-28
FOUNDER/LEADER: Eric Gill
Bleak & remote semi-ruined monastery leased by Gill after he left Ditchling (Sussex). Here a small group of families lived a frugal lifestyle whilst Gill carried on his sculpture & typography work.
GRID REF: SO256317
REF: Eric Gill.McCarthy/Utopian England

MAES-YR-HAF SETTLEMENT HOUSE 1927 -
House affiliated to the Educational Settlements Ass. set up by the Friends Coalfield Distress committee. Set up 52 'occupational clubs' with 9000 members, some in self-build clubhouses where the WEA ran classes in philosphy, social ideals, country dancing, radio listening, music, drama & singing. In 1932 a holiday home by the sea was acquired.

Other settlement houses were set up

at Mythr Tydfill, Risca, Bargoed & Rhymney, Pontypool, Dowlais, Brynmawr, Aberdare and Ponty Pridd.
REF: *Our Unemployed:; Can the past teach the present?. Margaret.R.Pitt.*

BRYNMAWR 1928-39
Small Quaker 'family' house started by Peter & Lillian Scott to do relief work in the town. Initially provided food, clothes, boot repairs and ran soup kitchen. Grew to include several small industries - bootmakers, furniture makers and small co-operative mine. Ran a District Poultry Ass. and organised several International Voluntary Service camps. Expanded further and became the Subsistance Production Society when they took over the Rhydw & Hafod farms, establishing a model piggery & planting 20,000 trees.
GRID REF: SO192119 31 Alma st.
REF: *Our Unemployed.*

LLANDEGVETH 1936-39
30 men worked the Court Perrott dairy farm as part of the Eastern Valley Subsistance Production Society (SPS).
GRID REF: SO192119
REF: *Our Unemployed.*

BEILI GLAS 1936-39
Small SPS site. Reared pigs and grew veg. Also produced stone, chippings, bricks and joinery for building.
GRID REF: SO192119
REF: *Our Unemployed.*

TREVETHIN 1935-39
Fruit farm unit for the SPS. Six flats were also built by the SPS.
GRID REF: SO192119
REF: *Our Unemployed*

PONTYMOILE 1936-39
3 small sites run by the SPS growing fruit & veg under glass. Grew 3000lbs of tomatoes in 1935.
GRID REF: SO192119
REF: *Our Unemployed.*

GRIFFITHSTOWN 1936-39
16-acre SPS site producing chickens, pigs & veg.
GRID REF: SO192119
REF: *Our Unemployed.*

PONTNEWYDD 1936-39
Rural SPS site produced 'Welsh honey' poultry & veg. Also woodwork shop.
GRID REF: SO192119
REF: *Our Unemployed.*

CWMBRAN 1936-39
Most southerly SPS site produced poultry, hay & veg.
GRID REF: SO192119
REF: *Our Unemployed.*

CWMAVON 1936-39
Central multi-purpose workshop for the SPS housed in the old brewery. From here a workforce of 200 ran a bakery, knitting, tailoring and shoe-repairs. Also various handicrafts, weaving & cabinetmaking. A canteen was set up along with a barber's, a dentist's and a confectionary shop. Acted as a central distribution point for other SBS sites in the area.
GRID REF: SO192119
REF: Our unemployed.

THE ISLAND FARMERS C1940s
Wartime co-operative farm.
GRID REF: SN005402
REF The Island farmers

Subsistance Production Society workshop Cwnavon

SCOTLAND

Scotland had its own homegrown utopian tendency as well as importing various schemes from South of the Border. Many later projects being attempts to stem mass emigration.

ST KILDA   C1500 -1950

A small archipelago of islands lying 110 miles west of the Scottish mainland - the remotest inhabited place in the British Isles. Varying in population over the years from 80-140 the St Kildans lived in isolation in what amounted to an island republic governed by its own island parliament. Living off seabirds and Soay sheep they held all goods in common, knew nothing of money until the mid 1800s and operated a system of barter right up until the islands were evacuated in 1930. The St Kilda Islands are in the care and keeping of the National Trust for Scotland which organises annual working parties to keep the cottages, cleits and other structures in good repair. There is also a small military base on Hirta.
GRID REF: NF104991
REF: The Life & Death of St Kilda. . / St Kilda. and other Hebridean Outliers.

BUCHAN HA   1784-1787

FOUNDER/LEADER: Elspeth Buchan Scottish prophetess, Elspeth Buchan and her followers the Buchanites moved to New Cample Farm in Nithsdale, Dumfrieshire after being hounded out of Irvine. They lived temporarily in an old barn whilst they built

NEW LANARK

WORLD HERITAGE VILLAGE

Surrounded by beautifull native woodland and close to the Falls of Clyde, the 200 year old cotton mill village of New Lanark has been saved for future generations as a living community and lasting monument to Robert Owen, mill owner and social pioneer.

But if you thought New Lanark was just history - think again! The new ride in the Visitor Centre, the `New Millennium Experience' will give you a glimpse of our future too! Meet Harmony, your guide from the future, and enjoy a magical journey across the frontiers of time. Amazing special efects and dazzling illusions bring the past - and the future - to life!

Open Daily: 11am to 5pm. all year. (except 25 Dec / 1 Jan)
Tel: 01555 661345
Website: **www.newlanark.org**

a rough community house known as 'Buchan Ha'. Here they suffered further persecution, but managed to stay on growing to 60 members until local magistrates forced them out.
GRID REF: Nithsdale
REF: *The Second Coming. JFC Harrison.*

New Lanark   1785 -
FOUNDER / LEADER: David Dale / Robert Owen.
Extensive cotton mill and tenement complex below the Clyde Falls, started by David Dale and made famous by the work of Robert Owen. After Owen sold his interest in 1828 the mills were run by the Walkers, a Quaker family, and later by the Gourock Ropework Company, who continued to operate the mills until the 1960s. Major restoration work has turned the site into a major tourist attraction.
GRID REF: NS880425
REF: *Historic New Lanark /Co-opera tion & Owenite Socialist Communities.*
www.robert-owen.com

Auchengibbert Farm 1787- 92
FOUNDER/LEADER: Elspeth Buchan
A wild moorland farm in the parish of Urr, Kirkcudbrightshire where the Buchanites moved after 'Buchan Ha'. Here they ran their own farm, made spinning wheels and span yarn for local factories. After Mrs Buchan death in 1791 the community broke up with some emigrating to America. 14 remaining members lived until 1808 at Larghill and then at Crocketford, the last Buchanite dying there in 1846.
GRID REF: Location Unknown
REF: *The Second Coming. Harrison.*

Catrine Mills   1787 - 1801
FOUNDER / LEADER: David Dale
Cotton mills, workers' housing and school built by David Dale in partnership with Richard Arkwright. Dale was a philanthropic Glasgow business man who set up the mills at New Lanark and whose daughter married Robert Owen. He also had interests in mills at Blantyre, Newton Stewart, Rothesay and Spinningdale.
GRID REF: NS511263
REF: *Historic New Lanark*

Tobermory   1788-1844
Settlement set up by the British Fisheries Society consisting of store house, customs-house and 2 streets of houses with large gardens and access to pasture and peat. By 1793 there were 32 settlers. Prospered later when Caledonian Canal opened. Sold 1844.
GRID REF: NM506554
REF: *British Fisheries Society 1786-1893.*

Ullapool   1788
Second British Fisheries Society settlement with storehouses, net drying sheds, school, 'Red Herring House', shops, inn, pier & breakwater along with 40 'thatched huts' each with half acre plots & grazing rights. Thomas Telford acted as surveyor for the society. By 1808 population reached 669.
GRID REF: NH128942
REF: *British Fisheries Society 1786-1893.*

Lochbay   1788-1830
British Fisheries Society settlement similar to Tobermory. More fertile land allowed settlers to live entirely from the land undermining attempt to set up fishery. Sold in 1830s
GRID REF: Location unknown
REF: *British Fisheries Society 1786-1893.*

Pultneytown   1803-1892
Most successful of the Brithish Fisheries Society settlements built on 390 acres next to the village of Wick. Planned by Thomas Telford. Laid out to follow contours of the land. Development was a rapid success with a resident population of 2000 by 1830 swollen to 7000 in the fishing season. Sold in 1892.
GRID REF: ND367503
REF : *British Fisheries Society 1786-1893.*

The Edinburgh Practical Society.   1822
Owenite society that claimed 500 families as members - ran its own co-operative store to raise funds to set up a community. Some evidence that some families lived communally in Edinburgh. Members went on to be active at the Orbiston community.
GRID REF: Location Unknown
REF: *Co-operation & Owenite Socialist Communities.*

Motherwell   1820's
Site proposed by the British and Foreign Philanthropic Society for the first Owenite Community. Robert Owen bought 600 acres of land, owned by Hamilton of Dalzell for the community. After 3 years of inactivity the scheme was overtaken by plans for the Orbiston Community nearby.
GRID REF: Location Unknown
REF: *Heavens Below*

Leather Workers Community
1820's

FOUNDER/LEADER: Abram Combe

Shortlived community experiment set up in Combe's Edinburgh Tanyard - the leather workers lived communally and operated a profit sharing scheme.

GRID REF: Location Unknown

REF: Co-operation & Owenite Socialist Communities.

Orbiston
1825 - 27

FOUNDER/LEADER: Abram Combe A.J. Hamilton

290 members of the community nicknamed 'Babylon' worked as weavers, blacksmiths, joiners, cabinet makers, wheelwrights, printers, painters, shoemakers, tailors, seamstresses and harness-makers. They ran a successful ironfoundery on the 291 acre site that included a 5 storey main communal building, school, apartments & communal dining facilities. 75 acres of the land was cultivated with vegetable garden & orchard. The land being manured with waste from the community sewage system. The community folded after disputes about levels of communality and the death of Abram Combe. The site was bought by Mrs Douglas, a local landowner who ordered all trace of the community to be removed. A housing estate now covers part of the site and the community is remembered in street names such as Babylon Rd., Community Rd., Hamilcombe Rd. & Register Avenue.

GRID REF: NS728530

REF: Co-operation & Owenite Socialist Communities / Adventures in Socialism

Colinsburgh Building Club
1826

Six blocks of 8 flats built as a mutual aid self-build scheme.

GRID REF: NO478433

REF: Building Communities.

Edinburgh Co-operative Building Co Ltd
1861 - 1945

Between 1861 & 1883 the co-operative built a series of model housing schemes on various sites throughout the city. Became ordinary building contractors in 1945.

GRID REF: Edinburgh.

REF: Colonies of Stockbridge. R.J Pipes.

Stirling Model Village
1880s

FOUNDER/LEADER : John Christie.

Proposed model village to have comprised of workers' cottages with land attached, for rent or sale, arranged around a square with a fountain and public hall.

REF: The Homesteads: Stirlings Garden Suburb.

Brig O'Turk Artists Colony
C1880

Summer colony for the 'Glasgow Boys'.

GRID REF: NN737066

REF: The Good & Simple Life

Cockburnspath Artists Colony
C1883-86

Coastal artists colony of the 'Glasgow Boys'. Edward Walton, James Guthrie, Joseph Crowhall & Arthur Melville. Were resident from 1883-6 afterwards returning during the summer months - could be seen with their easels pitched anywhere painting under umbrellas. Artists were drawn to the area right up to the 1960s.

GRID REF: NT776710

REF: Cockburnspath:A history of a People & a Place. S.Smith.Dunglass Mill Press 1999

Kirkcudbright Artists Colony
C1880s

Artists' colony set up under the influence of George Henry & E.A. Hornel from Glasgow School of Art. The colony features in the Dorothy Sayers Book *Five Red Herrings.*

GRID REF: NX687510

REF: The Good and Smple Life

Toynbee House
C1905

Glasgow University Settlement .

GRID REF: Location Unknown

REF: Listed in Labour Annual 1905

Queen Margaret's Settlement House
C1905

Womens University Settlement .

GRID REF: 75 Elliot St Anderston

REF: Listed in Labour Annual 1905

Vatersay
1907

Crofts set up after land raid by men from Barra. Government bought island at an exhorbitant price from Lady Cathcart to regularise the situation.

GRID REF: Off Barra

REF: Fit For Heroes? L.Leneman

Stirling Homesteads
1909-75

Small Homesteading scheme that grew out of the Garden City and Scottish Arts & Crafts movements. 10 Arts & Crafts style houses were built on the Stirling Castle estate - making them the only utopian experiment to be set up on Crown property. The homesteaders also worked smallholdings. The community continued as a co-partnership housing society until the early 1970s when the Crown made moves to end the experiment. A skeleton association still exists for some of the remaining homesteaders with the rest of the properties being sold off as they became vacant.

GRID REF: NS779942 Stirling
REF: The Homesteads: Stirlings Garden Suburb.

WESTERTON GARDEN SUBURB
1910 - 1970s

Tenants Co-partnership scheme consisting of 84 houses on Westerton Farm. WW1 interupted the scheme after only a third of the planned development was built. Went into voluntary liquidation in 197s and sold houses to sitting tenants.

GRID REF: NW edge of Glasgow.
REF: A Garden Suburb for Glasgow: The Story of Westerton. M.Whitelaw 1992

TIRREE   C1913 /18

Series of crofting Land Settlement schemes under the 1911 Smallholdings Act. on land owned by the Duke of Argyll, one of the few landowners sympathetic to the schemes. Later following a land raid a further scheme was set up for ex-servicemen.

GRID REF: Tirree
REF: Fit For Heroes? L.Leneman

SHETLAND   1914 /18

Series of crofting Land Settlement schemes creating new and enlarging existing holdings.

REF: Fit For Heroes? L.Leneman

GRETNA GARDEN VILLAGE
C1915-19

Estate built on modified Garden Suburb lines by the government for First World War munitions workers Estate was designed by Raymond Unwin & Courtenay Crickner and included a laundry, central kitchen, dentist's, post office, cinema, institute and school. The estate was alongside a large area of temporary accommodation 'huts', housing some 10,000 workers. The estate was used as a model for the 'Homes Fit for Heroes' programme after the war.

GRID REF:
REF: Homes Fit for Heroes. M.Swenarton

ROSYTH 'GARDEN CITY'   1916 -

Scheme on Admiralty land for workers at Rosyth Docks and on the Forth Bridge. Original plan for 3000 houses cut back by Admiralty. Some 150 houses built with YMCA, institute and bowling green by The Scottish Labour Housing Association.

GRID REF: NT103826
REF: The Story of Rosyth. 1982

ARABELLA FARM   1918

Land Settlement scheme under the Small Holdings Colonies Act. The 643-acre farm was split into 21 6 - 50acre holdings with central farm used as demonstration & training centre.

GRID REF: NG Easter Ross
REF: Fit For Heroes? L.Leneman

SOUTH UIST   1918 - 24

A number of crofting Land Settlement schemes were established after land raids despite the opposition of the owner of the island, Lady Cathcart.

GRID REF: NG South Uist
REF: Fit For Heroes? L.Leneman

LEWIS / HARRIS   1918 - 25

FOUNDER/ LEADER : W.H.Lever

Islands bought by W.H.Lever soap magnate and founder of Port Sunlight. Lewis was to be the 'Port Sunlight of Fishing'. Lever bought 350 British high street fish shops as outlets for the scheme. The Lewis project failed, but the fish distribution company became MacFisheries.

GRID REF: NG013864
REF: Lord of the Isles. N.Niclson 1960.

SHINNESS   1919

Croft Land Settlement scheme on the 16,000-acre farm of Shinness offered to the Board of Agriculture by the Duke of Sutherland. Holders ran the Shinness Sheep Stock Club Co-operative Soc. Houses on the scheme suffered from poor construction, but were not renovated till after WW2.

GRID REF: Shinness
REF: Fit For Heroes? L.Leneman

WEST WATTEN   1919

Crofting Land Settlement scheme.

GRID REF: Caithness
REF: Fit For Heroes? L.Leneman

EOLIGARRY   1919

Crofting land settlement scheme set up following threats of land raids.

GRID REF: NG Barra
REF: Fit For Heroes? L.Leneman

'THE PROMISED LAND' 1920/33

With flags flying and pipes playing ex-servicemen drove their stock on to farmland 'promised' to them as small-holdings by the Duke of Sutherland in protest at government inaction. They were persuaded to leave pending negotiations with the owner. 13 yrs later 13 holdings were created.
GRID REF: NG Kirkton
REF: Fit For Heroes? L.Leneman

ORMSAIGMORE 1921

Crofting Land Settlement scheme.
GRID REF: NG Ardnamurchan
REF: Fit For Heroes? L.Leneman

NORTH UIST 1921

Crofting Land Settlement schemes set up farms of Balranald and Paiblesgarry following land raids.
GRID REF: North Uist
REF: Fit For Heroes? L.Leneman

SUNART 1922

50,000-acre estate bought by the Board of Agriculture for smallholdings. Much of it was open moor & mountain and only a few holdings were set up.
GRID REF: Argyll
REF: Fit For Heroes? L.Leneman

KEOLDALE 1922

43 crofts established after long negoitiation and threats of land raids. Holders set up a Club-Stock Co-operative Society.
GRID REF: NG Keoldale
REF: Fit For Heroes? L.Leneman

STRATHERRICK 1922

Small Land Settlement scheme
GRID REF: NG Dell Farm
REF: Fit For Heroes? L.Leneman

BEOLARY 1924

Forestry commission farm bought for Land Settlement scheme by Board of Agriculture, 9 holdings established.
GRID REF: NG Glanelg Parish
REF: Fit For Heroes? L.Leneman

STRATHNAVER 1927

Croft Land Settlement scheme on the farm of Rhifial in an area previously notorious for its land clearances.
GRID REF: NG Strathnaver
REF: Fit For Heroes? L.Leneman

SCIBERCROSS 1930

Crofting Land Settlement scheme.
GRID REF: NG Scibercross
REF: Fit For Heroes? L.Leneman

'CAMPHILL HOUSE' 1939 -

Series of residential communites set up by Karl König and a small group of Austrian refugees. First at Kirkton House, a 25 acre estate nr. Insch. Then in the larger Camphill House on Royal Deeside with 170 acres. Murtle House and 35 acres were added in 1942 as the scheme expanded. They were the only educational provision for the mentally handicapped at the time and were supported by the Macmillan family. The Camphill Movement went on to found communities worldwide.
GRID REF: Nr Aberdeen
REF: Candle on the Hill: Images of Camphill Life. C.Pietzner. Floris Books.

IRELAND

Irish Radical history is significantly different from the rest of the British Isles being largely set in opposition to English occupation. I have included all information I could find - my experience of research elsewhere would point to there being other 'undiscovered' Irish utopian experiments.

BALLYTORE 1707 -

Kildare
Quaker settlement with meeting house, school, dispensary & savings bank alongside 'neat' cottages. Was set on fire by insurgents in 1798.
REF: Villages of Vision

GRACEHILL 1746 -

Antrim
FOUNDER/LEADER: B.Latrobe
Moravian settlement along lines of those in England with brothers & sisters choir houses, chapel, school and inn all set around a central square.
REF: Villages of Vision

NEW GENEVA 1782

Ambitious colonisation scheme by powerful men in London & Dublin. Was to have been modelled on the Swiss town of Geneva where middle-class liberals had overthrown the aristocratic rulers on the city council. Power had been restored by the intervention of foreign armies and the liberals were looking for a refuge. The Duke of Leinster offered them 2,000 acres to establish their protestant

colony and the English parliament granted £50,000 towards the scheme. Plans were put forward for a circular fortified town, but after the 1798 uprisings they were abandoned.
REF: *Villages of Vision*

STRATFORD-ON-SLANEY
1785-1846
FOUNDER/LEADER: Henry Stratford Prominent in the planning of New Geneva Henry Stratford set up a model village based on a combination of textiles and agriculture. Was settled and developed by Presbyterians from Paisley. At its height had 1,000 workers housing, church, chapel, benefit society and library. Was ruined by a combination of economic, political & religious disruption.
REF: *Villages of Vision*

BALLINDERRY   1825?
Nr Lisburn
Early co-operative land experiment.
REF: *Heavens Below*

PORTLAW   1825
Waterford
Quaker model industrial village built up around Malcolmson's cotton mills.
REF: *Villages of Vision*

CORK CO-OPERATIVE COMMUNITY   1814 - 1833
FOUNDER/LEADER:W.Thompson
Thompson was an 'improving' landlord He spent much of his time on his estate at Glandore, gave leases on generous terms to tenants, and instituted improved methods of cultivation. He laid out a model cottage farm, comprising a one-acre garden, and four acres devoted to the scientific rotation of crops and spade cultivation. This he let to "a peasant of good character " as an example to others. He also erected a school, where chiidren were taught spade cultivation `on the latest plan' and were given `all the produce they could grow.' He investigated the possibilities of producing silk and linen, and laid plans for establishing a deep-sea fishery near Glandore. Influenced by his involvement with the Owenite co-operative movement, of which he became leader when Owen was away in America, Thompson wrote a number of early socialist & feminist books including: *Practical Directions for the Speedy and Economical Establishment of Communities, on the Principle.s of Mutual Co-operation, United Possessions and Equality of Exertions and of the Means of Enjoyments.* He was a central figure in the Owenite attempts to set up communities and offered his estate in Ireland as a site for an Owenite community. When the Owenites showed no interest in his offer he himself began work at the 'townland' at Carhoogariff, where he built a 100ft high round tower for his own residence and as centre of operations. He directed the building of a row of cottages that was probably to form one side of the co-operative community, but Thompson died in 1833 before the community could be completed. He left a large legacy to the co-operative movement for the formation of communities - the will was contested by his heirs who tried to argue that anyone who wanted to set up co-operative communities must be insane. After a 25yr long legal process in which most of the estate was spent on lawyers' fees the court found in favour of the family.
REF: *William Thompson - Pioneer Socialist.R.Pankhurst.Pluto Press.1991*

ACHILL ISLAND   1830s
Mayo
FOUNDER/LEADER: Rev.Nangle
Failed attempt to convert Catholics by estabishing a model settlement.
REF: *Villages of Vision*

RAHALINE AGRICULTURAL & MANUFACTURINGASS.   1831
Co Clare
FOUNDER/LEADER: J.Vandeleur / E.T.Craig.
Owenite-inspired community set up by landower John Vandeleur after disturbances on his estate, with E.T. Craig the editor of the *Lancashire co-operator* as manager. A successful co-operative agricultural community was established on the 600 acre estate. Cottages and communal facilities were built, a school and library established. The community was run by an elected committee who introduced a labour credit system. Weaving was introduced and they brought in the first reaping machine to be used in Ireland. The community was wound up after 2 yrs existence when Vandeleur lost his estate in a bet.
REF: *Robert Owen & the Owenites in Britain & America / Co-operation & Owenite Socialist Communities.*

AGRICULTURAL COMMUNITY
C1800s Co Galway.
FOUNDER/LEADER: Lord Wallscott
Scheme similar to the Owenite community at Ralahine on the Wallscott Estate.
REF: *Labour in Irish History. James Connolly. Bookmarks 1987.*

BESSBROOK
1846
Antrim
FOUNDER/LEADER: J.G.Richardson
Two large squares with cottages & gardens set up by Quaker textile manufacturer with education and leisure facilities.
REF: *Villages of Vision*

COMMUNAL HOUSE
C1800s?
Dublin
Communal house run by Quakers at Ushers Quay mentioned by James Connolly in his history of Irish labour.
REF: *Labour in Irish History. James Connolly. Bookmarks 1987.*

THE SOCIETY OF WHITE FRIENDS
C1847
Dublin
Break-away Quakers, Joshua Jacob & Abigail Beale, set up their own sect numbering some 30 members who wore 'white Russia duck trousers' and plain leather shoes. On the estate of Lord Kilworden they lived by weaving and farming, living on a simple vegetarian diet whilst trying to establish 'a kind of Utopian Republic'.
REF: *Heavens Below p202*

'SMALL' COMMUNITY
C1800s?
Nr Dublin
'Small' community mentioned by James Connolly in his history of Irish labour. 9 miles from Dublin on 30 acres of land. Made and sold Jaunty cars, supported a priest and a school for 300.
REF: *Labour in Irish History. James Connolly. Bookmarks 1987.*

HAROLD CROSS
1850s
Dublin
Model workers cottages built by Quaker textile firm Pim.
REF: *The Emergence of Irish Town Planning 1880-1920. Turoe Press 1985.*

COOLE PARK
1897-1914
Nr Gort
Country house 'salon' run by Lady Augusta Gregory - "the woman behind the Irish Renaissance." The likes of W.B.Yeats, G.B. Shaw, J.M.Synge & Sean O'Casey all gathered at Coole.
REF: *Lady Gregory. M.L.Kohfeldt.*

THE IRISH SETTLEMENT SOCIETY
1892
London
London-based proposal to send 'settlers' to Ireland. The society "Sees that the troubles of Ireland arise from the unhealthy state of her social order as shown by the lack of men and women of culture and sympathy, and the mutual interchange of help and brotherhood which is essential to the true life of the nation. Among other things it proposes to organise and knit together in bands of union all who are living and working in Ireland, to help her people and encourage her industries and to extend the work by planting fresh settlers (mainly by twos) in various chosen districts..... to found clubs for men & women, to give addresses on agriculture, beekeeping, poultry, Hygiene etc and to encourage the visits of tourists."
GRID REF: Hon.sec. H.Orswood Anderton. 57 Clapham Common NE
REF: *Seed Time Jan 1892*

ALEXANDRA GUILD
1898
Dublin
Tenement scheme inspired by the work of Octavia Hill in London. Organised educational activities and holidays for children.
REF: *The Emergence of Irish Town Planning 1880-1920. Turoe Press 1985.*

IVEAGH HOUSE
1905 -
Dublin
5 storey lodging house for single men. 508 'cubicles' with communal dining room, smoking room & reading room. The scheme was extended 1912-15 with the addition of a recreation hall or "play centre" - inc. People's Palace with classrooms, gym & assembly hall.
REF: *The Emergence of Irish Town Planning 1880-1920. Turoe Press 1985.*

MARINO GARDEN VILLAGE
Dublin
C1916
1100 houses around central allotment area based on plan by Patrick Geddes and Raymond Unwin.
REF: *The Emergence of Irish Town Planning 1880-1920. Turoe Press 1985.*

INTERNATIONAL COMMUNITIES

The communities appearing in this section were either set up by British emigrants, or inspired by individuals or movements from the British Isles.

LEIDEN.   1609 - 1620
Holland

Temporary home of the Scrooby Separatists. Poverty and impending war made them plan to sail to Virginia, after considering South America & New Amsterdam.

REF: www.plimoth.org/library/holland.htm

JACOBOPOLIS   1622 - 24
USA

Henry Jacob left for the American Colonies, and established his new religious community of Jacobopolis in Virginia. Jacob died there in 1624.

REF: Website

MENNONITE COLONY   1663
Delaware, USA

FOUNDER/LEADER: P.C. Plockhoy

Peter Cornelius Plockhoy had come to England during the years of the Commonwealth and published a pamphlet: *A Way Propounded to make the Poor in These and Other Nations Happy, by Bringing Together Suitable and Well Qualifed People unto One Household Government, or Little-Common-Wealth.* Finding no takers

for his scheme he returned to Holland and obtained a contract to establish a colony of Mennonites in New Netherlands. The settlement was established at what is now Lewes, Delaware. However in 1664 the English conquered New Netherlands and in the process plundered "what belonged to the Quaking Society of Plockhoy to a very naile."

REF: Backwoods Utopias. A. Bestor

RADNOR QUAKER SETTLEMENT
C1680 USA

FOUNDER/LEADER: Richard Davies

Richard Davies, a hatter & 'Publick Friend' from Welshpool bought 5000 acres of the 'Welsh Tract' in Pennsylvania, divided it into smaller lots and sold it to the Welsh Quakers. The land produced abundant crops compared to Wales - a meeting house was built in 1717 and the local town was named Radnor.

REF:Friends in Radnorshire. MacPherson Verzon Books.

THE PHILADELPHIANS 1697-1706
Germany

FOUNDER/LEADER: Eva von Buttlar

Community inspired by the ideas of the English mystics Jane Leade and John Pordage. Eva and two of her adherents claimed to be the representatives of the earthly triad, Joseph, Mary, and Jesus. Furthermore, Eva herself professed to be the second Eve as Jesus Himself was the second Adam. In her society there was to be a complete community of goods, and, in addition to this, unlimited sexual inter-

course between its members.

REF: The Behmenists and the Philadelphians. Nils Thune .Uspala, 1948

THE SHAKERS   1774 - present
USA

FOUNDER/LEADER:Mother Ann Lee

First English-speaking sect to establish communal colonies in America. Local converts quickly outnumbered the original immigrants and a network of 18 communities was established. After Mother Ann Lee's death in 1784, she was succeeded as head of the sect by James Whittaker, one of her original English followers. The Shakers were the most successful communal sect in the US eventually going into decline due to their adherence to celibacy.

REF: Backwoods Utopias. A. Bestor

MORAVIAN SETTLEMENT   1740?
Savannah, Georgia USA

Moravian group visited by John Wesley.

REF: The Moravian Church in England 1728-1760. C.Podmore.

PITCAIRN ISLAND   1790 - present
South Pacific

FOUNDER/LEADER:F. Christian.

Final destination of the mutineers from the Bounty. Here over the years an island commonwealth developed based on a combination of seafaring traditions, Tahitian native culture and Seventh Day Adventism.

REF: Life & Death in Eden.Trevor Lummis. Victor Gollancz 1999

CAMBORD CASTLE   Late 1700s
France
FOUNDER/LEADER Robert Grubb/ Jean Marsillac.
Quaker-backed application made to establish an industrial, commercial and artistic community, with 80 to 100 workshops. The French Interior Minister was sympathetic. Outbreak of war made the scheme impossible.
REF: *Heavens Below*

YVERDON   C1800 - 1827
Switzerland
FOUNDER/LEADER: J.H.Pestalozzi. Highly-influential residential 'Free School' run by Swiss educator Heinrich Pestalozzi. The child-centred educational philosophy that he developed, underpins much of the English education system. The mystic, James Pierrepont Greaves taught for a while here and Robert Owen visited. Between them they introduced Pestalozzian ideas to England.
REF: www3.mistral.co.uk/dec/background.htm

TRISTAN DA CUNHA 1816-present
South Atlantic island republic set up after troops were stationed on the island during the Napoleonic wars.
REF: *Crisis in Utopia. P. Munch.*

NEW HARMONY   1824-27
Pennsylvania, USA
FOUNDER/LEADER: Robert Owen
Former colony of the German Rappite sect acquired by Owen for his grand experiment in founding the new moral world. Consisted of an entire small town and some 20,000 acres of surrounding land. Fell apart due to splits in the membership and financial instability. Is now a National Historic Landmark.
REF: *The Life & Ideas of Robert Owen /Backwoods Utopias*

MACLURIA / COMMUNITY No 2
1826 Pennsylvania, USA
A Methodist splinter group from New Harmony who objected to Owen's religious views. They set up on 1300 acres of uncleared land two miles from New Harmony. 80 to 150 people lived in 9 log cabins. Collapsed due to internal disagreements.
REF: *Backwood Utopias*

FEIBA-PEVELI / COMMUNITY No 3
1826-28
Pennsylvania, USA
A second splinter from New Harmony. Owen granted the group of English farmers 1400 acres of the best land. The name, Feiba-Peveli, came from a system devised by the architect, Stedman Whitwell, in which latitude and longitude were translated into letters, and pronunciation left to take care of itself. They built timber framed houses & log cabins with the luxury novelty of glass windows. The community made up of experienced farmers outlived New Harmony with the land quietly passing into individual ownership some years later.
REF: *Backwoods Utopias*

YELLOW SPRINGS.   1825
Greene County, Ohio, USA
75 to 100 families were involved in an attempt to emulate New Harmony, including professional and business men as well as farmers and labourers. The community fell apart after dissension caused it to split into factions.
REF: *Robert Owen & the Owenites in Britain & America.*

NASHOBA   1825-30
Tennessee, USA
FOUNDER/LEADER: Fanny Wright
Frances Wright, a young Scottish radical, purchased Nashoba, a 2000-acre plantation for a community of negro slaves. The aim was to buy or persuade benevolent masters to donate slaves who would be able to purchase their emancipation and at the same time prepare themselves for freedom by education. Several negro families were acquired by gift and purchase. After a visit to New Harmony Fanny became convinced of the necessity of religious and sexual emancipation. Nashoba then became an experimental, racially integrated community based on Owenite doctrines.
REF: *Eve & The New Jerusalem /Robert Owen & the Owenites in Britian & America. / Backwoods Utopias*

FRANKLIN COMMUNITY   1826
Haverstraw, Rockland County, USA
A group of 80 artisans, farmers and intellectuals set up on a 120 acre farm. The leaders were free-thinkers and deists: George Houston who had been jailed in England for publishing blasphemy, Abner Kneeland and Henry A. Fay - shortly to be joined by Robert Jennings from New Harmony. The community lasted for 5 months, ending amidst charges of dishonesty against

the managers.

REF: *Robert Owen & the Owenites in Britain & America.*

BLUE SPRING 1826 - 27

Nr Bloomington, Indiana, USA
Inspired by Robert Owen 27 members and their families lived on 325 acres in a group of log houses built in the form of a square, together with stores, granary and school.

REF: *Robert Owen & the Owenites in Britain & America.*

THE FRIENDLY ASSOCIATION FOR MUTUAL INTERESTS
1826 - 29

Kendal (now Massillon), Ohio, USA.
A 2000 acre estate settled by 150 local farmers, mechanics & woollen mill workers in an attempt to emulate Owen's community at New Harmony. The experiment was quietly abandoned after the members came to the conclusion that communitarian life did not benefit them substantially more than an individualised lifestyle.

REF: *Robert Owen & the Owenites in Britain & America.*

MAXWELL OWENITE COLONY
1827-8 Canada

FOUNDER/LEADER: Henry Jones
After the collapse of the Orbiston Community a supporter, retired naval officer Henry Jones, gathered a party of Scottish emigrants and sailed for Ontario where they established a new Owenite community.

REF: *The Toon O'Maxwell - an Owenite Settlement in Lambton City, Ontario. Ontario Hist. Soc. Papers & Records XII (1914) 5-12*

CAMPBELLITES C1827

Kirtland, Ohio, USA

FOUNDER/LEADER:Rev.A.Campbell
The Disciples of Christ or the Campbellites were founded by Scottish immigrant Alexander Campbell. They believed in the imminence of the second coming of Christ and lived communally holding all things in common. Many of the sect were converted to Mormonism and it was from the Campbellites that Mormon communalism stems.

REF: *The Second Coming. J.F.C. Harrison.*

THE 'PLAN' IN MEXICO 1828

FOUNDER/LEADER: Robert Owen
Following the collapse of New Harmony Owen tried to negotiate with the Mexican government for the concession of a territory 150 miles wide stretching from the Gulf of Mexico to the Pacific on which to carry out his 'Plan' for a New Moral World. Nothing came of the plan.

REF: *Robert Owen & the Owenites in Britain & America.*

MORRISANIA C1830s

New York, USA
English Owenite B.J.Timms was involved in a number of schemes in New York, the Sylvania Phalanx, a Co-operative Bakery and finally Morrisania - "the first co-operative village," a co-operative land-buying scheme.

REF: *The History of Co-operation.*

MANCHESTER & SALFORD COMMUNITY COMPANY 1834

Owenite society sent 23 members to Cincinnati in April 1834 to purchase land for a community.

REF: *Co-operation & Owenite Socialist Communities.*

FRUITLANDS 1843-44

Nr Harvard, USA

FOUNDER/LEADER:C.Lane & A.B.Alcott
Short-lived community set up on 90 acre farm by Charles Lane from the Ham Concorduim.

REF: *Search for a New Eden*

POTTERSVILLE C1844

Wisconsin, USA
Community set up by the Potters Union. - see Staffordshire for details.

REF: *The Staffordshire Potter. H. Owen*

ARTISTIC SISTERHOOD C1850

Munich
'Associated Home' set up by 3 English women artists, Anna Marie Howitt, Barbara Bodicha & Jane Bortha. They lived communally and shared studio space and pledged to found a "beautiful sisterhood in Art."

REF: *Artistic Brotherhoods in the Nineteenth Century.*

LA MAISON DES POETES
C1852

Pyrenees, France
Free-love commune founded by Léonone Labilliére who had visited both the Abode of Love & Oniedia communities and found them too repressive & patriarchal. Was an open house for impoverished artists, poets & musicians. Miss Esther Hersey sought sanctuary from the Abode of

Love here. Also ran a 'branch' in Paris.
REF: *The Temple of Love.*

ABRAMTSEVO   C1877 - 1890s
Russia
Artists' colony on the Mamonotov estate, influenced by the ideas of the English Arts & Crafts movement.
REF: *The Good & Simple Life.*

FONTAINEBLEAU   C1840 - 1900
France
The Fontainebleau Forest was popular with artists who formed a number of colonies notably at Barbizon & Grez. The Scottish author R.L.Stevenson was resident for a number of years.
REF: *The Good & Simple Life.*

BROCTON   1861
Lake Eyrie, USA.
FOUNDER/LEADER: T.L. Harris
After a lecture tour of Britain Harris gathered a group of followers in Scotland and formed the Brotherhood of the New Life. He established a community at Brocton on a 75 acre farm where his most high profile convert was the English MP L. Oliphant.
REF: *Heavens Below / Mdme. Blavatsky's Baboon.*

HAIFA   1882-88
Palestine
FOUNDER/LEADER L. Oliphant.
Community from where Laurence Oliphant promoted the colonisation of Palestine and his own blend of Islam & Christianity.
REF: *Mdm. Blavatsky's Baboon*

ADYAR   1882 -
Madras. India
FOUNDER/LEADER: H.P. Blavatsky
Theosophist headquarters established on a large estate bought for the society by a well-wisher at the mouth of the Adyar river. Here in a Mediterranean climate first Mdme. Blavastsky then Annie Besant presided. A large library of Buddhist texts was built up by Col. Olcott.
REF: *Mdme Blavatsky's Baboon/Annie Besant. A.Taylor*

LEVERVILLE   C1911
Belgian Congo / Zaire
Model settlements built for native workers on Lever Brothers Plantations.
REF: *Port Sunlight Guide*

NEW AUSTRALIA / LOMA ROUGA & COSME COLONY
1892-1905 Paraguay
FOUNDER/LEADER: William Lane
3 colonies set up after would-be settlers had sailed to South America from Australia on the Royal Tar. Offered free land and tax exemption by the Paraguay government, they first set up New Australia, building a series of houses and a large hall in clearings in the forest. They also built a 'cattle ring' for 2500 head of cattle. A second boatload the following year established Loma Rouga. Cosme colony was founded in 1894 as a series of small villages on a grassy plain. In 1897 five parties of new recruits arrived from England bringing numbers up to about 120. All the colonies struggled to sur-

vive and eventually the Paraguay government divided the communities into individual holdings.
REF: *Heavens Below*

RUSKIN   1894-1899
Yellow Creek, Tennessee, USA
FOUNDER/LEADER: J.A. Wayland
Small town based on the ideas of John Ruskin as put forward in the socialist paper The Coming Nation. Growing to 250 members the town had 75 buildings on 1800 acres inc: school, bakery, cafe, laundry, and workshops. It had a prosperous economy based on agriculture and cottage industry. The "Ruskin Rose" was propagated here.
REF: *Designing Utopia. M.H.Lang.*

THE ROYCROFTERS   1894-1938
East Aurora, nr Buffalo, USA
FOUNDER/LEADER: Elbert Hubbard
Following a visit to William Morris's workshops & press in England, Hubbard set up an idealised 'mediaeval manor' and workers' community producing 'mission' furniture, leather & metalwork on a system akin to the Guild & School of Handicrafts. The Roycrofters produced a magazine called *The Philistine* which brought a much simplified version of the Arts & Crafts philosophy to a wide American audience. They ran a hotel the Roycroft Inn whose motto was - Never mind, people will talk anyway.
REF: *Utopian Craftsmen.L.Lambourne*

SHANTI KUNJ - ABODE OF PEACE 1896 - Benares, India
FOUNDER/LEADER: Annie Besant
Small estate bought as the headquarters of the independent Indian section of the Theosophists. It consisted of a number of small houses, a meeting hall, offices, a printing press and a pharmacy. From here Annie Besant involved herself in the campaign for Indian independence.
REF: Annie Besant. A.Taylor

COGSLEA 1897-1961
West Mt., Airy, Philadelphia, USA
FOUNDER/LEADER: Violet Oakley
Community of women artists supported by the Woodward family who were developing the nearby Garden Suburb of Chestnut Hill. Inspired by a romantic version of the Arts & Crafts aesthetic they produced paintings, murals and stained glass in beautiful local stone houses. The community survived until the members died.
REF: Designing Utopia. M.H.Lang.

POINT LOMA 1897-1942
California, USA
FOUNDER/LEADER: K.Tingley
Community established on 500 acres when the American Theosophical Society split from the European branch after the death of Madame Blavatsky. The community built large domed 'temples' in which grand theatrical pageants were enacted under a regime known as Raga Yoga. They also carried out research into the cultivation of sub-tropical fruit and implemented an extensive afforestation programme planting a 40 acre forest on the Pacific coast.
REF: California Utopia. E.A. Greenwalt

THE UNITED CRAFTS 1898-1915
Syracuse, USA
FOUNDER/LEADER: Gustav Stickley
Initially inspired by the simplicity of Shaker furniture Gustav Stickley set up the United Crafts after a visit to Britain were he met C.F.A. Voysey and other Arts & Crafts Designers. The workshops were set up on Guild lines with a profit-sharing scheme for employees. Stickley did not share the antipathy to machines of his British counterparts and designed 'democratic' furniture for ordinary people that was sold mail order. The company also produced the highly-influential *Craftsman* magazine. A plan to build a model farm and community in New Jersey was cut short when they went bankrupt having invested in an Arts & Crafts skyscraper in New York.
REF: Utopian Craftsmen.L.Lambourne

DARMSTADT ARTISTS COLONY 1899 Darmstadt, Germany
FOUNDER/LEADER: Grand Duke Ernst Ludwig of Hesse
Inspired by the British Arts & Crafts Movement the Grand Duke of Hesse, an anglophile who had commissioned Baillie Scott and C.R.Ashbee to design interiors for his palace, established a small craft-based community at Darmstadt to realize the ideal of 'Gesamt-kunstwerk'. Joseph Maria Olbrich, the architect of the Sezession building in Vienna, designed houses and studios for most of the original artists. They produced a limited number of beautiful craft products, but relied heavily on subsidies from the local government & the Duke's patronage.
REF: The Arts & Crafts Movement. E.Cumming & W.Kaplan

ARDEN 1900 - present
Wilmington, Delaware, USA
FOUNDER/LEADER: W.Price / F. Stephens.
Arts & Crafts based community set up on lines of Henry George's single tax plan. Named after Arden Forest in Shakespeare's *As You Like It*. Financed by a loan from Joseph Fels. Intention was to show that a community of artists could support themselves producing fine objects for an urban market. Recently celebrated its centenary.
REF: Designing Utopia. M.H.Lang.
www.progress.org/archive/fold146.htm

ROSE VALLEY 1901-1910
Delaware Co., USA
FOUNDER/LEADER: W.Price
Second Arts & Crafts community set up by Price, again funded by Fels. Had many parallels with Chipping Campden. Set in carefully-restored old buildings the community suffered from divisions between the founder and the mainly foreign-born craftsmen.
REF: Designing Utopia. M.H.Lang.

BYRDCLIFFE COLONY 1902 - 1915
Woodstock, New York,
FOUNDER/LEADER: R.R.Whitehead
Arts & Crafts based community set up using an inherited fortune. Ralph

Whitehead had been converted to the ideals of John Ruskin at Oxford and later travelled to Italy with Ruskin. A complex of 30 buildings constructed of local materials housed craftsmen invited to try and combine the production of furniture, textiles, pottery and metalwork with callisthenics, drama & music. Their furniture proved too labour-intensive to sell profitably and the whole scheme relied on Whitehead's financial support. Many of the craftsmen only wanted to stay for the summer months and by 1915 it had become a private family estate.
REF: *The Arts & Crafts Movement.*

GODOLLO ARTISTS COLONY
1903   Hungary
The Godollo Artists Colony came perhaps the closest to fulfilling the artistic and social ideals put forward by Ruskin & Morris. Aladar Korosfoi-Kriesch a leading member of the colony wrote a book entitled *On Ruskin and the English Preraphaelites* in which he outlined a reforming role for artists in society and the belief that by making and using handcrafted folk objects people's lives could be transformed. By training local young people in weaving, pottery, woodwork and leatherwork in their studios they hoped to give them the means to stay on the land rather than emigrating to the cities or to America. They won international acclaim for their craft/design work based on traditional Hungarian and Transylvanian designs. The community played a key role in the development of indigenous Hungarian design and in fostering the myths and legends that would help forge a national identity for Hungary. They were responsible for an influential five-volume study -*The Art of the Hungarian People*- on vernacular furnishings and architecture.
REF: *The Arts & Crafts Movement.*

PHOENIX SETTLEMENT 1904 - 08
Natal, South Africa
FOUNDER/LEADER: M. K. Gandhi
Community established by Gandhi inspired by a single reading of John Ruskin's *Unto This Last.*
REF: http://www.anc.org.za/ancdocs/history/people/gandhi/bhana.html

TOLSTOY FARM   1908 -1914
Transvaal, South Africa
FOUNDER/LEADER: M. K. Gandhi
"Co-operative Commonwealth" set up by Gandhi as headquarters of his non-violent campaign. A mix of 70-80 Hindus, Muslims, Christians and Parsees lived on 1,100 acres of land with 1,000 fruit-bearing trees. 3 large buildings were put up in the first 6 months. One served as women's quarters, another as the men's residence with laundry and kitchen facilities. A third building was a combination of offices, workshop, and school.
REF: www.anc.org.za/ancdocs/history/people/gandhi/bhana.html

CITES JARDINS   C1911 - 1930
Paris, France
The Association Francaise des Cites Jardins was formed in 1903 and Garden Cities (Cites Jardins) were built around Paris by private enterprise and local government; Draveil in 1911, Petit Groslay in 1912, and Cite d'Ogremont in the 1930s.
REF: www.hmcm.co.uk/letweb/wormap.

PROZOROVKA   C1912
Russia
Vladimir Semionov, a pioneer Russian planner, lived and worked in London (1908-1912). Designed Prozorovka on the Moscow-Kazan railway using the Garden City as a model. Covering an area of 680 hectare, including 170 hectares for an 'outpark', 53 hectares designated for green planted areas within the town, and 335 hectares for housing. It was not completed due to the advent of WW1.
REF: www.hmcm.co.uk/letweb/wormap.

DACEYVILLE   1912 -
Sydney, Australia
State funded 'model residential environment' laid out on Garden City lines. A mixture of semi-detached and detached houses with extensive tree planting and private gardens.
REF: www.hmcm.co.uk/letweb/wormap.

HELLERAU
Germany
Factory village-cum-garden suburb, known as the German Letchworth, established by the industrialist Karl Schmidt. The original plan to build a small town of up to 15,000 inhabitants as a centre for William Morris style craft workshops was scaled down with less than 500 homes and only 4 factories being built.
REF www.hmcm.co.uk/letweb/wormap.

Colonel Light Gardens 1917

Adelaide, South Australia
Garden Suburb development.
REF: Colonel Light Gardens: model garden suburb. Christine Garnaut

The Den-en Toshi Co Ltd 1918

Tokyo, Japan
Japanese Garden City Company developed 150 hectares of land near Tokyo as Garden Suburbs.
REF www.hmcm.co.uk/letweb/wormap.

Abbey of Thelema 1920 -23

Sicily
FOUNDER/LEADER: Aleister Crowley
Archetypal sex & drugs commune set up by the so called 'wickedest man in the world' with a small band of followers. Here in squalid surroundings Crowley carried out his sex magick and occult practices until he was engulfed in scandal following the death of a commune member from gastro-enteritis.
REF: Aleister Crowley: The Beast Demystified. R.Hutchinson.

Institute for the Harmonious Development of Man 1922 -32

Château du Prieuré, Fontainebleau France
FOUNDER/LEADER: G.I. Gurdjieff
Community gathered around the esoteric guru G.I. Gurdjieff. Followers took part in seemingly meaningless arduous tasks in order to 'wake them up from spiritual sleep.'
REF: G.I. Gurdjief; The War Against Sleep. C.Wilson / www.gurdjieff.org

Rehavia 1922-24

Jerusalem, Israel.
Garden Suburb (Shechunat HaGanim) development designed by Richard Kaufmann on behalf of the Chevrat Hachsharat HaYishuv. The people who built the suburb were a Zionist elite of lawyers, businesspeople, academics, doctors and rabbis.
REF: www.jajzed.org.il/melitz/siteastext/rehavia/1.html

Sokol 1923

Russia
The Garden City concept survived the Russian Revolution and Sokol Garden City was built just outside Moscow. The designers were Victor Vesnin and Nikolai Markovnikov.
REF www.hmcm.co.uk/letweb/wormap

Sunnyside Gardens 1924-28

New York, USA
America's first "Garden City" built by the City Housing Corporation to a design by Clarence Stein and Henry Wright. It comprised 76 acres of ground with 1200 homes built around open common gardens.
REF www.hmcm.co.uk/letweb/wormap.

Juan Frenandez Island

C1920s Chile
An exiled group of communists were sent to an abandoned penal colony on 'Robinson Crusoe island', and 'invited' to form a communist colony if the spirit so moved them. Six months later they petitioned the Chilean Government for a return to the mainland and pledging to refrain from all agitation. Their request was granted.

REF: Communist and Co-operative Colonies. Charles Gide. 1930

Mariemont C1920s

Ohio, USA
A new town modelled on Letchworth Garden City. Founded by millionaires Mary and Thomas Emery.
REF www.hmcm.co.uk/letweb/wormap.

Canberra C1920s

Australia
Garden City principles were used for the layout of the city of Canberra and landscaping of the residential areas. One of the city's suburbs is named Letchworth, as a tribute to the world's first Garden City. Canberra has been called a "garden city run mad".
REF www.hmcm.co.uk/letweb/wormap.

Yallourn C1920s

Melbourne, Australia.
"Garden Town" for the workers at an open-cast coal mine, laid out on Garden City principles.
REF www.hmcm.co.uk/letweb/wormap.

Anarchist Colony C1929

Cooktown, Austraila
Group of anarchists, possibly connected with Whiteway, proposed to set up a colony here.
REF: www.takver.com/history/aia/aia00018

Arizona Abode of Love 1930s

Inspired by a visit to the Abode of Love in Somerset, an American photographer set up the Agapemone of America in Arizona. Here he produced the Soul-Babes Handbook which he sent to potential Soul-Babes in Europe encouraging them to come and join him. A number of Swiss women seem to have taken up his offer - they were later accused of using letters home as cover for spying for the Nazis.

REF: Temple of Love.

FRANKLIN FARMS   C1939
USA

FOUNDER/LEADER: P.D.Ouspensky

On the outbreak of war Ouspensky and a number of his English pupils migrated to a large estate at Mendham, New Jersey. While his wife supervised the pupils carrying out farm and household tasks as part of their psychological training, Ouspensky lectured in New York.

REF: http://www.gurdjieff.org

TRABUCO   1942-49
USA

FOUNDER/LEADER: Gerald Heard

'Club for Mystics' 60 miles south of Los Angeles set up by Heard who had moved away from the teachings of Swami Prabhavananda and wished to strike out on his own. He handed the community over to the Swami in 1949.

REF: Mdme. Blavatsky's Baboon.

FAROE ISLANDS   1948 - present
Atlantic Ocean

Islands granted independence by Denmark in 1948. The Faroese have built a thriving island economy implementing policies remarkably similar to those attempted by The Fifth Duke of Argyll on Islay and Lord Leverhulme on Harris/Lewis. They have built up the largest trawler fleet in Scandinavia, pursued a policy of decentralising employment throughout the islands and by the 1980s the Faroe islanders had the highest per capita national product in the world.

REF Scottish Islands. Ian Grimble

'BRANDO'S PITCAIRN'   1963
Tahiti

Marlon Brando, who starred as Fletcher Christian in the most famous movie of the Mutiny on the Bounty, not only lived with his Polynesian co-star/on-screen wife and called his first son Christian, but in 1963 bought an atoll of 13 tiny islets some 25 miles from Tahiti. Here he escaped from the pressures of Hollywood to his own south sea island utopia.

REF:Bounty:Beyond the Voyage.

SOME INTERESTING STATISTICS

Having read How to Lie with Statistics whilst studying A level sociology I am wary of statistical summaries. Nevertheless, with a fair amount of calculated guesswork where accurate information was not available, of some 350 groups that made-it into existence between 1600 &1945 the numbers break down as:

NUMBERS OF COMMUNITIES

1600 - 1800 :	30 or so predominantly religious based groups.
1800 - 1850 :	Over 70 mainly early socialist.
1850 - 1900 :	115 groups. 84% secular based.
1900 - 1950 :	116 groups. 79% secular based.

LIFESPAN OF COMMUNITIES

Age/Years	Religious	Secular
Less than 2	20.5 %	9%
2 to 5	27.25%	30%
5 to 10	13.5%	18.5%
10 to 25	8.25%	15.5%
25 to 50	12.5%	17.5%
50 to 100	11%	7%
100+	7%	2.5%

Religious groups fail to survive the first few years due mainly to persecution and few survive beyond 10years, though if they do they often manage to stabilise and reach a good age. A large number of all types of groups manage to survive for up to 5 years. Secular groups have a better % survival in the 5 to 50 year range though they often loose their initial radical edge as time progresses. And of those that reach a century of existence, whilst it is a higher % of religious based groups, the actual numbers are slightly in favour of secular communities.(7Rel. & 9Sec.)

BY WAY OF A CONCLUSION
UTOPIA BRITANNICA - FACT OR FICTION?

"The value of communities is not what they have done
but the revolution which they indicate is on the way. "

Emerson quoted by T. Adams in
How to Solve the Problem of Rural Depopulation. 1906

At the year 2000 inter-communities volleyball tournament, whilst I was halfway through the research for this book, a visitor said that they would never join an intentional (utopian) community because they were in reality pretty insignificant. This was pretty much a red rag to a bull. So gleaned from the previous pages are a few 'insignificant moments' from the history of intentional communities;

- The introduction and popularisation of the ideas of Italian educationalist Heinrich Pestalozzi by the Sacred Socialists and the Owenites which now underpin our entire education system so securely that few have ever heard of him let alone challenge his ideas.

- The clothes we all stand up in - otherwise known as 'Rational Dress' ("unusually comfortable, loose-fitting clothes") promoted by Godfrey and Ethel Blount, of Haslemere Peasant Industries, through the Healthy and Artistic Dress Union(1890) and pioneered in utopian communities up and down the country at the turn of the 20th century. (Oh, add to that, multi-width shoes introduced by Clarks.)

- Our entire Town and Country Planning system, carefully crafted by Raymond Unwin and his band of Arts & Crafts movement architects from the Garden City ideas of Ebenezer Howard. (On a recent flight to Denmark almost every North of England town viewed from a mile up appeared to be ringed by developments that bear all the hallmarks of Parker & Unwin Garden Village plans.)

- Social work - pretty much invented by Octavia Hill and the University Settlement Movement at the end of the 19th century.

- 4 Prime Ministers resident in utopian communities. Ramsay Mac Donald at the Fellowship of the New Life, Herbert Asquith educated by the Moravians at Fulneck, Clement Attlee, secretary of Toynbee Hall and Harold Wilson, homeowner in Hampstead Garden Suburb.

303

- Struggling a bit for successful sportsmen I will have to settle for tennis champion Fred Perry from the Brentham Club and vegetarian walking champion George Allen resident of Whiteway who smashed a whole week off the record for Land's End to John O'Groats in 1904.

- And finally perhaps the biggest utopian experiment of them all - the Welfare State. Penned by William Beveridge, former secretary at Toynbee Hall & editor of the Ruskinite paper *St George,* it was in essence an attempt to distil the experiences of 200 years of small-scale utopian experiment into a grand practical plan to deliver utopia to the masses.

The historic impact of small scale experimental utopian communities - misrepresented, maybe - insignificant, I don't think so.

As I have travelled round the country a sort of hidden historic landscape - Utopia Britannica - has revealed itself to me; a garden village here, a land settlement there, further on a religious community, in the next town a freehold land club, then a Chartist colony.... a landscape peppered with people's hopes and aspirations for a better world. My journeys led me to ask the inevitable: what happened to them? Like William Morris '... I pondered on all these things, and how men fight and lose the battle, and the thing that they fought for comes about in spite of their defeat, and when it comes, turns out not to be what they meant, and other men have to fight for what they meant under another name ....'   William Morris.*Dream of John Ball.*

Can we learn anything from our utopian ancestors? There seems to be what I have termed a 'utopian tendency' to human nature, an innate drive to make the world a better place. For some, the tendency works in relation to their immediate surroundings and close relatives, others are driven to apply it to the whole of society. Dr Pitzer of the Center for Communal Studies has put forward a developmental model for the study of communal living that helps to put things into a wider context. "Developmental communalism recognises three essential facts about communal living and collective economies. First they are universally available to peoples, governments and movements. Second, communal practices are often adopted out of necessity for security, stability and survival during the emergence of a people, a culture, a political programme or a religious or secular movement. Third, and possibly most important, that communal usage is sometimes altered or abandoned altogether for more relevant organisational strategies as new circumstances and opportunities arise, both preserving and perhaps invigorating the original culture, government or movement and its long term objectives."   D.Pitzer *Diggers & Dreamers 94/95*

The same could easily be said of all utopian experiments.

Sociologist N.Crossley has recently argued for seeing small scale social experiments which fall short of their complete aspirations as - Working utopias.

" they are working models..... having an educative role ...showing that things can be done differently."   N.Crossley

Working Utopias and Social Movements. Sociology 33(4), 809-30. 1999

And Lucy Sargisson sees the utopian tradition as having an even more positive role to play. 'Utopias, ... are an invaluable resource for political thought. Not only do they offer critique; but they also add to this imagination and play and creativity. In addition they are spaces (physical, fictional, imaginary and real) in which we can think about things differently..... as easily identifiable spaces, they can act as points of inspiration. Visitors from the mainstream can enter them and engage in utopian dialogue, returning marked by the encounter.."   Lucy Sargisson

Utopian Bodies and the Politics of Transgression.

One of the problems surrounding any discussion of attempts to set up ideal societies is the confusing interplay between fictional utopias and practical utopian experiments. When is a fiction a plan? Is a plan fiction? What happens when a plan is put into action? What about experiments with no plans; are they utopian? What if the reality doesn't match up to the plan: is the community a fiction? Lucy Sargisson in her book *Contemporary Feminist Utopianism* suggests that in women's science fiction utopia is no longer a fixed, completely-defined plan that can be deemed to have been attained or not, but instead a dynamic ongoing process that we have to participate in. Biologist W.H. Murdy talks about 'Participatory Evolution' and argues that we must learn to identify with future generations if our society is to survive and we are to continue to evolve as a species.Perhaps now that science provides us with theoretical models of the world that include chaos theory and fractal patterns we will be able to view our future as a many layered, multi-patterned dynamic opportunity. And maybe one day genetics will succeed where phrenology failed and come up with a gene for utopianism (or maybe that is just a bit too scary and dystopian!)

Perhaps utopianism has always been a dynamic ongoing participatory process. We just happen to view it through freeze-frame-snapshot-spectacles. If we take a long, wide-angle view of history, not artificially divided into centuries or separated by national boundaries, the sheer scale of wave after wave of utopian experiments looks less like a catalogue of broken dreams & more like a guidebook for the journey to that other place, a better place - the better place that is no-place - utopia.

The end of utopia was heralded long before the end of history; heralded long, hard and persistently by politicians, academics and social scientists of almost every hue & creed. Even its friends have struggled to appear confident about its future; Professor Armytage writing at the end of the 1950s can be forgiven for being rather down-beat at the end of Heavens Below, but even Dennis Hardy writing today in Utopian England struggles to convince himself that small-scale utopian experiments have a place or significance for 21st century society. Predicting the future, of course, is a dodgy business; the chances of looking foolish are high - not something one would wish to risk an academic reputation on certainly. Not that the risk of appearing foolish ever stopped any of our utopian experimenters in the past - it probably never even crossed their minds.

Frac-topia: Having fallen asleep at the console I awoke to find that instead of 25 minutes having passed, 25 years had quietly slipped away...........dozing off thinking of what the future might hold and waking up to find yourself there, was a bit too much of a co-incidence. Was this future a dream? Surprisingly the view out of the window - ....

Chris Coates 4.6.2001

AUTHORS BIOGRAPHY

Chris Coates; Born 1957 in Leicester a proud product of the comprehensive education system. Squatter, Street performer, carpenter, father, anarchist and communard, lived for twenty years at People in Common a small alternative community based in Burnley Lancashire that grew out of the radical underground of the 1970's. He was a founder member of a building co-operative and Altham Hardwood Centre an ecological timber co-operative specialising in sustainable use of English Oak. He has been one of the editors of Diggers & Dreamers, the Bi-Annual Journal and directory of communal living, since its inception in 1989 and before that a contributor to Communes Network. Currently works as a freelance consultant for community based building projects, balancing writing about communities with building them.

To conatct author e.mail: catandcoat@compuserve.com

ACKNOWLEDGEMENTS

This book is largely the distillation of the work of other writers. It would be impossible to list them all here. Obviously I have drawn on the work of any author mentioned in the various bibliographies, But a few who have travelled these utopian lanes before deserve special thanks for leaving clear signposts for others to follow; W.H.G Armytage, J.F.C Harrison, Gillian Darly, Dennis Hardy, Fiona MacCarthy & Colin Ward. I would also like to thank numerous anonymous local librarians who gave freely of their time and knowledge in particular the staff at Lancaster library who patiently ordered a whole mini-library of obscure books for me. Also the host of anonymous website authors and designers whose sites I visited. People I met on my various visits to the sites of historical communities invariably welcomed me, sometimes literally into their homes. Thanks are due to those who supported me through the writing; my partner Catriona Stamp, Jonathan How, William Morris, Various Diggers & Dreamers Editors, Patrick Upton, members of People in Common who put up with me for 20 years - there is nothing like having lived it to deepen the understanding, and Bob Sproule whose idea it was all that time ago. Finally I would like to thank my Grandmother Gladys Bone (1904-2000) who without knowing it made the difference.

Picture Credits: I have tried to trace sources for all photo's and illustrations, where it has not been possible to trace the publisher or author I has chosen to print those that I thought important. I apologise if this is in anyway offends anyone. Thanks for permission to use pictures go to: Kibbo Kift Foundation, Kate Evans(illustration in Diggers article), Dennis Hardy, Diggers & Dreamers. Cover by: Jonathan How & Catriona Stamp. Many pictures and photos are from my own personal archive. I have a comprehensive slide collection and would be happy to give a short illustrated talk to anyone interested.

Chris Coates 2001

Recommended Bibliography

The books listed below are the best starting points for anyone interested in finding out more about the communities mentioned in Utopia Britannica. Along with these titles I would recommend anything on the subject by Colin Ward, Fiona MacCarthy, Dennis Hardy and J.F.C. Harrison.

Heavens Below: Utopian experiments in England 1560-1960. W.H.G. Armytage.
Routledge and Kegan Paul 1961 - Out of print.
Professor Armytage's seminal work is a 'lucid and fascinating history of "ideal settlements" from the days of the Levellers to the Garden City.' Until the 1970s Heavens Below was the only work on utopian experiments and is still much referred to and quoted. Armytage wrote widely on the subject of utopias and many of his articles and pamphlets can be found in library collections. Heavens Below is meticulously researched and referenced and was the starting point for much of the research carried out for Utopia Britannica.

Villages of Vision. A study of Strange Utopias. Gillian Darley
The Architectural Press 1975. (2nd Ed Paladin/Granada 1978) Out of Print.
All over Britain there are villages that were artificially introduced - strange or pretty arcadias invented for aesthetic, philanthropic or political reasons, for convenience and for ideals, built by conscience-stricken aristocrats, industrialists, by idealists and by landscape gardeners seeking the right effect. Villages of Vision charts the development and growth of these communities, where the Englishman's desire for `a place in the country' has resulted in a curious mixture of romance and megalomania.

Alternative Communities in Nineteenth Century England. Dennis Hardy
Longmans. London 1979. Out of Print.
Detailed study of utopian communities, communal religious sects and back-to-the-land initiatives from the 1800s. Hardy's study includes in-depth profiles of many communities with maps, historic & contemporary photographs and illustrations, along with analysis of the various movements that gave rise to them.

The Architectural and Social History of Co-operative Living. Lynn F. Pearson
Macmillan Press. 1988. Out of Print.

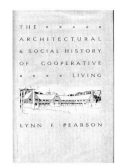

The Co-operative Housekeeping movement of the 19th & 20th centuries set out to improve women's lives through domestic revolution. The co-operative home, with private rooms centred on a core of communal facilities was to take the place of the private house. The movement was connected to the Garden City and Arts & Crafts movements. The book traces the history of the movement and includes details of a number of Co-operative Housekeeping schemes carried out in the UK.

The Good & Simple Life. Artists Colonies in Europe and America. Michael Jacobs.
Phiadon. 1985. Out of Print.

In the 2nd half of the 19th century, a growing interest in outdoor painting caused groups of artists to settle in village communities to live & work. The study of these 'artist colonies' throws new light on the major artistic developments in Europe and America at the time. The movement is examined through descriptions of colonies in France, Scandinavia, Russia, Germany, Hungary, Britain and the USA. A vivid narrative of life in the colonies reveals personal conflicts and adolescent antics which belie the ideals of the movement.

Designing Utopia. John Ruskin's Urban Vision for Britain and America. Michael H. Lang
Black Rose Books. 1999. www.web.net/blackrosebooks.

Designing Utopia presents a broad overview of John Ruskin's life; the development of his views on architecture and urban design, as well as his views on social justice; how his vision was developed from his writings; and his efforts at practical application of that vision. It also looks at the work of a long line of progressive architects and planners and the buildings and communities they designed.

Utopian England. Community Experiments 1900-1945. Dennis Hardy
E. &F.N. Spon. 2000. Available from bookshops.

England in the early part of the twentieth century was rich in utopian ventures, diverse and intriguing in their scope and aims. Two world wars, an economic depression, and the emergence of fascist states in Europe were all a spur to idealists; to seek new limits, to escape from the here and now, and to create sanctuaries for new and better lives. Utopian England explores this fascinating history of utopian ideals, the lives of those pursued them, and the utopian communities they created.

INDEX